On Shakespeare and Early Modern Literature

On Shakespeare and Early Modern Literature

Essays

JOHN KERRIGAN

OXFORD
UNIVERSITY PRESS

OXFORD

UNIVERSITY PRESS

Great Clarendon Street, Oxford OX2 6DP

Oxford University Press is a department of the University of Oxford.
It furthers the University's objective of excellence in research, scholarship,
and education by publishing worldwide in

Oxford New York

Auckland Bangkok Buenos Aires Cape Town Chennai
Dar es Salaam Delhi Hong Kong Istanbul Karachi Kolkata
Kuala Lumpur Madrid Melbourne Mexico City Mumbai Nairobi
São Paulo Shanghai Taipei Tokyo Toronto

Oxford is a registered trade mark of Oxford University Press
in the UK and in certain other countries

Published in the United States
by Oxford University Press Inc., New York

British Library Cataloguing in Publication Data

Data available

Library of Congress Cataloging in Publication Data

Kerrigan, John. On Shakespeare and early modern literature:
essays/John Kerrigan.
p. cm
Includes index
1. English literature—Early modern, 1500–1700—History and criticism.
2. Shakespeare, William, 1564–1616—Criticism and interpretation. I. Title.
PR423.K47 2001   820.9'003—dc21   22001033990

ISBN 0-19-924851-6
ISBN 0-19-926917-3 (pbk.)

1 3 5 7 9 10 8 6 4 2

Printed in Great Britain
on acid-free paper by
Biddles Ltd,
King's Lynn, Norfolk

TO KIM WALWYN

Preface

These essays are selected from work of the last two decades. Throughout that period I was publishing on poetry, drama, and the novel across a wide historical range. Even so, Shakespeare and early modern literature kept attracting me. The experience is common enough. Though the texts taught in schools and universities are more and more often twentieth-century, adventurous readers and playgoers still find their way back to a body of writing which, in its linguistic and social richness, has probably never been equalled. This book variously engages with that early modern legacy, reassessing well-known works and giving some neglected ones fresh attention.

Those familiar with Renaissance studies will not find it hard to detect here a number of responses to the sometimes turbulent development of the subject. Most obviously, the recent essays are more historical than the earliest—'Astrophil's Tragicomedy', 'Milton and the Nightingale', and 'Between Michelangelo and Petrarch' (all given as lectures in 1982, though polished for publication later). Elsewhere poststructuralist overtones are audible, while '*Henry IV* and the Death of Old Double' (written 1988) appreciatively but critically tests the routines of the emerging new historicism. For me the point to establish against Stephen Greenblatt and his disciples was that the subversive energies of Shakespearian drama are more intimately and potently active in dialogue and its on-stage performance than in social contexts. While the essays in this book explore in different ways the relationship of plays, poems, and romances to such factors as genre, the rules of rhetoric, courtesy literature, and historical crisis, they retain a belief in the capacity of verbal artefacts to respond with transformative power to the circumstances that create them.

Both parts of the book begin with essays on a subject which used to be considered dull. But I came to textual scholarship just as Peter Blayney's work on *King Lear* was encouraging young Shakespearians to challenge the editorial consensus. 'Shakespeare as Reviser' was written in the first flush of the enterprise (1983, rev. 1987), and it catches something of the excitement that many of us felt. How things have moved on in this field it would take another book of essays to explain, but a reaction to some of the changes can be found in 'The Editor as Reader' (1996), which shifts the focus from authorial agency and argues that insufficient attention has been paid—not just by editors, but by critics—to the interaction between variant texts and varying readers.

Though textual studies are now almost fashionable, it still might seem severe to start both parts of the collection in this way. The gesture seems right, however, because much of what follows is informed by reading habits and emphases that I developed through my involvement with textual scholarship—an activity that requires the fullest engagement with the material intricacy of writing, its incoherences and architectonic potential, its specificity yet frequent provisionality (especially in theatre-scripts). Beyond that, there is a slightly different logic to the two halves of the book. The Shakespeare essays are organized more or less in order of composition, regardless of when they were published; in Part II it has seemed more useful, after the opening, general essay, to follow the chronology of the authors discussed. Here and there I have corrected errors and added or removed words. About a dozen footnotes have been introduced to help less specialized readers. This policy of minimal intervention means that the pieces differ, though not inappropriately, in the levels of modernization imposed on old spelling, titles, and so forth.

The production of these essays has been an erratic process, steadied by friends and colleagues. I hope that those who have provided information, or who have read draft material, will accept this generalized but warm thanks. I am grateful to my mother and brothers; to Anne and John Barton, Helen Small, and Kate Plaisted; and to many at St John's College, Cambridge. The dedication to this book records a special attachment. One further debt I must record is to Jeremy Maule, an exemplary scholar who died young. When I was working on Thomas Carew it was Jeremy who, among similar encouragements, suggested I look at the miscellany in the Boxley Abbey papers where I found 'T.C.' (I fear he was sceptical about any attribution), and who mentioned Thornton Shirley Graves's article on clubs, in which a document listing 'M^r: Tho: Carew' is reprinted. This convivial but private, institutionally committed but elusive man gave an enormous amount to the world, and had more to give. Those who knew him miss him.

'William Drummond and the British Problem' is a new essay. I am grateful to those who published the other pieces in the first place. Essay 1 initially appeared in Christopher Ricks (ed.), *English Drama to 1710*,

Sphere History of Literature, rev. edn (London: Sphere Books, 1987); 2 in Yasunari Takada (ed.), *Surprised by Scenes: Essays in Honour of Professor Yasunari Takahashi* (Tokyo: Kenkyusha, 1994); 3 and 5 were published in *Shakespeare Survey*, 41 (1988) and 50 (1997); 4 and 10 in *Essays in Criticism*, 40 (1990) and 42 (1992); 6 in James Raven, Helen Small and Naomi Tadmor (eds.), *The Practice and Representation of Reading in England* (Cambridge: Cambridge University Press, 1996); 7 in Toshiyuki Takamiya and Richard Beadle (eds.), *Chaucer to Shakespeare: Essays in Honour of Shinsuke Ando* (Cambridge: Boydell and Brewer, 1992); 9, a Chatterton Lecture, appeared in *Proceedings of the British Academy*, 74 (1988), and 11, under the slightly fuller title 'Revenge Tragedy Revisited: Politics, Providence and Drama, 1649–1683', in *Seventeenth Century*, 12:2 (Autumn 1997).

Contents

Part I

Shakespeare

CHAPTER 1

Shakespeare as Reviser (1987)

If you want to study Wordsworth's revisions you can go to Dove Cottage where, surrounded by lakes and tourists and daffodils, you may pull sheaf upon manuscript sheaf from the shelves, each traced with 'turnings intricate of verse'. If your interests are Miltonic or Tennysonian, Cambridge has the papers and, in the chequered shade of the Wren Library, you can watch *Comus* and *In Memoriam* come to life in the authors' hands. With Shakespeare the situation is different. No manuscripts stand behind his *Collected Works*: our *Richard III*s and *Cymbeline*s are based on early printed texts, trimmed, corrected and judiciously corrupted by editors. The Shakespearian originals have been lost beyond recall—some, perhaps, consumed in the fire that destroyed the first Globe theatre in 1613, and others, certainly, marked up by the printers and then thrown away. From time to time, someone will claim that Shakespeare's papers are hidden in the roof of Anne Hathaway's cottage, or under the tombstone guarded by the poet's sharp curse in Holy Trinity Church. But such notions are more curious than scholarly, and only based on wishing. Nothing seems to survive in the dramatist's hand beyond certain pages in a play apparently not performed and a scattering of signatures on legal documents.

The play, *Sir Thomas More*, was kept from the stage by censorship. As Master of the Revels, responsible for vetting drama, Edmund Tilney judged the chronicle, with its racial unrest and food riots in the reign of Henry VIII, unacceptably close to Elizabethan politics. '[Le]aue o[ut] ye insur[rection] wholy', he commanded its authors, '& ye Cause ther off'. That such an omission would eviscerate the work may or may not have struck him. But Munday and Chettle, aware that their play required a scene resembling the uncensored riot in *2 Henry VI*, seem to have turned at this point to Shakespeare.[1] What he wrote did not, perhaps, persuade

---

[1] The evidence is usefully summarized in *The Riverside Shakespeare*, ed. G. Blakemore Evans et al. (Boston, 1974), the source of quotations from *More* and of the line references in this essay. Early texts are quoted from *Shakespeare's Plays in Quarto: A Facsimile Edition*, ed. Michael J. B.

Tilney, but it has wit, moral weight, and metaphoric ingenuity. It is also littered with second thoughts. 'Whates a sorry parsnyp to a good hart', asks John Lincoln, a rioter, in the manuscript. Yet he first called parsnips 'watrie'. 'The removing of the straingers . . . cannot choose but much advauntage the poor handycraftes', cries Betts, but he reached that resonant 'advauntage' by way of a deleted 'helpe'. Not for nothing are working sheets called 'foul papers'. Throughout this scene, words, phrases, and even speech prefixes, though added last (Shakespeare composed the riot as a cacophany and then identified the voices), are subject to inky-fingered revision.

'Wee haue scarse receiued from him a blot in his papers', declared Heminge and Condell in their preface to the Folio—that posthumous collection which is the only source we have for half the plays—and the comment has been used to challenge not only the authorship of Lincoln and Betts's riot but the idea that Shakespeare was a self-revising writer. The Folio compilers do not stop, however, at their assertion of blotlessness. 'But', they add, 'it is not our prouince, who onely gather his works, and giue them you, to praise him.' E. A. J. Honigmann has shown that fluency was such a modish accomplishment in the period that not to praise Shakespeare for it would be tantamount to saying he couldn't write.[2] Admittedly Jonson echoed the phrase, declaring in *Discoveries* that his rival should have 'blotted' lines which, strictly construed, made no sense. Yet in the Folio, where a considered panegyric was called for, Jonson struck a balance between Art and Nature, celebrating Shakespearian ease but at the same time insisting, in what reads like a conscious correction of Heminge and Condell, on the artistry of Shakespeare as reviser. 'Yet must I not give Nature all', he writes:

> Thy Art,
> My gentle *Shakespeare*, must enioy a part.
> For though the *Poets* matter, Nature be,
> His Art doth giue the fashion. And, that he,
> Who casts to write a liuing line, must sweat,
> (such as thine are) and strike the second heat
> Vpon the *Muses* anuile: turne the same,
> (And himselfe with it) that he thinkes to frame;

Allen and Kenneth Muir (Berkeley, 1981) and *The First Folio of Shakespeare: The Norton Facsimile*, ed. Charlton Hinman (New York, 1968).

[2]   *The Stability of Shakespeare's Text* (Lincoln, Nebr., 1965), 22–8.

> Or for the lawrell, he may gaine a scorne,
>> For a good *Poet's* made, as well as borne.
> And such wert thou.[3]

Certainly, the loose ends, confused attributions, double versions of single exchanges, and other textual tangles which characterize plays printed from Shakespearian foul papers most plausibly stem from variant thoughts.[4] Not all point to the sweat of striking a second heat. Often Shakespeare changed things on the hoof, blotting as he went, and sometimes he did not trouble to stop and delete what had become rejected text. On occasion, however, he made foul-paper changes significant enough to deserve Jonson's strenuous description. Theseus' speech at *A Midsummer Night's Dream* V. i. 2–22, for instance, originally compared 'Louers, and mad men'; but Shakespeare returned to it at a late stage of composition and, made self-conscious perhaps by what he had achieved, squeezed into the margins, to the confusion of the printer, a number of lines about poetry, including these famous words:

> The Poets eye, in a fine frenzy, rolling,
> Doth glance from heauen to earth, from earth to heauen.
> And as imagination bodies forth
> The formes of things vnknown: the Poets penne
> Turnes them to shapes, and giues to ayery nothing,
> A locall habitation, and a name.[5]

Every reader of the early plays will sense a great leap forward. We seem to find at the point of revision a born poet being made. Can it be doubted that striking a second heat here shaped and, in Jonson's image, 'turned' the poet with his 'formes of things vnknown', through the labour of re-writing?

Whatever is learned from such a crux will be inseparable from the text; but since, in revision as elsewhere, Shakespeare works impersonally, that is not inappropriate. Compare a speech in *Hamlet*, where Laertes encounters Ophelia, driven mad by her father's death (IV. v. 154–64). In the second edition of the play, a quarto (i.e. paperback made of sheets folded

---

[3] 'To the memory of my beloued, The AVTHOR MR. WILLIAM SHAKESPEARE', *First Folio of Shakespeare*, ed. Hinman, 9–10, p. 10.

[4] Roughly a third of the three dozen plays survive in this form. For a classic account see W. W. Greg, *The Shakespeare First Folio* (Oxford, 1955), especially on *Errors*, *2 Henry IV*, and *Timon* (though this is now considered a collaboration with Middleton).

[5] Lineation corrected. The standard analysis remains J. Dover Wilson (ed.), *A Midsummer Night's Dream* (Cambridge, 1924), 'The Copy . . . 1600' Section C.

twice, into four) printed from foul papers, Ophelia enters and Laertes cries,

> O Rose of May,
> Deere mayd, kind sister, sweet *Ophelia,*
> O heauens, ist possible a young maids wits
> Should be as mortall as a poore mans life.

Coming upon this passage later—presumably while copying from foul to fair—Shakespeare decided that 'poore' was unhelpfully unfocused, since, meant to imply pathos ('poor chap'), it also suggested a degree of poverty at odds with Polonius' worldly status. The counsellor to kings was no 'poore man'. So, as the Folio (based on a transcript near the prompt-book) shows, he substituted 'old' for 'poore'. But as soon as Shakespeare registered his objection to the word, the objection itself worked on his imagination, and he was prompted to add to his speech lines developing the suppressed suggestion of value:

> . . . as mortall as an old mans life?
> Nature is fine in Loue, and where 'tis fine,
> It sends some precious instance of it selfe
> After the thing it loues.

The shift from age to worth, which in F (Folio) and the modern editions which follow it seems a disjunction, is, for readers aware of the divergence from Q (quarto), associative and Shakespearian. It is as though the 'poore mans life', bodied forth in re-imagining, had yielded its ambiguity in re-vision.

That paragraph is contentious. Almost all scholars accept the idea of rethinking within foul papers, and the majority believe that, in copying, Shakespeare made changes. A text like *Love's Labour's Lost* will thus be agreed to reflect both rewriting in draft (as with Q's two versions of Berowne's great speech on Love (IV. iii. 285–362)) and tinkering between foul papers and a transcript, evidenced by F's divergence from Q.[6] Resistance sets in, however, with plays like *Hamlet* which vary at many points between 'good' quarto and Folio. For reasons which have more to do with the history of textual bibliography than evidence from the theatre and print-shop, many still reject the message of early editions: that Shakespeare revised *Othello* and *King Lear* as surely as he did *Troilus and*

---

[6]   Stanley Wells, 'The Copy for the Folio Text of *Love's Labour's Lost*', *Review of English Studies,* NS 33 (1982), 137–47.

Cressida, extensively and in detail, and that Laertes was not meant from the outset to call Polonius 'old'. Hence the most recent editor of *Hamlet*—Philip Edwards, in the New Cambridge series (1985)—accepts the principle of revision but reckons only the 222 and 83 lines unique to Q2 and F part of a rewrite, though evidence from the period suggests that authorial (including collaborative) revisions are characterized by local variants while larger cuts and inserts can indicate non-authorial adaptation.[7] (There are doubtful passages of this kind in *Macbeth* and *Measure for Measure*,[8] and Hamlet himself adds 'a speech of some dosen lines, or sixteene lines' to *The Mouse-trap* (ii. ii. 541–2).) Worse, the magisterial New Arden (1982) rejects authorial revision at every point but one (spurning, like Edwards, the *c.*1,300 local variants), and judges the Folio lines on boy players an insert only because they conflict with the editor's early date for the tragedy.

Yet this passage, ii. ii. 337–62, belongs to a sequence of variants affecting Rosencrantz and Guildenstern. The King's faithful ministers in the prose analogues, they become in Q2 fellow students of the Prince and Claudius' gullible agents. The Folio, as one would expect in rewriting, moves further from the received story. (A similar drift away from source can be found in Shakespeare's revision of Sonnet 2, and in the reworked war in *King Lear*.[9]) F *Hamlet*'s friendship with the pair is stressed, not only in the 'ayrie of Children' insert but in added banter (bluntly starting 'Let me question more in particular:') about bad dreams and ambition (ii. ii. 239–69). Then, in the bedchamber scene, F cuts Hamlet's hostile speech, 'Ther's letters seald, and my two Schoolefellowes, | Whom I will trust as I will Adders fang'd, | They bear the mandat[e] ...' (iii. iv. 202–10). This omission can hardly be accidental since, while Q2 confirms the Prince's suspicions by having Rosencrantz and Guildenstern arrive after his speech in Claudius' company, F has the King enter to Gertrude alone, leaving the pair to be called for. Harold Jenkins, in his New Arden, invokes the 'Adders fang'd' to support Hamlet when, confronted by Horatio's cool reaction to the rewritten commission and their death, 'So

---

[7] John Kerrigan, 'Revision, Adaptation, and the Fool in *King Lear*', in Gary Taylor and Michael Warren (eds.), *The Division of the Kingdoms: Shakespeare's Two Versions of 'King Lear'* (Oxford, 1983), 195–245.

[8] iii. v and iv. i. 39–43, 125–32 in the tragedy (probably Middleton), i. ii. 1–84 and, it has been argued, iv. i. 1–20 in the problem play.

[9] Gary Taylor, 'Some Manuscripts of Shakespeare's Sonnets', *Bulletin of the John Rylands University Library*, 68 (1985), 210–46; 'The War in *King Lear*', *Shakespeare Survey*, 33 (1980), 27–34.

Guyldensterne and *Rosencrans* goe too't', the Prince replies, 'Why man, they did make loue to this imployment' (v. ii. 56–7). 'Hamlet assumes them to be willing for the worst' Jenkins says, noting III. iv. 202–7, 'and we are probably meant to assume it too and to accept the poetic justice of their end.' This feckless comment is a warning against conflation. For Hamlet's response is Folio-unique and linked to the chain of variants. Stung by Horatio's criticism, and less sure of the pair's complicity in F than Q2, Hamlet shrugs off blame with a bawdy jest.[10]

As the exchange unfolds, the texts drift purposefully apart. Girding at Horatio's coolness, Hamlet asks in F whether it is not 'perfect conscience, | To quit' the King 'with this arme?', now that the commission gives proof of his villainy, and he anticipates what will be cut from Q2 a few lines later: Gertrude's suggestion that he apologize to Laertes before the duel (v. ii. 67–80). The Folio emphasis on pace is striking:

Hor. It must be shortly knowne to him from England . . .
Ham. It will be short,
   The *interim's* mine, and a mans life's no more
   Then to say one:

and it so clearly anticipates those gaps in F which reduce the exchange with Ostric[11] (106–43) and remove entirely the anonymous Lord who comes in 1604 to make sure Hamlet will fight Laertes (195–208) that Professor Jenkins's refusal to notice links begins to look perverse. But then, Philip Edwards cannot give much weight to a single word like 'one', though the ghost first appears on 'The bell then beating one' (I. i. 39), and in the clash of 'fell incensed points' a man's life hangs on 'one' sword-thrust:

Ham. Come on sir.
Laer. Come my Lord.
Ham. One.
Laer. No.
Ham. Iudgement.
Ostrick. A hit, a very palpable hit. (Q2)[12]

---

[10] For 'goe too't' see *King Lear* IV. vi. 111–13; for 'make loue', *Hamlet* III. iv. 93–4.

[11] So the courtier is named at most points in Q2—*Ostrick(e)*, contracted in speech prefixes—presumably because his foppish headgear is plumed with ostrich feathers, but perhaps on account of his affected gait ('This Lapwing runnes away with the shell on his head' (185–6)) and his folly.

[12] V. ii. 280–1. Contrast the iterative 'one's added to *Othello* at the same point in a tragic economy and in the context of 'Iustice' and 'her Sword' (V. ii. 16–20). What makes for pace at Elsinore stresses protraction in the later ending.

'[I] do so much of my work by the critical, rather than the imaginative faculty',[13] Yeats confessed, and we're inclined to think this un-Shakespearian. What the new work on revision has revealed, however, is a poet willing to engage with his own work critically, as reader and re-thinker. That meshing of Shakespearian imagery and echo which works across scenes and situations to complicate our responses, and which has seemed instinctive, now starts to look deliberate. If the reshaping of *Hamlet* from Q2 to F may be readily summed in general terms—cuts to hasten the arrival of the ghost (I. i. 108–25, I. iv. 17–38), a softening of sensual denunciation in the bedchamber (III. iv. 71–6, 78–81, 161–5, 167–70), a blunting of our scepticism towards Fortinbras so that he more securely refigures Old Hamlet, that other smiter of the Polacks (IV. iv. 9–66)—the *details* of revision change our idea of Shakespeare. He becomes a self-considering artist, verbally conscious down to the chiasmus 'One./No', and too preoccupied with complex material to warble native woodnotes wild. Moreover, the bias of his self-criticism must influence our own. For the first time, analysis can gain some purchase on the plays from inside. It is liberating, and creative of better discipline, to establish with exactness that Shakespeare thought some of his inspirations better than others, and not a few dispensable. We need not accept his judgements, but they are inextricably part of the texts they address. Meanwhile any impulse to view the plays as fixed entities—verbal icons for actors—should be resisted. Shakespeare's imagination seems to have thrashed around within a story, establishing an area of textual potential, and he then reworked his material as the development of sources through drafts which were subject to second and, we may gather, third thoughts. His plays achieved completeness only in the spontaneity of performance, from a book which then might be revised.

A corollary of this is that certain analyses can be found, in the deepest sense, Shakespearian. When John Bayley, for instance, wrote his essay 'Time and the Trojans',[14] he will not have known that, as it now appears, Q *Troilus and Cressida* precedes F, reproducing the foul papers of a text lying behind the play as it was probably performed at the Inns of Court, while F stems from the prompt-book of a public theatre version revised from the work found in Q.[15] Even when faced with a blurred text,

---

[13] To Fiona MacLeod, ? November 1901, in *The Letters of W. B. Yeats*, ed. Allan Wade (London, 1954), 358.

[14] *Essays in Criticism*, 25 (1975), 55–73.

[15] Gary Taylor, '*Troilus and Cressida*: Bibliography, Performance, and Interpretation', *Shakespeare Studies*, 16 (1983), 99–136. For an interesting but unpersuasive attempt to revive

however, Bayley detected in it a distinctive quality of timelessness. Despite the long perspective of history through which its events are seen, he argued, and despite the looming fall of Troy, its characters are allowed no felt past or future. And so we look from foul papers to the second prompt-book to find that Shakespeare has interpolated six extraordinary lines in Agamemnon's greeting of Hector. 'Worthy [of] armes', he says in both texts, 'as welcome as to one, | That would be rid of such an enemy.' Then, F alone,

> But that's no welcome: vnderstand more cleere
> What's past, and what's to come, is strew'd with huskes,
> And formelesse ruine of obliuion:
> But in this extant moment, faith and troth,
> Strain'd purely from all hollow bias drawing:
> Bids thee with most diuine integritie,

—back to shared text—'From heart of very heart, great *Hector* welcome' (IV. v. 165–70). It is at least as easy to see why those words are in the play as it is to see why they are in Agamemnon's speech; and when that happens in Shakespeare it is always worth asking, Why?

Most changes in *Troilus and Cressida* are of this kind, affecting the dialogue rather than staging and structure. Shakespeare tautens (e.g. Thersites' list of plagues (v. i. 20–3)) and dilates (I. iii. 354–6), cuts (II. i. 29–30) and interpolates (IV. iv. 144–8). Rare words he replaces with familiar ones, while obvious terms become exotic. Sometimes he seems merely to fidget, making 'worthy' 'Noble' and 'such like' 'so forth'; yet work on Middleton, Chapman, Jonson, and Dekker shows that meddling with indifferent substitutions is the hallmark of a closely revising author.[16] Only once do the early texts indicate a major adjustment. Where Q has Troilus dismiss Pandarus before the epilogue (v. x. 32–4), F duplicates the dismissal at the end of v. iii. If F was printed from a copy of Q annotated against the Globe prompt-book, it follows either that the company book kept both options open (rather as F *Macbeth* allows the hero to be killed on- or offstage) or that the Folio printer ignored the collator's deletion, if it was made, of v. x. 32–56. At all events, the tangle shows Shakespeare first ending the play with a seamy, cynical epilogue, and then deciding to finish with Troilus' 'Hope of reueng[e] shall hide our inward woe'. No

Nevill Coghill's theory that F precedes Q see E. A. J. Honigmann, 'The Date and Revision of *Troilus and Cressida*', in Jerome J. McGann (ed.), *Textual Criticism and Literary Interpretation* (Chicago, 1985), 38–54.

[16] Kerrigan, 'Revision, Adaptation', 205–13 and nn. 45–66.

more than hollowly affirmative, the revised conclusion at least spares its audience the foul aftertaste of Pandarus' bequeathing his diseases.

More connectedly than *Hamlet*, and more searchingly than *Troilus*, the text of *Othello* has been rethought and recast.[17] Between Q and the post-1606 prompt-book-related F, Shakespeare works along fault lines in the story, ambiguating afresh points at which the audience's sympathy seems too readily assured. The dialogue is shot through with shifting emphases, rhythms, and, above all, possessives and pronouns. A Roderigo 'I' becomes 'you' in Iago's alchemical presence (II. i. 281); 'he ecchoes me. | As if there were some monster in his thoughts' is echoically 'thou' and 'thy' in F (III. iii. 106–7); Desdemona's wedding sheets distressfully switch from 'our' to 'my' (IV. ii. 105). Tiny examples; but the subtlest attention is paid in revision to that which holds between characters, and between characters and their senses of self. Consider Desdemona's murder, v. ii. 80–91. In Q, she cries 'O Lord, Lord, Lord' as Othello strangles her, and the line is both the 'prayer' she was denied at line 83 and an anguished protest, couched in the language of obedience, to the Moor, her lord.[18] At once, a banging on the door begins—like the knocking on the castle gate, after Duncan's murder—and also the process of anagnorisis, with Emilia's 'My Lord, my Lord, what ho, my Lord'; and the narrowed obsessive Moor for a moment thinks this Desdemona's voice, displaced. (Emilia's voice will again become her mistress's, singing the added willow song at v. ii. 246–8.) 'What voyce is this?' he asks, 'not dead? not yet quite dead?' In F, 'O Lord, Lord, Lord' is deleted and 'What voyce is this?' correspondingly becomes 'What noise', which takes Emilia's cry to be other. Look at a modern edition like the Riverside, or Norman Sanders's New Cambridge (1985), and you find the quarto line plus, ineptly, 'What noise'.

This detail is chosen as a hard case. F regularly removes references to God because an Act of Parliament, passed in 1606, forbade stage blasphemy. While the Shakespeare prompt-books did not suffer as keenly as, say, *Dr Faustus* under this dispensation, undesirable changes were still forced on the text. When discussing revision, it is important to remember that while certain variants (such as the inserted fly scene, III. ii, in *Titus Andronicus*) were in Shakespeare's power, others were not. Censorship

---

[17] Though Johnson comments shrewdly on the play's revision in a note to the F-only willow song (IV. iii. 31–53, 55–7), the pioneering work is by Nevill Coghill, 'Revision after Performance', in *Shakespeare's Professional Skills* (Cambridge, 1964). See also E. A. J. Honigmann, 'Shakespeare's Revised Plays: *King Lear* and *Othello*', *Library*, 6th ser. 4 (1982), 142–73.

[18] Cf. 'Who is thy Lord? | He that is yours, sweet Lady', F IV. ii. 101, another added possessive twist.

kept the 'deposition scene', *Richard II* iv. i. 154–318, off page and stage during Elizabeth's lifetime; the Master of the Revels probably objected to *King Lear* i. iv. 140–55, missing in F;[19] and 'O Lord, Lord, Lord' was expunged by law. So many distinctive variants are linked to oaths in *Othello*, however, that it looks as though Shakespeare himself purged the promptbook. Many of the changes from Q to F—6 lines unique to the former, 160 added, about 1000 variants in common text—are not of the kind that can be readily attributed to a book-keeper, or scribe, or drunken compositor. Some stand alone, like the dozen lines given Roderigo to clarify the plot (i. i. 121–37), but others connect thematically and by means of stage tableaux.

Thus F thrice foregrounds Brabantio's assertion that Othello seduced his daughter 'with Drugs or Minerals', 'Spels, and Medicines, bought of Mountebanks' (i. ii. 65, 72–7, i. iii. 63). The Moor assures the Duke that he used no 'forced courses' to 'poyson' Desdemona, but that when he told the story of his life she 'with a greedie eare | Deuour[ed] vp [his] discourse'. 'This onely', he says, 'is the witch-craft I haue vs'd' (i. iii. 110–70). At first blush the answer clears his name, but that image of an ear glutted with charm, glanced at several times in the scene, once by Iago, may give us pause. 'Thou know'st we worke by wit, and not by wi[t]chcraft' the Ensign later reminds Roderigo, yet the 'poyson' he uses on Othello (iii. iii. 325, F only) is called, in the F-dilated epileptic fit, 'Medicine' (iv. i. 38–43). The 'Drugs' and 'Minerals' poured in dead King Hamlet's ear become verbal in *Othello*; but they are not the less dangerous for that. There may be no 'witchcraft' in Renaissance Venice; but there remains as in *Macbeth* the corrosive 'suggestion' that lies like truth.

My claim is not that the Moor deceives, but that the inserts about magic are concerned with suasion too. There is a strong centripetal tendency in the tragedy, referring disparate material towards the temptation that precipitates Othello's downfall, and the i. iii argument about feeling and fabling decidedly looks forward to Acts III and IV. So, indeed, does its account of Turkish strategy. For in revising the Senate scene Shakespeare chose not to trim what might be thought an excrescence, but to expand. What are we to make of the Turkish to-and-fro, the feint towards Rhodes before the attack on Cyprus? 'Tis a Pageant', a senator answers, 'To keepe vs in false gaze'. His analysis of what is against what

---

[19] Gary Taylor, 'Monopolies, Show Trials, Disaster, and Invasion: *King Lear* and Censorship', in Taylor and Warren (eds.), *Division*, 77–119; Annabel Patterson, *Censorship and Interpretation* (Madison, 1984), 58–73.

merely seems (17–35) offers an example of caution beside which Othello can ultimately be judged, deluded as he is by false gazing and Iago's pageant with Cassio. And it is spun out in F:

> . . . If we make thought of this,
> We must not thinke the Turke is so vnskillfull,
> To leaue that latest, which concernes him first,
> Neglecting an attempt of ease, and gaine
> To wake, and wage a danger profitlesse.

While the Duke and others are baffled by this manœuvring, the sage First Senator is sceptical, explains in balanced phrases why, and immediately after the addition has his doubts confirmed by the arrival of a messenger from Cyprus. This may be the most extreme example in *Othello* of public affairs reflecting private experience, but the links are there, and Shakespeare's enlargement of the speech points towards his wishing them registered.

At all events, this takes us to the cluster of variants which must concern us most—in the temptation, fall, and vengeance of the Moor. We also find there a counter-instance to the Bayley essay: criticism which contradicts the movement of authorial feeling. Dr Leavis, notoriously, saw Othello's behaviour in these scenes as imperceptive and egotistical. Rejecting Bradley's image of the Noble Moor, he emphasized the hero's responsiveness to Iago, and wrote of his succumbing 'with a promptness that couldn't be improved upon'.[20] Scholarship may have recomplicated the picture, but critics, always wary of siding with the credulous, remain closer to Leavis than they should. For we can deduce from the drift of variants that, after sailing close to the wind in Q, Shakespeare worked to protect Othello. His Folio 'promptness' not only could be 'improved upon': it had been in the quarto. Caution seems evident from the outset in F. While Q Othello calls Iago's suspicions 'horrible counsell', they constitute in F III. iii. 93–162 'Some horrible Conceite'—less information than a fancy. Strikingly 'conceits' replaces 'coniects' a few lines later (148–9), where F Iago defensively plays up Othello's 'Wisedome'. Meanwhile, 'close denotements' in Q's exploratory exchange become uncommitted 'dilations, working from the heart' (123) in Folio, much as F's 'For *Michael Cassio*, | I dare be sworne, I thinke that he is honest' pulls back the devil's horns more sharply than Q's 'I dare presume' (125). Towards the

---

[20] 'Diabolic Intellect and the Noble Hero: or The Sentimentalist's Othello', repr. in F. R. Leavis, *The Common Pursuit* (London, 1952).

end of this sequence, we notice, quarto Othello's explosive 'Zouns' (154) is replaced by a baffled but genuinely interrogative 'What dost thou meane?'

Howsoever that may be, by the end of the scene Shakespeare is unmistakably concerned to make the Moor less amenable. In both texts, Othello returns to the stage, after Desdemona's loss of the handkerchief and Iago's exchange with Emilia, enraged and hating his tempter. He wishes he had remained ignorant, bids farewell to the plumed troops, and insists on 'ocul[a]r proofe'. Erratic in Q, he immediately proclaims Iago's honesty and has to be prompted by the Ensign into thinking once more about evidence. 'I should be wise, for honestie's a foole', Iago says, 'And looses that it workes for:' half-line pause, characteristic of his methods:

> I see sir, you are eaten vp with passion,
> I doe repent me that I put it to you,
> You wou'd be satisfied.
> *Oth.*   Would, nay, I will.

With the handkerchief to hand, and a plot ripening, Q Iago can risk encouraging the Moor to seek the proof he has already part-forgotten (III. iii. 382–3, 391–3). That does not happen in F; there Othello inherits Iago's half-line and says:

>   By the World,
> I thinke my Wife be honest, and thinke she is not:
> I thinke that thou art iust, and thinke thou art not:
> Ile have some proofe. My name that was as fresh
> As *Dians* Visage, is now begrim'd and blacke
> As mine owne face. If there be Cords, or Kniues,
> Poyson, or Fire, or suffocating streames,
> Ile not indure it. Would I were satisfied.

This may not be the most limber, intelligent blank verse, but its inflexible antitheses at least show Othello weighing in a balance the evidence he has heard against what he knows of the Ensign and Desdemona. Instructively, he echoes the First Senator's added idiom, with its 'If we make *thought* of this, | We must not *thinke*', its 'ease, and gaine' and 'wake, and wage'. And Othello demands, for himself, 'some proofe'.

In F this speech is a watershed, a parting of the ways, and when Iago offers 'some proofe' by mentioning the handkerchief—that scarlet-dabbled token lifted from revenge tragedy, strawberry-spotted like wedding sheets, and woven perhaps with 'witch-craft'[21]—Othello's collapse is correspondingly extreme. His debasement is registered in the vindictive oath, expanded in F into a highly dramatic set-piece. As Othello and his Ensign kneel together (III. iii. 453–69), the revised Moor rants about the Propontic and the Hellespont and swears 'by yond Marble Heauen' to act against his wife. 'Do not rise yet', Iago answers, effective in both texts but painfully attractive in the Folio as an instant parodist:

> Witnesse you euer-burning Lights aboue,
> You Elements, that clip vs round about,
> Witnesse that heere *Iago* doth giue vp
> The execution of his wit, hands, heart,
> To wrong'd *Othello*'s Seruice . . .

Now this revision, like the congruent one in the second big Iago/Othello scene, extending the Moor's epileptic fit (from IV. i. 35–7 to 43), might seem theatrically opportunistic. But the charge of crowd-pleasing can be discounted because the changes are linked to variants elsewhere in the tragedy, while both are consistent with Shakespeare's slightly more protective attitude towards the Folio Moor at this point in the action. 'Nature would not inuest her selfe in such shadowing passion, without some I[n]struction', for instance, in the epileptic speech, shows F Othello even at the point of breakdown thinking through the possibility of delusion. In a hideous sense, it is his willingness to think about unthinkable evidence which precipitates his collapse. 'It is not words that shakes me thus', he says: '(pish) Noses, Eares, and Lippes: is't possible'. The question is not asked in Q, and neither is the mesh which entangles the Moor so intricately displayed. The speech may lie at the limits of sanity, but nothing in it is redundant. 'O diuell' it ends in F: both 'Oh *Desdemon*!' (F v. ii. 281)[22] and 'If that thou bee'st a Diuell, I cannot kill thee [*Wounds Iago*, no more]' (v. ii. 287). Even the exclamation ('pish') works, as a classic instance of an Iago word carried into Othello's language; and it is carried from one sexually heightened Folio moment, in the exchange with Roderigo at II. i. 257–70, to another.[23]

[21] Kyd, *The Spanish Tragedy* II. v; Shakespeare, *3 Henry VI* I. iv; Tourneur, *The Atheist's Tragedy* II. i; Sigmund Freud, *Introductory Lectures on Psychoanalysis* (1916–17), trans. James Strachey, Pelican Freud Library vol. i (Harmondsworth, 1973), no. 17, 'A lady, nearly thirty years of age . . .'; *Othello* III. iv. 55–75, recalling Brabantio's additions (above, p. 12).

[22] The 'demon' in '*Desdemon*'—a form which occurs after the jealousy (I owe this point to Anne Barton), in F—matching the 'hell' in 'Othello', is seen at least as clearly in Cinthio's source (where the Moor has no name): 'Disdemona' there means, as in the New Testament, 'unfortunate', but it also reads 'Hades/*demon*/feminine ending'.

[23] 'Pish' occurs nowhere else in Q/F, and only once in the rest of Shakespeare.

And then, the combination of 'yond Marble Heauen' with Iago's kneeling and the 'euer-burning Lights aboue' generates, in F only, one of the most alarming ironies introduced by Shakespeare as reviser. Having developed III. iii, that is, the poet went on to add an echoic sequence in which Desdemona kneels to the Ensign (IV. ii. 150–9). 'By this light of heauen', she says in both texts, 'I know not how I lost him'. But F goes on:

> Heere I kneele:
> If ere my will did trespasse 'gainst his Loue,
> Either in discourse of thought, or actuall deed,
> Or that mine Eyes, mine Eares, or any Sence
> Delighted them [in] any other Forme,
> Or that I do not yet, and euer did,
> And euer will, (though he do shake me off
> To beggerly diuorcement) Loue him deerely,
> Comfort forsweare me.

Shakespeare once more associates heaven, light, and kneeling with a sweeping vow—for this is Desdemona's version of the Propontic speech; and his doing so involved more than a black structural joke. If, in Desdemona's genuflection, we see evidence of the Ensign's growing power, F also protects Othello from the hasty rebuke of those who blame the outcome entirely on him. Another, outside the circle of macho camaraderie, and with less reason to trust Iago, bends the knee.

Yet the editors neglect this. Norman Sanders, for example, concedes second thoughts but, like his New Arden precursor (1958), he uses signs of revision to underwrite eclecticism. Divergence is for him a local phenomenon and his *Othello* is 'arrived at by treating each pair of variants as a separate entity'.[24] This procedure reduces textual criticism to a lucky dip, since the well-printed substantive prizes are all Shakespearian. Professor Sanders does not choose to hear the resonance of F IV. ii in the F-only willow song and its aftermath—that argument between Desdemona and Emilia in which both swear 'by this Heauenly light' (IV. iii. 65–6). He does not pause to examine the Folio bolstering of Emilia there, against her mistress's rapt romanticism (86–103), nor trace through Act V the comic relativism which, associated with Iago's wife, tells against the Moor's stoic posturing (in, especially, the Folio-unique V. ii. 151–4, 185–93, and 246–8 vs. 266–72 and F variants at 338 and 342). His conflating policy makes him miss Shakespeare returning upon himself, visibly busier than everywhere else except Q and F *King Lear*.

[24] *Othello*, ed. Norman Sanders (Cambridge, 1984), 206.

For that play, finally, lies at the heart of the matter. Indeed, Peter Blayney made it the *start* of the matter when he showed that a grubby *Lear* published in 1608 was textually confused because of circumstances in Nicholas Okes's print-shop.[25] Previous editors had dismissed Q as a 'bad' text, derived from the same lost original as F, yet supplementing it. The actors playing Goneril and Regan had hastily assembled and dictated the text from papers filched out of Shakespeare's closet. Or an assiduous stenographer, visiting the Globe many times, had botched together a draft of the play and sold it to the printer with verse lined as prose plus all sorts of passages, oddly, not in the prompt-book. But Blayney showed that Okes's press was not equipped to print plays, so that, quite quickly, the compositors ran out of wooden blocks to fill the margins for verse and had to set it as prose instead. And he traced, precisely, a shortage of full stops—plays use them heavily, after each speech-prefix as well as in the text—which meant dialogue full of commas, seeming underpointed and eccentric. In short he showed that foul papers lay behind Q, with an authority distinct from F. Subsequent work has supported Blayney on stylistic as well as bibliographical grounds, and a growing consensus suggests that Q was set from papers preceding a prompt-book used for the first performance of the play in 1606, while F was printed from a copy of a reprint of the quarto annotated against a prompt-book of the play as revised on or from a copy of the first quarto probably put together in 1609–10. In a nutshell, Q and F approximate early and late versions of *King Lear*, both apparently authorial but separated by three or four years' hard writing and by the experience of producing plays like *Coriolanus* and *Pericles*.

Massive in scale and intricate in detail, Shakespeare's reworking of *King Lear* offers the most extreme and revealing evidence of his willingness to rethink. The blots in *Sir Thomas More*, interlinings of the *Dream*, foul to fair changes in *Hamlet*, and post-prompt-book further thoughts there and in *Troilus* perhaps and certainly in *Othello*: changes of each kind apparently recur in *Lear*. Some 285 lines in Q are cut from F, with a further 120 added. In common text, there are about 800 variants. And the changes affect most roles in the play. There is that sharp cutting in the second third of the tragedy which, combined with the removal of references to French involvement in the War for Britain, transforms the pace and temper of the play's drift towards catastrophe. Rapid and unsettling, F lacks the choric exchanges and static soliloquies which lend Q its

---

[25] A Cambridge Ph.D. leading to *The Texts of 'King Lear' and their Origins*, i: *Nicholas Okes and the First Quarto* (Cambridge, 1982).

amplitude.[26] There is the exaltation of Cordelia and diminution of Kent, the constraining of Edmund and refraction of the Fool.[27] Albany is strong in Q and has the play's last lines; in F, Edgar is more powerful, and he increasingly appropriates speeches from quarto Albany until he inherits the kingdom.[28] There is hardly a character in the play not caught up in revision. No scene is free from rewriting of some sort. At half a dozen points, conflation produces nonsense. And Q's family tragedy is more complex and political in F.

For, if one had to isolate the 'most important' strand in revision, it would start from the abdication speech.[29] In Q, Shakespeare does nothing to make Lear seem sagacious. The old man sits there with his map, like Hotspur and the rebels in *1 Henry IV*, presumptuously putting asunder a kingdom which Nature has assembled from 'shady forrests, and wide skirted meades'. Peremptory and self-concerned, the King offers no reason for his abdication beyond a desire to shake the 'cares and busines' of government from his shoulders:

> Meane time we will expresse our darker purposes,
> The map there; know we haue diuided
> In three, our kingdome; and tis our first intent,
> To shake all cares and busines of our state,
> Confirming them on yonger yeares,
> The two great Princes *France* and *Burgundy*,
> Great ryuals in our youngest daughters loue,
> Long in our Court haue made their amorous soiourne,
> And here are to be answerd, tell me my daughters,
> Which of you shall we say doth loue vs most,
> That we our largest bountie may extend,
> Where merit doth most challenge it,
> *Gonorill* our eldest borne, speake first?

[26] Taylor, 'War in *King Lear*', and, for a useful caution suggesting theatrical involvement, 'The Structure of Performance: Act Intervals in the London Theatres, 1576–1642', in John Jowett and Gary Taylor, *Shakespeare Reshaped, 1606–1623* (Oxford, 1993).

[27] Michael Warren, 'The Diminution of Kent', and Kerrigan, 'Revision, Adaptation', in Taylor and Warren (eds.), *Division*, 59–73, 195–245, but also Taylor, 'War in *King Lear*', and R. A. Foakes, 'Textual Revision and the Fool in *King Lear*', *Trivium*, 20 (1985), 33–47.

[28] Michael Warren, 'Quarto and Folio *King Lear* and the Interpretation of Albany and Edgar', in David Bevington and Jay L. Halio (eds.), *Shakespeare, Pattern of Excelling Nature* (Newark, Del., 1978), 95–107; Steven Urkowitz, *Shakespeare's Revision of 'King Lear'* (Princeton, 1980), ch. 5.

[29] I. i. 36–54. My account of this speech overlaps with Thomas Clayton, ' "Is this the promis'd end?": Revision in the Role of the King', and MacD. P. Jackson, 'Fluctuating Variation: Author, Annotator, or Actor?', in Taylor and Warren (eds.), *Division*, 121–41, 313–49, and Gary Taylor, *Moment by Moment by Shakespeare* (London, 1985), ch. 5.

The weight of this falls on paternal authority and filial love. Lear seems recklessly ready to sacrifice the realm for the sake of his comfort and a few words of flattery. All those fears of division and dissent fostered in the Elizabethan and Jacobean mind by tracts and homilies would have come to life when Shakespeare's projected audience heard this. It is worth recalling what that audience consisted of. We are told by the Stationers' Register and title-page of Q that the original *Lear* was performed at court during the Christmas Revels of 1606. Since we know that certain other plays belonging to Shakespeare's company were written with King James's interests in mind—*Macbeth*, for instance, which shows the origins of the Stuart succession in Banquo and Fleance—it is natural to wonder what this tragedy might have offered the King. Significantly, at just this time James was trying to persuade Parliament to accept the unification of Scotland with England and Wales, something not finally achieved until the eighteenth century. Q is not propaganda, but its first scene does present a view of national unity which would have been recognized at the time as conforming to that of the King.

In the Folio, by contrast, Shakespeare allows certain complicating factors inherent in his material to surface.

> Meane time we shal expresse our darker purpose.
> Giue me the Map there. Know, that we haue diuided
> In three our Kingdome: and 'tis our fast intent,
> To shake all Cares and Businesse from our Age,
> Conferring them on yonger strengths, while we
> Vnburthen'd crawle toward death . . .

What else was Lear to do? Critics are forever telling the King what he should not have done, and they quote *Gorboduc* to prove it. But what positive steps could the old man take to ensure the safety of the realm? Given his lack of a male heir, was he to respect primogeniture and leave the state in Goneril's less than ideal hands? Or make the best of an intractable problem by ensuring that at least part, the best part it seems, of Britain should be ruled by the kind and honest Cordelia? If the latter, was it not wise of Lear to divide the kingdom—or as Q reminds us at 1. i. 4 'kingdomes'—before his own death, given that, while alive, he could act as figurehead and arbiter, helping consolidate the potentially unstable system of tripartite government? You can watch the political issues surface. Quarto 'To shake all cares and busines of our state' uses 'state' to mean 'condition', 'of' as 'off'; F makes the line less ambiguous, while transforming 'all cares . . . of our state' into one phrase in a two-line parenthesis opened after 'Tell me my daughters': '(Since now we will di-uest vs both of Rule, | Interest of Territory, Cares of State)'. The change can scarcely be random since it rings, a few lines later, in Kent's variant—remarked by Dr Johnson as evidence of revision—'Reuerse thy doome', 'reserue thy state' (149). In Q, the counseller questions Lear's judgement in the love-trial; in F he engages with the issue of abdication.

At the same time, F Albany and Cornwall join Cordelia's suitors—ciphers in Q but associated in revision with wealth and territory, with 'The Vines of France' and 'Milke of Burgundie' (84).[30] The Folio reminds us of the redistribution of power which Lear's demotion must entail: to husbands and to foreign states as well as daughters. 'Our son of *Cornwal*, | And you our no lesse louing Sonne of *Albany*' it adds, at some risk of becoming a catalogue,

> We haue this houre a constant will to publish
> Our daughters seuerall Dowers, that future strife
> May be preuented now . . .

That last clause is, of course, crucial. Coleridge writes of Shakespeare's characteristic preference for 'expectation' over 'surprize',[31] and the Folio supports his insight, for, while 'prevented' means 'staved off' in Jacobean English, it also implies 'brought forward'. Unanticipated in Q, tragedy is courted while striven against in F. And it takes effect complexly. That obsessive rerun of Q's filial love-trial, the mock-trial (III. vi), goes, while Lear's developing political awareness is emphasized in lines about 'the strong Lance of Iustice', a rare addition to the stripped Act IV.[32] The family drama becomes as contingent as it is paradigmatic. Goneril is in revision, if not exactly pleasant, less opaquely evil.[33] It is Regan, not her sister, who in F slaps down Cordelia after the love-trial. When Oswald neglects

---

[30]   A laden rift marked by Keats in his F facsimile. By no means a textual bibliographer, and unread in Q (the play he knew was at this point virtually identical with F), Keats nevertheless on the first page of facsimile (*c*.88 lines) underscored almost half the added text (totalling *c*.9 lines)—with a stroke in the margin also against the enriched 36–41—but only *c*.3 lines common to Q/F. Since the markings show us, in a concrete form, Keats reading Shakespeare like Shakespeare returning to himself, it is uncanny, and moving, to find on the opposite page 'On sitting down to read King Lear once again' in holograph. For some related thoughts see Randall McLeod, 'UN*Editing* Shak-speare', *Sub-Stance*, 33/4 (1982), 26–55.

[31]   Samuel Taylor Coleridge, *Shakespearean Criticism*, ed. Thomas Middleton Raysor, 2 vols., 2nd edn. (London, 1960), ii. 199.

[32]   IV. vi. 165–70. See, especially, Roger Warren, 'The Folio Omission of the Mock Trial: Motives and Consequences', in Taylor and Warren (eds.), *Division*, 45–57.

[33]   Randall McLeod, '*Gon.* No more, the text is foolish.', in Taylor and Warren (eds.), *Division*, 153–93.

Lear, Kent trips him, and Goneril demands a reduction in the King's hundred knights (I. iv), the confrontation is prepared by her in Q but not in F. Throughout the early text, she is impetuous. Revision increases Lear's impatience, and there is a real sense in F of Goneril's cruelty interacting with and responding to provocation. Cuts and close changes make her quarrel with Albany better tempered (IV. ii); and, in the long last scene, F Goneril is attractively self-possessed. It is she, for example, who has the presence of mind to exclaim, when Albany challenges Edmund, 'An enterlude'. And where the quarto Goneril says, somewhat obviously, to Regan's 'Sick, ô sicke', 'If not, Ile nere trust poyson' (v. iii. 95–6), the revised sister darkly remarks, 'If not, Ile nere trust medicine.'

The glint of Iagesque irony here, 'poyson' becoming 'Work on my medicine, worke' (*Othello* IV. i. 44–5), is lost in conflation. But the change shows us Shakespeare revising intently. Three scenes earlier, and in a happier part of the family drama, Cordelia had been reunited with the King, recuperating from madness in sleep. In Q, a Doctor arranges Lear's wakening. But in F his lines are either abolished or given to a Gentleman, while Cordelia revives the King—takes him, in Lear's vivid phrase, 'out o'th'graue' (IV. vii. 24–47). Cerimon is, as it were, ousted by Marina. And a comparison with late Shakespeare seems inevitable. For the Doctor is in Q a Paulina figure, stage-managing the recovery, calling for music to rouse the King. In F, 'Please you draw neere, louder the musicke there' is cut, and Cordelia's 'kisse' proves cordial:

> O my deere Father, restauratian hang
> Thy medicine on my lippes, and let this kisse
> Repaire those violent harmes, that my two Sisters
> Haue in thy Reuerence made.

'Restauratian hang | Thy *medicine*'. Having in F thrust this into prominence by making it the key to Lear's recovery, Shakespeare chose—as so often with decisive dramatic moments—to root it firmly into the play's verbal texture. 'If you have poyson for me, I will drinke it', the restored King says (71). In the alteration of 'poyson' to 'medicine' three scenes later, we can see the reviser pointing a subliminal contrast in the family plot.[34]

And he had good reason to bear those 'lippes' in mind. Not for nothing did Shakespeare work against the practice of his late romances in removing the music. He emphasized the restorative medicine hanging on

[34] For a broader context, see *Sonnets and A Lover's Complaint*, ed. John Kerrigan (Harmondsworth, 1986), 422.

Cordelia's lips to anticipate the tender concentration with which Lear bends over his daughter when she is 'hang'd' and he seeks to bring her out of the grave (v. iii. 258–75). The effort is vain; she cannot be restored; Cordelia, as in the love-trial, says nothing (272–5); and both deaths begin,

> my poor Foole is hang'd: no, no, no life?
> Why should a Dog, a Horse, a Rat haue life,
> And thou no breath at all?

In Q Lear utters 'O, o, o, o', the groans which represent, in F *Hamlet,* a death rattle, but which are here, as in the fifth act of *Othello,* where the Moor sees what he has done to Desdemona, a terrible cry of despair. He faints, and wills himself to die, with 'Breake hart, I prethe breake.' In F those words are given to Kent, who seeks a loyal death like Enobarbus and Iras,[35] and Lear dies attending not to his own heart but to Cordelia's lips:

> Pray you vndo this Button. Thanke you Sir,
> Do you see this? Looke on her? Looke her lips,
> Looke there, looke there.

The ending has 'surprised' critics when they should have profoundly 'expected' it. Shakespeare, as Coleridge helps us notice, struck a second heat to lend the lines meaning. He did not make them suddenly transcendent, raising the King above tragedy as Bradley and his followers argued. But neither did he pitch Lear's death into pointlessness and the theatre of the absurd. The conflated text encourages such critical extremism because it obscures, with its quarto Doctor and music plus the Folio ending, the steady particularity of Shakespeare's design. As far back as III. iv, we find F adding 'Come, vnbutton heere' to give us the measure of Q/F 'Pray you, vndo this Button'. In such variants we glimpse Shakespeare as reviser intimately at work, preparing an outcome in which what tells are echoes of a known situation carrying into silence. Lear here realizes what time not being up might mean, and deixis suggests what could be said, given more words, about the love-trial and F's redoubled 'Nothing' (I. i. 88–9), and Desdemona coming back to life as Cordelia won't, and Pistol killing his prisoner on stage, and the order of dancers in *Much Ado,* and the history of editing in the eighteenth century[36]—about, in short, all the perplexed issues raised by being a character in Shakespeare's revised text.

---

[35] *Antony and Cleopatra* IV. ix; V. ii. 292–305.

[36] *Henry V,* ed. Gary Taylor (Oxford, 1982), 65–6; Stanley Wells, 'Editorial Treatment of Foul-Paper Texts: *Much Ado About Nothing* as Test Case', *Review of English Studies,* NS 31 (1980), 1–16, pp. 8–10; Steven Urkowitz, 'The Base Shall to th' Legitimate: The Growth of an Editorial Tradition', in Taylor and Warren (eds.), *Division,* 23–43.

CHAPTER 2

Between Michelangelo and Petrarch
Shakespeare's Sonnets of Art (1994)

The year 1494 found Michelangelo in Bologna: young, brash, and full of promise. Behind him lay his first major work, the *Madonna of the Steps*, a low relief carved with all the delicate solidity of Donatello, though left—like so many of Michelangelo's most emotional compositions— unfinished. Before him lay Rome, and a whole series of sculptural tri- umphs: the *Bacchus*, the *Pietà*, the bronze and marble *David*s of 1501–2, and the first designs for the Julius tomb. But, for twelve months or so, the young artist stayed in Bologna, at the house of Gianfrancesco Aldrovandi, carving very little, yet drawing, writing, and reading. Michelangelo had already encountered—in the circle of Lorenzo de' Medici—Ficino, Poliziano, and Pico della Mirandola; and he must have absorbed, during those years in Florence, the Neoplatonic doctrines which were to influence him for the rest of his life. Now, in Bologna, he steeped himself in the poets. 'Every evening', writes a contemporary biographer, Al- drovandi made Michelangelo 'read from Dante or from Petrarch and now and then from Boccaccio, until he fell asleep'.[1] Just how important Pe- trarch became can be judged from a sketch made for the two statues of David. Down the margin of the page, beside the strong right arm of the marble giant, the artist has written: 'Davicte cholla fromba | e io chollarco | Michelagniolo || Rocte lalta cholonna el ver . . .'[2]—at which point the text breaks off. 'David with the sling, and I with the bow; Michelangelo. The high column is broken, and the gre . . .' This jotting has puzzled art historians for many years, and its secrets are not quickly unlocked. If, however, we follow the clues offered by that last line, with its arresting quotation from the *Canzoniere*, we can make some progress towards

---

[1] Ascanio Condivi, 'Life of Michelangelo Buonarroti', in George Bull and Peter Porter (trans.), *Michelangelo: Life, Letters, and Poetry* (Oxford, 1987), 1–73, p. 18.

[2] See e.g. Howard Hibbard, *Michelangelo*, rev. edn. (Harmondsworth, 1978), 53–4.

understanding what it meant to write artful sonnets, in English as well as Italian, after Petrarch.

David could represent many things in 1502—not least, in republican Florence, opposition to the Medici family, the political Goliath of Tuscany. But his standard significance, sanctioned by centuries of biblical exegesis, was 'fortitude'. No doubt it was this tradition which led Michelangelo to model his marble *David* on the *Fortitude* which Nicola Pisano had carved into a column in the Pisan Baptistry. As images of stubborn strength, the pillar and David would persist. Leonardo, in 1504, doodles a sketch of Michelangelo's statue among pilastered buildings in his notebook. In Apianus and Amantius' *Inscriptiones sacrosanctae vetustatis* (1534) the broken column is classicized as a vulnerable emblem of immortality.[3] Puttenham, 'in Italie conuersant with a certaine gentleman', helped disseminate the motif in England, observing, in his *Arte of English Poesie*, that 'By this figure is signified stay, support, rest, state and magnificence.'[4] Michelangelo's mind will have passed from David to Petrarch's 'broken column', then, because he associated both with 'fortitude'. A second link is provided by artistic ambition. *Canzoniere* 269 is a love-lament. It bewails the sudden deaths of Petrarch's patron Giovanni Colonna, and of Laura. 'Rotta è l'alta colonna e 'l verde lauro' the line reads in full: 'the high column is broken, and the green laurel.'[5] While Giovanni is identified with 'una colonna' broken short, the laurels of creative success (such as were granted Petrarch by Robert of Naples in 1341)[6] are put in question. Preparing to carve his first important Florentine statue, and (as often when sketching major work) full of self-doubt, Michelangelo quoted Petrarch to record his fears of blasted fame. There is a third connection, the most subtle but far-reaching. 'Davicte cholla fromba | e io chollarco': the weapon which Michelangelo means to wield against Goliath is primarily a running-drill, the 'bow' used to turn the shaft which engraves fine details on sculpture. But it associates, inevitably, with the 'bow' used by the god of love. In Michelangelo's verse, bows repeatedly tend to the erotic, and his best-known drawing, the *Saettatori*,

---

[3] Reproduced in Elizabeth Cook, *Seeing through Words: The Scope of Late Renaissance Poetry* (New Haven, 1986), 27.

[4] Ed. Gladys Doidge Willcock and Alice Walker (Cambridge, 1936), 91, 97.

[5] All verse quotations from *Opere di Francesco Petrarca*, ed. Emilio Bigi, 2nd edn. (Milan, 1964).

[6] On this strain see Robert M. Durling, 'Petrarch's "Giovene donna sotto un verde lauro"', *Modern Language Notes*, 86 (1971), 1–20 and John Freccero, 'The Fig Tree and the Laurel', *Diacritics*, 5 (1975), 34–40.

shows archers—figured as their own bows and arrows—making passionately towards a seductive-looking Herm. From the 'fromba' to the 'arco' then; David's 'sling' suggests Michelangelo's 'bow'. Then, from the 'bow' as running-drill to Cupid's 'bow', and so to Petrarch's love-lament. Yet there is more to the glissade. For the bow of eros, in Petrarch as in Michelangelo, effectively is a running-drill, a tool for shaping images.

At almost every level of composition, the love poetry of the *Canzoniere* shows a calculated asymmetry. As the reader grasps one structure, it dissolves into another, producing irregularities that rather intimate the shifting formulations of life than Dantesque movement towards 'l'amor che move il sole e l'altre stelle' (*Paradiso* xxxiii. 145). Instead of dividing centrally at a major canzone like the *Vita nuova*, the *Rime sparse* break unevenly between 263 poems supposedly written during Laura's lifetime, and 103 composed 'In morte'. Such a disproportion recalls the shape of individual sonnets, where settled octave rhyme schemes give way to a range of possible sestets. The effects of love are adumbrated: a promise of order is apparently grasped, but frustrated by what ensues. Syntax and figuring show a similar drift towards irresolution. Consider 132, at the mid-point of 'In vita' (and the first of Petrarch's sonnets to be translated into English). 'S'amor non è, che dunque è quel ch' io sento? | ma s'egli è amor, per Dio, che cosa e quale . . .?' The poet asks whether it is love he feels, and, if so, what that 'viva morte' and 'dilettoso male' might be. At the end of the sonnet, trembling and burning in oxymoronic suspense, he is not much the wiser: 'e tremo a mezza state, ardendo il verno.' Though it owes much to the *dolce stil nuovo* of Dante and his contemporaries, the sonnet's idiom has an innovative insecurity which comes from the dispersal of the subject in a dialectic of turbulent emotion. Speculating and suffering, it can reach no end in itself. 'Se', Petrarch begins; and parallel 'if' clauses—so common in the *Canzoniere* and its progeny (including the verse of Michelangelo)—take up the entire octave, and spill over (a dramatic effect) into the sestet. Questions recur too, suspending the self in uncertainties, shying from declaration. Petrarch does not resolvingly figure love as a 'lord of terrible aspect', like Dante in the *Vita nuova*, nor as a winged putto stirring hot coals in the lover's breast. One has only to read a few lines of Chaucer's version of the *Canticus*—'If no love is, O God, what fele I so? | And if love is, what thing and which is he? | If love be good, from whennes cometh my woo?'[7]—to see that, with that

---

7 *Troilus and Criseyde*, I. 400–2, in *The Riverside Chaucer*, gen. ed. Larry D. Benson, 3rd edn. (Boston, 1987).

apostrophe and those strong cadences, one cannot talk of a Petrarchan tone in fourteenth-century English. Not until Wyatt does vernacular verse begin to match the subtle music of a passion which, as it begins, ends (and so has no end) in the *io*.

Poem 132 is no more than typical in its parallelism, its painful stalling at 'If? . . . If? . . . If?' Anaphora is characteristic, together with lists which offer little for the mind to catch at, though much to traverse:

> Benedetto sia 'l giorno e 'l mese e l'anno
> e la stagione e 'l tempo e l'ora e 'l punto
> e 'l bel paese e 'l loco ov'io fui giunto
> da' duo begli occhi che legato m'ànno . . .

Canzoniere 61 should be dull, it so firmly follows one syntactical structure, yet it has become an anthology piece. Language is here refined towards pure extension, continuously penultimate. 'Sentioque inexpletum quiddam in precordiis meis semper', Petrarch admitted in the prose *Secretum*:[8] 'in my heart I always feel something unfulfilled.' These sonnets do not close, like Shakespeare's, with pointed logic or a deft reversal. Indeed, they rarely deploy the couplet. Petrarch writes memorable last lines, but their greatness lies in what they absorb, not what they foreclose. Labouring in the *Trionfi* to build coherent iconographical worlds of Love, Chastity, Death, Eternity, the poet of the *Canzoniere* incites extremes to meet. Consecutive lyrics, such as the more religious Good Friday poem ('Padre del ciel . . .') which follows 61, are thus yoked by antithesis, like the 'living death' and 'delightful harm' of 'S'amor non è'. 'Of all the pleasing things I ever read or heard,' Petrarch wrote in *De remediis utriusque fortune*, 'almost nothing impressed itself more deeply . . . than Heraclitus's dictum: all things are ruled by strife.'[9] Swayed towards paradox, he produced a style which can be misunderstood if read through that of such mannered and mechanical followers as Serafino and Il Tebaldeo. Traces of this misconception mar even the best recent translation, by Robert M. Durling, as when he renders that final line of 132 ('e tremo a mezza state, ardendo il verno'), 'and I shiver in midsummer, burn in winter'.[10] Petrarch prefers the imbalance of a gerund, 'ardendo' (all matter for Heraclitus, we recall, was such a kind of 'burning'), and the reader is left with protraction. Significantly, 'verno'—which might have shut the sonnet by opposing

---

[8] *Opere*, ed. Bigi, 580.

[9] Preface to Bk. II, quoted and trans. Nicholas Mann, *Petrarch* (Oxford, 1984), 82.

[10] *Petrarch's Lyric Poems: The 'Rime sparse' and Other Lyrics*, trans. and ed. Robert M. Durling (Cambridge, Mass., 1976).

'state'—fails to do so because, though a standard poeticism for 'inverno' ('winter'), it can also mean 'vernal, spring-like', so that the 'winter' which concludes the sestet advances insidiously into spring, while the poet burns.

The problem of closure has an erotic aspect: sonnets cannot resolve because Laura remains unattainable. When Michelangelo's contemporary Pietro Aretino wrote his *Sonetti lussuriosi*, twenty-nine pornographic poems designed to accompany drawings by Giulio Romano, he found the inconclusive Petrarchan form inadequate for his purpose. For him, copulation called for the couplet, so he added to his fourteen-line lyrics heavily rhymed codas.[11] Yet Byron's question, 'Think you, if Laura had been Petrarch's wife, | He would have written sonnets all his life?',[12] seems clumsy. More suggestive is John Berryman's

> Seventy springs he read, and wrote, and read. . . .
> Also there was Laura and three-seventeen
> Sonnets to something like her . . . twenty one years . . .
> He never touched her.[13]

A famous canzone, translated by Spenser among others, describes Laura as: a doe with a human face, a ship with silken tackle, a laurel tree full of birdsong, a clear fountain, a phoenix with purple wings, and, finally, a lady clad in a garment seemingly of gold and snow.[14] In all these visions, including the last, we see 'something like' Laura. It is the imagined St Augustine of the *Secretum* who tells us that the woman herself died young and plain, worn out with childbearing. The poetic *io* seems ignorant of this Laura, in thrall to an elusive image. That is why Byron's gibe is inappropriate. Laura is everything to long for, yet (and therefore) never to be attained. While not possessed, she is in the poet's possession. Always inseparable from him, she seems closest when he is most alone. Hence the many poems which involve Petrarch in lonely wandering. 'I' l' ò piú volte (or chi fia che m' il creda?)', he writes in 129,

> ne l' acqua chiara e sopra l'erba verde
> veduto viva, e nel troncon d' un faggio,
> e 'n bianca nube, sí fatta che Leda

---

[11] For illustrated examples see e.g. Lynne Lawner's parallel-text *I modi: The Sixteen Pleasures* (London, 1988).

[12] *Don Juan* III. 63–4, in Lord Byron, *The Complete Poetical Works*, vol. v, ed. Jerome J. McGann (Oxford, 1986).

[13] *Collected Poems 1937–1971*, ed. Charles Thornbury (London, 1990), 108.

[14] *Canzoniere* 323; 'Epigrams' in *A Theatre for Worldlings* (1569).

> avria ben detto che sua figlia perde
> come stella che 'l sol copre col raggio;
> e quanto in piú selvaggio
> loco mi trovo e 'n piú deserto lido,
> tanto piú bella il mio pensier l' adombra.

Petrarch sees Laura in clear water, on the green grass, in the trunk of a beech tree, limned by cloud. And do we not find in that last phrase—where thought 'shadows forth' the object of desire—the poet revered by Michelangelo, the Petrarch who elsewhere called Laura 'an idol sculpted in living laurel'? For this is a canzone in which Laura's visage is drawn in stone: 'Ove porge ombra un pino alto od un colle, | talor m' arresto, e pur nel primo sasso | disegno co la mente il suo bel viso.' The bow of love becomes a creator's running-drill, shaping the lineaments of desire. 'Davicte cholla fromba | e io chollarco | Michelagniolo.'

The idea that lovers and artists shape the world alike runs deep in post-Petrarchan writing:

> S'egli è che 'n dura pietra alcun somigli
> talor l'immagin d'ogni altri a se stesso,
> squalido e smorto spesso
> il fo, com'i' son fatto da costei.
> E par ch'esempro pigli
> ognor da me, ch'i' penso di far lei.

The opening conceit of Michelangelo's madrigal,[15] probably written for Vittoria Colonna—that very Petrarchan name—acquires gravity as the *io* becomes end and beginning. Burckhardtian views of 'the Renaissance', emphasizing Petrarchan inwardness, neglect this dialectic, but it was arguably the *Canzoniere*'s greatest bequest. 'Ogni depintore depinge se medesimo', as Cosimo de' Medici said: 'every painter paints himself.'[16] Such views had become commonplace by the time Michelangelo sculpted *David*. Behind them lies Plato's *Timaeus*, the medieval tradition of *Deus artifex*, and, more largely, the Christian belief that God, loving man, made him in his own image. Artist and lover conceive similarly divine images, but their powers are woefully circumscribed by the limitations of mortal hands. This lends undercurrents of despair, of grim absurdity, to Michelangelo's most heroic achievements—as the ribald, tailed sonnet 'I' ho già fatto un gozzo in questo stento' suggests. At work

---

[15] Poem 242 in the *Rime*, ed. Ettore Barelli (Milan, 1975); all verse quotations from this edn.
[16] See e.g. David Summers, *Michelangelo and the Language of Art* (Princeton, 1981), 233.

in the Sistine Chapel, the artist imagines (and sketches) himself[17] as a 'bow', 'com'arco soriano', not bent by the mind but cramped in body at the top of his scaffolding.

Such frustration can be more sublimely expressed:

> Non ha l'ottimo artista alcun concetto
> c'un marmo solo in sé non circonscriva
> col suo superchio, e solo a quello arriva
> la man che ubbidisce all'intelletto. . . .

Michelangelo discerns an ideal image in the stone he addresses; but he cannot, like God, simply will a thing into effect, and his skill works against him, 'l'arte' ruining what is conceived:

> Amor dunque non ha, né tua beltate
> o durezza o fortuna o gran disdegno
> del mio mal colpa, o mio destino o sorte;
> se dentro del tuo cor morte e pietate
> porti in un tempo, e che 'l mio basso ingegno
> non sappia, ardendo, trarne altro che morte.

One begins to see why so many of the artist's works were torn or smashed in anger as he saw his execution blurring and distorting the *concetto*. It also becomes clear why his most challenging works were often left unfinished. 'His imagination was so powerful and perfect', writes Michelangelo's disciple Vasari, 'he often discarded work in which his hands found it impossible to express his tremendous and awesome ideas; indeed, he has often destroyed his work.'[18] From that early *Madonna of the Steps*, the line runs through the *Taddei Tondo*, the Florentine *St Matthew*, the *Dying, Rebellious, Young* and *Bearded Slaves* to the late *Rondanini Pietà*. Numbers of his most powerful poems are fragments—like the harrowing sestet 'In me la morte, in te la vita mia'—and his most complete poems are unpolished. Even the sublime marble *David* is unresolved, for the sculptor has left, on the crown of the giant's head (where only he and God could see it), a small area of unworked marble. It is as though Michelangelo felt that rough Italian and unworked stone kept his works tied to the ideal image in his soul, a harsh idiom and raw marble preserving the conception from ruin. This would explain why Michelangelo tended to finish only those works he cared about least, and why the

---

[17] Poem and caricature are reproduced in *Rime*, ed. Barelli, 38.
[18] *The Lives of the Artists*, sel. and trans. George Bush, rev. edn. (Harmondsworth, 1971), 418–19, cf. p. 404.

homosexual artist found it more difficult to complete statues of men than statues of women.

Such considerations may seem distant from Petrarch. But continuities of form, figuring, and syntactical structure between the poets are secured by a shared, frustrated desire for transcendence through love's imaging. Contradiction might be no more than a verbal tic in Bembo and his contemporaries, but the 'burning ice' and 'living death' of Michelangelo's songs and sonnets have a Petrarchan concentration. Much of his work can seem constituted by antithesis, from the tense cross-hatching used to sketch his nudes to such larger oppositions as those on the Medici tomb between *Dawn* and *Dusk*, *Day* and *Night*, and the Active and Contemplative Lives. Why was he so upset when Benedetto Varchi insisted that painting and sculpture were one, not contrary arts? And why was he obsessed by the oval (that circle with opposed extremities), anticipating baroque design by admitting it into his architecture, while inventing, it is said, a compass for drawing the ellipse? Nowhere is this commitment more evident than in the male nudes he created in such abundance. Almost invariably these display *contrapposto*: an antithetical disposition of the limbs. Recall the Florentine *Victory*, the *Creation of the Sun and Moon* in the Sistine Chapel, the *Saettatori*, or (for that matter) the marble *David*. It might seem far-fetched to insist on a link, but throughout this period—as the poem/pillar/statue configurations of Puttenham, Herrick, and others suggest—sculpture, painting, and poetry were nearly-related modes. Language itself shows this: *contrapposto* is an Italian version of Latin *contrapositum*, used by rhetoricians to render the Greek *antithesis*. Michelangelo found in the Petrarchan sonnet what he admired in the classically posed male nude: a divided, exacting form which could express his sublime but thwarted aesthetic.

There is a celebrated passage on literary imitation and painting in the Moral Epistles of Seneca the Younger: 'Etiam si cuius in te comparebit similitudo, quem admiratio tibi altius fixerit, similem esse te volo quomodo filium, non quomodo imaginem; imago res mortua est.'[19] For Seneca, the proper measure of resemblance in *imitatio* is that which holds between father and son, not between a picture and what it reproduces. He

---

[19] *Ad Lucilium epistulae morales*, ed. and trans. Richard M. Gummere, 3 vols. (London, 1917–25), ii. 280 (Ep. 84. 8): 'Even if there shall appear in you a likeness to him who, by reason of your admiration, has left a deep impress upon you, I would have you resemble him as a child resembles his father, and not as a picture resembles its original; for a picture is a lifeless thing.'

writes of the dead completeness of art-objects in a spirit almost as extreme as that of the despondent Michelangelo: 'non sappia, ardendo, trarne altro che morte.' The virtue of good imitation (Seneca goes on to say) is that it so deeply impresses what it borrows with its own form that deciding which of two texts copied the other becomes impossible. The practice, as well as theory, of good imitation is exemplified by a letter of Petrarch's to Boccaccio:

> curandum imitatori ut quod scribit simile non idem sit, eamque similitudinem talem esse oportere, non qualis est imaginis ad eum cuius imago est, que quo similior eo maior laus artificis, sed qualis filii ad patrem. In quibus cum magna sepe diversitas sit membrorum, umbra quedam et quem pictores nostri aerem vocant, qui in vultu inque oculis maxime cernitur, similitudinem illam facit.[20]

This follows the Moral Epistles in cautioning against the idea that literary imitation should be as precisely reproductive as portraiture, but Petrarch's account of painting is less hostile. Indeed, he pointedly adopts the language of painters to describe that divergence from source which imitation should display. The visage of the secondary text ought to be shadowed with the 'air' of the father. Since recent work on Renaissance literary theory has found that *imitatio* was not clearly distinguished from *translatio*, *paraphrasis*, and *allusio*,[21] we can demonstrate what Petrarch was warning against by quoting Wyatt:

> Caesar, when that the traitor of Egypt
> With th'honourable head did him present,
> Covering his gladness, did represent
> Plaint with his tears outward, as it is writ. . . .[22]

Matching as closely as possible the rhythms and sound-patterns of *Canzoniere* 102, Wyatt shows how inert initial trochees and feminine chiming,

---

[20] *Le familiari*, ed. Vittorio Rossi and Umberto Bosco, 4 vols. (Florence, 1933–42), iv. 206 (XXIII. 19). In Morris Bishop's selection, *Letters from Petrarch* (Bloomington, Ind., 1966), the following trans. is offered: 'A proper imitator should take care that what he writes resembles the original without reproducing it. The resemblance should not be that of a portrait to the sitter—in that case the closer the likeness is the better—but it should be the resemblance of a son to his father. Therein is often a great divergence in particular features, but there is a certain suggestion, what our painters call an "air," most noticeable in the face and eyes, which makes the resemblance' (pp. 198–9).

[21] e.g. Thomas M. Greene, *The Light in Troy: Imitation and Discovery in Renaissance Poetry* (New Haven, 1982), 51–2. For overviews, cf. G. W. Pigman III, 'Versions of Imitation in the Renaissance', *Renaissance Quarterly*, 33 (1980), 1–32, Richard S. Peterson, *Imitation and Praise in the Poems of Ben Jonson* (New Haven, 1981), ch. 1, David Quint, *Origin and Originality in Renaissance Literature: Versions of the Source* (New Haven, 1983).

[22] Quotations from *Sir Thomas Wyatt: The Complete Poems*, ed. R. A. Rebholz (Harmondsworth, 1978).

based on Petrarch's hendecasyllabics, can become. Some wrought arcs of phrasing, such as that which ends this sonnet's octave—'His cruel despite for to disgorge and quit'—are feats of vocal imitation ('per isfogare il suo acerbo despitto'), yet Petrarch's 'air' is repeatedly lost in ellipsis, bluntness, and redundancy.

Where Wyatt diverges from source, moreover, at the end of his sonnet, it is to react against Petrarch's open plangency by speaking of 'sport and play'. In the turbulent court of Henry VIII, where imprisonment and execution were a continual threat and patronage made the difference between high office and ruin, Wyatt is drawn to those facets of the *Canzoniere* which are interested in secrecy. This strain in the *Rime sparse* encouraged him to cultivate a cloaked, resistant idiom firmly braced within the rhythms of Tudor English. But the resulting interplay of accent and emotion is very different in imaginative texture from even those parts of the *Canzoniere* which present public experience as private loss:

> The pillar perished is whereto I leant,
> The strongest stay of mine unquiet mind;
> The like of it no man again can find—
> From east to west still seeking though he went—
> To mine unhap, for hap away hath rent
> Of all my joy the very bark and rind . . .

This is the sonnet quoted by Michelangelo in 1502. Yet, in Wyatt's version, pathos and insecurity are compensated by metrical assurance. 'I leant' counterpoints and partly offsets the seeking of 'went', and 'mind' at the same pitch 'finds' itself. Wyatt's syntax goes some way towards reconstructing Petrarchan complexity, but not in his terms. English, as Jiří Levý has shown,[23] has a phonetic logic which leads to sonnet closure. The Italian hendecasyllabic, ending on an upturn, and the iambic pentameter, are weighted differently, and this generates for English Petrarchans a difficult-to-harness, though sometimes effective, tension between stated weakness and voiced strength.

What is the 'air' of Wyatt? Drawn by Holbein, his face flickers with unease, mouth tensed, eyes evasive and on guard. Surrey, by contrast, projects through the same artist's portraiture a clearer, less defensive image, vulnerable but self-contained, topped out smartly with a plumed hat. As in the case of Wyatt, Holbein might have been drawing the verse:

---

[23] 'The Development of Rhyme-Scheme and of Syntactic Pattern in the English Renaissance Sonnet', *Acta Universitatis Palackianae Olomucensis*, 7, Philologica, 4 (1961), 167–85.

Set me wheras the sonne dothe perche the grene,
Or whear his beames may not dissolve the ise;
In temprat heat wheare he is felt and sene;
With prowde people, in presence sad and wyse;
Set me in base, or yet in highe degree,
In the long night, or in the shortyst day . . .[24]

Avoiding the jolts of Wyatt, Surrey is partly successful in imitating the smooth-filed eloquence of *Canzoniere* 145. His performance is less concerned with the relations between self and public life than with ease of manner. Yet, by line 4, Surrey has so tired of Petrarch's oppositions that he ignores the drift of the sun's car from east to west and substitutes 'With prowde people . . .'. As an assertion of aristocratic hauteur, imperatively desiring to suffer in the best company, this is awkwardly at odds with the paradox which reverts to Petrarch: 'Set me in base, or yet in highe degree.' It is not, however, so inept as the antithesis of line 6: 'In the long night, or in the shortyst day.' Petrarch here creates a double opposition, between day and night, long and short: 'ponmi a la notte, al dí lungo ed al breve.' Surrey responds with a merely ostensible balance, because a 'long night' and 'the shortyst day' go together (in December). These antitheses are not thought—never mind felt—through. The music of Petrarch is emulated, but little of his substance remains. Only in the couplet, when, in the manner of Wyatt, Surrey rejects the anguished penultimacy of his original ('continuando il mio sospir trilustre') for the sake of an almost defiant containment—'Yours will I be, and with that onely thought | Comfort my self when that my hape is nowght'—does *imitatio* flicker with an access of emulative creativity.[25]

It might seem eccentric to approach Shakespeare from this angle, to place his artful sonnets between the statues, pictures, and poems of Michelangelo and the Petrarch of these learned Henricians. If it does, that is because scholarship continues to lay false emphases. Though few would now explicitly subscribe to the eighteenth-century notion of the Bard as fancy's child, a poet who needed not the spectacles of books, there is a persistent reluctance to acknowledge his affiliation with the self-conscious literary humanism of Petrarch, Erasmus, Buchanan, Montaigne. There are several reasons for this, but all are reinforced by the use made of Shakespeare in a western educational system which, to preserve his valuable centrality, cannot afford to stress his erudition and historical distance. It

---

[24] Quoting *Henry Howard, Earl of Surrey: Poems*, ed. Emrys Jones (Oxford, 1964).
[25] On *aemulatio* see e.g. Quintilian, *Institutio oratoria*, 10. 2. 9–10.

is true that, thanks to such scholars as T. W. Baldwin, G. K. Hunter, Emrys Jones, and Joel Altman, readers have been alerted to the way in which early Shakespearian drama and, to a lesser extent, the mature plays are enriched by their relations to humanistic theatre and historiography. It has also become customary to stress the grammar-school Ovidianism of *Venus and Adonis* and *Lucrece*. But the *Sonnets* seem to have been rescued from Victorian, autobiographical reading only to find themselves (for the most part) subject to the self-referential obsessions and dispersals of formalism and deconstruction. When read as Shakespeare's diary, or with the assumption that lyric poems constitute their own fields of reference, these texts cannot communicate their 'imitative' complexity. More recent, new historicist attempts to relate them to 'the discourse of patronage' (was there only one?), and other modes of cultural circulation,[26] might be preferable to speculative effusions about the love-life of the Earl of Southampton, but, working Shakespeare into the socio-political dynamics of early modern England, they do little to clarify his place within traditions of learned writing.

That the *Sonnets* are exercises in *imitatio* is often, though, strikingly apparent. Numbers 153–4, for instance, can scarcely be understood without reference to a European-wide anacreontic cult spawned by the Greek Anthology. These poems are as evidently erudite and emulative as anything by Wyatt or Surrey. Yet, although their intertextual allegiance has been reconstructed by James Hutton,[27] they remain out of focus for most readers because so much that is 'imitative' elsewhere in the sequence—especially of Sidney and Daniel—is overlooked or patronized, as though literary 'debts' implied artistic immaturity, or were residual impurities which should have been purged by the heat of composition. It is a striking feature of the *Sonnets*, however, that they make elegant, explicit, and highly purposeful use of Erasmus. They allude, more or less at the outset (both in the 1609 ordering and, it would seem,[28] chronologically), to a

---

[26] e.g. John Barrell, 'Editing Out: The Discourse of Patronage and Shakespeare's Twenty-Ninth Sonnet', in his *Poetry, Language and Politics* (Manchester, 1988), 18–45, Patricia Fumerton, '"Secret Arts": Elizabethan Miniatures and Sonnets', *Representations*, 15 (1986), 57–97, repr. in Stephen Greenblatt (ed.), *Representing the English Renaissance* (Berkeley, 1988), 93–133.

[27] 'Analogues of Shakespeare's Sonnets 153–4: Contributions to the History of a Theme', *Modern Philology*, 38 (1941), 385–403, repr. in his *Essays on Renaissance Poetry*, ed. Rita Guerlac (Ithaca, NY, 1980), 149–68.

[28] On dating see A. Kent Hieatt, Charles W. Hieatt, and Anne Lake Prescott, 'When Did Shakespeare Write Sonnets 1609?', *Studies in Philology*, 88 (1991), 69–109, and, for the manuscript version of Sonnet 2, Mary Hobbs, 'Shakespeare's Sonnet II—"A Sugred Sonnet"?', *Notes and Queries*, 224 (1979), 112–13, Gary Taylor, 'Some Manuscripts of Shakespeare's Sonnets', *Bulletin of the John Rylands Library*, 68 (1985–6), 210–46.

letter in *De conscribendis epistolis* which expounds that model of father–son resemblance which Seneca and Petrarch have taught us to read as an image of successful *imitatio*.[29] Even if the sonnets on breeding were actually written to persuade a beautiful, negligent nobleman to produce an heir, the textual situation is one which not only makes an old wooing theme new (the lovely youth as Laura) but renders uniquely integral the theme of imitation. Sidney punctuates *Astrophil and Stella* with poems about feebly imitative poetry, mocking the Petrarchism of the Pléiade and, to a lesser extent, his Tudor predecessors.[30] Shakespeare can be less explicit because, in a continuous shadowed conceit, the proliferation of imitative texts is figured as conceiving children.

This helps explain the relative coolness of his urgings to breed. In Sonnets 1 to 15 we always sense a better argument—let poetry reproduce you—waiting in the wings. The poet's promise to 'engraft' the youth,[31] first raised in the couplet of 15, becomes a compound undertaking to defeat 'decay', to produce childlike poems and to generate further sonnets by thinking about the means and morality of such production. Moreover, as a 'graphic' act (the ambiguity is there in 'engraft'), writing has a painterly aspect. Not least because of the manuscript circumstances of early circulation,[32] imitative script moves the pen into a form of portraiture:

> Now stand you on the top of happy hours,
> And many maiden gardens, yet unset,
> With virtuous wish would bear your living flowers,
> Much liker than your painted counterfeit:
> So should the lines of life that life repair
> Which this time's pencil, or my pupil pen,
> Neither in inward worth nor outward fair
> Can make you live yourself in eyes of men.
> To give away yourself keeps yourself still,
> And you must live drawn by your own sweet skill.

When Shakespeare writes this in Sonnet 16, he demonstrates his imitative resourcefulness by avoiding dead reproduction. Whatever Seneca or

[29] See T. W. Baldwin, *On the Literary Genetics of Shakspere's Poems and Sonnets* (Urbana, Ill., 1950), 183, notably for the mediating role of Thomas Wilson's *Arte of Rhetorique* (1553, rev. 1560). For Erasmus' use of father–son resemblance to characterize *imitatio*, emulating Seneca and Petrarch, see e.g. Pigman, 'Versions of Imitation', 9.

[30] e.g. 3, 6, 15.

[31] Quotations from *The Riverside Shakespeare*, ed. G. Blakemore Evans et al. (Boston, 1974).

[32] Cf. Shakespeare, *Sonnets and A Lover's Complaint*, ed. John Kerrigan (Harmondsworth, 1986), 10, 441 ff.

Petrarch might assume, painters are rarely (he reminds us) good at like-nesses. As cleverly, he develops the idea that script resembles portraiture to suggest that breeding children involves an impulse to draw the counte-nance of a child. The young man should become both the painter and that father whose 'air' is imitated in a son's visage. When the noble youth demurs, Shakespeare advances verse as a means of survival first parallel to, then a substitute for, drawing stemmata. By 'copy[ing] what . . . is writ' in the friend, the poet can create his simulacra, poetic children. Gradually, through sonnets later than the triumphant 19 and literary-critical (almost Sidneian) 21, the mimetic action of writing gives way to an inner genera-tion of the other which makes the poet father the youth—that object of address and devotion who finally becomes 'my lovely boy' (126). The ironies as well as hopes implicit in this development resemble those dis-covered by earlier artists wielding a running-drill. 'It is probably in the na-ture of any profound erotic desire', Yasunari Takahashi shrewdly remarks, in a discussion of *Izutsu*, 'that it annihilates the rational demarcation of subject/object, active/passive, and self/other.'[33] Where Petrarch becomes a laurel in Canzone 23, or is turned to 'pietra morta' after drawing Laura's face in the 'pietra viva' of 129, and where Michelangelo finds himself cold and pale like the statue that he is carving, Shakespeare writes, ''Tis thee (myself) that for myself I praise, | Painting my age with beauty of thy days' (62).

The idea that Shakespeare goes on about 'painting' because he puri-tanically detested cosmetics—a notion still found in the commentaries—requires heavy qualification. For him, the polarity is not between vile daubing and virtuous nakedness because the opposite of being falsely coloured is being (what Sonnet 20 calls) 'with Nature's own hand painted'. It is because the excuse is routine, not because it is necessarily false, that Sonnet 101 is apologetic about its apology, ' "Truth needs no color with his color fix'd, | Beauty no pencil, beauty's truth to lay . . .".' When Olivia pulls aside her veil (like the 'curtain' over a 'picture') to re-veal her beauty to Cesario, and insists against his/her insinuation that her colours are 'in grain' (*Twelfth Night* I. v. 230 ff.), the artifice lends the scene brittle intensity but does not reduce her value. ''Tis beauty truly blent,' Cesario murmurs (in a sudden escape from prose), 'whose red and white | Nature's own sweet and cunning hand laid on.' Leo Salingar is

[33] 'How to Present a Japanese Ghost: Touring Europe with a Noh Troupe', *Temenos*, II (1990), 5–20, p. 10.

right to warn us, in 'Shakespeare and the Italian Concept of "Art"',[34] that for this dramatist 'art' often carried deceitful connotations; but the greater danger lies in our neglecting the sophistication of passages which use 'art' artfully:

> Mine eye hath play'd the painter and hath stell'd
> Thy beauty's form in table of my heart;
> My body is the frame wherein 'tis held,
> And perspective it is best painter's art.
> For through the painter must you see his skill,
> To find where your true image pictur'd lies,
> Which in my bosom's shop is hanging still,
> That hath his windows glazed with thine eyes.
> Now see what good turns eyes for eyes have done:
> Mine eyes have drawn thy shape, and thine for me
> Are windows to my breast, wherethrough the sun
> Delights to peep, to gaze therein on thee.
> > Yet eyes this cunning want to grace their art,
> > They draw but what they see, know not the heart.

The epistemological puzzling of Sonnet 24 can put off even readers accustomed to John Ashbery and A. R. Ammons. As an attempt to grapple with the self-othering paradoxes of Petrarchan tradition, however, it is formidably accomplished. Though it lacks the fluid, associative figuring of the *Canzoniere*, its clever play on 'eyes'—those crystal windows which open into 'I'—is more than routinely conceited. For this 'eye' has the strength to sketch and apparently engrave (line 1 of the quarto reads 'steeld'), to depict images in hard matter, like Michelangelo's 'arco'. 'Form', 'image', and 'art' might not have the Neoplatonic reach and resonance of cognate terms in the sculptor's sonnets, but they do begin to show how the poet can become the youth's sweetly skilled drawer. His bosom is an artful cabinet, anticipating Paulina's gallery in *The Winter's Tale*.

Various later sonnets are rooted in Sonnet 24. The pair on eye/heart disputation, 46 and 47, for instance, make adroit, if slightly chilly, use of the breast-as-closet with 'love's picture' topic. As significant as this continuity, however, is the proximity of all three poems to sonnets about dreaming. Of these, 43 is the most searchingly paradoxical, but the earlier couple, 27–8, have a key role in developing the poet's authority as other-

---

[34] *Renaissance Drama Newsletter*, Supplement 3 (Warwick, 1984), repr. in Salingar's *Dramatic Form in Shakespeare and the Jacobeans* (Cambridge, 1986), 1–18.

reproducer. If lonely wanderings bring out the visionary in Petrarch, the author of *The Taming of the Shrew* and *The Tempest* deepens the subjectivity of his 'I' by 'Looking on darkness' and finding, in that 'eye''s scope, a world of 'imaginary sight' (27). The power of optic beams to configure and effectively realize a loved object fascinated Shakespeare, but in the *Sonnets* he elaborates what might have remained within the sphere of commonplace by fusing this capacity into the 'I''s reproductive scheme. The poet begins to suggest that his 'eye/I' is inherently 'conceptual', painting ahead of perception what the mind desires to see. To that extent Shakespeare's position recalls Michelangelo's

if one considers all that is done in this life, one will find that every man unconsciously is engaged in painting this world, both in creating and producing new forms and figures, in dressing variously, in building and filling in spaces with buildings and houses, in cultivating the fields and ploughing the land into sketches and pictures . . .[35]

Yet the bravura sweep of this points up the troubled, counter-energies of those sonnets concerned with the astigmatism of lovesick 'eyes'. Some of the bleakest poems to the dark lady, such as 137 ('Thou blind fool, Love') and 148 ('O me! what eyes hath Love put in my head'), deal with moral blindness and erotically-warped sight. The related baroque iconography which opens *A Lover's Complaint*, and the 'fickle maid''s extravagant blazoning of the young man's beauty, show similar anxieties being explored.[36]

    It is in Sonnets 113–14, however, that Shakespeare modulates the paradoxes of Petrarchan seeing towards that distinctive late-play phenomenology which makes an island both barren and (to other eyes) fertile, which turns a statue (when looked at differently) into a woman, and which, with disconcerting frequency, renders the world plastic to the senses. Number 113 might begin with a commonplace ('Since I left you, mine eye is in my mind'), but its psychological blurs and strong rhymes—'Seems seeing, but effectually is out'—quickly suggest the mental confusions and physical violence of Jacobean theatre ('Out, vild jelly!').[37] When the poet says that regardless of what is looked at (rude or gentle,

----

[35] Quoted from *Four Dialogues on Painting*, trans. A. F. G. Bell (London, 1928), in Leonard Barkan's stimulating essay, '"Living Sculptures": Ovid, Michelangelo, and *The Winter's Tale*', *ELH* 48 (1981), 639–67, p. 654.

[36] See John Kerrigan (ed.), *Motives of Woe: Shakespeare and 'Female Complaint'. A Critical Anthology* (Oxford, 1991), esp. 34–7, 41–3.

[37] *King Lear* III. vii. 83.

crow or dove) the eye 'shapes them' to the young man's 'feature', his thought is still in touch with Petrarchan plangency. But its pathos conceals a danger which the last line of 113 concedes—'My most true mind thus maketh mine [*read* m'eyne] untrue'—and which 114 develops:

> Or whether doth my mind being crown'd with you
> Drink up the monarch's plague, this flattery?
> Or whether shall I say mine eye saith true,
> And that your love taught it this alcumy,
> To make of monsters and things indigest
> Such cherubins as your sweet self resemble,
> Creating every bad a perfect best
> As fast as objects to his beams assemble?

These mustering 'beams' would be happier in operation did not 'plague' and 'flattery' suggest that the transformation of bad to good involves something like deception. The 'cherubins' recall 'Angelo', as well as the treacherous youth of *A Lover's Complaint* (316–19). Even in this form, the passionate sight which dreamingly sees in 27–8 and 43 has acquired an instability which alarms. It is virtually the sight of Leontes, putting Hermione's life at the 'level' (an eyesight word)[38] of his 'dreams':

> O, 'tis the first, 'tis flatt'ry in my seeing,
> And my great mind most kingly drinks it up;
> Mine eye well knows what with his gust is 'greeing,
> And to his palate doth prepare the cup.
>   If it be poison'd, 'tis the lesser sin
>   That mine eye loves it and doth first begin.

The sestet of 114 gives us the poet as King of Sicilia, the monarch who drinks and sees the spider, astigmatically discerning what the poisoned mind's eye desires. Against Leontes' sight, in this dispensation, naked truth does not stand; there can only be (in Kent's words) better seeing. The *theatrum mundi* is painted every way, like the vivid timberwork of the Globe. It is the artistry of a Paulina, a new perspective, 'best painter's art', which provides the antidote to poison.

Significantly, Paulina gives the cast of *The Winter's Tale* a guided tour of her gallery before introducing them to the stone Hermione. They are acclimatized to wonder. Whatever Shakespeare's reason for exchanging Sicily and Bohemia in his sources, making Leontes rule where Robert Greene's Pandosto had not, one effect is to associate the gallery with an

---

[38] e.g. *A Lover's Complaint*, 22.

island off the Italian coast and so with the High Renaissance of Bembo and Michelangelo. 'Julio Romano', supposed sculptor of the statue (as well as notorious illustrator of Aretino's sonnets), is 'that rare Italian master . . . who, had he himself eternity and could put breath into his work, would beguile Nature of her custom' (v. ii. 97–9). Interestingly, this artist is said to have 'perform'd' his 'piece' (96). There is more than a hint in the scene's unfolding that Shakespeare, arch-exploiter of theatrical metaphor, means to use stage space to configure the psychological paradoxes of Italian art, much as he had, in *Hamlet*, employed it as a locus of memory. Certainly the Queen's descending reruns old sonnet images, reaching back to Dante's *Rime petrose*, his stony rhymes. Hermione is a variation on the topos of the flint-hearted mistress, aloof for sixteen years, deciding to accept love. She is Pygmalion's maiden—the subject of Petrarch's poem on Martini's portrait of Laura—brought to life out of marble by Venus. And she is also, obviously but most subtly, an actress or boy-actor, pretending to be pretending to be a statue. What happens when the marble warms is that one frame of reference (which allows for the actress's inadequacy as a statue) shifts into another (the inadequacy read, instead, as what now appears). The statue does not change, but is regarded as mortal. When the audience conceives her differently, she becomes what Michelangelo called a 'living sculpture'.[39] She is indeed, as Paulina warns, freshly painted, yet painted with Nature's own hand. Moreover, the characters grouped round the pedestal are touched by that astonishment which has a Gentleman report of the Kings' reunion: 'Who was most marble there chang'd color' (v. ii. 89–90). Perdita stands 'like stone' before her mother; Leontes ('does not the stone rebuke me | For being more stone than it?') is 'numb' as Hermione awakens (v. iii. 37–42, 102). The desire of those round the plinth to find loved life in stone, to trace in marble the lineaments of a desired object, fixes them in that pale numbness plotted by Petrarch, and turned by Michelangelo's running-drill.

[39] Cf. Barkan, '"Living Sculptures"', 653.

CHAPTER 3

Keats and Lucrece *(1988)*

Among the papers at Keats House, Hampstead, is a marked-up copy of Shakespeare's *Poetical Works*,[1] ignored, in large part, both by Keatsians and by students of his 'Presider'.[2] Caroline Spurgeon may give us, in her classic study, the gist of Keats's notes to the plays, *Venus and Adonis*, and the *Sonnets*; but, like every other praiser of Keats's 'Shakespearian' qualities,[3] she neglects the marks and remarks which criss-cross *A Lover's Complaint* and *Lucrece*. The omission is a grave one, not only because it reinforces assumptions about what is distinctively 'Shakespearian' which Keats, allowed a hearing, might correct, but because the gathering of poems—a loan perhaps, then gift, from J. H. Reynolds[4]—was so constant a companion and informing an influence during Keats's productive years that it deserves the fullest attention from those who wish to understand the growth of his genius.

Perhaps the most surprising feature of this volume is the dense underlining it shows throughout *A Lover's Complaint*. The poem has been read closely and with enjoyment. Keats and Reynolds, parleying, it appears,

---

[1] *The Poetical Works of William Shakespeare* (London, 1806), no editor cited, published for Thomas Wilson. Shakespeare's poems are quoted from this edition (long s modernized, as throughout the essay); for line references, and quotations from the plays, the Oxford *Complete Works* (1986) is employed.

[2] *The Letters of John Keats 1814–1821*, ed. Hyder Edward Rollins, 2 vols. (Cambridge, 1958), i. 142.

[3] *Keats's Shakespeare: A Descriptive Study* (London, 1928). The critical tradition goes back to Richard Woodhouse (letter to John Taylor, *c*.27 Oct. 1818, *Letters*, ed. Rollins, i. 388–90). Furthered by Arnold's essay 'John Keats' (1880) and Middleton Murry's *Keats and Shakespeare* (London, 1925), it still offers insights (see, for example, chs. 8 and 9 of Jonathan Bate's *Shakespeare and the English Romantic Imagination* (Oxford, 1986) and R. S. White, *Keats as a Reader of Shakespeare* (London, 1987)).

[4] The title-page is inscribed 'John Hamilton Reynolds to John Keats 1819' but, given the correlation between its marking and Keats's comments in letters written before that date, Spurgeon is probably right to suppose 'that Reynolds lent this volume to Keats some time before he actually gave it him for his own' (*Keats's Shakespeare*, 38). The famous epistle from Burford Bridge, on 'beauties in the sonnets' and '"cockled snails"' (*Letters*, ed. Rollins, i. 187–90), proves 'Shakespear's Poems' an inspiration by 22 Nov. 1817, and a book worth mentioning to Reynolds rather than (in the same day's correspondence) to Benjamin Bailey.

through annotation, underline, endorse each other's underlining with verticals in the margin, redouble those, and add enthusiastic footnotes. Opening the book now, one seems to eavesdrop on literary conversation in the Keats circle—dialogue which continued until the circle broke and Keats set sail for Italy and death, taking this volume with him and inscribing, opposite the first stanzas of *A Lover's Complaint*, 'Bright star, would I were stedfast as thou art . . .' The pleasure apparent in the Hampstead markings should give us pause. Academic ears may judge the complaint 'from the same belfry' as 'Shall I die?', or damn it as 'ostensibly efficient',[5] but Reynolds will scribble, against an especially complex and heavily marked passage (141–7), 'a very characteristic stanza', and opine of the lines 'O father, what a hell of witchcraft lies | In the small orb of one particular tear' (288–9), 'perhaps as fine as anything in his plays'.

By no means all the underlining in this 'fine' and 'characteristic' poem can be attributed, but a continuity in practice with other parts of the book suggests that, as Spurgeon concluded of the volume's *Sonnets*, after a thorough examination of all Keats's Shakespearian notes, 'by far the greatest amount of marking is by Keats'.[6] Certainly, when the relaxed confidence of the pen-work—less crisply angular than Reynolds's—is added to the quality of what is underlined, it is impossible not to think the tracing of lines 29–35 and 101–3 Keatsian. Responding to the maid's abandonment, the poet of 'La Belle Dame sans Merci' would seem to underscore the description of her 'untuck'd' hair 'Hanging her pale and pined cheek beside'. Pleased by its fresh natural imagery, its figuring of moody weather, the poet of 'I stood tip-toe' picks out a passage on the youth's exquisite anger: 'such a storm | As oft 'twixt May and April is to see, | When winds breathe sweet, unruly though they be.' Even Shakespeare's interest in duplicity, which leads to an involution some find alienating, strikes a sympathetic chord. The image of letters 'With sleided silk feat and affectedly | Enswath'd, and seal'd to curious secrecy' (48–9), the stanza on poisoned yet restorative tears (295–301), the lines on 'subtle matter' and 'tragick shows' (302–8): these are respectively underlined, marked with triple and with single verticals in the margin.

Moreover—and this must particularly strike those who have, like the present author, sought to relate *A Lover's Complaint* to the *Sonnets* published with it in 1609—the Hampstead markings reinforce the long

---

[5] Andrew Gurr, 'Mulberrying', *London Review of Books*, 8/5 (6 Feb. 1986), quoting p. 20; Barbara Everett, 'Mrs Shakespeare', *London Review of Books*, 8/22 (18 Dec. 1986), quoting p. 9.

[6] Spurgeon, *Keats's Shakespeare*, 39.

poem's emphasis on persuasion by means of sexual charm, jewelled gifts, and derivative, panegyrical 'similies'. Picking out the stanza on the young man's 'browny locks' (85–91), this book underlines 'paled pearls, and rubies red as blood', 'deep-green emerald', 'heaven-hued saphire' (198, 213, 215), and the clause about 'deep-brain'd sonnets' (209). Indeed, not content with underscoring 'O then advance of yours that phraseless hand, | Whose white weighs down the airy scale of praise' (225–6), it marks the second line with no fewer than eight parallel verticals in the margin. 'Whose white weighs down the airy scale of *praise.*' Everything one might readily say about Keats and the limitless founders on that final word. The poet may have been drawn to the 'phraseless hand' through a fascination with what cannot be circumscribed in verse, but the annotator's attention to the 'airy scale' shows us a reader discovering the pivot on which the lover's seduction, and the maiden's poem, revolve.[7]

Interestingly, the lines marked most heavily in the Hampstead *Lucrece*—a text in which Reynolds's hand cannot be discerned—once more involve 'praise' and its Shakespearian corollary, 'fame'.[8] Tarquin, it will be recalled, rides 'From the besieged Ardea all in post' to the house of Collatine, where, encountering the chaste Lucrece, he is smitten. To ingratiate himself, Shakespeare says:

> He stories to her ears her husband's fame,
> Won in the fields of fruitful Italy;

[7] Compare *The Sonnets and A Lover's Complaint*, ed. John Kerrigan (Harmondsworth, 1986), 17–18. Also marked in the Hampstead copy: l. 14 (underlined), l. 17 (underlined), ll. 22–3 (vertical in left margin), ll. 27–8 (vertical in left margin), ll. 29–35 (double verticals in left margin, trebled for l. 31, and the underscored 32), ll. 58–60, 'Sometime . . . hours' (underlined), ll. 71–7 (vertical in left margin, doubled for l. 73, with 'tell your judgement I am old' underlined), l. 82, 'Love lack'd a dwelling' (underlined), l. 84 (underlined, with vertical in left margin), ll. 99–103 (vertical in left margin, trebled for l. 100, and ll. 101–3, with 'maiden-tongu'd' as well as 'was he such a storm . . . though they be' underlined), ll. 120–6 (vertical in left margin trebled for l. 126, with a cross against l. 122 keyed to note 'himself'), l. 132, 'dialogu'd' (underlined), ll. 141–7 (vertical in left margin, quadrupled for l. 147, with a squiggle beside l. 144, and keyed to 'a very characteristic stanza'), l. 148 (underlined), ll. 162–8 (vertical in left margin), l. 193 (underlined), l. 196 (double verticals in left margin), ll. 197–203 and 204–5 (vertical in the left margin, plus the underscored l. 198), ll. 211–17 (vertical in margin, plus the two underlined phrases), l. 219 (underlined), ll. 237–8 (vertical in left margin, doubled for l. 238), ll. 244–5 (vertical in left margin, trebled for l. 245), l. 261 (underlined), l. 278 (underlined), ll. 288–9 (four or five verticals in left margin, with a cross keyed to the judgement noted above, 'This is perhaps as fine . . .').

[8] The full list reads: ll. 106–12 (vertical in left margin doubled, with three verticals to the right, for the underscored ll. 106–7), ll. 141–2 (double verticals in left margin), ll. 197–201 (vertical in left margin, with ll. 197, 198, and 200 underlined), ll. 211–17 (vertical in left margin), ll. 568–71 (underlined with vertical in left margin), l. 715 (underlined), ll. 944–5 (double verticals in left margin), ll. 946–52 (vertical in left margin, with ll. 947–8 underlined), ll. 1007–8 (vertical in left margin), l. 1497 (underlined), ll. 1835–41 (vertical in left margin and l. 1835 underlined).

> And decks with praises Collatine's high name,
> Made glorious by his manly chivalry,
> With bruised arms and wreaths of victory:
>> Her joy with heav'd-up hand she doth express,
>> And, wordless, so greets heaven for his success. (106–12)

The entire stanza is marked with a vertical line in the left margin, and five added verticals plus underlining—more emphasis than anywhere else in the poem—stress 'He stories to her ears her husband's fame . . . fruitful Italy'. That such an emphasis is justified becomes apparent when one considers the form of the whole; for this is another seductive moment on which a poem turns. Indeed, the passage should remind us of a disjunction in the *Sonnets*' and *A Lover's Complaint*'s account of praising fame.[9] In the original narrative, after all, recorded by Ovid and Livy and repeated in 'The Argument' to *Lucrece*, Collatinus and others at the siege of Ardea proclaim the 'virtues' of their wives 'in their discourses after supper'. To prove this virtue substantial they set out as a party for Rome, only to discover all the wives except Lucrece disporting themselves. Inflamed by 'Lucrece' beauty', Tarquin returns to Ardea with the other generals, but then steals back to Rome and commits the rape. In the poem, by contrast, there is no prior encounter, no occasion on which Tarquin might have been tempted by the woman. Instead, it is suggested, Collatine's 'boast of Lucrece' sovereignty . . . Braving compare', prompted Tarquin to gallop from the siege and pour his own venomous compound of praising fame into Lucrece's 'ears' (33–42).

That this divergence from Ovid and Livy was deeply intended can be deduced from a play admired by the young Keats, *Cymbeline*.[10] There, once again, a husband's 'boast' precipitates tragedy; for it is Posthumus' public vaunting of Innogen's 'virtue' which prompts Giacomo to test her, creeping across the rushes of her bedchamber like, as he declares, Tarquin. Indeed, while Collatine becomes 'the publisher | Of that rich jewel', his wife (33–4), Posthumus wagers with Giacomo a 'diamond' identified with Innogen (I. iv. 70–166). The Hampstead annotations should be recalled. By marking those jewels which the youth received as love tokens, then purveyed to seduce the maid—the 'emerald', 'heaven-hued saphire', and

---

9 *Sonnets*, ed. Kerrigan, 21–9.
10 For his schoolboy enthusiasm see Charles and Mary Cowden Clarke, *Recollections of Writers* (London, 1878), 126. The continued significance of this play is attested by, for example, the letter to Woodhouse on 'the poetical Character' (27 Oct. 1818, *Letters*, ed. Rollins, i, 386–8), in which 'as much delight in conceiving an Iago as an Imogen' points up in the contrast a link with *Othello* where both overlap with *Lucrece*.

'diamond'—they alert us to a Shakespearian link between reification and sexual treachery. *Cymbeline* remains indicative. With the 'diamond' at stake, Giacomo climbs out of a trunk in which, he claims, his valuables are kept, and suggestively slips a bracelet from Innogen's wrist. It is this token, added to the news of his wife's birthmark, which pitches Posthumus into the world of *Othello.* The bangle and crimson mole, 'cinque-spotted', like the strawberry-spotted handkerchief, fetishistically translate the female body into its disposition and adjuncts, and advance a narrative of tragic deception inaugurated, for Shakespeare, in the soldiers' tents and 'at a feast' in Rome, with Posthumus' and Collatine's attempts to lend their wives' 'virtue' value.

For Collatine to 'boast of Lucrece' sovereignty', in a text concerned, like *Julius Caesar*, with conflict between tyrannical and republican values, is ironic. By vaunting his wife's virtue, Shakespeare implies, Collatine puts it on a level with Tarquin's regal pride, and betrays the principles associated for Elizabethan readers with his house. But a secondary sense of the word, emerging as the poem unfolds, is at least as important. In the period, 'sovereignty' could mean 'the dignity attaching to certain dispositions of heraldic bearings',[11] and for Collatine to 'boast' his wife's 'sovereignty' is for him to blazon her in ways which tellingly anticipate the perceptions of his enemy. Even the blushes and pallor which greet Tarquin's arrival are gold and silver on the 'field' or background of the 'shield' of Lucrece's countenance:

> This heraldry in Lucrece' face was seen,
> Argued by beauty's red, and virtue's white.
> Of either's colour was the other queen,
> Proving from world's minority their right:
> Yet their ambition makes them still to fight;
> > The sovereignty of either being so great,
> > That oft they interchange each other's seat. (64–70)

If the ambiguity of 'sovereignty' is productive here, less so, perhaps, is the association of blazoning with the narrator. Not for nothing has this passage become the focus of feminist commentary.[12] Yet the phrase 'was seen'

---

[11] George Wyndham (ed.), *The Poems of Shakespeare* (London, 1898), 227, quoting John Gwillim's *Display of Heraldrie* (London, 1610 [1611]), at p. 43, a passage which in turn invokes Gerard Legh's *Accedens of Armory* (London, 1562) as authority.

[12] See Coppélia Kahn, 'The Rape in Shakespeare's *Lucrece*', *Shakespeare Studies*, 9 (1976), 45–72, p. 51, and Nancy Vickers, '"The blazon of sweet beauty's best": Shakespeare's *Lucrece*', in Patricia Parker and Geoffrey Hartman (eds.), *Shakespeare and the Question of Theory* (London, 1985), 95–115, an admirable essay which reached me too late to contribute to my argument.

should not be overlooked; coinciding with 'heraldry', it introduces Tarquin as perceiver. The whole encounter is shaped by the emergence of Sextus' gaze from Shakespeare's. To read from line 50, his arrival, to line 84, with its 'silent wonder of still-gazing eyes', is to find benign strife heightened into what is seen as self-division by a 'traitor eye' (73). While the narrator presents red and white as intermingled, with virtue never not governing beauty on Lucrece's 'shield', the rapist reads it as a sign of battle. The heraldic 'field' is, in his eyes, militarized and divided, a 'silent war of lilies and of roses | Which Tarquin view'd in her fair face's field' (71–2). Like Thomas Heywood, in a congruent section of 'Oenone and Paris', Sextus finds in the 'strife' of 'white and redde' evidence of unconscious 'shame'.[13] He construes Lucrece's 'blushes' as sexual incitement.

If Tarquin misreads, Lucrece fails to interpret. Innocence makes her illiterate, incapable of discerning Sextus' intent. As the narrator remarks:

> But she that never cop'd with stranger eyes,
> Could pick no meaning from their parling looks,
> Nor read the subtle-shining secrecies
> Writ in the glassy margents of such books;
> She touch'd no unknown baits, nor fear'd no hooks;
>   Nor could she moralize his wanton sight,
>   More than his eyes were open'd to the light. (99–105)

Tarquin is a learned edition or black missal. He carries notes in his eyes like comments in a margin; and they point, as index-fingered glosses did in Elizabethan books, towards dark matter, clear lust. The Princess in *Love's Labour's Lost* has Boyet on hand to interpret the King of Navarre's 'heart's still rhetoric disclosèd with eyes' (II. i. 229). Those 'eyes', he explains, 'glassed' and glossing the King's intent, 'Did point you to buy them', just as 'His face's own margin did quote such amazes | That all eyes saw his eyes enchanted with gazes' (242–7). Unable thus to read, and lacking good counsel, Lucrece sees only eyes 'open'd to the light', glancing rather than 'parling'. Her failure to 'moralize' is a major lapse in the terms set by this poem, where the coding of character and its interpretation are decisive activities.

Hence the nature of Tarquin's self-doubt, a dozen stanzas later, as he contemplates the rape in prospect. Combining images from heraldry and the book, he says:

[13] London, 1594, quoting Joseph Quincy Adams's edition, Folger Shakespeare Library Publications, 5 (Washington, 1943), 13.

> my digression is so vile, so base,
> That it will live engraven in my face.
>
> Yea, though I die, the scandal will survive,
> And be an eye-sore in my golden coat;
> Some loathsome dash the herald will contrive,
> To cipher me, how fondly I did dote. (202–7)

The lines should remind us that blazoning constructed male as well as female identity. At once a means of maintaining ancient distinctions and of endorsing social advancement, heraldic ciphers articulated late Elizabethan and Jacobean culture to an extent it is easier to underestimate than analyse. Even those inclined to believe, with the King in *All's Well*, that 'honours thrive | When rather from our acts we them derive | Than our foregoers' (ii. iii. 136–8), thought such 'nobility' worth 'display'. Henry Peacham, for example, insists in *The Compleat Gentleman* that 'meannesse of birth and beginning' are consistent with 'Honor' and 'Nobilitie', yet he goes on to elaborate, in loving detail, the principles '*Of Armorie, or Blazon of Armes, with the Antiquity and Dignitie of Heralds*'.[14]

The fascination is understandable. In order to mediate between the self and society, heraldry developed an idiom expressive enough to rival the language of the book. The two modes are visibly continuous in Emblem Books like Peacham's *Minerva Britanna*, which includes devices used in late Elizabethan Accession Day Tilts. And it is in this context, with Sidney's device of '*Speravi* "dashed through, to shew his hope therein was dashed"',[15] that we should read the 'loathsome dash' in Tarquin's 'coat'. Dedicated to Southampton—a direct descendant of the York Herald, William Wriothesley, and notable contributor to Accession Day tournaments—*Lucrece* is bound up with the Essex circle and their Sidneian world of Protestant knighthood. It makes bookish heraldry the locus of serious concerns. When Collatine's wife meets an 'attaint' in rape (825), dishonour is registered in the chivalric image as surely as self-disgust in the idea of infection. Lucrece has been, the word suggests, touched by an opponent's lance and disgraced in the lists.[16] Through her, she feels, Collatine's scutcheon is sullied, and a 'loathsome dash' has been marked in the family, as well as Tarquin's, face:

[14] London, 1622, quoting pp. 3, 138.
[15] Cited by Roy Strong, *The Cult of Elizabeth: Elizabethan Portraiture and Pageantry* (London, 1977), 144.
[16] Compare, for example, the use of 'untainted' in Sonnet 19.

O unseen shame! invisible disgrace!
O unfelt sore! crest-wounding, private scar!
Reproach is stamp'd in Collatinus' face,
And Tarquin's eye may read the mot afar,
How he in peace is wounded, not in war.

(827–31 (1806 italics))

Just what is at stake here becomes clear if one compares the stanzas from 'Saint Agnes' Eve'[17] which so impressed Hood, the Pre-Raphaelites, and, a few streets away from Keats House, Gerard Manley Hopkins.[18] Porphyro, of course, gains access to Madeline's chamber with the help of a Shakespearian nurse, old Angela. There he lurks in the cupboard, like Giacomo in the trunk, till his beloved arrives. 'A casement high and triple-arch'd there was', writes Keats,

All garlanded with carven imag'ries
Of fruits, and flowers, and bunches of knot-grass,
And diamonded with panes of quaint device,
Innumerable of stains and splendid dyes,
As are the tiger-moth's deep-damask'd wings;
And in the midst, 'mong thousand heraldries,
And twilight saints, and dim emblazonings,
A shielded scutcheon blush'd with blood of queens and kings. (208–16)

The 'colours' which *Lucrece* details with heraldic exactness[19] are blurred here in organic images of fruits and flowers and fabrics. Instead of Collatinus' 'mot' we find a '*moth*'s deep-damask', and the Shakespearian idea of damasking is steeped afresh in dappled pigment felt as texture. It is dimness which enthralls Keats, the tactile thickening of moonbeams, and the aura of an aristocratic past. Yet his responsiveness to this last does not subsume Madeline in her scutcheon. While the 'shielded' window records her nobility, like heraldic glass in Peacham,[20] an erotic warmth flushes those 'queens and kings' with a contrary Keatsian blush, and the casement casts images which cannot contain the body:

---

[17] All quotations are from Jack Stillinger (ed.), *The Poems of John Keats* (London, 1978), who notes on p. 629 Keats's consistent use of this title—also standard in the early transcripts—in his letters. The now-familiar title preferred in the first edition (1820) may have been provided by its publisher, Taylor; compare below, p. 58 and n. 34.

[18] George H. Ford, *Keats and the Victorians: A Study of his Influence and Rise to Fame, 1821–1895* (New Haven, 1944), 8, 85, 128–31; Hopkins, 'The Escorial', esp. stanza 6.

[19] For these 'tinctures' see *OED*, 'colour', *sb*. 2b.

[20] See, for example, *The Art of Drawing with the Pen* (London, 1606), 63–5 (I4^r–KI^r).

Full on this casement shone the wintry moon,
And threw warm gules on Madeline's fair breast,
As down she knelt for heaven's grace and boon;
Rose-bloom fell on her hands, together prest,
And on her silver cross soft amethyst,
And on her hair a glory, like a saint:
She seem'd a splendid angel, newly drest,
Save wings, for heaven:—Porphyro grew faint:
She knelt, so pure a thing, so free from mortal taint. (217–25)

We are still in the realm of heraldry, but the 'taint' which St Agnes' eve
may bring is far from 'attaint' at some Accession Day tilt. The identity
granted Lucrece by the coincidence of body and blazon is here thrown
free of symbolism. If the ruddy 'gules' which cast their light on Madeline's
breast blush for her, they no more fix a meaning than they are her blood.
The woman remains herself, and the 'Rose-bloom' is an intimation, almost an answer to her prayer 'for heaven's grace and boon'. What is in
Shakespeare a matter of reading, here takes on depth and opacity. In *The
Eve of St Agnes* character is sexualized by a bodying forth in light, not by
interpretation.

Narrative objectivity of the kind projected by Beckett and Robbe-
Grillet is hardly Keats's aim. Objects in his romance carry a strong affective charge, are felt out inwardly as the more significant for not signifying.
Hence the palpable rightness of Porphyro's heaped and candied fruit, and
there being nothing to make of it. What the draft accounts of Madeline's
undressing reveal is the same instinct at work: a poet labouring to image
the desirable 'object' without reduction, to celebrate eros without
voyeurism. Whether Keats succeeds in this, any more than Shakespeare
unambiguously distinguishes his narrator's attentive, from Tarquin's 'traitor', eye at lines 50–84, is debatable. He remains perhaps for most readers,
'the voyeur . . . also | somewhat embarrassed'.[21] But his intent seems clear
in those revisions which remove, for instance, the strip-tease 'Loosens her
fragrant boddice *and doth bare*' and wrong sort of physicality in 'Loosens
her *bursting* boddice' (app. crit., 225/226), while developing the image,
neither reticent nor fetishistic, so near yet removed from Shakespeare's
'emerald', 'saphire', and 'diamonds', of 'warmed jewels' unclasped 'one by
one' (228).

---

[21] Amy Clampitt, 'Chichester', from 'Voyages: A Homage to John Keats', in *What the Light
Was Like* (London, 1986), 57–9, p. 59.

Moreover, Keats sets up tremors of irony designed to unsettle an identification of rapt poet with desiring intruder. Thus, 'Seemed a splendid angel, newly dressed, | *Save wings*, for heaven' (223–4) slyly rescues Porphyro's admiration, in the nick, for love. And it is the attempt to fictionalize Madeline which prompts this flicker of dissent. In Porphyro's effort to assimilate her to 'The carved angels' of her father's house, 'ever eager eyed . . . With hair blown back, and wings put crosswise on their breasts' (34–6), we recognize the same claim that the scutcheoned window makes upon her, and which Keats denies. While Lucrece is 'a virtuous monument' under Tarquin's 'unhallowed eyes' (391–2), a stony image of her own perfection that 'stories' her 'fame',[22] Madeline becomes 'a mermaid' or nesting bird (231, 235–9)—vocal yet scriptless, anonymous creatures. It comes as no surprise, in this context, to find Keats varying an immediate source, Richard Polwhele's *The Fair Isabel*:

> Thro' diamond panes of storied glass
> Scarce could the light of morning pass.
> Yet 'twas enough, through each dim pane,
> The room with richer tints to stain;
> Colouring, upon the shrine below,
> The crucifix with finer glow,
> And from its polish'd brilliance raying,
> And on the Virgin's image playing,
> But, where an amber radiance fell,
> Illumining fair ISABEL!
> No muse, in sooth, could paint it true—
> So soft it was, and sombrous too![23]

That word 'storied' could not appear in Keats—does not appear, indeed, even in draft, among obvious echoes. Moonlight, in his poem, spreads the scutcheon's blush over Madeline without growing into meaning.

Likewise the obscurity of books. In *The Eve of St Mark*, which Keats began shortly after 'Saint Agnes' Eve', the omniscient narrator, with a more commanding pitch of address ('Upon a Sabbath day it fell'), places in his tale a heroine who reads while she is 'storied'. 'A curious volume, patch'd and torn' (25) prompts Bertha's fantasies, and, oddly, when 'she

---

[22] On the ambiguities of 'Monument' see *OED*, esp. 2, 4b, and 5c ('A written document . . . A piece of information given in writing . . . An enduring evidence or example . . . A carved figure, statue, effigy').

[23] Quoted by Ian Jack, in *Keats and the Mirror of Art* (Oxford, 1967), 194–5. Also, compare Milton, *Il Penseroso*, ll. 159–60.

read[s] awhile', it is 'With forehead 'gainst the window pane' (48–9).
Thus drawn inside the frame of her intelligence, 'with bright drooping
hair, | And slant book full against the glare', Bertha might escape us; but
Keats brings the book to life in the 'monsters' and 'wildest forms and
shades' which play about her in the lamplight as she reads, and then indeed quotes the volume—in the literated substantiality of pseudo-
Chaucerian Englyshe (67–114). By contrast, Angela's intelligence is glazed
into opacity, 'Like . . . an aged crone | Who keepeth clos'd a wond'rous
riddle-book, | As spectacled she sits in chimney nook' (129–31), and
Madeline, Bertha's equivalent, is as obscure. The scutcheoned window is
a dense medium of annunciation, and not, like Bertha's textual metonym,
a lucid barrier the mind is pressed against. You would not find, in *The Eve
of St Agnes*, 'subtle shining secrecies | Writ in the glassy margents of such
books', where glosses are glass for textual deciphering. Since the body in
'Saint Agnes' Eve' is illegible, Madeline lies between the sheets in bed
'Clasp'd like a missal where swart Paynims pray' (241). The image has
given Keats's editors pause, but it is there to protect the girl from reading.
She is, Keats tells us as directly as he could, a closed book. While Tarquin
misreads, and Lucrece fails to moralize, *The Eve of St Agnes* removes its
heroine from interpretation.

These texts might seem so different as not to be worth comparison. But
Lucrece is, in my view, the missing source of 'Saint Agnes' Eve'. Tradition-
ally, it has been supposed that a popular superstition, discovered in Burton's *Anatomy of Melancholy*, prompted Keats to write the poem. Local
debts, like the one to Polwhele, and several involving Milton, were then
incurred. But, while superstition explains Madeline's going to bed on this
night to dream about her lover, Porphyro's unexpected arrival in her father's castle and his slipping to her room to ravish her when she is, at best,
half-asleep, then the lovers' hasty departure before dawn—these struc-
turally echo Shakespeare's poem. That Angela, the nurse, was inherited
from *Romeo and Juliet*, along with the antagonism between the lovers'
families, has been long accepted. The text is littered with ideas from
Hamlet, *Measure for Measure*, and *The Tempest*. So why not a further, and
informing, debt to Shakespeare?

Certainly, this would explain the sharing of motifs. When Tarquin
creeps towards Lucrece's chamber, for instance, the doors grate accusingly
and

> As each unwilling portal yields him way,
> Through little vents and crannies of the place

> The wind wars with his torch to make him stay,
> And blows the smoke of it into his face,
> Extinguishing his conduct in this case;
> But his hot heart, which fond desire doth scorch,
> Puffs forth another wind that fires the torch. (309–15)

In the rushes of the corridor he finds 'Lucretia's glove, wherein her needle sticks' and, drawing it out of the matting, he is pricked. By prosopopoeia we learn, 'this glove to wanton tricks | Is not inur'd; return again in haste; | Thou seest our mistress' ornaments are chaste.' But Tarquin still misreads, and presses on to ravishment. As the narrator says:

> He in the worst sense construes their denial:
> The doors, the wind, the glove that did delay him,
> He takes for accidental things of trial. (317–26)

Shakespeare's implication is not Keats's, that objects are sensately realized in otherness, but that, in a discursive Rome, misreading is as guilty as not reading is ill-advised.

The Eve of St Agnes offers us, again, a 'gusty floor' and rhetoric of doors. Yet objects in this text are freed of meaning or inexplicably—like moonlight through dense glass—graced by it. When Porphyro follows Angela 'through a lowly arched way, | Brushing the cobwebs with his lofty plume' (109–10), the lover's passage is fraught with suggestion. Youth, we might deduce, sweeps up Decay. Yet the event remains untranslatable. As Chesterton observed of the plume on Marmion's helmet, it is not described for the sake of what it tells us about Scott's hero but because the plume is a plume. Equally when Madeline leads Angela down the staircase 'To a safe level matting' (190–6), or goes on to open her chamber door:

> Out went the taper as she hurried in;
> Its little smoke, in pallid moonshine, died:
> She clos'd the door, she panted, all akin
> To spirits of the air, and visions wide:
> No uttered syllable, or, woe betide!
> But to her heart, her heart was voluble,
> Paining with eloquence her balmy side;
> As though a tongueless nightingale should swell
> Her throat in vain, and die, heart-stifled, in her dell. (199–207)

That self-communing which is an aspect of the St Agnes' eve superstition here underlines the contingency of what occurs. Where Tarquin's light is blown out as a warning, and rekindled in an Ovidian touch by his ardent breath, Madeline's gutters as event. Only in the sidelong glance at Philomel's ravishment does Keats incite interpretation.

It is an important cue, and rare. Shakespeare boxes actions in with glozing, so that, though his poem unfolds in a narrative present, it feels distant from the reader. Keats employs a staple perfect, but the events of 'Saint Agnes' Eve' seem immediate and unfabled because objects are unglossed and because the narrator's few interventions suggest he does not control the outcome of his tale. 'Let no buzz'd whisper tell', he is wont to cry, when Porphyro enters the castle, 'All eyes be muffled, or a hundred swords I Will storm his heart' (82–4). Engaged yet by no means omniscient, the Keatsian narrator brings these lovers to life by standing near the reader. Such tension as the plot evokes depends on this detachment— on an acted-upon resistance to storying, a relinquishment of narrative power. Hence Keats's deletion at an early stage of the push-start that the first Woodhouse transcript gave the fable: 'Follow, then follow to the illumined halls, I Follow me youth—and leave the Eremite' (27/28). And hence the adding and subtracting of the preparatory stanza on Porphyro's heaped fruit (54/55), as Keats seeks to reconcile narrative coherence with narratorial reticence. All of which calculated detachment makes the tongueless nightingale, dying in her dell, remarkable. For an allusion to Tereus' rape, and his cutting out his victim's tongue, is unmistakable here, though it supplements event with story and merges Madeline with legend.

As it happens, the lines support the claim that 'Saint Agnes' Eve' is in debt to Shakespeare's poem. 'Come Philomel', Lucrece cries after the rape:

> Come Philomel that sing'st of ravishment,
> Make thy sad grove in my dishevel'd hair.
> As the dank earth weeps at thy languishment,
> So I at each sad strain will strain a tear,
> And with deep groans the diapason bear:
> > For burthen-wise I'll hum on Tarquin still,
> > While thou on Tereus descant'st, better skill.
>
> And whiles against a thorn thou bear'st thy part,
> To keep thy sharp woes waking, wretched I,
> To imitate thee well, against my heart
> Will fix a sharp knife, to affright mine eye;
> Who, if it wink, shall thereon fall and die.
> > These means, as frets upon an instrument,
> > Shall tune our heart-strings to true languishment. (1128–41)

This fable recurs, of course, in *Titus Andronicus*, where the tongueless Lavinia reveals her rape by referring to a copy of Ovid, and it returns much later in *Cymbeline*, where Giacomo discovers that Innogen before going to sleep has turned the leaf of her book down at the ominous tale. The story, as a story, seems to have been Shakespeare's familiar recourse when figuring rape. But the fable is not Keatsian, and the need to make sense of its presence in 'Saint Agnes' Eve' has provoked over-reading of the kind which might have been corrected by a glance towards *Lucrece*. To judge the poem a 'fantasy of eroticized destructiveness', because the myth of Philomel images 'shattering and loss',[24] is to mistake the work by neglecting not only Keats's humane particularity, but that of Shakespeare's mediating text.

This is not to imply that a debt to *Lucrece* counts against 'dark' readings. Keats deploys his nightingale in ways which support Jack Stillinger's description of Porphyro as 'villainous seducer'.[25] Emphasizing the bird's Shakespearian 'eloquence', and the 'Paining' of its 'side' as though 'against a thorn'—not a motif found in *Lemprière* or Ovid—Keats then calls her 'heart-stifled', choked, dumb. A violent side of the fable is invoked here, and, significantly, this transumption marks the first of several stressed allusions to Madeline's moaning, panting, weeping, or venting 'witless words with many a sigh' (303). Against this background of silence and incoherence, Porphyro's 'voice' becomes an image of erotic force. He may rouse Madeline with 'La belle dame sans mercy', but Chartier's fifteenth-century dialogue between hapless wooer and articulate lady is, for Keats, a foil to what occurs. 'Give me that voice again' is Madeline's first imperative on waking up (312). Like the author of *A Lover's Complaint*, Keats associates female responsiveness with a vocalism which is ultimately Echo's: iterative, insecure, and inclined to prompt, 'rape me with the musick of thy tongue'.[26]

But can there be rape by request, and are we dealing with *The Rape of Madeline*? Up to a point, both questions are the same. 'Wide awake', though 'still' beholding 'the vision of her sleep' (298–9), Madeline cries, 'Oh leave me not in this eternal woe' (314), and no resistance to Porphyro

[24] Beverly Fields, 'Keats and the Tongueless Nightingale: Some Unheard Melodies in "The Eve of St Agnes"', *Wordsworth Circle*, 19 (1983), 246–50.

[25] 'The Hoodwinking of Madeline: Scepticism in *The Eve of St Agnes*', *Studies in Philology*, 58 (1961), 533–55.

[26] James Shirley, *Narcissus, Or, The Self-Lover*, in *Poems* (London, 1646), stanza 80. This is not the place to explore Shakespeare's use of Narcissus and Echo as a link between the early *Sonnets* and *A Lover's Complaint*.

is recorded in any form of the text. Few juries would convict on such evidence. Yet it seems significant that, in revising the poem to 'remove an opening for doubt what took place',[27] Keats placed the word 'still' under such strain that its ambivalence—temporal yet adversative—was lost, and Madeline slipped back into sleep:

> and still the spell
> Unbroken guards her in serene repose.
> With her wild dream he mingled, as a rose
> Marrieth its odour to a violet.
> Still, still she dreams, louder the frost wind blows. (318–23, app. crit.)

In heightening the sexual explicitness (and making 'with the violet' more intrusively 'to . . .'), Keats did not need to seal Madeline in 'repose', returning her to those 'poppied' slumbers which Stillinger associates with the rape of Clarissa. It might be claimed that 'Still, still she dreams' adds a note of desire and assent, since it emphasizes wish-fulfilment in the wakeful-sleeping state. But our reading of this sequence has been more hindered than helped by that cliché, as it has become, of Keatsian criticism: 'The Imagination may be compared to Adam's dream—he awoke and found it truth.'[28] While there are Miltonic resonances at this point (not all of them reassuring), the most significant echo, ignored by Keats's editors, is Shakespearian and suggestive of deception, substitution, and sexual threat. For Innogen, waking among the bushes and herbs, finds dream life 'still', as though in sleep, melled with the real:

> The dream's here still; even when I wake it is
> Without me as within me; not imagined, felt.
> A headless man? The garments of Posthumus?
> I know the shape of 's leg; this is his hand,
> His foot Mercurial, his Martial thigh . . . (IV. ii. 308–12)

This woman thinks she wakes beside a lover and husband, but her partner is the man who, one scene earlier, vowed to rape her.[29]

To look again at Woodhouse's report is to find Keats coming clean about the Tarquin streak in Porphyro. When his friend called the rewrite 'unfit for ladies', Keats declared that:

---

[27] Woodhouse to John Taylor, 19 Sept. 1819, *Letters*, ed. Rollins, ii. 163.
[28] Ibid. i. 185.
[29] As R. S. White observes (*Keats as a Reader*, 82), the same sequence from *Cymbeline* lies behind Isabella's mourning for the decapitated Lorenzo (*Isabella; or, The Pot of Basil*, ll. 393–472). Evidently IV. ii. 293–334 made a deep impression on the poet.

he does not want ladies to read his poetry: that he writes for men—& that if in the [original version] there was an opening for doubt what took place, it was his fault for not writing clearly & comprehensibly—that he sh[oul]d despise a man who would be such an eunuch in sentiment as to leave a <Girl> maid, with that Character about her, in such a situation: & sho[ul]d despise himself to write about it &c &c &c—and all this sort of Keats-like rhodomontade.

This is explicit and, even allowing for bluster, unlovely. 'With that Character about her' seems particularly dubious. It is what gets said about raped hitch-hikers, or women on the streets after nine. Angered by the threat of censorship, Keats has lined up behind Porphyro and obscured his own position by clarifying the poem. As always, the verse is more subtle than Keats in its defence. But some of the same problems as arise with Shakespeare's blazoning cling to Porphyro's reduction of Madeline, after their 'Solution sweet', to 'beauty's shield, heart-shaped and vermeil dyed'. Is this flimsily the language of heraldry ('N.B. the *heart* in blazon is . . . called a *body heart*'), or richly the idiom of Spenser?[30] How much interpretative weight should be attached to the line's completing a set of rosy guled images assembled by Keats with deliberation and meshed with the narrator's 'voice'?[31]

In *his* handling of ravishment, Shakespeare is unflinchingly responsible. Though Lucrece blames herself for being raped, the poem makes it clear that her resistance was staunch. There is no trace in Shakespeare of that covert desire which makes, for instance, Britten's *Rape of Lucretia* fraught. When Kathleen Ferrier or Janet Baker sings to Tarquin, 'In the forest of my dreams | You have always been the Tiger', there is a Keatsian sense of the rape as dream life taking its affective course. This tiger appeals to unconscious appetites in the chastely housebound Lucretia; and, in one of the opera's finest moments, Tarquin hymns 'the linnet in [her] eyes' that 'Lifts with desire, | And the cherries of [her] lips . . . wet with wanting'. 'Can you deny', he asks, 'your blood's dumb pleading?' 'Yes, I deny,'

---

[30] Joseph Edmondson, *A Complete Body of Heraldry*, 2 vols. (London, 1780), ii, Qq2ʳ; *The Faerie Queene*, for example, I. v. 9. 6, I. xi. 46. 3, II. x. 24. 7.

[31] Erotic thoughts flush Porphyro's brow 'like a full-blown rose' (in draft 'more rosy than the rose') at ll. 136–7, they contribute to Madeline's annunciation via 'warm gules' and 'Rose-bloom' (again the app. crit. shows 'rose' being rationed at ll. 217–22), and they issue in the 'rose' which 'Blendeth . . . with' or 'Marrieth' the 'violet' at ll. 320–2. For 'gules' as roseate, and 'derived from . . . the Arabic word *gule*, a red rose', see William Berry, *An Introduction to Heraldry* (London, 1810), 55, and *Encyclopoedia Heraldica, or Complete Dictionary of Heraldry*, 4 vols. (London, 1828–40), i, Ee2ᵛ, and for 'gules' as 'vermeil' (so that Madeline is finally subdued to the scutcheon), see James Dallaway, *Inquiries into the Origin and Progress of the Science of Heraldry in England* (Gloucester, 1793), 405.

she says, but Britten's music points up the ambivalence of such affirmative negations. Shakespeare avoids them. Indeed, the motif of dream life is raised in his poem to extinguish, at Tarquin's arrival, the idea of desire. We are asked to 'Imagine her as one in dead of night', and one

> From forth dull sleep by dreadful fancy waking,
> That thinks she hath beheld some g[h]astly sprite,
> Whose grim aspèct sets every joint a shaking;
> What terrour 'tis! but she, in worser taking,
>   From sleep disturbed, heedfully doth view
>   The sight which makes supposed terrour true. (449–55)

Lucrece awakes to find a dream truth, but there is no doubting its nightmarish tenor. Moreover, Tarquin's appeal to the 'blood's dumb pleading' is, in Shakespeare, set among words and images only too familiar by this stage of the poem. 'The colour in thy face', he declares,

> (That even for anger makes the lily pale,
> And the red rose blush at her own disgrace)
> Shall plead for me, and tell my loving tale:
> Under that colour am I come to scale
>   Thy never-conquer'd fort; the fault is thine. (477–82)

There is no music, whether from the English Chamber Orchestra under Britten or Madeline's 'lute', to enforce this claim. 'Colour', 'the lily pale', 'the red rose', and Tarquin's martial imagery ominously recall his misreading Lucrece's blazon (50–84), and the false 'disputation' which made him think that blushing 'beauty pleadeth' (183–280). Now, as then, he 'construes' blushes 'in their worst sense' and proceeds.

In the rape itself, Lucrece is withheld. Ravishment, Shakespeare implies, is the act of one, begotten on itself like jealousy. In the interpreted foreground which is this poem, the question with which Renaissance commentators on the story busied themselves, 'Did Lucrece enjoy the rape?',[32] is not answered because it has no room to crystallize. Tarquin fills the scope of our attention, and, remarkably, the images culturally fabricated for Lucrece are transferred to him. Instead of hers, his female soul is spotted; his is the virgin-like 'consecrated wall' smashed down (719–28). This makes him his own worst enemy. He ravishes himself. Even so, Lucrece is convinced of her pollution. In an important echo of the narrator's description of Tarquin, she finds her soul's house

---

[32] For an instructive summary, see Ian Donaldson, *The Rapes of Lucretia: A Myth and its Transformations* (Oxford, 1982), esp. ch. 2.

> sack'd, her quiet interrupted,
> Her mansion batter'd by the enemy;
> Her sacred temple spotted, spoil'd, corrupted,
> Grossly engirt with daring infamy. (1170–3)

Robbed of honour, Lucrece laments. Indeed, drawing on the conventions of the Complaint, and thus invoking a form through which women poets emerged into English,[33] a mode in which women's powerlessness was typically transmuted into eloquence, Shakespeare allows his heroine to lament at lengths which might be felt to distort a poem called *The Rape of Lucrece*. But those words, emphasizing Tarquin's action, appear on no title-page until 1616.[34] The title printed during Shakespeare's lifetime coincides with the heroine in ways which make acutely suggestive the drift of her plaint. 'Make me not', she appeals to 'night',

> object to the tell-tale day!
> The light will shew, charàcter'd in my brow,
> The story of sweet chastity's decay,
> The impious breach of holy wedlock's vow:
> Yea, the illiterate that know not how
> > To 'cipher what is writ in learned books,
> > Will quote my loathsome trespass in my looks. (806–12)

The 'object' which would be opaquely illegible in Keats becomes in Shakespeare 'something presented to the sight' for reading, and Lucrece, previously ignorant of the self's 'glassy' essence, begins to construe herself as *Lucrece*. A definite shift in her stance is apparent. When deciding how to clear herself, Lucrece explicitly images herself as text. She will summon her kinsmen, she announces, knife herself, and bravely declare: 'How Tarquin must be us'd, read it in me' (1195). Whether or not Shakespeare approves the suicide, he seems concerned to show in Lucrece an initiation by violence into reading.

Thus, after the rape, she becomes as obsessively concerned with life's and language's dissembling interpretable surfaces as the philosophical

---

[33] Note the recent work on Cambridge University Library MS Ff.1.6: Rossell Hope Robbins, 'The Findern Anthology', *PMLA* 59 (1954), 610–42; Richard Beadle and A. E. B. Owen, 'Introduction' to the facsimile edition of *The Findern Manuscript Cambridge University Library MS Ff.1.6* (London, 1978); Kate Harris, 'The Origins and Make-up of Cambridge University Library MS Ff.1.6', *Transactions of the Cambridge Bibliographical Society*, 8 (1983), 299–333; and, most directly, Elizabeth Hanson-Smith, 'A Woman's View of Courtly Love: The Findern Anthology Cambridge University Library MS Ff.1.6', *Journal of Women's Studies in Literature*, 1 (1979), 179–94.

[34] The standard edited form reproduces Q1's head and running-title and echoes Harrison's entry in the Stationers' Register, 'the Ravyshement of Lucrece'.

rhetoricians—Puttenham, for instance, in the closing chapters of *The Arte of English Poesie.*[35] Writing to Collatine, her pen hovers uneasily over the page, seeking words neither 'curious-good' nor 'blunt and ill'. What Collatine will deduce from the note becomes of pressing concern, since in its natural artfulness, she knows, he will construe her. Her sorrow needs communication, but not its cause, and the letter becomes a paradox in which ' "woes are tedious, though . . . words are brief" ' (1296–309). Even the groom commanded to take the note is caught up in interpretative scrutiny. Blushing at the greatness of his charge, he is read as reading Lucrece's shame, and she blushes in return (1331–58). Shakespeare and Embarrassment. The scene is an awkward rerun of Tarquin's first encounter, in which the rush of blood was read only on his side. Lucrece then had no desire to 'moralize', but the rape makes her, if anything, morbidly prompt to 'pick' messages from 'parling looks'.

Ill fame, meanwhile, haunts her. Having displaced covert lust as a motive from the ravishment, Shakespeare chose to stress the idea that Lucrece succumbed because Tarquin threatened to kill a churl and put him in bed beside her. 'If thou deny', he declares,

> some worthless slave of thine I'll slay,
> To kill thine honour with thy life's decay;
> And in thy dead arms do I mean to place him,
> Swearing I slew him, seeing thee embrace him.
>
> So thy surviving husband shall remain
> The scornful mark of every open eye;
> Thy kinsmen hang their heads at this disdain,
> Thy issue blurr'd with nameless bastardy:
> And thou, the author of their obloquy,
> Shall have thy trespass cited up in rhimes
> And sung by children in succeeding times. (513–25)

Among Tarquin's hundreds of words, these are the ones which stick; Lucrece recalls them just before her suicide. What frightens her is 'infamy' (1638), and a blurring of those 'lines to time'—both 'issue, offspring' and 'self discoursed'—marked in the Hampstead *Sonnets.*[36] Lucrece imagines herself misconstructed as a fable, storied in false 'rhimes' and dishonoured by what she 'authorised'. Everything inward and organic is dis-

---

[35] On Puttenham, and Renaissance semiotic suspicion in general, see Frank Whigham, *Ambition and Privilege: The Social Tropes of Elizabethan Courtesy Theory* (Berkeley, 1984), esp. chs. 2 and 4.

[36] Sonnet 18.

counted at this point. Instead we find what Keats underscored—fame, storying, a desire for praise—made cruelly explicit, and formative of behaviour.

The problems raised by Tarquin pursue Lucrece into her account of the painted cloth. The most extended act of reading in the poem, this is also the one most completely bound up with inherited obloquy. For the fabric stories the fall of Troy, and its betrayal by Sinon, the Greek spy remembered as a hypocrite. In him we find depicted what a lasting slur can mean, and through Lucrece's efforts he becomes an image of Tarquin. But not without close reading. Stanza by stanza, Shakespeare elaborates the enigmas of appearance. With Ajax and Ulysses, for instance, 'The face of either 'cipher'd either's heart; | Their face their manners most expressly told' (1396–7). Yet the latter, when scrutinized, is, despite his 'mild glance', 'sly'. Nestor may be honest, but the painting arrests his lifted hand, which 'beguil[es] attention, charm[s] the sight' (1404) in ways that now prompt caution. Like Chapman in the ecphrasis of Hero's scarf,[37] Shakespeare makes his artefact an icon of moral ambivalence. Indeed, like Chapman in the final stanza of that interpretative puzzle, *Ovid's Banquet of Sense*, he exploits a prevalent mistrust of foreshortening and shadowing[38] to provoke textual suspicion:

> For much imaginary work was there;
> Conceit deceitful, so compact, so kind,
> That for Achilles' image stood his spear,
> Grip'd in an armed hand; himself, behind,
> Was left unseen, save to the eye of mind:
>   A hand, a foot, a face, a leg, a head,
>   Stood for the whole to be imagined. (1422–8)

Reading, Lucrece finds a reflex of her grief in Hecuba and Priam, in Troilus and in Hector. Gaining authority, she supplements the 'painted woes' with speech, and 'sad tales doth tell'—in a verse underlined in the Keats text—'To pencil'd pensiveness and colour'd sorrow' (1492, 1496–7). Yet Sinon, whose 'enchanting story' (1521) betrayed Ilion as Tarquin's deluded her, poses a challenge to her 'advised' acumen. Like Ulysses 'mild' and plausibly 'ciphered', he seems at first miscalculated by the painter. Only when Lucrece remembers Tarquin can she comprehend Sinon: '"It

---

[37] *Hero and Leander* (London, 1598), Sestiad IV, at H2ᵛ–4ʳ.

[38] For a suggestive account of this mistrust, see Lucy Gent, *Picture and Poetry, 1560–1620: Relations between Literature and the Visual Arts in the English Renaissance* (Leamington Spa, 1981).

cannot be"', she says, construing that 'painted' surface, '"But such a face should bear a wicked mind"' (1539–40).

Keats learned something similar in 1818. 'A year ago', he wrote to George, 'I could not understand in the slightest degree Raphael's cartoons—now I begin to read them a little.'[39] Yet the qualities he learned 'to read' in those tapestry designs[40] were evidently different from the lurid, articulate, and shadowed effects encountered by Lucrece. 'And how did I learn to do so?', Keats went on:

> By seeing something done in quite an opposite spirit—I mean a picture of Guido's in which all the Saints . . . had each of them both in countenance and gesture all the canting, solemn melo dramatic mawkishness of Mackenzie's father Nicholas.

Granted, the ecphrastic setting of Madeline's chamber includes 'dusk curtains' and a 'carpet' with 'Broad golden fringe' (281–5). But these objects are, like the candied fruit, felt out inwardly, unfigured save in mass and line. Nothing could be less like Lucrece's 'tear[ing] the senseless Sinon with her nails' (1564), enwoofing herself with the storied surface, than the affective enmeshing of curtained bed and fringed carpet and Madeline's closed eyelids and Porphyro's musing 'entoil'd in woofed phantasies' (in stanza 32 of the later poem). Nor can one imagine Keats lingering to decode the 'arras, rich with horseman, hawk, and hound' (358) which lies behind the lovers as they elope. The vague richness of Keats's influential drapery[41] has all the dense obliquity of the scutcheon in his window. It tells us something about the lovers' status, as the hunt reminds us of their need for haste, but the fabric does not intrude into the foreground to engage, be read by, and read with, the characters.

Lucrece's tearing Sinon is a dramatic motif that leads away from drama. To read Middleton's *The Ghost of Lucrece* is to realize just how untheatrical Shakespeare has chosen to be, and to sense why this 'graver labour' stands outside the mainstream of his development. When Keats wrote to Taylor in 1819, 'I wish to diffuse the colouring of St Agnes eve throughout a Poem in which Character and Sentiment would be the figures to such drapery', he was pointing, through that distinction between human nature and the textual arras (extrapolated from the lovers' elopement), a way towards his 'writing of a few fine Plays—my greatest ambition—when I

[39] *Letters*, ed. Rollins, ii. 19.
[40] Now in the Victoria and Albert Museum, the fragmentary NT cycle was lent by the Prince Regent to the British Institution, piecemeal, during 1816–19.
[41] Ford, *Keats and the Victorians*, 36, 87.

do feel ambitious'.[42] By reducing the distinction, Shakespeare excluded the free, unstable qualities which would make his poem potential theatre. True, Lucrece stabs herself in the closing phase of the story, but her action has none of the emotive shock we feel when, for instance, the Countess of Salisbury whips out her daggers in *Edward III* and invites the King to swear to kill if he wants her adulterous love (III. ii). Equally, when Heywood in his Red Bull *Rape of Lucrece* has Collatine ask,

> Why how is't with you *Lucrece*, tell me sweete?
> Why do'st thou hide thy face? and with thy hand
> Darken those eyes that were my Sonnes of joy,
> To make my pleasures florish in the Spring?[43]

the shoddiness of the poetry cannot wreck that moment of human truth which asks, 'Why do'st thou hide thy face?' This, Shakespeare decides not to be interested in. Instead he describes a heroine who, to earn herself an honourable 'place i' th' story', subdues her nature and narrates what we know.

Philomel had been otherwise. Locked in the woodland hut by Tereus, she wove a tapestry to communicate her situation to her sister, and between them they ravaged the rapist by feeding him his children in that bloody banquet which Shakespeare appropriated for the end of *Titus Andronicus*. Philomel may use a sedentary art to further her revenge, but she does not lapse into passivity. Lucrece, a placid spinner among her maids in 'The Argument', neglects even that labour in the poem itself. Instead of inactivity, and rather than filling Ithaca and Rome full of moths or mots—in Valeria's scornful image (I. iii. 84–6)—Philomel uses female craft to challenge masculine violence. She does not, like Lucrece, scratch at the face of evil, but, like Clarissa writing to Anna Howe of the plots to punish Lovelace, she creatively transcends her plight and seizes the initiative. Lucrece invokes Philomel at her most passive, warbling her betrayal in the depths of a grove. Moreover, she fastens on that apocryphal addition which makes the nightingale lean against the thorn, inciting herself to song by the pain of what she has suffered. The prick, as so many Renaissance wits observed, is something that the bird does not flinch from, and in Lucrece's developing an idea of self-slaughter from this emblem (above, pp. 53–4) we find her accepting a masochism which the legend

---

[42] *Letters*, ed. Rollins, ii. 234.
[43] London, 1608, quoting from the expanded 1638 text, ed. Allan Holaday, Illinois Studies in Language and Literature, 34 (Urbana, Ill., 1950), 120.

known to Shakespeare questioned. One should read *Lucrece* with a poem such as Gascoigne's 'Complaynt of Phylomene'—where the nightingale merges with Nemesis—in mind. The painted cloth, not in Livy and inserted by Shakespeare with a purpose, reminds us how dispassionately fabled is Lucrece's self-destruction.

Even so, she changes. Our experience of the text may be statically self-explicative, but tragedy here makes room for metamorphosis, with something of the spirit of *Titus Andronicus*, by cultivating the temporal. Hence the present tense in which the narrative unfolds, and the meditation on Time which rings like a passacaglia through the closing phases of the poem, from the rape itself to Old Lucretia's lament. 'The perfect' may be, for the reasons Susanne K. Langer offers, 'the characteristic tense of story',[44] but Shakespeare needs a present to grow through and recoil from. For what Lucrece learns to value in this much-storied realm is intimate with storying itself. As in *Julius Caesar*, we observe identity formulating itself to be construed. Living in the present, characters such as Brutus and Lucrece continuously look back on themselves, from the vantage-point of fame, hoping to find themselves perfect. They prepare for death with such lines as 'Brutus' tongue | Hath almost ended his life's history' (v. v. 39–40), or appeal for vengeance by retreating from the moment into a seeing the self as past. 'For she that was thy Lucrece,—now attend me; | Be suddenly revenged on my foe' (1682–3).

Again, and finally, Keats can help. To extraordinary effect, his narrative slips in and out of its conventional perfect to play an ending game with time:

> The arras, rich with horseman, hawk, and hound,
> Flutter'd in the besieging wind's uproar;
> And the long carpets rose along the gusty floor.
>
> They glide, like phantoms, into the wide hall;
> Like phantoms, to the iron porch, they glide;
> Where lay the Porter, in uneasy sprawl,
> With a huge empty flaggon by his side:
> The wakeful bloodhound rose, and shook his hide,
> But his sagacious eye an inmate owns:
> By one, and one, the bolts full easy slide:—
> The chains lie silent on the footworn stones;—
> The key turns, and the door upon its hinges groans.

---

[44] *Feeling and Form: A Theory of Art Developed from 'Philosophy in a New Key'* (London, 1953), 264.

> And they are gone: ay, ages long ago
> These lovers fled away into the storm. (358–71)

In Keats, temporal recoil carries the characters out of fiction. Haunting breaks with the perfect of 'arras' and gusted 'carpets', and in gliding through the hall the lovers seem immediate yet distant, like things less tangible than art can render and more the residue of lives once lived. That Porter may come squarely before us 'in uneasy sprawl', yet 'lay the Porter' fixes him in the past tense of the 'story'. He belongs with the fabric, is figured in drapery together with the dog that 'rose' and sank like carpeting (360, 365–6). It is the poem's last door that springs decisively into the present. Poised at the liminal, its key 'turns' and hinges 'groan'. Across that threshold the lovers step, and all at once the tenses fold. 'They are', Keats writes, but 'they are' also 'gone', and nothing more can be told of them. Through the storm, across the southern moors,[45] they vanish into the not-story we read as life. While Lucrece turns the tenses back to begin the process of storying herself, Keats's couple escape our scrutiny.

If their poem ends where life begins, those left behind in the fable are pointedly deprived of life:

> Angela the old
> Died palsy-twitch'd, with meagre face deform;
> The Beadsman, after thousand aves told,
> For aye unsought for slept among his ashes cold. (375–8)

The contrast with *Lucrece* could scarcely be more conclusive. There death almost becomes what it cannot be, 'an event of life',[46] since the heroine's existence continues after the suicide. Indeed, the self-inflicted wound of lines 1723–4 is conspicuously a prologue to the slow fabling of blood, as currents of black and crimson gore surround Lucrece's corpse and are set off by a 'watery rigol': a heraldry of death, 'moralized' by the poet (1737–50). Nor does the tale end with this gory effusion, 'bubbling' like the 'fountain' which flows from raped Lavinia's lips.[47] Cleopatra in defeat had offered herself and her women, with some irony, as 'scutcheons and . . . signs of conquest' to 'Hang in what place [Octavius] please' (v. ii. 131–2). The dead Lucrece becomes such an icon of triumph, for her corpse is carried through the streets and deployed against the royal house,

---

[45] Replacing 'dartmoor blak' and 'the bleak Dartmoor' in draft (l. 351), phrases which put the pair too clearly on the map and allow reading to pursue them.

[46] Ludwig Wittgenstein, *Tractatus Logico-Philosophicus*, trans. D. F. Pears and B. F. McGuinness (London, 1961), 6.4311.

[47] Compare with *Lucrece*, ll. 1734–5 and 1737–41, *Titus Andronicus* II. iv. 18–19 and 22–5.

fomenting rebellion. Like Julius Caesar's in the tragedy, read as a lecture to the Roman mob, Lucrece's 'bleeding body' contrives, book-like, 'to publish Tarquin's foul offence' (1850–2). Its argument is written in history. Fame and honour ripple from the death, through Livy and Ovid into the poem Shakespeare writes. That narrative self-consciousness which leads Keats to mark the limits of artifice prompts Shakespeare to encode the historicity of his text. If suicide is the end of the heroine's woes, it is so by virtue of its securing a storied fame, and our reading, as she did the tapestry, and Keats her, *Lucrece.*

CHAPTER 4

Henry IV *and the Death of Old Double* (1990)

I

Towards the end of his second book of *Essais*, Montaigne turns aside from such large themes as virtue and anger to describe an infant prodigy. 'I saw two dayes since a child,' he reports,

> whom two men and a nurce . . . carried about with intent to get some money with the sight of him, by reason of his strangenes. . . . Under his paps he was fastned and joyned to an other child, . . . face to face, and as if a little child would embrace another somewhat bigger. . . . His Nurce told me, he made water by both privities.[1]

Appalled yet fascinated, Montaigne details a creature as grotesque as anything in Shakespeare. To think of his 'Monstrous Child' is to recall Othello's anthropophagi and Iago's 'beast with two backs', or that bizarre episode in which Stephano stumbles upon a double-bodied marketable monster: Trinculo under Caliban's cloak.[2] Both writers draw on a European-wide literature of marvels, ranging from encyclopaedias of classical chimeras, through quasi-scientific books of wonders, down to the ballads which stuff Autolycus' pack,[3] and both display a scepticism and speculative reflexivity which complicate their relations with those discourses.

When Montaigne deciphers the infant hieroglyph, he writes from literary precedents[4] but with a figurative involution of his own. 'This double body,' he declares,

---

[1] Quotations from *Essays*, trans. John Florio, introd. L. C. Harmer, 3 vols. (London, 1965), ii. 439.

[2] *Othello* I. i. 118–19, *The Tempest* II. ii; quotations from *The Complete Works*, gen. eds. Stanley Wells and Gary Taylor (Oxford, 1986).

[3] See Jean Céard, *La Nature et les prodiges* (Geneva, 1977) and Katharine Park and Lorraine J. Daston, 'Unnatural Conceptions: The Study of Monsters in Sixteenth- and Seventeenth-Century France and England', *Past and Present*, 92 (1981), 20–54; also Dudley Wilson, 'Publications Relating to Births of Conjoined Twins and Hermaphrodites in France, 1570–1707', in *The Monstrous*, Durham French Colloquies, 1 (Durham, 1987), 104–20.

[4] Maurice Rat refers to Boaistuau's *Histoires prodigieuses* (VI and XXXV) in his notes to the

and these different members, having reference to one onely head, might serve for a favorable prognostication to our King, to maintaine the factions and differing parties of this our kingdome under an unitie of the lawes. But least the successe should prove it contrary, it is not amisse to let him runne his course: For in things already past the[re] need no divination. *Ut quum facta sunt, tum ad conjecturam aliqua interpretatione revocantur* (Cic. *Divin.* ii) . . . *Those which we call monsters are not so with God, who in the immensitie of his worke seeth the infinitie of formes therein contained.* And it may be thought, that any figure [which] doth amaze us, hath relation unto some other figure of the same kinde, although unknown unto man. . . . Wee call that against nature, which commeth against custome. (pp. 439–40)

Orthodoxy prompts the reader to expect a prediction of strife,[5] but Montaigne finds a hopeful message in even this body politic's diversity-in-unity. Elaborating his emblem through some rapid shifts of style—vernacular insouciance, Latinate authority—he divines, not without wry hindsight, what Warwick in 2 *Henry IV* calls 'the hatch and brood of time'. His prose moves reflectively towards creative recognition, breeding out of the divided child a 'world of figures'—in a phrase used by Shakespeare's Worcester—which, licensed by divine immensity (and underwritten by St Augustine),[6] both questions customary order, and, more obscurely, intimates what Montaigne makes explicit elsewhere, that his essays are 'crotesques et corps monstrueux, rappiecez de divers membres', his own nature a 'monster' and 'expresse wonder'.[7]

That Montaigne can chime with Warwick and Worcester[8] in the two parts of *Henry IV* means next to nothing in itself. Renaissance plays, though, have more in common with grotesques than their 'strangenes' being shown for money. Philosophers increasingly understood the

---

Œuvres complètes (Paris, 1962). Cf. Ambroise Paré's *Des monstres et prodiges* (1573, etc.), trans. Janis L. Pallister (Chicago, 1982), 15–16, 30.

[5] e.g. 'On Physiognomy', where Montaigne quotes Ovid ('*Hostis adest dextra laeváque à parte timendus* . . .') and declares of the frame of order: 'Oh monstrous Warre: Others worke without; this inwardly and against hir selfe: And with her owne venome gnaweth and consumes her selfe' (iii. 295). Cf. P. Archambault, 'The Analogy of the "Body" in Renaissance Political Literature', *Bibliothèque d'humanisme et Renaissance*, 29 (1967), 21–53, David George Hale, *The Body Politic: A Political Metaphor in Renaissance English Literature* (The Hague, 1971), and 'Monstres et maladies', ch. 4 of Géralde Nakam, *Les 'Essais' de Montaigne: miroir et procès de leur temps* (Paris, 1984).

[6] See Marie-Thérèse Jones-Davies (ed.), *Monstres et prodiges au temps de la Renaissance* (Paris, 1980), 5–6, 10.

[7] *Œuvres complètes*, 181 (invoking the fish/woman of Horace's *Ars poetica*, 4); *Essays*, iii. 282, cf. i. 43–4 (comparing his essays to the fleshly misconceptions of solitary women).

[8] 2 *Henry IV* III. i. 81, *1 Henry IV* I. iii. 207.

monstrous as commensurate with the artful because both evidenced through addition the fertility of nature. Bacon's denunciation of 'the fashion to talk as if art were something different to nature' is inseparable from this theory of monsters, in which 'the passage from the miracles of nature to those of art is easy; for if nature be once seized in her variations, and the cause be manifest, it will be easy to lead her by art to such deviation as she was at first led by chance.'[9] The analytic grotesquerie of late Shakespeare most evidently adumbrates this vision, but grafting and chimeric variation are not restricted to Bohemia and Cymbeline's Britain. Signs of the kind provided by Cloten's headless trunk, that problematic image of the body politic, also figure in earlier Histories. If Shakespeare ever thought kingship uncomplicatedly the apex of 'natural' order, in the manner of the Homilies, he explores in the second tetralogy—as surely as Montaigne comparing Henry III's control of faction to a double-bodied monster—the grotesquerie of artful government. After the split deformities of Richard III, which make him a supreme self-observing actor but also epitome of disunion in the realm,[10] come works which acknowledge the duplicity by which the king's 'two bodies' compose a divided 'body politic'. Even cool prose defining those doctrines inclines to gemination: 'The ideas are related', Marie Axton notes—'closely related', for David Hale, 'This dual nature of the [two-bodied king] as both microcosm and part of the macrocosm.'[11] It is hard not to strike a playful note when elaborating such constitutional theory, and the risibility which colours the accounts of Maitland and Ernst Kantorowicz[12] should not be dismissed as anachronistic. Shakespeare proliferates 'figures' under and of King Henry with a sceptical sense of incipient absurdity in artful doubling.

Take the first appearance of Shallow and Silence. From the troubled darkness of a palace chamber (the King is '*in his nightgown*'), the scene shifts to a Gloucestershire morning, early. We have just heard Henry rehearse his isolation: the falling away of Northumberland (once 'like a brother' to him), Prince Harry pointedly not mentioned. The garrulous, amiable Justices, by contrast, insistently celebrate their kinship:

    [9] Park and Daston, 'Unnatural Conceptions', 44, quoting *Description of the Intellectual Globe*, ch. 2, and *Novum organon* II. 29.

    [10] Cf. Michael Neill, 'Shakespeare's Halle of Mirrors: Play, Politics, and Psychology in *Richard III*', *Shakespeare Studies*, 8 (1976), 99–129.

    [11] *The Queen's Two Bodies* (1977), 12; *The Body Politic*, 15–16.

    [12] F. W. Maitland, 'The Crown as Corporation', repr. in *Collected Papers*, ed. H. A. L. Fisher, 3 vols. (Cambridge, 1911), iii. 244–70; Ernst H. Kantorowicz, *The King's Two Bodies: A Study in Medieval Political Theology* (Princeton, 1957).

Shallow. . . . And how doth my good cousin Silence?
Silence. Good morrow, good cousin Shallow.
Shallow. And how doth my cousin your bedfellow? And your fairest daughter and mine, my god-daughter Ellen?
Silence. Alas, a black ouzel, cousin Shallow.
Shallow. By yea and no, sir, I dare say my cousin William is become a good scholar. He is at Oxford still, is he not?
Silence. Indeed, sir, to my cost.
Shallow. A must then to the Inns o' Court shortly: I was once of Clement's Inn, where I think they will talk of mad Shallow yet. (*Part 2* III. ii. 3–14)

There is a warmth and quirky affirmation here far more confident than anything at Westminster. As surely as in the court scenes, however, Shakespeare deals with power and inheritance. The Justices discuss the reproduction of a rural élite—Ellen, attractive and marriageable, William retracing his Uncle's career-moves[13]—and their present authority is demonstrated by the lot of the recruits, waiting just offstage or (if Folio directions are followed) already blocked out behind them. Early audiences would have seen the pair as more than rustic babblers. The government of Elizabethan England extended power far from the centre, and rule (as we shall see) lay disproportionately with the old. *Acts of the Privy Council* demonstrate Westminster's involvement with local minutiae, but also its determination to support JPs as limbs and members of the crown. And Gloucestershire was no backwater; it remained from the fourteenth to the seventeenth century a crossroads between north and west, with thriving ports and affluent hinterland.[14] The county recurs in the tetralogy[15] for some of the strategic reasons that made it, during the 1590s, a heavily guarded area (open to Spanish invasion) in which there was heavy impressment which Justices (against local resistance) were instructed to impose.[16]

Nor should the post-Restoration tendency of theatre to find rural life inane obscure the importance of Shallow's farm. The years 1595–8 saw

[13] 'The same names recurred generation after generation in the lists of Justices . . . for Gloucestershire,' writes Joan Johnson, *Tudor Gloucestershire* (Gloucester, 1985), 114–15.

[14] e.g. William Bradford Willcox, *Gloucestershire: A Study in Local Government 1590–1640* (New Haven, 1940), ch. 1.

[15] It sees the start of Bolingbroke's campaign against Richard (landing at Berkeley Castle) and the beginnings of unrest after the regicide (*Richard II* V. vi. 2–3). Prince Harry heads through it towards Bridgnorth (*Part 1* III. ii. 175–6), anticipating Falstaff in this scene. Indeed the murder of a local magnate, Gloucester, Thomas Woodstock, initiates the 'revolution of the times'.

[16] e.g. *Calendar of State Papers Domestic, 1591–1594*, 495, *1595–1597*, 400, *Acts of the Privy Council, 1595–6*, 48, 53, 157–8, 262–3, 304, 323–4, 327–8, *1596–7*, 240–1, 268–9, 277–8, 292–5, 343–6, 468–9, *1597*, 24, 101–3 and 105, 106–7, 160–2 and 164, *1597–8*, 46, 251, 527–8, 631, *1598–9*, 573–6.

famine and rioting in the West Country, which JPs were required to quell.[17] Hardship had been felt earlier: Queen Elizabeth's last visit to the locality, in 1592, prompted an entertainment at Sudeley Castle in which 'an olde Shepheard' spoke less than idyllically about country life.[18] *2 Henry IV* was written against a background of deep recession. Grain shortages pushed up prices from 1594. Central government required the likes of Shallow and Silence to share resources with Shakespearian Warwickshire: 'poore people . . . specially at Stratford uppon Avon, Alcester and other places thereaboutes.'[19] By 1597 the problem had assumed national proportions and rye was being imported from as far away as Poland to relieve London, Bristol, and Gloucester itself. For early audiences, Shallow's farm, far from being a bucolic retreat, would be a venture of immediate interest. The price of a yoke of bullocks, the prospect of 'pigeons' for supper, were the matter of daily politics. Moreover, the language of husbandry was charged with political implications. Ploughing, reaping, manuring, the keeping of bees: thanks not least to the *Georgics*, a standard text at grammar schools, these activities were thought to reflect as well as belong to the flourishing Commonwealth. On Shallow's busy acres, where even 'the headland' on which the plough turns is prudently sown, and where a Justice's daily agenda includes the bill for horseshoes and 'a new link to the bucket', the exercise of government becomes palpable, and the 'decaying', 'almost Chekhovian' farm celebrated by critics[20] is hard to find.

'Then was Jack Falstaff, now Sir John, a boy, and page to Thomas Mowbray, Duke of Norfolk', Shallow goes on:

Silence. This Sir John, cousin, that comes hither anon about soldiers?
Shallow. The same Sir John, the very same. I see him break Scoggin's head at the
   court gate, when a was a crack, not thus high. And the very same day did I
   fight with one Samson Stockfish, a fruiterer, behind Gray's Inn. Jesu, Jesu, the
   mad days that I have spent! And to see how many of my old acquaintance are
   dead. (23–33)

[17] My account draws on Buchanan Sharp, *In Contempt of All Authority: Rural Artisans and Riot in the West of England, 1586–1660* (Berkeley, 1980), chs. 2 and 3, H. P. R. Finberg (gen. ed.), *The Agrarian History of England and Wales*, iv, ed. Joan Thirsk (Cambridge, 1967), chs. 4 and 9, Willcox, *Gloucestershire*, 135–9, Penry Williams, *The Tudor Regime* (Oxford, 1979), 327–38; also *APC, 1595–6*, 180–1, *1596–7*, 152–3, 226–8, 335–6, 339–40, 479–80, *1597*, 119, 362–3, *1597–8*, 314–17.

[18] John Nichols (ed.), *The Progresses and Public Processions of Queen Elizabeth*, 3 vols. (London, 1823), iii. 136–7.

[19] *APC, 1597–8*, 316–17.

[20] Quoting here A. D. Nuttall, *A New Mimesis: Shakespeare and the Representation of Reality* (London, 1983), 159.

Moving, and moved by cadence, is Shallow's shift from 'The same Sir John, the very same', where we join with him in sensing how that double phrase belies him, obscures a loss of years ('the *very same* day did I fight . . .'), to the doubled 'Jesu, Jesu', and his subsequent reflections upon death. But the drift towards doubling develops its own momentum as it reflects back to Shallow complacent echoes of his profundity:

> *Shallow.* Certain, 'tis certain; very sure, very sure. Death, as the Psalmist saith, is certain to all; all shall die. How a good yoke of bullocks at Stamford fair?
> *Silence.* By my troth, I was not there.
> *Shallow.* Death is certain. Is old Double of your town living yet?
> *Silence.* Dead, sir. (35–41)

Beyond, now, and somewhere before character is the rhythm of stage circumstance, uttered in two actors who double themselves as Justices,[21] having doubled other roles in this large-cast play.[22] The pair of actor/ Justices, who will be interrupted by that unresolved double of Sir John Russell, Bardolph,[23] '*and one with him*' (as Q puts it), speak a veritable dialect of doubling: in phrase, 'very sure, very sure' (the recurrent figure is *geminatio*),[24] in imagery ('How a good *yoke* of bullocks'), and then, with a question answered before it is asked ('Death is certain'), through a name that seems spoken by the scene: 'Is old Double of your town living yet?'

Silence's answer 'Dead, sir' elicits from Shallow a tribute which, like Hamlet's reverie over Yorick, brings a buried man back to life. That the Prince of Denmark is haunted by the past is, tonally and supernaturally, apparent. But it stands high among points of comparison between *Henry IV* and *Hamlet* that the Histories dilate into retrospection. Indeed, if the Oxford editors are right, Shakespeare added in revision those Folio-only passages in *Part 2* which recall Bolingbroke's triumphant entry into London, Hotspur 'in speech, in gait, | In diet . . . the mark and glass' of soldiership, Richard throwing down his warder at the tilts between Hereford and Norfolk.[25] Not only does retrospection become more resonant as the

[21] 'Where "actor" and "character" were inevitably fused within the same person, they nevertheless remained distinguished from one another for the beholders . . . This dual conception . . . This double image . . . was their stage realism'; Glynne Wickham, *Early English Stage: 1300–1660*, ii (London, 1963), 24.

[22] See e.g. Stephen Booth, 'Speculations on Doubling in Shakespeare's Plays', in '*King Lear*,' '*Macbeth*,' *Indefinition, and Tragedy* (New Haven, 1983), 127–55, developed by Richard Fotheringham, 'The Doubling of Roles on the Jacobean Stage', *Theatre Research International*, 10 (1985), 18–32.

[23] John Jowett, 'The Thieves in *1 Henry IV*', *Review of English Studies*, NS 38 (1987), 325–33.

[24] Cf. Patricia Parker, *Literary Fat Ladies: Rhetoric, Gender, Property* (London, 1987), 71–3.

[25] I. iii. 85–108, II. iii. 23–45, IV. i. 101–37; see John Jowett and Gary Taylor, 'The Three Texts of *2 Henry IV*', *Studies in Bibliography*, 40 (1987), 31–50.

two parts of *Henry IV* unfold before an audience: the idea of looking back became more important for Shakespeare in composition. And since we find him working towards the tonalities of *Hamlet*, it is not surprising that he should, as at Elsinore, render ambiguous those moments when the past returns. Just as the graveyard proves a turning-point in the tragedy,[26] so Shallow's tribute to old Double oscillates between reminiscence and *memento mori*:

Jesu, Jesu, dead! A drew a good bow; and dead! A shot a fine shoot. John o' Gaunt loved him well, and betted much money on his head. Dead! A would have clapped i'th' clout at twelve score, and carried you a forehand shaft a fourteen and fourteen and a half, that it would have done a man's heart good to see. . . . And is old Double dead? (42–51)

Renaissance prints and paintings frequently show a young person contemplating a skull. The idea of shared mortality invests such icons with doubleness. Does Hamlet hold Yorick's skull, or is the silent, bony icon somehow his own death's head? Doubling in Gloucestershire draws on the same uncanniness, as Silence 'speaks[s] like a death's-head' (Falstaff's words to Doll (II. iv. 236–7)), and bids Shallow remember his end. It is mortal enough for a tender prince to meditate in a graveyard: to be 'old' as well as 'Double' makes 'Death' utterly 'certain'. Shallow's question is almost tautological, since 'double' could mean 'ghost, apparition'. Hence the bizarre resonances of that quarto stage-direction, '*Enter Bardolfe, and one with him*'—the latter mute, unspeaking, a figure of Silence. Faces are often significant in *Henry IV*, but the blaze of Bardolph's countenance carries a prodigious reminder: his master makes 'as good use of it as many a man doth of a death's head, or a *memento mori*' (*Part I* III. iii. 28–30). What speaks of old Double registers at levels deeper than dialogue the common predicament of man.

If that projects 'old Double' beyond grotesque bone-rattling, it does not leave politics behind. Figuring ramifies in these plays as in Montaigne, where 'any figure . . . hath relation unto some other figure of the same kinde'. If Falstaff tells his death's head, 'I am old, I am old' (273), we know what that doubleness makes 'certain'. 'Old', 'death', and 'doubling' suffuse the lexis of *2 Henry IV*; nowhere else in the canon do the words 'figure' so richly together,[27] so that Shallow's question articulates a central

---

[26] See John Kerrigan, 'Hieronimo, Hamlet and Remembrance', *Essays in Criticism*, 31 (1981), 105–26, esp. pp. 119–20.

[27] Though *King Lear* uses 'old' as often, *Macbeth* 'double' more frequently, and *Romeo and Juliet* together with *Richard III* outstrip *2 Henry IV* for 'dead'.

trope. Psychoanalysis would gloss this with reference to Sigmund Freud and Otto Rank, to their belief that doubling has become ominous. In primitive cultures, Rank argues, 'the double' is 'a guardian angel, assuring immortal survival to the self', but it 'eventually appears as precisely the opposite, a reminder of the individual's mortality, indeed, the announcer of death itself'.[28] Shakespeare, though, is less determinate. Death's joke, old Double, can be suggestive not least because a large part of the little we are told of him is unlikely. Falstaff, lamenting at the end of this Gloucestershire scene, 'Lord, Lord, how subject we old men are to this vice of lying' (298–9), will pick out for special comment Shallow's pretended intimacy with Gaunt. And how could Gaunt love Double for shooting a 'forehand shaft', level, over 290 yards—a shot only possible with a heavy-calibre machine-gun? Yet Falstaff is by his own admission 'old, old' when he denounces Shallow's mendacity, and the Cretan Liar factor is inseparable from all these reminiscences. Attend to Double's name, as the only sure thing about him (apart from his death being 'certain'), and that very name elaborates the enigma—not so much because the scene's other speaking names can be unreliable ('Samson Stockfish a fruiterer', 'Feeble', most gallant of recruits) as because unreliability is in the nature of what it is to be Double. 'Double-dealing', 'double knavery', 'double meaning', 'double self': even, simply, just to 'double', as the toiling and troubling witches doubly do, is steadily, in Shakespeare, duplicitous. Shallow's need to glorify the past, like Hamlet's desire to make his own old Double, Old Hamlet (and he is not so named in the sources), tower above Elsinore like Hyperion, compounds death with deception.

It is time to recall Montaigne's 'Monstrous Child': that double-bodied infant who prompts thoughts about a faction-racked king. For there is one old Double in *Henry IV* whose 'death' is not only 'certain', but also decisive in ending an action which, expected to conclude with *Part 1*—by the rebels and many auditors (else the *Part 2*-as-afterthought theory would not be so tenacious)—is delayed through long illness while other mortuary announcements are made. When Northumberland dismisses Lord Bardolph's good news, sensing Hotspur's 'death' to be 'certain', or when Shallow asks knowingly about Double, the processes of invention, by which 'any figure . . . hath relation unto some other figure of the same kinde', anticipates the inevitable news flash. 'And is old Double dead?' is, in other words, a way of saying this, in Gloucestershire:

[28] *Beyond Psychology* (1941; New York, 1958), 76.

Pistol. Under which king, besonian? Speak, or die.
Shallow. Under King Harry.
Pistol.   Harry the Fourth, or Fifth?
Shallow. Harry the Fourth.
Pistol.   A foutre for thine office!
  Sir John, thy tender lambkin now is king. . . .
Falstaff.   What, is the old King dead? (v. iii. 114–20)

'Dead, sir.' And if that amounts to declaring that the high political denouement is written in the speech rhythms, in the staged configuration,
of Shallow's first exchange with Silence, it also leads to the thought that
old Double may be dead rather doubly. It might appear monstrous to die
and come back to life. Yet, grotesquely binary as the old King is, the con-
ventional resolutions 'Not Amurath an Amurath succeeds, | But Harry
Harry' and 'weep that Harry's dead . . . But Harry lives' (v. ii. 48–9, 59–60)
are high-minded 'king's two bodies' versions, mutually figures and parodies, of his uncanny dying and reviving in a chamber called Jerusalem.

  The episode in which Hal takes the crown from his seemingly dead father is, of course, reported by both Holinshed and *The Famous Victories of
Henrie the Fifth*. Shakespeare seems also to have known Daniel's account
in *The Civile Wars*.[29] But in none of these sources is the situation made so
ambiguous. Other nobles, not the Prince, judge the King defunct in
Holinshed, and they 'covered his face with a linnen cloth' before his heir
entered the chamber. Daniel moves the Prince in and out of the room so
quickly that doubts about motivation cannot form. Only in the King's
rebuke as reported by the *The Famous Victories* do we get a clumsy hint
of what Shakespeare manages to convey: the subliminal possibility of
design.

> Why how now my sonne?
> I had thought the last time I had you in schooling,
> I had given you a lesson for all,
> And do you now begin againe?[30]

For Shakespeare suggests that a test is set by the King—that lack of trust
in the Prince which lingers from *Part 1* is given scope, and the impulse to
instruct—not out of any intention to deceive, but as it is Henry's 'nature'
to be double, as he can't but counterfeit the death which is certain. 'By his
gates of breath | There lies a downy feather which stirs not' (IV. iii. 162–3).

---

[29] See Geoffrey Bullough (ed.), *Narrative and Dramatic Sources of Shakespeare*, 8 vols. (London, 1957–75), iv. 277.   [30] Ibid. 318.

Deader than Cordelia, he is nothing of the kind. Harry, interestingly, passes this test in the terms set by his father: even if he is guilty of wishing the old King into his grave (as Bolingbroke did King Richard), he purges himself by being double about what was said to the crown. We hear what the Prince says, and the quite different words he reports, yet (like his father, who does not claim to believe him) cannot but respect his 'Pleading so wisely in excuse' (309). It is wrong to think of the King responding, reassured, to filial emotion, exhibited (according to Warwick only) in the Prince's tears in the ante-room; it is enough between doubles that affinity be what is looked for, between one king and '[him]self deceased' (as the *Sonnets'* prolepsis puts it), that the counterfeiting be true.

As my double use of 'counterfeit' implies, *Parts 1* and *2* seem to me extendedly in parallel. Previous accounts of the plays' relations, by G. K. Hunter, Sherman H. Hawkins, and others,[31] argue that rebellion shapes both texts, until, with the ironic counterpointing of Gaultree against the battle of Shrewsbury, comparison ends. If, however, one registers counterfeiting in Jerusalem chamber, then the action replay seemingly curtailed by blood-royal double-dealing at Gaultree retains its momentum at least as far as the death of Henry. Douglas thinks 'the old King dead' on killing Sir Walter Blunt, only to find that he has destroyed a 'likeness', 'Semblably furnished like the King himself' (*Part 1* v. iii. 21). For Douglas, that sends Blunt into eternity in the company of a double whom editors fail thoroughly to gloss because the idea that fools are 'shadows' of kings ('Who is it that can tell me who I am?' [*King Lear* ii. iv. 212]) is so tenacious but obscure in Shakespeare: 'A fool go with thy soul, whither it goes!' (22). But while Douglas stretches commentators, what he further says of Blunt, 'A borrowed title hast thou bought too dear' (23), is more transparent to us than to him. The audience's political scepticism is elicited by quibbling. If 'A borrowed title' in the language of rebellion makes Blunt resemble Henry because neither is entitled to the crown, the 'title' not finally belonging to a king (but to his heirs in perpetuity) is, in all obedience, essential to the seemliness of kingship.

Having charged around Shrewsbury field in pursuit of an impossible referent, a king with no 'borrowed title', Douglas comes on Henry and cries, 'What art thou | That counterfeit'st the person of the king?' (v. iv. 26–7). Henry's reply is, 'The King himself, who, Douglas, grieves at heart | So many of his shadows thou hast met | And not the very King.' But

[31] '*Henry IV* and the Elizabethan Two-Part Play', *Review of English Studies*, NS 5 (1954), 237–48; '*Henry IV*: The Structural Problem Revisited', *Shakespeare Quarterly*, 33 (1982), 278–301.

Douglas's response carries the scars of his having looked for an absolute and encountered irreducible doubleness: 'I fear thou art another counterfeit; I And yet, in faith, thou bearest thee *like* a king' (34–5). At Flint Castle York had said of Richard, 'Yet looks he like a king', and in so doing had drawn attention to the schism of self-alienation which would contribute to that monarch's fall (III. iii. 67). On the night before Agincourt, Henry V will walk in disguise, yet be open about his doubly being himself with the troops, and still remain unknown:

Pistol. The King's a bawcock and a heart-of-gold,
   A lad of life, an imp of fame,
   Of parents good . . .
                What is thy name?
King Harry. Harry *le roi.*
Pistol. Leroi? A Cornish name. Art thou of Cornish crew? (IV. i. 45–51)

Bolingbroke operates between these extremes, between the potentially split self-staging of Richard and the unreflecting doubleness of his son. That is as much his historical as psychological position. In the development of the second tetralogy towards ideal Christian Kingship—otherwise known as Anointed Duplicity—Henry IV is transitional, no more than 'like' when not 'counterfeit'. Hence the significance of the fat knight's reaction to being attacked by Douglas, yet, 'like' Henry ('figures' proliferate), getting away with his life:

'Sblood, 'twas time to counterfeit, or that hot termagant Scot had paid me, scot and lot too. Counterfeit? I lie, I am no counterfeit. To die is to be a counterfeit, for he is but the counterfeit of a man who hath not the life of a man. But to counterfeit dying when a man thereby liveth is to be no counterfeit, but the true and perfect image of life indeed. (V. iv. 112–18)

The parallels are eloquent. Henry IV's 'counterfeit dying' in *Part 2* is 'the true and perfect image of life itself' which, if it 'be no counterfeit', seems very 'like' it.

Highly relevant is the King's cowardice, which not even a Maurice Morgann could argue away. Holinshed writes of him having three replicas, but also of killing thirty-six rebels. This is not what Shakespeare shows. Henry on stage is no more valiant than Sir John, and 'many march . . . in his coats' at Shrewsbury (V. iii. 25). When Douglas comically cries, 'Now by my sword, I will kill all his coats. I I'll murder all his wardrobe, piece by piece' (26–7), 'O monstrous!' comes to mind, 'Eleven buckram men grown out of two!' (II. v. 223–4)—not 'one'. Certainly Gads Hill in performance is not much less a battle of counterfeits (Sinklo, Burbage, and company) than Shrewsbury with its few fighters and exiguous '*Alarums*'. Prince Henry's valour in the fray earns respect, but the King's 'devices' are so politic that his death in 'counterfeit' seems 'discretion', like running away from a robbery or profiting from the valour of others. Falstaff again:

The better part of valour is discretion, in the which better part I have saved my life. Zounds, I am afraid of this gunpowder Percy, though he be dead. How if he should counterfeit too, and rise? By my faith, I am afraid he would prove the better counterfeit. Therefore I'll make him sure . . . (v. iv. 118–23)

The Prince's reaction to Sir John's resurrection adds to the scepticism generated by Henry's 'counterfeiting' in both parts of *Henry IV*. 'I saw him dead, | Breathless'—no downy feather stirring; 'Art thou alive?', he asks, 'Thou art not what thou seem'st' (131–5). The knight's response is a triumphant witty compound which monsters identity by merging 'art' as being with the 'art' of 'seeming': 'No, that's certain: I am not a double man. But if I be not Jack . . . then am I a jack. There is Percy. [*He throws down Hotspur's body*]' (136–8). Hijacking (to play out the pun) an emblem of father/son affinity, derived from Aeneas' carrying Anchises out of Troy—an image used uncomically by, for instance, Young Clifford in the first tetralogy[32]—Sir John proves himself not double (not a 'liar' because not a 'ghost') by throwing down a dead double (so demonstrably being single), even though, as his being both jack and Jack reminds us, his singularity could scarcely be less duplicitous.

II

Montaigne's essay 'Of the Resemblance Betweene Children and Fathers', is even more divagatory than most of his mature pieces; but one passage in it partly carries on where 'Of a Monstrous Child' left off, and, by shedding light on the monstrousness in there even being children, suggests why Sir John's bearing Hotspur on his back has to do with duplicitous doubleness in the Prince of Wales becoming 'King Harry'. 'Wee neede not goe to cull out miracles,' he writes,

and chuse strange difficulties: me seemeth, that amongst those things we ordinarily see, there are such incomprehensible rarities, as they exceed all difficulty of miracles. What monster is it, that this teare or drop of seed, whereof we are

---

[32] *2 Henry VI* v. iii. 61–5.

ingendred brings with it; and in it the impressions, not only of the corporall forme, but even of the very thoughts and inclinations of our fathers? (ii. 495–6)

This begins among the mysteries of Shakespeare's early sonnets, where reproduction is miraculous but uncomplicated, an imitative endorsement of both kinship and identity. In support, Montaigne cites Aristotle, who 'reporteth of a certaine Nation, with whom all women were common, where children were allotted their fathers, only by their resemblances'. These 'resemblances', at once visible and psychological (dictating 'thoughts and inclinations'), may have awkward consequences, as Faulconbridge's mother discovers in *King John*; but the process remains unproblematic.

Characteristically appealing from Aristotle to experience, however, Montaigne goes on to discuss less mimetically symmetrical factors. 'How beare they these resemblances', he asks of the monstrous seed,

of so rash, and unruly a progresse, that the childes childe shall be answerable to his grandfather, and the nephew to his uncle? . . . It may be supposed, that I am indebted to my father for this stonie quality; for he died exceedingly tormented with a great stone in his bladder. He never felt himself troubled with the disease, but at the age of sixtie seaven yeares . . . I was borne five and twenty yeares before his sicknes, and during the course of his healthy state his third child. Where was al this while the propension or inclination to this defect, hatched? . . . He that shal resolve me of this progresse, I will believe him as many other miracles as he shall please to tell mee . . . (p. 496)

The text ends up as far from the early sonnets as Shakespeare himself in the Histories. Paternity, Montaigne observes, may be never more than part-evident, the proof long-delayed and unwelcome. Evidences as odd as gallstones can demonstrate the affinity. It may emerge, in what Warwick calls the 'hatch and brood of time', as late as a final illness, and prove descent from the father by resembling not him but an uncle or a grandfather.

The idea of patrilineal succession is central to the second tetralogy where it meshes with beliefs by which 'the family served as a metaphor for the state; in conventional political thought the king was a father to his people, the father king in his household.'[33] These interconnected theses, widespread (though not unchallenged) in early modern England, at once underpin and flaw Henry IV's kingship. Richard II's abuse of Hereford's

---

[33] Susan Dwyer Amussen, *An Ordered Society: Gender and Class in Early Modern England* (Oxford, 1988), 1.

lineal rights licenses the exile's return, and it remains an unstated but powerful advantage for him that his sons promise continuity where childlessness—Queen Elizabeth's 'I am Richard II, know ye not that?'[34]—cannot. Of several silences associated with Bolingbroke, however, the most telling is his failure to mention Gaunt in *Henry IV*. The line which should descend to him from Richard does not, precipitating a complex of doubts which is not the King's alone. His classically exact, but unusually inverted, articulation of family romance—

> O, that it could be proved
> That some night-tripping fairy had exchanged
> In cradle clothes our children where they lay,
> And called mine Percy, his Plantagenet!
> Then would I have his Harry, and he mine. . . . (*Part I* 1. i. 85–9)

—finds an echo in the Prince's diffused, resentful uncertainty about the legitimacy of his relations with his king/father. That tardiness or lack of clear proof in the blood-line which Montaigne addresses, exacerbated by generational conflict, draws Prince Harry to a life which he despises ('I know you all . . .') but adopts in order to demonstrate that he will not conform to his so-called father's wishes and play the decorous part of heir apparent. He prefers what his first soliloquy calls 'the unyoked humour of . . . idleness' (1. ii. 193), where 'idle', as in *Hamlet* ('I must be idle' (III. ii. 88)), implies 'unstable, zany'. 'Upholding' wild company, he assumes an 'antic disposition'.

That the Prince's predicament resembles that of Hamlet has been insufficiently brought out. Yet the King adumbrates the paradigm when lecturing his son in *Part I*, a speech which caught the attention of at least one early auditor.[35] Contrasting his own reserve in youth with Richard, who 'Grew a companion to the common streets, | Enfeoffed himself to popularity' and fell, he warns: 'And in that very line, Harry, standest thou' (III. ii. 68–9, 85). The Prince is 'lineally' related to an anointed blood-legitimate king, yet the officially designated heir (again, like Hamlet) of a politic usurper who contrived that king's death. When writing 'in that very line', Shakespeare will have known (from Holinshed and elsewhere)

---

[34] The Queen reportedly went on to relate the historical figure to Shakespeare's play: 'this tragedy was played 40tie times in open streets and houses.' De la Warr MSS, quoted in E. K. Chambers, *William Shakespeare: A Study of Facts and Problems*, 2 vols. (Oxford, 1930), ii. 326–7.

[35] See the transcription of Edward Pudsey's commonplace book in Hilton Kelliher, 'Contemporary Manuscript Extracts from Shakespeare's *Henry IV, Part I*', *English Manuscript Studies 1100–1700*, 1 (1989), 144–81, pp. 157–8.

that the historical Prince was close to Richard, fought with him in Ireland, and was knighted by him—like the Black Prince, say, dubbed by his father Edward III. Is the King Prince Harry's psychological parent, or, as Hamlet says of Claudius, 'A little more than kin and less than kind' (I. ii. 65)? 'For all the world', he continues, weeping, 'As thou art to this hour was Richard then, | When I from France set foot at Ravenspurgh, | And even as I was then is Percy now' (93–6). The tears need not be taken at face value, any more than the Prince's snuffling at his father's 'counterfeit' death. Shakespeare alerts us to their canniness by parodying them beforehand, in Sir John's Eastcheap travesty (II. v). That Henry's 'Pleading so wisely' involves more persuasion than evidence is clear. *Richard II* shows us a ruler who could better be accused of hauteur than of 'popularity'. Indeed the King complains of Hereford's

> courtship to the common people . . .
> Off goes his bonnet to an oysterwench.
> A brace of draymen bid God speed him well,
> And had the tribute of his supple knee . . . (I. iv. 23–32)

This account, which squares with Bolingbroke's reception by the masses in Act V (ii. 7–21), is complicatingly more like the suspect populism of his son, 'sworn brother to a leash of drawers', than the staid 'rareness' and 'solemnity' advocated by Henry. But that is what experience, and Montaigne, lead us to expect, setting limits to the tragic comparison. There is, between the Prince and his father, a subterranean set of resemblances finally more redeemable than those between Hamlet and Claudius. *Henry IV*'s Elsinore dilemma can be eased by Bolingbroke's becoming a 'figure' of old Double.

Likeness and dislike run deep through the Prince's role until the closing stages of *Part 2*. He may not be as learnedly distrait as Hamlet, but his madcap conduct is as much a distraction, his coded utterances are as pregnant, as those of the tragic hero. Consider that tavern scene in which Sir John theatrically weeps, and its inset playlets—rehearsing, like Hamlet's dramatic tableaux, matters of concern to the Prince. Recent criticism has reduced to a dialectic of power the sequence in which Harry boasts his proficiency to 'drink with any tinker in his own language', implies that Francis might rob and leave his master, and has Poins prompt cries of 'Anon, anon, sir!' (*Part 1* II. v. 1–109).[36] Linguistically the episode is far

---

[36] e.g. Stephen Greenblatt, 'Invisible Bullets', revised in *Shakespearean Negotiations: The Circulation of Social Energy in Renaissance England* (Oxford, 1988).

richer: its 'Anon' routine,[37] for instance, sets off Sir John's men in buck-ram speech in ways which fully signify only when the parallel episode in *Part 2* puts Falstaff under Francis's constraints.[38] Psychologically, too, re-lations between Prince and drawer do not neatly fit a circuit of exploita-tion. David Bevington has added to the case for identification between the pair by noting that the Prince's list 'Tom, Dick, and Francis' (8) pri-vately quibbles with 'Tom, Dick, and Harry'.[39] But there are two young Harrys in the play, and Dr Johnson was right to indicate how pointedly the episode ends with a gibe at Hotspur's fixed humour. When the Prince compares Francis's, 'fewer words than a parrot . . . his eloquence the par-cel of a reckoning' to 'Percy's mind . . . he that kills me some six or seven dozen of Scots at a breakfast' (99–104), the play's close texture illuminates his guilt that, trapped in life's apprenticeship, he has not buckled down to its reckonings with the assiduity of his rival. Hotspur, that 'paraquito' (as Kate has just called him (II. iv. 83)), is compounded in Francis too, and the playlet revolves their drama. Hence the Prince's interest in the drawer's rebellion against his master and anxiety at the very thought.

'But Francis', he declares,

Francis. My lord.
Prince Harry. Wilt thou rob this leathern-jerkin, crystal-button, knot-pated,
 agate-ring, puke-stocking, caddis-garter, smooth-tongue, Spanish-pouch?
Francis. O Lord, sir, who do you mean?
Prince Harry. Why, then, your brown bastard is your only drink! For look you,
 Francis, your white canvas doublet will sully. . . . (66–74)

Those looking for a discourse of power find 'a revolt against authority . . . closed off . . . with a few obscure words'.[40] Shades of obscurity seem not to matter when language is construed as an instrument of 'social practice'. Prince Harry, though, knows a hawk from a handsaw. In Tudor rhetoric, 'doublet' translates *geminatio*: 'when we rehearse one and the same worde twise together', as in 'Anon, anon, sir!'[41] Nor is 'white canvas' properly the cloth of doublets; it is the stuff of drawers' aprons, while doublets are single items joined and separate—clothing of a *Henry IV* kind. To

[37] Cf. *The Rare Triumphs of Love and Fortune* (1582, pub. 1589), Ciiiʳ, a play which Shakespeare apparently knew.

[38] When Hal and Poins pounce as drawers, the tongue-tied 'No, no, no, not so . . . No abuse, Hal; none, Ned, none; no, faith boys, none' (II. iv. 313–28; cf. 260–1, 285) clearly recalls *Part 1*'s 'Anon, Anon' parroting.

[39] *Henry IV, Part 1* (Oxford, 1987), 178.

[40] Greenblatt, *Shakespearean Negotiations*, 44.

[41] Thomas Wilson, quoted by *OED*. Cf. Parker, *Literary Fat Ladies*, 69–70.

respond to the Prince's 'obscurity' is to think, not only into the speech pattern of his unprivileged 'sworn brothers' ('Anon, anon, sir! Score a pint of bastard in the Half-moon'), but of buckram men and Henry's battlefield wardrobe, and the other vizards and suitings which bespeak covertness in the play. With some help from Hamlet's 'sullied flesh', Harry decodes in contradiction: 'Why then, stick to your apprenticeship as Prince, blot though it is not to be in a legitimate line, and accept that your coat of office (the "canvas doublet" of an oddly elevated prentice) will be tainted with that bastard stain'; 'Why, accept your sense of not being Bolingbroke's son, and don't aspire to the snow-white doubleness ("doublet" can mean a "double") that he wants, since it can never be more than corrupt.' This intractable field of meaning, hinting both loyalty and rebellion, is reactivated at the equivalent point in *Part 2*, where the Prince and Poins step forward as a double, clad in their 'sworn brothers'' canvas aprons, and Falstaff cries,

> Some sack, Francis.
> *Prince and Poins (coming forward)*. Anon, anon, sir.
> *Sir John*. Ha, a bastard son of the King's!—And art not thou Poins his brother?
> (II. iv. 284–7)

Some of these 'bastard' anxieties are allayed by Shrewsbury, battle of 'counterfeits'. Given an unhistorically youthful Hotspur, it becomes possible for the Prince to dramatize his father's changeling fantasy and emerge from the struggle 'more himself'. The decisive lines are familiar. Hotspur's 'Harry to Harry shall, hot horse to horse, | Meet and ne'er part till one drop down a cor[se]' (IV. i. 123–4); the Prince's 'Two stars keep not their motion in one sphere, | Nor can one England brook a double reign' (V. iv. 64–5): for both young warriors rivalry is imagined as twinning, merging, splitting, and the death of a double. With Harry Percy killed, the Prince confirms he is heir apparent and proves himself, rather than Hotspur, his father's son. The 'Base inclination'—bastard, illegitimate tendencies—imputed by Henry IV (III. ii. 125) is acted away. To some extent Shakespeare stresses filial affection by having Harry, rather than Holinshed's Earl of March, save the King from the sword of Douglas. But his son's explication, when thanked for 'this fair rescue', is awkward. By declaring 'I might have let alone | The insulting hand of Douglas over you . . .' (V. iv. 52–3), he intimates an alternative entertained. It is not surprising that the King should evade his son's Danish talk of 'poisonous potions' and 'treacherous labour' by turning to questions of battle: 'Make up to

Clifton; I'll to Sir Nicholas Gawsey' (57). The incompleteness of reconciliation seems appropriate. Certainly, if what has been claimed so far is true, proof of the son's affinity with his father could only partly resolve the perplexities through which he labours. As the memory of Richard's murder becomes fainter, in *Part 2*, the *Hamlet* paradigm becomes less pressing. Yet the King, who is eventually prepared to admit, as he does not in *Part 1*, the 'indirect crook'd ways' which brought him to the 'crown', remains almost to the end a usurper, a Claudius-figure spared from death (as in the chapel scene) by the Prince, rather than fully legitimate.

Backsliding on Prince Harry's part, or laziness on Shakespeare's, cannot in any case explain why *Part 2* finds him again among his cronies and, 'essentially mad/e' or not,[42] 'idling' time away. His implication in the fate of the drawer involves a relative powerlessness which *Part 2* sets out to detail. 'Five year! By'r Lady, a long lease for the clinking of pewter.' Keith Thomas has shown that 'the sixteenth and seventeenth centuries are conspicuous for a sustained drive to subordinate persons in their teens and early twenties and to delay their equal participation in the adult world'.[43] High among the factors was a 'wider dissemination of apprenticeship'. But the same process—enshrined in laws which discounted, for instance, statutes passed before a monarch was 24—affected princes as well as prentices. The play which many think the 'seed' of Shakespeare's tetralogy (though this essay will end with a better candidate), *Woodstock*, turns on Richard II's discovery that, being a year older than he thought, he can shake off Gloucester's protectorship. Hamlet's complaint that 'the grass grows . . .' is so commonplace as to be a proverb (III. ii. 330). For the many apprenticed or employed in domestic service, delay was only part of the problem. They shared in the lives of adopting families, like kin, but outwardly filial relations could easily tilt into harshness. The 'mutual dissatisfaction' which Ralph Houlbrooke records between men and their masters indicates the psychological interest which the Prince's alienation from his father/master would have held for early audiences.[44] At the same time, his concession that 'the relationships built up between the most conscientious masters and their . . . servants sometimes resembled those between parents and children, especially when masters had no children of

---

[42] The F3 variant at *Part 1* II. v. 498 points a pun on Harry's legitimacy, his being a 'true prince' or pejorative 'natural', which brings the phrase into *Hamlet* (III. iv. 171–2).

[43] 'Age and Authority in Early Modern England', *Proceedings of the British Academy*, 62 (1976), 205–48, p. 214.

[44] *The English Family 1450–1700* (London, 1984), quoting p. 176.

their own' points up redemptively sembling elements in subordination to which Falstaff, typically, proves most sensitive. When Sir John speaks of the childless Shallow's servants, for instance, he uses images which recall Montaigne's 'Resemblance Betweene Children and Fathers':

It is a wonderful thing to see the semblable coherence of his men's spirits and his. They, by observing him, do bear themselves like foolish justices; he, by conversing with them, is turned into a justice-like servingman. (*Part 2* v. i. 57–61)

Falstaff diagnoses more than family likeness: he describes a process of imaging close to that described in Montaigne's 'Of the Force of Imagination', sceptically adumbrating means by which a world is 'figured' out of 'figures' of authority.[45] In doing so, significantly, he recalls a rare word used only once again in *Henry IV*—of the royal likenesses 'Semblably furnished' at Shrewsbury. The duplicitous kingly seemliness of *Part 1* finds a distant reverberation in the socialized commerce of *Part 2*.

Seen from this perspective, the tetralogy moves out of the elevated milieu of *Richard II*, where feudal bonds and kinship-lines possess a diagrammatic clarity, through the fuller but largely aristocratic world of *Part 1*, in which Prince Harry's drama of legitimation can be centrally expressive of social values, into the highly interactive, devolved culture of *Part 2*, where affinities fan out from the blood-line into service, adoption, and friendship. The first London scene of the sequel presents Falstaff, now equipped with a page, interviewed by the Lord Chief Justice—but not without vigorous mediation by his servant (i. ii). Then the Prince is discovered bantering with Poins about the latter's innumerable bastards, while Poins jests back about those who 'never prick their finger but they say "There's some of the King's blood spilt"', and Falstaff, previously so unkinned, signs his letter 'John with my brothers and sisters . . .' (ii. ii. 22/3–5, 104–6, 124). From the narcissism of Richard II, who plays out his abdication by shattering a mirrored self, and who carries the semblabling logic of the early sonnets into the prison scene ('beget[ing] | A generation of still-breeding thoughts' and construing the King's divided nature as the 'imaginative' progenitor of a realm (v. v. 1–32))—from that, we move to a play in which Prince Henry's inheritance of his father's abstract body seems relatively notional, a trope of political rhetoric, given the multifaceted countenances of resemblance in society. When the King finally calls Harry 'the noble image of my youth' (iv. iii. 55), his words seem more

---

[45] *Essays*, i. 92–104; cf. iii. 155–6.

a conventional way of saying 'I want the Prince to succeed me' than would have been the case in *Richard II*, or—where they had been so desired and resisted—*Part 1*.

Prince Henry responds to this change in the time by manipulating the motif as propaganda. After announcing 'Not Amurath an Amurath succeeds, | But Harry Harry' and 'weep that Harry's dead . . . But Harry lives' (v. ii. 48–9, 59–60), he reruns the whole play of metaphors with an apprehensive Lord Chief Justice—'the person of your father', as he calls himself, excusing Harry's prison custody, 'The image of his power . . . The image of the King . . . your most royal image . . . in a second body' (72–89). The Justice's argument is textbookish, almost a reading out of Plowden. But the new monarch puts the theme to work, demonstrating succession by speaking as his father (107–11) and drolly utilizing the old King's death to expunge his madcap image. Since, as he claims through the inverting sophistry of reflection, 'My father is gone wild into his grave,' he will elevate the Lord Chief Justice into 'a father to my youth' (111–23). Significantly, there is covert resemblance in even this divergence from paternity. Bolingbroke, we are told in *Part 1*, 'by this face, | This seeming brow of justice' won credence when seeking the crown (IV. iii. 84–5). *Part 2* exceeds what precedes it in the use of 'immasked' (Poins's coinage) and expedient 'faces'. While Richard II conceives no kingly visage but his own, young Harry is a prince of 'countenances', expert with vizard and buckram.

It matters, indeed, that 'Double' is not the only duplicitous figure named in Shallow's orchard:

Davy. I beseech you, sir, to countenance William Visor of Wo'ncot against
 Clement Perks o'th' Hill.
Shallow. There is many complaints, Davy, against that Visor. That Visor is an
 arrant knave, on my knowledge.
Davy. I grant your worship that he is a knave, sir; but yet God forbid, sir, but a
 knave should have some countenance at his friend's request. . . . I beseech
 you let him be countenanced.
Shallow. Go to; I say he shall have no wrong. (v. i. 32–45)

Advancement given or denied by Henry V belongs to the same drama of advantage. While the JP biddably 'countenances' 'that Visor', Falstaff's show of 'face' at the coronation prompts Henry (as 'son' of the Lord Chief Justice) to adopt the 'face . . . of justice'. The very rhythms of performance augur double-dealing: within four lines F v. v generates five doublets.[46] Sir John's promise, 'Shallow, I will make the King do you grace. I will leer upon him as a comes by, and do but mark the countenance that he will give me' (5–8) is foredoomed by this figuring. And the text is fraught, below the drama of 'leer' and 'face', with the stuff of 'immasked' kingship:

Falstaff. Fear not your advancements. I will be the man yet that shall make you great.
Shallow. I cannot perceive how, unless you give me your doublet . . . (v. v. 77–81)

But scepticism so intricately orchestrated is compatible with large design. The 'Monstrous Child' that can figure for Montaigne doublebodied kingship, or the 'infinite . . . forms' in a 'drop of seed' that bring intense though delayed resemblance, belong to a 'Shakespearian' generosity of vision which finds 'nature' more 'imaginative' than 'custom'. Henry IV, that old 'counterfeit', does not die of gallstones, but of the apoplexy recorded in Holinshed. His death is rendered 'Montaignean', nevertheless, through signs not in the chronicles—signs exposed by the play to ironic interrogation (Doll's 'unfather'd' and 'loathly' cushion),[47] yet congruent with 'monstrous' nature, with a leaping over times and generations, and with doubts about legitimacy allayed by disease and death:

Gloucester. The people fear me, for they do observe
   Unfather'd heirs and loathly births of nature.
   The seasons change their manners, as the year
   Had found some months asleep and leap'd them over.
Clarence. The river hath thrice flow'd, no ebb between,
   And the old folk, time's doting chronicles,
   Say it did so a little time before
   That our great-grandsire Edward sicked and died. . . .

(*Part 2* iv. iii. 121–8)

The 'figure' Shakespeare has introduced here is the progenitor of Richard II, Harry the Fourth, and Harry the Fifth, and his significance can hardly be overstated. Edward III, scourge of the French, father of seven sons, head of both the Lancastrian and Yorkist royal houses, is in Tudor history the great exemplar. When the young King Richard, in

---

[46] Two grooms, 'More rushes, more rushes'; then we are told that 'The trumpets have sounded twice' (which suggests blasts offstage); ''Twill be two o'clock ere they come . . .'
[47] v. iv; for forged pregnancies under the heading of monsters see Paré, *Des monstres*, trans. Pallister, ch. 23.

Woodstock, consults the chronicles to discover his age, it is with a stirring account of Edward's and the Black Prince's campaign in France that he is greeted (II. i). As Gloucester the Protector lies in his cell, at Calais, it is the ghosts of the Black Prince and Edward III that appear to him warning of murder (v. i). Woodstock's death, before *Richard II*, prompts Shakespeare's Duchess of Gloucester to call up the whole bloodline to incite Edward's son, Gaunt, to revenge (I. ii. 9–25). It is to his father's memory that Gaunt appeals in his deathbed speech to Richard (II. i. 104–8). York, in the same scene, looks back to Edward as a king whose 'hands were guilty of no kindred blood, | But bloody with the enemies of his kin' (172–84). And it is to Edward, notoriously, that Canterbury appeals as Henry V busies 'giddy minds | With foreign quarrels':

> Look back into your mighty ancestors.
> Go, my dread lord, to your great-grandsire's tomb,
> From whom you claim; invoke his warlike spirit,
> And your great-uncle's, Edward the Black Prince,
> Who on the French ground played a tragedy,
> Making defeat on the full power of France . . . (I. ii. 102–7)

Perhaps predictably then, the promised seed of the second tetralogy, a more fertile source of its figures than *Woodstock*, is *The Reign of King Edward the Third*, published in 1596. This is not the place to explore that fine play, partly or wholly by Shakespeare, celebrated in Heywood's *Apology for Actors* (1612) and familiar to early audiences of the mature Histories.[48] Even to recall the plot is, though, in this context highly suggestive. For it begins in England, with Edward told about his rights in France, obscured by Salic Law. There is a threat from Scotland, some risk of political instability. The action mounts to an invasion of France, to sieges and battles against great odds, in which the vaunting French are with God's help (and English archery) miraculously vanquished. In short, *Edward III* is doubled in *Henry V* so closely that the latter seems a recapitulation, the closing of a historical cycle. This does not imply a return to Tillyard's providential history, with Henry V predestined to reclaim the glories of his Oldest Double. On the contrary, the young King's campaign in France, by setting out to recapitulate that of his great progenitor, takes on a picturesque air of performance: for all its courage and purpose, it becomes 'a tragedy', in Canterbury's words, 'played' upon a familiar field of rushes.

---

[48] For some first steps see Richard Proudfoot, '*The Raigne of King Edward the Third* (1596) and Shakespeare', *Proceedings of the British Academy*, 71 (1985), 159–85.

The unease which flickers for audiences across Henry's role, even when not exposed to the ironic shafts of a Pistol or Williams, would have been more evident and articulate for viewers in the 1590s, aware of him enacting a part—that of Edward—often witnessed on the London stage. They would have noted a diminution in Henry's very strengths: cold-blooded, not least in love, without the dangerous heat of Edward's womanizing; killer of French prisoners, against his great-grandsire's mercy to the burghers of Calais. But they would also have construed his characteristics—the opportunism and theatricality—through that 'revolution of the times' which is the story of *Henry IV*. Lacking even the hidden wrongs of *Richard II's* aristocratic order (Woodstock murdered, the King's vaguely hinted vices), *Edward III* is a History Play staged before history starts. Politics are there the extension of family interest, family interest that of the nation. A sequence such as the one recalled by the Archbishop, in which the Black Prince wins his spurs and is knighted by his father (III. v.), strikes a note of burnished clarity which points up everything doubtful about Shrewsbury. That simpler world is lost in the course of the pentalogy. The tendency vainly to recall the past, which emerges in the writing and revision of *Henry IV*, finds its logical conclusion in the return of Edward III. But Henry V's campaign is a brilliant, continuous piece of counterfeiting. It answers the question, 'And is old Double dead?' by a feat of theatrical 'doubling' for king and company as patently virtuosic as any in Elizabethan drama.[49] Movement through the plays towards a forging of 'CRONICLE History'[50] involves a narrowing of scope, until doubling becomes the countenance of acting itself. Yet this loss of sceptical amplitude should not be confused with an abolition of irony. That *Henry V* increasingly makes a spectacle out of events, concluding with scenes often disconcertingly close to those in *The Famous Victories*, does not prevent us recognizing the kind of player Prince Harry has become.

[49] See e.g. Thomas L. Berger, 'Casting *Henry V* ', *Shakespeare Studies*, 20 (1988), 89–104.
[50] Title-page of *Henry V* in quarto (1600).

CHAPTER 5

Secrecy and Gossip in Twelfth Night *(1997)*

Renaissance secrecy is no longer quite as secret as it was. Art historians and iconologists have returned to the myths and emblems explored by Panofsky and Edgar Wind, and reassessed (often sceptically) their claims to hermetic wisdom. Thanks to Jonathan Goldberg and Richard Rambuss, we now have a better understanding of the early modern English secretary,[1] and of how his pen could produce, in Lois Potter's phrase, *Secret Rites and Secret Writing.*[2] Not just in popular biographies of Marlowe and Shakespeare,[3] but in such Foucauldian accounts of high culture as John Michael Archer's *Sovereignty and Intelligence,*[4] the world of Renaissance espionage is being analysed afresh. William W. E. Slights has written at useful length about conspiracy, fraud, and censorship in middle-period Jonson.[5] And, though the tide of Puttenham studies has now begun to ebb, students of Elizabethan England are still profiting from the work done by Daniel Javitch and Frank Whigham[6] on what *The Arte of English Poesie* calls 'false semblant' or 'the Courtly figure *Allegoria*'[7]—a line of enquiry which leads back to the civilized dissimulation advocated by Castiglione, but also to the politic ruthlessness of 'l'art machiavélien d'être secret'.[8]

---

[1] Jonathan Goldberg, *Writing Matter: From the Hands of the English Renaissance* (Stanford, Calif., 1990), Richard Rambuss, *Spenser's Secret Career* (Cambridge, 1993).

[2] Lois Potter, *Secret Rites and Secret Writing: Royalist Literature, 1641–1660* (Cambridge, 1989).

[3] e.g. Charles Nicholl, *The Reckoning: The Murder of Christopher Marlowe* (London, 1992), Graham Phillips and Martin Keatman, *The Shakespeare Conspiracy* (London, 1994).

[4] John Michael Archer, *Sovereignty and Intelligence: Spying and Court Culture in the English Renaissance* (Stanford, Calif., 1993).

[5] *Ben Jonson and the Art of Secrecy* (Toronto, 1994); for his comments on Shakespeare see pp. 25–30.

[6] Daniel Javitch, *Poetry and Courtliness in Renaissance England* (Princeton, 1978), Frank Whigham, *Ambition and Privilege: The Social Tropes of Elizabethan Courtesy Theory* (Berkeley, 1984).

[7] George Puttenham, *The Arte of English Poesie*, ed. Gladys Doidge Willcock and Alice Walker (Cambridge, 1936), 186.

[8] Michel Senellart, 'Simuler et dissimuler: l'art machiavélien d'être secret à la Renaissance', paper at 'Le Secret à la Renaissance', Colloque IRIS 1996.

These investigations have not advanced in a state of mutual ignorance, but they have, inevitably, suffered from a degree of exclusive specialism. What interests me is how different modes of concealment operated together. For I have found it impossible, in thinking about *Twelfth Night*, to separate iconography from secretarial inscription (as when Malvolio unpicks the Lucrece seal of silence on Maria's riddling letter), or to divorce Sebastian's intelligence-gathering, among 'the memorials and the things of fame' in Illyria,[9] from that rhetorical discretion in him which is equally recommended in courtesy literature.[10] At the same time, *Twelfth Night* pushes one's perception of Renaissance secrecy beyond the usual categories. It makes one return, for instance, to courtesy literature to notice what it says about that irregular but ubiquitous practice, the circulation of secrets as gossip, and to wonder how the gendered speech-patterns which Castiglione and his successors discuss might bear on the reticences and self-concealments involved in the construction of sexual identity.

By gesturing towards social practice, I am, of course, begging questions, and it is worth saying at once that Elizabethan London was not, in my view, full of cross-dressed maidens in love with dukes. There is plainly much to be said against the current historicist tendency to discount the made uniqueness of particular Shakespearian play-scripts for the sake of readily meshing them with circumstantial contexts. Formalist criticism had its drawbacks, but its respect for the artful integrity—for the shifting, secret coherence—of such elusive works as *Twelfth Night* remains, in my view, admirable. On the other hand, there is no doubt that, as Richard Wilson (among others) has shown with *As You Like It*,[11] mature Shakespearian comedy goes much further in internalizing and articulating political conflict than traditional criticism realized. Good productions of *Twelfth Night*—such as John Barton's in 1969—have always been alert to the tensions which arise between kin-status and the dignity of office (Sir Toby vs. Malvolio), to the insecurity of a figure like Maria, whose social rank is ambiguous, and to the importance, in Illyria, of jewels and cash changing hands. Above all, in this connection, *Twelfth Night* is interested

---

[9] *Twelfth Night*, ed. J. M. Lothian and T. W. Craik (London, 1975), III. iii. 23.

[10] e.g. James Cleland, 'Ηρω-παιδεία, *or The Institution of a Young Noble Man* (1607), Bks. V, chs. 7–9, and VI ('shewing a young Noble mans Dutie in Travailing')—esp. pp. 258–62, on sight-seeing as gentlemanly espionage (the pursuit of 'manie secrets').

[11] 'Like the Old Robin Hood: *As You Like It* and the Enclosure Riots', *Shakespeare Quarterly*, 43 (1992), 1–19; repr. as ch. 3 of his *Will Power: Essays on Shakespearean Authority* (Hemel Hempstead, 1993).

in service. It explores the fraught relations which often held, in early modern households, between employment and eroticism. This dialectic is most active in the Viola–Orsino plot,[12] but it also significantly contributes to the misfortunes of Malvolio. Too often, critics view his gulling as an incidental intrigue. When he asks his mistress, however, in Act V, 'tell me, in the modesty of honour, | Why you have given me such clear lights of favour' (v. i. 334–5), he lands on a complex word which catches his outraged feeling that his preferment (both real and imaginary) cannot have stemmed from nothing in Olivia's heart. The play punishes the steward for believing that the more precisely he obeys his mistress's wishes the more he will deserve her favour (in every sense), even while it allows, in Cesario/Viola's relations with Orsino, a ripening into love of what is erotically problematic in Elizabethan ideas of service.

One way of developing these claims is to make an oblique approach to *Twelfth Night* through the autobiography of Thomas Whythorne: the Tudor poet and musician who was employed in a series of noble households before his death in 1596. Though the memoir which he compiled in the late 1570s lacks great events, it is altogether enthralling because of its attentiveness to social detail, its intricacy of self-criticism and rationalization, and its almost neurotic sensitivity to the role of flirtation, deceit, and gossip in the politics of favour. Like Gascoigne's *Adventures of Master F.J.*—a work which probably suggested to Whythorne how his occasional poems could be linked by commentary and narrative—the *Book of Songs and Sonnets, with Long Discourses Set with Them* is particularly alive to the use and abuse of secrecy. Thus, as autobiographical writing starts to emerge from the commonplaces which begin the memoir, Whythorne describes a friend who once told a woman 'the very secrets that were hidden in his heart', only for her to 'blaz[e] abroad that which he had told her to keep in secret'.[13] Similarly, the first of many love intrigues in which he played a part involves a girl who wooed him by leaving a note threaded through the strings of his gittern. His typically wary reply praised her for proceeding 'secretly', but gossip made the affair 'known all about the house' and the girl was promptly discharged (pp. 22–3). Throughout his memoir, Whythorne describes situations in which secrecy and dissimulation

---

[12] Cf. Lisa Jardine's excessively darkened judgements, in *Reading Shakespeare Historically* (London, 1996), 72–7.

[13] *The Autobiography of Thomas Whythorne: Modern Spelling Edition*, ed. James M. Osborn (London, 1962), 19.

shadow-box with each other and attempt to evade the tattling which his epigram, 'Of secret things', calls '*blab*' (p. 224).

The episode which bears most interestingly on *Twelfth Night*—though it can only be loosely contextual—comes shortly after the dismissal of the gittern girl, while Whythorne was still at the age which he calls 'adolescency' (p. 11). Like the young Cesario waiting upon Olivia, Whythorne found his way to the household of a beautiful young widow. Even before he accepted a position as her tutor and 'servingman', he was wary of enduring 'the life of a water-spaniel, that must be at commandment to fetch or bring here, or carry there' (p. 28). His resentment mounted when he discovered how manipulative his mistress could be. Whythorne vividly describes the sort of emotional pressure which could be brought to bear on a man whose position as a servant resembled that of a biddable suitor:

Many times when I was not nigh unto her, although she had appointed me to wait on her cup when she sat at meat, she would bid me come nigher unto her. And therewithal scoffingly she would say to those that were with her, 'I would fain have my man to be in love with me, for then he would not be thus far from me, but would be always at mine elbow.' And then would she sometimes put a piece of good meat and bread on her trencher, and forthwith bid me give her a clean trencher, for the which I should have that of hers with the bread and meat on it. (p. 29)

The problem for Whythorne, however—as he chooses to remember the situation—was that, while he disliked these coercive games, he had to flirt with a mistress towards whom he was clearly attracted (not least in her exercise of power) because 'open contempt might breed such secret hate in her toward me' (p. 30). Innured, like F.J., to duplicity, and hoping for advancement, he recalls deciding that, 'if she did dissemble, I, to requite her, thought that to dissemble with a dissembler was no dissimulation . . . But and if she meant good will indeed, then I was not willing to lose it, because of the commodities that might be gotten by such a one as she, either by marriage or otherwise' (pp. 30–1). As a result, when the widow told him 'how she would have me to apparel myself, as of what stuff, and how she would have it made' (though cross-gartering is not specified), he 'feathered his nest' by accepting money from her to buy clothes and other finery (p. 32). He also wrote to her in secret, and was, like Malvolio, deceived by an encouraging letter which, he later discovered, had been written by her 'waiting gentlewoman' (p. 34). By now, of course, gossip was rife (the attempt at secrecy assured that)—'our affairs were not so closely handled but they were espied and much talked of in the house' (p. 36)—and the problem of his mistress having to disguise any signs of love which might, in themselves, be dissimulated added to Whythorne's difficulty in deciding whether she could be won. The 'comical' affair (as he calls it) reached its climax when he appeared before her, not exactly in yellow stockings, but in 'garments of russet colour (the which colour signifieth the wearer thereof to have hope). And one time I did wear hops in my hat also; the which when my mistress had espied, she in a few scoffing words told me that the wearing of hops did but show that I should hope without that which I hoped for' (pp. 40–1). Thanks to his quibbling wit, Whythorne was able to deflect this rebuff, but his suit thereafter cooled.

If one moves too hastily from this material across to Viola and Malvolio, the contrasts are overwhelming. Where Whythorne describes his affair in such calculating and duplicitous terms that even an impression of mutual vulnerability cannot offset his cynicism, *Twelfth Night* shows Viola concealing what she is to persist in faithful service. Unlike Rosalind, who seems, at least initially, pleased by the experimental scope which men's attire affords, she speaks of frustration and self-division, and the dissembling which her disguise entails is not embraced with relish. Malvolio, rather similarly, is constrained by the habit he adopts. His alacrity in putting on yellow stockings may smack of the self-promotion which infuriates Sir Toby, but his inability to see (as Whythorne instantly would) that he is being made a fool of stems as much from his eagerness to obey Olivia as from ingrown pride. Yet these differences between the memoir and *Twelfth Night* should not distract attention from their shared early modern fascination with the ambiguities of service, and their interest in how secrecy relates to what Cesario calls 'babbling gossip' (I. v. 277).

Certainly these issues are prominent in Viola's opening scene. When she questions the Captain about Illyria, he can tell her of the Duke's love for Olivia—that obsession of his 'secret soul' (below, p. 100)—because 'murmur' has put it about. 'What great ones do,' he observes, 'the less will prattle of' (I. ii. 32–3). Gossip is equally active around the Countess's reclusive life. The Captain knows of her resistance to Orsino because, again, of report: '(They say) she hath abjur'd the company | And sight of men' (40–1). Olivia's withdrawal into mourning for the death of her father and brother naturally attracts Viola, because she fears herself equally bereft, and she cries out for a position in her household which she imagines will bring emotional consonance: 'O that I serv'd that lady' (41). Though the motif is merely incipient, the play is beginning its exploration of the knot which ties employment to love. Hence the Captain's reply, 'That were hard to compass, | Because she will admit no kind of suit, | No, not the Duke's' (44–6), where the idea of suing to serve is inextricable from a lover's suit.

In Shakespeare's chief source, Barnabe Riche's novella 'Of Apolonius and Silla', the Captain is a villain whose designs on Silla's virtue are only foiled by tempest and shipwreck. Early audiences of *Twelfth Night* may or may not have recalled this when they saw Viola come on stage with the Captain, but Shakespeare alludes, through the heroine, to the possibility that he might be as he is in Riche:

> There is a fair behaviour in thee, Captain;
> And though that nature with a beauteous wall
> Doth oft close in pollution, yet of thee
> I will believe thou hast a mind that suits
> With this thy fair and outward character.
> I prithee (and I'll pay thee bounteously)
> Conceal me what I am, and be my aid
> For such disguise as haply shall become
> The form of my intent. (47–55)

This is touchingly complex because Viola's youthful moralism about appearances slips into an equally youthful trust, while she raises doubts about dissimulation in the same breath as she proposes concealment. But its deeper interest lies in its showing us how secrets are made: produced through interaction with possible or actual disclosure. For what is only known to yourself is not a secret—it might merely be too humdrum to speak of—except in so far as the taboo on its disclosure anticipates that disclosure, or in so far as you might feel (as Viola/Cesario will later feel) that you are sharing the secret with your self as with another person.

Unlike Silla, Viola does not explicitly disguise herself in men's clothes to avoid sexual predators. While she may share this motive, the scene points towards a practical desire to secure a court position and an impulse to escape from herself. It is as though, by becoming Cesario, she hoped to leave Viola to grieve in secret. That is, paradoxically, why her suit to serve the Duke can resemble Olivia's immurement. Just as the Countess resolves to withdraw into a nun's asexuality, and thus becomes a 'cloistress' (1. i. 28), so Viola proposes to be a eunuch—if not for the kingdom of heaven, then at least to sing at court. 'I'll serve this duke', she says:

Thou shalt present me as an eunuch to him.
It may be worth thy pains; for I can sing,
And speak to him in many sorts of music,
That will allow me very worth his service. (55–9)

These lines have baffled editors not least because they seem to go from singing to speech but then return to music. What Viola is saying, however, in a play which is much concerned with that branch of rhetoric which Feste calls *vox* (v. i. 295), is that she is not only musically competent but has the flexible *pronunciatio* of a courtier. 'The pleasure of speech,' writes Stefano Guazzo, in Pettie's 1581 translation of *The Civile Conversation*, 'so wel as of Musicke, proceedeth of the chaunge of the voyce, yea . . . the change of the voice, like an instrument of divers strings, is verie acceptable, and easeth both the hearer and the speaker.'[14] 'If Nature haue denied you a tunable accent,' James Cleland urges in 'Ηρω-παιδεία, *or The Institution of a Young Noble Man* (1607), 'studie to amend it by art the best yee maie' (p. 186). Interestingly, when Viola concludes the scene by urging 'silence' on the Captain (61), he sustains her rhetorical concerns by promising to avoid the speech-style which Thomas Whythorne calls '*blab*': 'Be you his eunuch, and your mute I'll be: | When my tongue blabs, then let mine eyes not see' (62–3).

At once the blabbers enter, as Maria, Sir Toby, and, a few lines later, Sir Andrew come on stage. Maria is eager for Toby to avoid expulsion from Olivia's household by moderating his behaviour, but when she urges, 'confine yourself within the modest limits of order', he replies: 'I'll confine myself no finer than I am' (i. iii. 8–10). We have by this point become so accustomed to characters *seeking* confinement—Orsino lying 'canopied with bowers' (i. i. 41), the Countess's enclosure in mourning—that Toby's quibbling excess, as he sprawls through the play's first prose dialogue, is bound to appeal. As the scene goes on, however, the superb inconsequentiality of Maria's wit when she toys with Sir Andrew, and his stupefying inability to get a grip on language, test the audience's patience. We feel assailed as well as amused by the prattle and networking chat which conduct books typically chastise by citing Plutarch's *De garrulitate*. This challenge to the audience mounts. As the RSC director John Caird has noted, it creates problems in production that Sir Toby 'goes on and on and on' during Acts II and III.[15] Even in i. iii., Shakespeare points up the

---

[14] *The Civile Conversation of M. Steeven Guazzo*, trans. George Pettie (Bks. I–III) and Bartholomew Young (Bk. IV), introd. Sir Edward Sullivan, 2 vols. (London, 1925), i. 129.
[15] Bill Alexander, John Barton, John Caird, and Terry Hands, *Directors' Shakespeare: Approaches to 'Twelfth Night'*, ed. Michael Billington (London, 1990), 22.

garrulity of networking. Sir Andrew's reputation has reached Maria, for instance, from those she refers to as 'the prudent' and Toby calls 'scoundrels and substractors' (32–5). Where report is offered sceptically by the Captain, gossip is here the stuff of life.

Anthropological work on gossip has stressed the importance of verbal trivia in maintaining social bonds. Max Gluckman, for instance, argues that scandalous chat draws participants together while serving to exclude others because access to conversation depends on inside knowledge. 'The right to gossip about certain people is', he says, 'a privilege which is only extended to a person when he or she is accepted as a member of a group.'[16] This account can be squared with the way the lighter people network in *Twelfth Night* in opposition to the aloof Malvolio. But Gluckman's critics are right to insist that gossiping is by no means always collective, and that a group can turn out, once inspected, to be full of conversational partitions.[17] In that sense, the garrulous in *Twelfth Night* form an interestingly fractious set, with Fabian and Feste as satellites, and Sir Toby prepared to bamboozle Andrew with what sounds like friendly chat, in ways which make it easier for him to scorn and reject him in Act V. But Sir Andrew is not the only one left behind in the conversational flow. Everyone who works on gossip would agree that the morsels of information and rumour which it retails must have some element of obscurity, some secret component worth disclosing, since they would otherwise not be passed on. *Twelfth Night* respects this principle to the point, almost, of defiance, by including material which may well have been written to exclude early audiences from what the play's in-crowd knows, and which certainly excludes us now. Who, for instance, is Mistress Mall, and why should we care about her picture?

In the drinking scene of Act II, the obscurities of prattling accumulate. What is Sir Toby on about when he says, 'My lady's a Cataian, we are politicians, Malvolio's a Peg-a-Ramsey' (II. iii. 76–7)? The clown calls this 'admirable fooling' (81), and it does, indeed, resemble the patter of Feste, which rings in Andrew's empty head, and which he now babbles out: 'thou wast in very gracious fooling last night, when thou spok'st of Pigrogromitus, of the Vapians passing the equinoctial of Queubus' (22–4). This replication of proliferating nonsense recalls Plutarch's comparison of gossip to the porch or gallery at Olympia which 'from one voice by sundry

[16] 'Gossip and Scandal', *Current Anthropology*, 4 (1963), 307–16, p. 313.
[17] e.g. Robert Paine, 'What is Gossip About? An Alternative Hypothesis', *Man*, NS 2 (1967), 278–85.

reflections and reverberations . . . rendered seven ecchoes'. When speech comes 'to the eares of a babbler,' he says, 'it resoundeth again on every side . . . insomuch, as a man may well say: That the conducts and passages of their hearing reach not to the braine . . . but onely to their tongue.'[18] Babbling of this sort climaxes in the drinking scene for obvious reasons. It hardly needs Plutarch to tell us (though he does so more than once) that drunkenness provokes 'much babling and foolish prattle' (p. 194). What we can misunderstand, historically, is that the folly of babbling was— partly because of Plutarch—so routinely associated with drink that when a commentator such as Thomas Wright seeks to explain garrulity, he gravitates to talk of 'foolery' and alehouse metaphors: 'he that wil poure foorth all he conceiueth, deliuereth dregges with drinke, and as for the most part, presently men apprehend more folly than wisdom, so he that sodainely vttereth all he vnderstandeth, blabeth forth moore froath than good liquor.'[19] This is the mixture of assumptions which Malvolio provocatively ignites when he stalks in and rebukes the drinkers for choosing 'to gabble like tinkers' (88–9).

It should now be clear why the Captain's word 'blab' refers as much to a style of speech as to the betrayal of secrets. Early modern accounts of the psychology and practice of gossip start, as it were, from rhetoric.[20] The blabber was a verbal incontinent, whose itch to gabble whatever was in his mind would lead (as Plutarch warned) to rash disclosure. Avoid making friends, advises Wright, with the 'blabbish, and . . . indiscreet' because they will not 'keep secret, or conserue thy credit, and so with one breath they blow all away' (pp. 119–20). The corresponding virtue to this vice was called 'discretion'—a word which, symptomatically, has etymological and semantic links with 'secrecy'.[21] Time and again, in conduct books, gentlemen are advised to be discreet. The courtier, Castiglione says, 'shall be no carier about of trifling newes . . . He shall be no babbler [but keep]

---

[18] 'Of Intemperate Speech or Garrulitie', in *The Philosophie, Commonlie Called, The Morals Written by the Learned Philosophy Plutarch of Chæronea*, trans. Philemon Holland (1603), 191–208, p. 192.

[19] *The Passions of the Minde in Generall*, rev. edn. (1604), 107.

[20] Contrast the more recent views surveyed in e.g. Patricia Meyer Spacks, *Gossip* (1985; Chicago, 1986), ch. 2. For work by social historians on the practice of 16th- and 17th-century gossip see e.g. J. A. Sharpe, *Defamation and Sexual Slander in Early Modern England: The Church Courts at York*, Borthwick Papers, 58 (York, 1980) and Steve Hindle, 'The Shaming of Margaret Knowsley: Gossip, Gender and the Experience of Authority in Early Modern England', *Continuity and Change*, 9 (1994), 391–419.

[21] Cf. Sissela Bok, *Secrets: On the Ethics of Concealment and Revelation* (1982; Oxford, 1986), 286 n. 7.

alwayes within his boundes.'[22] In Guazzo, who is almost anti-courtly, at moments, in his mistrust of easy eloquence,[23] there is an equally firm resistance to what Cleland calls 'pratling' and 'Babling' (p. 189). 'Blaze neuer anie mans secret,' Cleland says, 'nor speake of that which discretion commandeth you to conceale, albeit it was not commended to your silence' (p. 190).

This has a gendered aspect, in that, while gentlemen are encouraged discreetly to converse, women are incited to a discretion which can be absolute. It is the anti-feminist Lord Gaspar who maintains, in Castiglione, 'that the verye same rules that are given for the Courtier, serve also for the woman', and the sympathetic Julian[24] who argues that 'in her facions, maners, woordes, gestures and conversation (me thinke) the woman ought to be muche unlike the man' (pp. 215–16). Like the courtier, he argues, women should be 'discreete' and avoid 'babblinge', but they should concentrate, further, on cultivating 'sweetnesse' and reticence (pp. 216–18). English writers were as confident as Guazzo that 'a young man is to be blamed, which will talke like an olde man, and a woman which will speake like a man' (i. 169). Nor was it just the fools, including Sir John Daw in *Epicoene*, who believed that '*Silence in woman is like speech in man.*'[25] In *The English Gentlewoman* (1631), Richard Brathwait pushes his praise of 'Discretion' to the point of insisting that 'bashfull silence is an ornament' in women (p. 89). Against the background of a prejudice which assumed (as it still does) that women are more garrulous than men,[26] he writes: 'It suites not with *her* honour, for a *young woman* to be prolocutor. But especially, when either men are in presence, or ancient Matrons, to whom shee owes a ciuill reuerence, it will become her to tip her tongue with silence' (ibid.).

In 'The Table' to *The English Gentlewoman*, Brathwait cites the apothegm, '"Violets, *though they grow low and neare the earth, smell sweet-*

[22] *The Book of the Courtier*, trans. Sir Thomas Hoby (1561), introd. Walter Raleigh (London, 1900), 124.

[23] For contexts see e.g. Daniel Javitch, 'Rival Arts of Conduct in Elizabethan England: Guazzo's *Civile Conversation* and Castiglione's *Courtier*', *Yearbook of Italian Studies*, 1 (1971), 178–98, pp. 188–9.

[24] See e.g. Gaspar's remarkable anticipation, out of Aristotle, of Freud on the castration complex in women, and Julian's reply: 'The seelie poore creatures wish not to be a man to make them more perfect, but to have libertye, and to be ridd of the rule that men have of their owne authoritie chalenged over them' (pp. 226–7).

[25] *Epicoene or The Silent Woman*, ed. L. A. Beaurline (London, 1966), II. iii. 109.

[26] Cf. e.g. Lisa Jardine, *Still Harping on Daughters: Women and Drama in the Age of Shakespeare* (Brighton, 1983), ch. 4.

est: and Honour *appears the fullest of beauty, when she is humblest*' ' (††2).
As Gerard's *Herball* confirms,[27] the Latin word '*Viola*' was used in Elizabethan England as another name for the violet, a flower which, in general,
was associated with modesty. What Cesario inherits from Viola is the discretion which a female upbringing made second nature to gentlewomen.
What he gains, as it were, over Viola is permission to speak out—even
when men are present. These claims are not in conflict with traditional accounts of the role, but they do, I think, point up the hybridity of Viola's
performance. To think about her in relation to courtesy literature is to notice those comical moments when she overplays the courtly rhetoric—as
when Cesario impresses Sir Andrew (always a bad sign) by praying for the
heavens to 'rain odours' on Olivia, or, more oddly, when Andrew sur-
prises us by speaking French, and exchanges such exquisite salutations
with Cesario that both are satirically construed.[28] As strikingly, to look at
Viola in the light of Guazzo, Cleland and other conduct writers is to recognize the acute importance of discretion in the play.

While describing his affair with the widow, Whythorne glumly notes: 'It
is a common matter among servants, . . . if any one of them be in favour
with their masters or mistresses above the rest, by and by all the rest of the
servants will envy him or her, and seek all the means and ways that they
can imagine to bring them out of credit' (p. 36). Again, it would be wrong
to read too directly from this into *Twelfth Night*. Because critics have neglected the politics of favour, however, they have missed the edginess of
Viola's first exchange as Cesario, when s/he comes on stage with Valentine, who was trusted, in I. i, with the task of visiting Olivia, but who is
now losing his influence. 'If the Duke continue these favours towards
you,' Valentine says, 'you are like to be much advanced: he hath known
you but three days, and already you are no stranger.' This could be spoken
neutrally, but Cesario's reply indicates that the actor playing Valentine
should give his words some salt: 'You either fear his humour, or my negligence, that you call in question the continuance of his love. Is he incon-
stant, sir, in his favours?' (I. iv. 1–7). The question is fascinatingly pitched,
given the erotic range of 'favour', since the constancy which Cesario
hopes for in his master is not one which Viola, who now loves the Duke,
would unambiguously welcome—at least in Orsino's relations with
Olivia.

[27] John Gerard, *The Herball or Generall Historie of Plantes* (1597), 701.
[28] III. i. 86–7, 72–3. On courtly excess in 'Salutation . . . complements, false offers, &
promises of seruice' see e.g. Cleland, *Institution*, 176 ff.

One thing is clear immediately, though: Valentine is right to envy Cesario's progress with Orsino. As soon as the Duke appears, his cry is for Cesario, and for the rest to stand 'aloof' (12). Drawing his servant downstage, no doubt, into the theatre-space which signifies and facilitates intimate conversation, he says:

> Cesario,
> Thou know'st no less but all: I have unclasp'd
> To thee the book even of my secret soul.
> Therefore, good youth, address thy gait unto her,
> Be not denied access . . . (12–16)

In the Italian comedy *Gl'ingannati*—a probable source for *Twelfth Night*—the Viola-figure says to Clemenzia, when asked why she attends her lover in disguise, 'Do you think a woman in love is unhappy to see her beloved continually, to speak to him, touch him, hear his secrets . . .?'[29] Shakespeare's emphasis is more on the intimacies of disclosure than on the content of those 'secrets' which are, in any case, the stuff of Illyrian gossip. This is not a process which can be represented, entirely, through dialogue. It depends on proximity and touch between actors, and on the boy or woman playing Cesario having a demeanour which promises that discretion described in Bacon's 'Of Simulation and Dissimulation': 'the *Secret* Man, heareth many Confessions; For who will open himselfe, to a Blab or a Babler? But if a man be thought *Secret*, it inviteth Discoverie.'[30]

Cesario gains access to Olivia by means of stubborn pertness, but his suit is then advanced because he is a '*Secret* Man'. As Bacon adds, with worldly acumen: 'Mysteries are due to *Secrecy*. Besides (to say Truth) *Nakednesse* is uncomely, as well in Minde, as Body; and it addeth no small Reverence, to Mens Manners, and Actions, if they be not altogether Open' (ibid.). If there is a technology of mystery, Cesario exemplifies it. Olivia's veil of mourning cannot but advertise the celebrated beauty it conceals, and she is right (though her modesty is false) to worry about prosaic nakedness when the lacy screen is lifted to reveal 'two lips indifferent red . . . two grey eyes, with lids to them' (I. v. 250–1). Cesario, whose 'smooth and rubious' lips are so meshed into gender ambiguity that their very nakedness tantalizes (I. iv. 32), has a nature more covert and estranged, which, because of Viola's recessive psychology, is not just dis-

---

[29] Trans. and excerpted as *The Deceived*, in Geoffrey Bullough (ed.), *Narrative and Dramatic Sources of Shakespeare*, vol. ii (London, 1958), 286–339, p. 296.

[30] *The Essayes or Counsels, Civill and Morall*, ed. Michael Kiernan (Oxford, 1985), 20–3, p. 21.

guised by clothes. His embassy goes in stages. At first, he attracts attention by presenting himself as a forward page-boy, seeking to recite a script of compliments,[31] but he intrigues Olivia by modulating into a more inwardly performative role which plays on the comeliness of secrecy while expressing, with a twist of pathos, Viola's sense of being mysterious to herself as she comes to terms with loving the Duke: 'and yet, by the very fangs of malice I swear, I am not that I play' (184–5). Orsino has told his servant to 'unfold the passion of my love' (I. iv. 24), but, as Cesario quickly discovers, that secret is too open to entice. It is almost an objection to the Duke, for Olivia, that his qualities are manifest and talked of: 'Of great estate, of fresh and stainless youth; | In voices well divulg'd' (I. v. 263–4). Cesario, by contrast, has a secret allure—the allure of secrecy; and he uses it to secure a private audience by promising revelation: 'What I am, and what I would, are as secret as maidenhead: to your ears, divinity; to any other's, profanation' (218–20).

These lines are alive with risk. As Georg Simmel has noted, in his classic account of secrecy: 'the secret is surrounded by the possibility and temptation of betrayal; and the external danger of being discovered is interwoven with the internal danger, which is like the fascination of an abyss, of giving oneself away.'[32] Cesario's mention of a 'maidenhead' produces secrecy from what is hidden by anticipating disclosure. He alludes to the 'she' in Cesario, and 'she' alludes to something so essentially intimate that her feelings for Orsino come to mind. Yet the process of tempting Olivia into private conference, of enticing her (and the audience) with intimations of a sexual secret more real than maidenheads merely talked of,[33] goes along with an urge on Viola's part to be done with her intolerable disguise and give herself away by blabbing. For as Simmel adds: 'The secret puts a barrier between men but, at the same time, it creates the tempting challenge to break through it, by gossip or confession—and this challenge accompanies its psychology like a constant overtone' (ibid.).

The overtone is most audible, a few lines later, in the willow cabin speech. If I loved you, Cesario tells Olivia, I should

---

[31] Compare (but also contrast) ll. 169–96 with Mote at *Love's Labour's Lost* V. ii. 158–74, addressing the Princess and her ladies.

[32] 'The Secret and the Secret Society', pt. 4 of *The Sociology of Georg Simmel*, ed. and trans. Kurt H. Wolff (New York, 1950), 307–76, p. 334.

[33] The effect of elusive enigma was enlarged, no doubt, for early audiences aware of being addressed by a boy (playing a woman playing a boy), especially given medical doubts concerning the existence, in reality, of the hymen: see e.g. Helkiah Crooke, Μικροκοσμογραφια: *A Description of the Whole Body of Man*, 2nd edn. (1631), 256: 'It hath beene an old question and so continueth to this day, whether there be any certaine markes or notes of virginity in women . . .'

> Make me a willow cabin at your gate,
> And call upon my soul within the house;
> Write loyal cantons of contemned love,
> And sing them loud even in the dead of night;
> Halloo your name to the reverberate hills,
> And make the babbling gossip of the air
> Cry out 'Olivia!' O, you should not rest
> Between the elements of air and earth,
> But you should pity me. (272–80)

The speech is emotionally electric because, by positing herself as Orsino wooing Olivia, Viola is imagining what it would be like to woo the Duke,[34] while seducing Olivia into imagining what it would be like to be wooed by Cesario.[35] But the energy of the utterance, as it moves through double, endstopped lines to the suddenly freed enjambment and exclamatory caesura after 'gossip of the air',[36] also stems from her frustrated impulse to babble out what she is. Given the fact that Shakespeare varied his characters' names from those in the sources, it can hardly be accidental that, if 'the babbling gossip of the air' *did* cry out 'O-liv-ia', the rebounding echoes would reverberate into something very like 'Vi-o-la'—a word which is, for innocent audiences, a secret within the secret until, near the end of the play, Sebastian greets Cesario by saying '"Thrice welcome, drowned Viola"' (v. i. 239).

Characterization in mature Shakespeare is angled into complexity by what holds between roles as well as by what is written into them. The lucid symmetries and parallels which shape such early comedies as *Errors*

---

³⁴ To woo, that is, as Viola (if a woman might be so assertive), rather than compoundly, as in II. iv, where the attraction of Cesario/Viola's eye to 'some favour that it loves' (which riddlingly means the Duke's 'favour' (24–5)), prompts him/her to utter the half-betraying speech about 'concealment', 'My father had a daughter lov'd a man . . .' (108–19). Symptomatically, in the exchange which follows, Bacon's observation, 'he that will be *Secret*, must be a *Dissembler*, in some degree. For Men are too cunning, to suffer a Man, to keepe an indifferent carriage . . . They will so beset a man with Questions, and draw him on, and picke it out of him' (p. 21) is ratified both by Orsino's leading interrogation ('But died thy sister of her love, my boy?' (120)) and by Cesario/Viola's dissimulation ('I am all the daughters of my father's house, I And all the brothers too' (121–2)), which slurs into poignant honesty, as s/he hopes for Sebastian's survival ('. . . and yet I know not' (122)), but which remains sufficiently in touch with the deviousness of his/her opening ploy to recall (for instance) the explicitly seductive discretion of F.J. when he woos Dame Elinor with a lute song composed by 'My father's sister's brother's son' (Gascoigne, *The Adventures of Master F.J.*, in Paul Salzman (ed.), *An Anthology of Elizabethan Prose Fiction* (Oxford, 1987), 3–81, p. 28).

³⁵ For another perspective see John Kerrigan (ed.), *Motives of Woe: Shakespeare and 'Female Complaint'. A Critical Anthology* (Oxford, 1991), esp. pp. 20–3, 41–5.

³⁶ Folio punctuation mostly conforms to the rhetorical shape of the passage, though, as routinely, it divides the run-on 'air I Cry' with a comma.

and *Love's Labour's Lost* give way, from *Much Ado* onwards, to a recognizably more mannerist procedure in which analogies are elliptical and overdetermined, and characters who seem unlike can be, in fluctuating ways, related. No case is more extreme, perhaps, than the coupling of Cesario and Malvolio. Yet the resemblances are there. Both gentlemen are upwardly mobile suitors (respectively unwelcome and coerced) of Olivia. In the echoing cluster of names which lies at the heart of the play, 'Malvolio' is more involved with 'Olivia' and 'Viola' than is, for instance, 'Orsino'. And this reflects, perhaps, a similarity rooted in source-material, given that, in 'Of Apolonius and Silla', the Viola-figure is thrown into the dark house reserved, in *Twelfth Night*, for Malvolio, when the Duke gathers, from gossip among servants, that the Countess has fallen in love with his man.

It is in their role as servants, however, that the two are most closely aligned. As I noted in relation to Whythorne, both are equally subject to the politics of favour. At first, Malvolio is as successful as Cesario. If Orsino finds it natural to turn to his discreet young servant when thoughts about Olivia well up, Olivia calls for that 'known discreet man', her steward (I. v. 95), both in sending Cesario her ring, and, later, in III. iv, when she comes on stage with Maria, but talks, rather, to herself about how to win the Duke's handsome ambassador. 'I speak too loud,' she says, checking her own indiscretion: 'Where's Malvolio? He is sad and civil, | And suits well for a servant with my fortunes: | Where is Malvolio?' (4–7). The word 'sad' here does not mean 'gloomy', as in modern English. The steward is grave and close. He can observe the decorum which Puttenham praises when he says that a man should be 'secret and sad' in counsel (p. 292). This quality is defined, of course, against the babbling indiscretion of Sir Toby and his friends. Towards the end of III. iv, Cesario will say that he hates 'babbling drunkenness' (364). It is a trait which Malvolio shares, as we know from his denunciation, in the drinking scene, of those who 'gabble like tinkers' and keep 'uncivil rule' (II. iii. 89, 122).

To insist that Malvolio feels the same urge as Viola/Cesario to disclose a hidden nature through babbling would be false to the glancing way in which parallels work in *Twelfth Night*. His yellow stockings and forced smile do involve an element of disguise, since they belie his 'sad and civil' self; but they owe more (I shall argue) to adornment, and they cannot be patly compared to the costume which stirs up in Cesario a desire to reveal the Viola in him. Yet the steward is not as indifferent to 'babbling gossip' as he would like the world to suppose. Even before he reads the forged letter, he is fantasizing about Olivia by recalling, 'There is example for't. The Lady of the Strachy married the yeoman of the wardrobe' (II. v. 39–40). This snippet from Illyrian gossip columns is every bit as trivially topical, or, more likely, pseudotopical, as Sir Toby's allusion to Mistress Mall. Indeed the plot against Malvolio can be understood, in early modern terms, as designed to bring out the babbler in the discreet man, by emptying his language. 'My masters, are you mad?', the steward asks the drinkers (II. iii. 87). When denounced as a madman and locked up, he is not just confined as finely as Sir Toby Belch could wish: his words—once so commanding in the household—are discredited and trivialized, then mocked as empty verbiage. 'Malvolio,' Sir Topas cries, 'thy wits the heavens restore: endeavour thyself to sleep, and leave thy vain bibble babble.'[37]

It is easy to see how the courtesy literature which sheds light on Cesario can also illuminate his double, Sebastian. In the elaborate, even stilted idiom of his first exchanges with Antonio, in the reserve and sturdy valour with which he engages Sir Andrew and Sir Toby, and in his discreet handling of the secret betrothal to Olivia, he conforms with the ideals laid out in such texts as Henry Peacham's *Compleat Gentleman* (1622). The plot against Cesario's more eccentric co-rival, Malvolio, might seem harder to relate to conduct books. In practice, though, even the courtly Castiglione is more tolerant of what Fabian calls 'sportful malice' (v. i. 364) than a modern reader might expect. *The Book of the Courtier* describes, indeed, a series of 'Meerie Pranckes' which bear comparison with *Twelfth Night*. In one of them, an unfortunate man is persuaded by his companions that the dark room in which he has been sleeping is illuminated by the—actually, unlit—candles which they carry. Like Sir Topas visiting Malvolio, they cry, with incredulity, 'Say'st thou that house is dark?' (IV. ii. 35) until— lacking the steward's resilience—the poor man is convinced of his blindness, repents his sins, and prays to Our Lady of Loreto, whereupon his friends undeceive him (pp. 193–5). Almost as cruel is the tale told by Monsieur Bernarde about the occasion when he fell a-wrestling, in sport, with Cesar Boccadello on the Bridge of Leo. When passers-by made to separate them, Bernarde cried, 'Helpe sirs, for this poore gentilman at certein times of the moone is frantike, and see now how he striveth to cast himselfe of the bridge into the river' (p. 197). Cesar was instantly set upon, and the more he struggled and protested, the more apparently justified and inevitable his confinement (like Malvolio's) became.

---

[37] IV. ii. 98–100; cf. e.g. the 'jangling bibble babble' of 'praters' in Plutarch's 'Of Intemperate Speech' (p. 193).

There are, Castiglione says, 'two kyndes of Meerie Pranckes . . . The one is, whan any man whoever he be, is deceyved wittilie . . . The other, whan a manne layeth (as it were) a nett, and showeth a piece of a bayte so, that a man renneth to be deceyved of himself' (p. 191). The plot against Malvolio is a fine example of this latter, more sophisticated form of joke. It is always surprising, when one returns to the play, to discover just how deeply the steward is mired in fantasies about Olivia *before* he finds the letter. Yet Malvolio does need some enticement to run himself into the net, and Maria's letter is well judged to appeal not only to his ambitions but to his pride in managing secrets. It is relevant, in this regard, that her writing parodies secretaryship—or, as likely, abuses a secretarial office which she has discharged on other occasions—by conducting the sort of covert correspondence with a suitor which such a servant might expect to handle for her lady (as when the devious secretary in Gascoigne writes to F.J. on Elinor's behalf). In a secretary, discretion was essential. As Angel Day notes, in *The English Secretary*, 'in respect of such *Secrecie* . . . the name was first giuen to be called a *Secretorie*'.[38] Equally integral, however, was the idea of imitative substitution. The secretary, Day reports, will be 'a zealous imitator' of his master, down to the 'forme and maner' of his penmanship.[39] This is the context of Maria's announcement, 'I can write very like my lady your niece; on a forgotten matter we can hardly make distinction of our hands' (II. iii. 160–2). She is indicating that her letter will not be a forgery so much as a duplicitous secret.

The hermeticism of the missive is compounded, for it is wrapped in mysteries—ornamented by secrets—from the tantalizing address on its outside ('*To the unknown beloved . . .*' (II. v. 92)), through the seal which closes it up (but which also dis-closes its matter, by hinting that Olivia is the author), into the enigmas of its message:

> *I may command where I adore;*
> *But silence, like a Lucrece knife,*
> *With bloodless stroke my heart doth gore;*
> *M.O.A.I. doth sway my life.* (106–9)

This 'secrete conceit'—to use Puttenham's phrase for the posies and ana-grams of amorous courtiers (p. 102)[40]—is a subplot version of those

---

[38] *The English Secretary*, rev. edn. (1599), pt. 2, p. 102.

[39] *English Secretary*, pt 2, p. 130; cf. Rambuss, *Spenser's Secret Career*, 43.

[40] For examples beyond Puttenham (esp. pp. 108–12), see e.g. [Sir John Mennis], *Recreation for Ingenious Headpeeces* (1654), P5ʳ–Q4ʳ, R3ʳ–4ʳ. On verse composition, more broadly, as 'secret intercommoning'—a compromise formation between self-consuming inwardness and full dis-closure (below, pp. 110–11)—see Gascoigne, *Adventures of Master F.J.*, 40–1.

riddles which elsewhere in the play (and especially in Cesario/Viola's lines) have an ontological aspect. And it does, more locally, raise the thought that Malvolio's cultivated discretion (his chosen mode of being) is a form of self-advertisement. For the ornate secrecy of the letter is calculated to command attention: it engages in a covert exhibitionism which the steward finds congenial. To that extent it recalls Simmel's insight, that 'although apparently the sociological counter-pole of secrecy, adornment has, in fact, a societal significance with a structure analogous to that of secrecy itself' (p. 338). In other words, the secrecy of the letter has much in common with the yellow stockings, cross-gartering, and fixed smile which it encourages its recipient to adopt.

This claim may sound unlikely, but I am encouraged to advance it by the cogency of Simmel's observation that, while man's desire to please may include outward-going kindness, there is also a

wish for this joy and these 'favors' to flow back to him, in the form of recognition and esteem, . . . [B]y means of this pleasing, the individual desires to *distinguish* himself before others, and to be the object of an attention that others do not receive. This may even lead him to the point of wanting to be envied. Pleasing may thus become a means of the will to power: some individuals exhibit a strange contradiction that they need those above whom they elevate themselves by life and deed, for they build their own self-feeling upon the subordinates' realization that they *are* subordinate. (ibid.)

Even before he finds the letter, Malvolio's attentiveness to Olivia and his contempt for those like Sir Toby exemplifies a power-seeking desire for 'favours'. His attraction to the countess has less to do with eroticism than with a longing for the unruly, over whom he elevates himself, to become his subordinates: his daydream about Toby curtsying to him, and being required to amend his drunkenness, shows that he cannot imagine life in the household (certainly not an agreeable life) without having the lighter people to condescend to. In preparation for the happy day when he will be made Count Malvolio, he distinguishes himself before others by means of a singular discretion (so unlike their collective gabbling) which is actually a form of ostentation. We are not surprised when Maria reports that Malvolio 'has been yonder i' the sun practising behaviour to his own shadow this half hour' (ii. v. 16–18) because he is that recognizable type: a secret exhibitionist. The invitation to put on yellow stockings, cross-gartered, is, in one sense, ludicrous and improbable, because it contradicts those 'sad and civil' qualities which attract Olivia's praise. But it is hardly surprising that Malvolio takes the bait, because, as Simmel says,

'Adornment is the egoistic element as such' (p. 339), and the strange garb—which the steward claims he already owns, and which he may indeed have worn, at least in fantasy (II. v. 166–8)—amplifies and gives expression to his desire for singularity without compromising his attentiveness to Olivia: on the contrary, it is a way of 'pleasing' her.

Simmel goes on to notice that adornment does not express the organic nature of the person adorned, but depends on superfluousness and impersonality. Jewels and precious stones are typical of its highly external relationship with the person, but yellow stockings and cross-garters work to similar effect because they divide up and cut into the wholeness and ease of the body (they obstruct, indeed, Malvolio's circulation (III. iv. 19–20)). One might compare Simmel's example of new clothes as against old: the former 'are particularly elegant', he says, 'due to their being still "stiff"; they have not yet adjusted to the modifications of the individual body as fully as older clothes have' (p. 341). There is a vein of comedy here, of course, because, as Bergson points out in *Le Rire*, laughter is provoked by superimpositions of mechanical rigidity on the organic flow of the body. The ornaments seemingly requested by Olivia, the clothes which Malvolio puts on to mark his new status, are laughable even as—and for precisely the same reason that—they signify advancement. For adornment can be a mark of status regardless of the market-value of the materials used, and Malvolio's attire shares the usual property of adornment in bringing together, or parodying (since Olivia cannot bear yellow), what Simmel calls 'Aesthetic excellence' and the '*sociological* charm of being, by virtue of adornment, a representative of one's group' (p. 343)—with the added delight, in this case, for Malvolio, that, by becoming a count, he will represent the dignity of Olivia's house to the consternation of Sir Toby and his ilk. Beyond that, and underwriting it, is secrecy: the ultimate bait. To assume yellow stockings and be cross-gartered puts Malvolio's discretion on display, without abolishing it, because the new garb allows him, as he thinks, to share a secret with Olivia, to signal an ambition and grasp of courtly intrigue (hence 'I will read politic authors' (II. v. 161–2)) which she will understand and appreciate while the drinkers and babblers will not.

That this exhibitionistic secrecy is designed to please Olivia only with the intention of gratifying Malvolio is compatible with the sickness of self-love which she diagnoses when he first comes on stage (I. v. 89). From a psychoanalytical perspective, indeed, the yellow stockings are narcissistic fetishes while the cross-gartering looks auto-erotic. This line of enquiry could bear a Lacanian twist, given that the anagrammatic relations which hold between 'Olivia' and 'Malvolio'—pointed up by the disjection of those names ('*M.O.A.I.*') in the letter—register, at the level of the sign, her role in reflecting Malvolio's constitutive desire back on himself. Freudian speculation aside, there is certainly something masturbatory about the steward's complacent cry, as Sir Toby and the rest move in to take the yellow-stockinged madman away: 'Let me enjoy my private' (III. iv. 90). This recoil into self-pleasuring is not restricted, of course, to the steward. Critics often call Orsino (rather loosely) a narcissist, and his early remark—before Cesario's charms get to work—'for I myself am best | When least in company' (I. iv. 37–8) would have suggested to an Elizabethan audience, with its inherited disapproval (to simplify somewhat) of solitariness,[41] a similarly troubling mind-set. The conduct literature is emphatic in its insistence on affective sociality. '*Self-Loue* is the greatest disease of the minde,' according to James Cleland, and it has 'beene the cause of manie *Narcissus* his changing among you Nobles' (p. 241). There is, in other words, an important Renaissance distinction between the socially produced (and socially productive) quality called secrecy and suspect, anti-social solitude.

It is entirely in line with this that Stefano Guazzo celebrates discretion but bends his dialogue towards showing how arguments for civil conversation can persuade his brother, William Guazzo, from abandoning society: 'And now my joye is the greater', William's interlocutor, Anniball Magnocavalli, says at the end, 'that I understande how readie and willinge you are to caste of the obscure and blacke Robe of Solitarinesse, and in liew of that to revest and adorne your selfe with the white and shininge garment of Conversation' (II. 215). The danger was, inevitably, that discretion could become exaggerated into self-absorption. Malvolio's antisocial vanity bears out Nashe's observation in *Pierce Penilesse his Supplication to the Divell* (1592): 'Some thinke to be counted rare Politicans and Statesmen, by being solitary: as who would say, I am a wise man, a braue man, *Secreta mea mihi: Frustra sapit, qui sibi non sapit* [My secrets are my own; he is wise in vain who does not know his own business], and there is no man worthy of my companie or friendship.'[42]

---

[41] See Janette Dillon, *Shakespeare and the Solitary Man* (London, 1981), chs. 1–2.

[42] *The Works of Thomas Nashe*, ed. R. B. McKerrow, corr. by F. P. Wilson, 5 vols. (Oxford, 1958), i. 137–245, p. 169.

Much is now being written about the way Renaissance culture developed modern ideas about privacy by building and exploring the uses of secluded chambers and closets.[43] This emergent mentality is reflected in the appeal which *Twelfth Night* makes to varieties of privy space. Somewhere offstage Andrew has his 'cubiculo' and Toby his own retreat. But it matters that we should learn of the former by Toby saying, 'We'll call thee at thy cubiculo' and of the latter by his remark (to Feste or Maria) 'Come by and by to my chamber' (III. ii. 50, IV. ii. 73–4). The babblers are social in their privacy, where Malvolio seeks to be private even in the open spaces of Olivia's great house. That is why the 'dark room' (III. iv. 136)— that dramatically overdetermined locale—is such an apt punishment for his pretensions: locked up there he is both cast out of society and thrown in upon himself. He is forced into a solitude which represents, but which is also maliciously designed to induce, asocial derangement. But he is also given a chance—I shall end by suggesting—to reassess the value of what Nashe calls 'companie or friendship'.

I referred, a little earlier, to ontological riddling. What I mean by that is the presence of, and counterpoint between, such claims, in Cesario/ Viola's part, as 'I am not that I play' and 'I am not what I am' (I. v. 185, III. i. 143). As disguise and confusion mount, even simple indicative statements such as 'I am the man' (when Viola deduces that Olivia has fallen for Cesario) are deceptive, twisting into dubiety and delusion: 'if it be so, as 'tis, | Poor lady, she were better love a dream' (II. ii. 24–5). 'Nothing that is so, is so', the clown will later quip (IV. i. 8–9). Sebastian calls this 'folly', but Olivia is alert to the instability of so-ness when, a few lines later, she thanks him for agreeing to be ruled by her by saying, quite simply, but, by now, with some perplexity, 'O, say so, and so be' (64). This line of enigmatic quibbling, of instability in the indicative of being, runs all the way through the play to its perhaps redemptive reformulation when Cesario meets Sebastian: 'A natural perspective, that is, and is not!' (v. i. 215). It matters to the Malvolio plot because, in his attempt to subvert the steward's sanity, Feste turns such riddling against him. '"That that is, is,"' he tells Sir Toby (with the assurance that, by this point, what is is not): 'so I,

[43] See e.g. Orest Ranum, 'The Refuges of Intimacy', in Roger Chartier (ed.), *Passions of the Renaissance*, trans. Arthur Goldhammer (Cambridge, Mass., 1989), vol. iii of *A History of Private Life*, 207–63, Patricia Fumerton, *Cultural Aesthetics: Renaissance Literature and the Practice of Social Ornament* (Chicago, 1991), ch. 2, and Alan Stewart, 'The Early Modern Closet Discovered', *Representations*, 50 (1995), 76–100.

being Master Parson, am Master Parson; for what is "that" but "that"? and "is" but "is"?' (IV. ii. 15–17).

Malvolio does not doubt that Master Parson is Master Parson, even when Feste presents himself in that guise without disguise—just in a different voice. By the same token, however, he persists in a stubborn belief that 'that' is 'that' and 'is' 'is'. He has a self-centred clarity about what he credits which carries him with some dignity through Feste's peculiar questions about Pythagoras' metempsychosis, and whether the soul of one's grandam might haply inhabit a bird. No audience can entirely warm to Malvolio's self-assurance, unchanged since the letter scene, but his persistent protestations of sanity seem the more admirable as his opponents' pranks become redundantly sadistic. Their cruelty is particularly marked in respect of the motif of 'companie or friendship', because, if the plot to incarcerate Malvolio is justified in so far as it obliges him to confront what it means for a man to be truly solitary, it abandons any claim to the moral high ground when Feste assists the steward by bringing him writing materials and agreeing to take a letter to Olivia, but then suppresses the missive—an event of such moment that Shakespeare underscores it in that otherwise null episode where the clown refuses to divulge the letter's contents to Fabian (v. i. 1–6).

I have touched, several times, in this essay, on the social dimension of secrecy, and stressed how it is produced, in the early modern period, out of civil intercourse. It should be clear, in consequence, at this late stage, why 'companie or friendship' is so important in *Twelfth Night*. Obviously, in this play of cross-dressing and variant sexuality, there is an interest in the mergings of heterosexual love with same-sex friendship, and with the friendship in heterosexual love as well as the eroticism of same-sex amity. But secrecy impinges on, and gives rise to, friendship (as in the shaping confidences shared between Sebastian and Antonio) because, although the period knew that—as the cynical commonplace put it—three can keep a secret when two of them are away, it was also aware that not to confide a hidden thing was to go the readiest way to public exposure or self-destruction. In trying to 'keepe love secrete', says Lord Julian in *The Book of the Courtier*, it is bad to be 'over secrete' and better to trust a friend with your feelings so that he can help you conceal what you will otherwise, certainly, betray (pp. 284–5). Recall Duke Charles the Hardy, Bacon advises, in his essay 'Of Frendship', who, because he 'would communicate his Secrets with none', damaged his wits. 'The Parable of *Pythagoras* is darke, but true; *Cor ne edito; Eat not the Heart*. Certainly, if a Man would give it a hard Phrase, Those that want *Frends* to open themselves unto, are Canniballs of their owne *Hearts.*'[44]

Bacon's fable from Pythagoras is not the same as Feste's, but something close to what the clown says can be found in Cleland's *Institution*, where, immediately after explaining why a man's friend should not be 'a great pratler', he enthuses:

O how much am I bound to Gods bounty amongst al the rest of his benefits to-wardes me, in sending me such a friend! . . . In the very first daie of our meeting . . . I found my minde so changed and remooued into the place of his, which before that time was in me. Hitherto I could neuer excogitate anie reason why I shoulde loue him, but *Pythagoras* his μετεμψύχωσις, and that hee is another my selfe. (p. 197)

Why is a friend so valuable? Cleland's answer is typical of the period: because he is a person 'in whom I dare better trust, and vnto whom I dare discover the most secret thoughtes of my minde with greater confidence then I am able to keepe them my selfe' (ibid.). So the dialogue between Feste and Malvolio about the steward's grandmother and a woodcock is not just random nonsense, and more than an insult to the old lady's intelligence. It contributes to the close texture of *Twelfth Night* a riddling reminder that, notwithstanding the resistance of the self-centred steward, the soul can be said, at least in amity, to migrate from one body to another. This is what Viola/Cesario means when s/he speaks of calling 'upon my soul within the house' (above, p. 102), and what Orsino invokes when he promises the assembled lovers that 'A solemn combination shall be made | Of our dear souls' (v. i. 382–3).

Malvolio is often seen as excluded from this finale. In one of the best essays on *Twelfth Night,* Anne Barton stresses the fragmentariness of its ending by pointing out that, like Sir Toby and Sir Andrew, the steward 'comes as a figure of violence and leaves unreconciled'. At the end of *As You Like It,* 'Jaques had walked with dignity out of the new society; Malvolio in effect is flung.'[45] This is largely true. Yet the charmed circle of amity does not actively dismiss Malvolio: if anything, Olivia and Orsino do the opposite, acknowledging, in an echo of his own words, that 'He hath been most notoriously abused' and commanding, 'Pursue him, and entreat him to a peace: | He hath not told us of the captain yet' (v. i. 378–80).

---

[44] *Essayes*, ed. Kiernan, 80–7, p. 83.

[45] '*As You Like It* and *Twelfth Night*: Shakespeare's "Sense of an Ending"' (1972), repr. in her *Essays, Mainly Shakespearean* (Cambridge, 1994), 91–112, p. 110.

What Orsino reminds the audience of here is that Malvolio is holding 'in durance', at his own suit, the Captain who arrived with Viola in the third scene of the play. This character, almost forgotten, is now freshly important, because he holds Viola's 'maiden weeds' (272 ff., 251 ff.). I am not myself persuaded that clothes were so constitutive of identity for Shakespeare's original audience that Cesario cannot become Viola until those very clothes are recovered from the Captain. Even Orsino, piquantly intrigued at being affianced to a boy, only says that 'Cesario' will keep his masculine name until 'in other [unspecified] habits you are seen' (386).[46] Yet the gesture of deferral—as against fragmentation—is unmistakable, and compatible with a denouement which straggles its endings out, from the pre-emptive coupling of Maria and Toby, through the betrothal but delayed marriage of Olivia and Sebastian, to the as-yet-unrealized resolution of the Cesario/Viola–Orsino romance. In that delayed conclusion, space is made for Malvolio, his hold over Viola's weeds confirming what his anagrammatic link with her name implies. These characters belong together. Until the steward is reconciled, comedy will not be consummated. Just how he will be persuaded remains one of the secrets of the play.

[46] Contrast Stephen Orgel, *Impersonations: The Performance of Gender in Shakespeare's England* (Cambridge, 1996), 104.

Part II

Early Modern Literature

CHAPTER 6

The Editor as Reader: Constructing Renaissance Texts (1996)

The practice of editing literary texts was transformed, during the 1920s and 1930s, by the innovative and assiduous researches of Alfred W. Pollard, R. B. McKerrow, and W. W. Greg. Between them, the New Bibliographers discovered a number of crucial facts about early modern printing, about the rules which governed 'copyright' before 1709, and about the textual status of such landmark volumes as the Shakespeare first Folio. They also formulated principles which continue to shape editorial thinking across a range of post-medieval periods. Greg's famous paper 'The Rationale of Copy-Text' (1950) is not, in fact, narrowly addressed to questions of authorship and authority, but, by encouraging editors confronted with variant texts to base their editions on sources as close as possible to authorial manuscript, Greg implied a model of literary production which became, in the work of his most gifted followers—Fredson Bowers and G. Thomas Tanselle—explicitly intentionalist.[1] For textual scholars in this tradition, it is the job of an editor to identify and strip out corruptions introduced by scribes and printers in order to recreate, as accurately as possible, the 'ideal' work intended by the author. Such an approach construes the literary text in quasi-Kantian terms, as an end in itself, free of historical contingency and the accidents of material circumstance. It also, and connectedly, pays little or no attention to the role of the reader.

---

[1] W. W. Greg, 'The Rationale of Copy-Text', *Studies in Bibliography*, 3 (1950), 19–36. See, repeatedly, Fredson Bowers, *Textual and Literary Criticism* (Cambridge, 1959), *Bibliography and Textual Criticism* (Oxford, 1964), *Essays in Bibliography, Text, and Editing* (Charlottesville, Va., 1975); G. Thomas Tanselle, 'The Editorial Problem of Final Authorial Intentions', *Studies in Bibliography*, 29 (1976), 167–211, repr. in his *Selected Studies in Bibliography* (Charlottesville, Va., 1979), *Textual Criticism since Greg: A Chronicle, 1950–1985* (Charlottesville, Va., 1987), *A Rationale of Textual Criticism* (Philadelphia, 1989); and, for a discriminating overview, James McLaverty, 'The Concept of Authorial Intention in Textual Criticism', *Library*, 6th ser. 6 (1984), 121–37.

Over the last twenty-five years, this approach has come under pressure. D. F. McKenzie's demonstration, in 1969, that the lucid patterns of compositor behaviour posited by Bowers and his associates do not match the erratic work-schedules of actual seventeenth-century printers induced scepticism about bibliographical explanations based on the 'logic' of the printing process.[2] Editors noticed that Greg's views of authorship and copy-text were not easily reconciled with the collaborative features of those Renaissance play-scripts which most interested him.[3] More generally, changes in the discipline of literary criticism rendered intentionalism and formalism problematic. As Marxist and post-structuralist critics modified perceptions of authorship and textuality, and as reader-response and reception theory heightened awareness of the contribution made by audiences to literary meaning, the work of Bowers and Tanselle began to look like the bibliographical wing of the—increasingly discredited— New Criticism. Though a great deal of editing still takes place in the shadow of Greg, textual scholars are being tempted beyond formalism. D. F. McKenzie, for instance, has encouraged them to recognize what is lost when the literary work is construed as a self-contained object—a 'verbal icon' or '*well-wrought Urn*'[4]—and urged them to analyse such 'non-book texts' as maps, prints, music, electronic forms of data storage, and film.[5] Meanwhile, Jerome J. McGann has pointed towards new ways of thinking about literature by maintaining, against Bowers and Tanselle, that textual criticism should not be cultivated for exclusively editorial ends but become part of an integrated programme of textual-historical enquiry.

McGann's work on the theory of editing first bore fruit in *A Critique of Modern Textual Criticism* (1983). This civilized polemic points up the drawbacks of an editorial practice which, wedded to false intentionalism and fixated on authorial manuscript, ignores the part played in the creation of literary artefacts by the process of publication. It urges textual critics to recover the breadth of historical and philological interest shown by the great German scholar-editors of the early nineteenth century. In

---

[2] D. F. McKenzie, 'Printers of the Mind: Some Notes on Bibliographical Theories and Printing-House Practices', *Studies in Bibliography*, 22 (1969), 1–75.

[3] See, most trenchantly, T. H. Howard-Hill, 'Modern Textual Theories and the Editing of Plays', *Library*, 6th ser. 11 (1989), 89–115.

[4] *Bibliography and the Sociology of Literary Texts*, The Panizzi Lectures 1985 (London, 1986), ch. 1, esp. pp. 16–17 (citing catch-phrases of the New Criticism, originally associated with W. K. Wimsatt, Jr., and Cleanth Brooks).

[5] *Bibliography and the Sociology of Literary Texts*, chs. 2–3.

The Beauty of Inflections (1985), McGann reconnects bibliography with historical scholarship and practical criticism, working through examples from Blake, Poe, and others to demonstrate the importance of those determinants of literary meaning which lie in the circumstances of publication and reception, beyond authorial control—a claim furthered by the contextualizing commentary of his seven-volume edition *Lord Byron: The Complete Poetical Works* (1980–93). More recently, in *The Textual Condition* (1991), McGann has pushed his argument to extremes. On the one hand, he examines the part played by such apparently external agents as publishers, reviewers, and audiences in creating the interactive 'human event' called literature, and, on the other, he shows how such inwardly bibliocentric minutiae as typeface, layout, and paper quality should not be regarded as incidental features of what contains or transmits 'the authorial text' but as signifying components of the textual phenomena.

Together, McGann's books constitute the most influential contribution to editorial theory and practice since the birth of the New Bibliography. To examine them in relation to the history of reading, however, is to identify a grave deficiency. Given his belief that 'texts' become 'poems' only when they enter the public realm and interact with audiences,[6] McGann is damagingly indifferent to the variety and complexity of reading practices. It is understandable that, in the *Critique*, where he engages directly with the arguments of Bowers and Tanselle, he should replicate their neglect of the reader.[7] More troubling is the suppression of individual reading in *The Beauty of Inflections*. There is a Marxist-theoretical strain in this book which leads McGann to collectivize the literary audience. He is no more willing to privilege individual reading responses than he is to value biographical criticism of authors: both, by implication, involve a false social geography. As a result, when he finds Coleridge saying, of scripture, 'the conflicts of grace and infirmity in your own soul, will enable you to discern and to know in and by what spirit they [i.e. biblical figures] spake and acted,—as far at least as shall be needful for you, and in the times of your need', he turns a Protestant concern with personal grace and salvation into a historical materialist point about the reader being 'subject to time-specific cultural limitations'.[8] Similarly, when he quotes

---

[6] *The Beauty of Inflections: Literary Investigations in Historical Method and Theory* (Oxford, 1985), 114–15.

[7] For undeveloped exceptions see *A Critique of Modern Textual Criticism* (Chicago, 1983), 48, 60.

[8] *Beauty of Inflections*, 149.

Tennyson's remark, 'Poetry is like shot-silk with many glancing colours. Every reader must find his own interpretation according to his ability, and according to his sympathy with the poet,' he glosses away the subjectivism with a faintly Stakhanovite (and certainly Bakhtinian) account of *The Princess*: 'Tennyson worked hard to fashion a poetic vehicle that was not merely designed to accom[m]odate different views and alternate readings, but that actively anticipated those differences—that (as it were) called out to them, and that offered Victorian readers a place where they would find their differences reconciled.'[9] For McGann, the contexts of poetry work together with the words on the page to 'enforce' reader-responses. This is the verb he uses when, discussing an Emily Dickinson lyric as it appears in two different editions and an anthology, he insists that the 'bibliographical environments . . . enforce very different reading experiences'.[10]

The same impulse to deny the agency of readers by finding their responses hard-wired into (and so 'anticipated' by) the literary work in its material setting remains apparent in *The Textual Condition*. Here, McGann invokes reader-centred theories of interpretation only to reject them. Reacting against the idealism which he finds in both Tanselle and the post-structuralist Paul de Man, he yokes these unlikely bedfellows with the most dexterous of reader-response critics, Stanley Fish,[11] and sets them against his own position. There is no question of a McGann-accredited reader construing, say, an advertisement as a lyric poem. To do so would constitute a mistake, or an illicitly creative act. Nor, apparently, should we think of responses to the 'shot-silk' of poetry taking shape in pre-verbal fields of irridescent neurological activity; that would lead to talk of minds, and compromise materialism. 'Reading appears always and only as text', McGann insists, 'in one or another physically determinate and socially determined form. This is not to deny either the reality or the importance of silent and individual reading. It is merely to say that textuality cannot be understood except as a phenomenal event, and that reading itself can only be understood when it has assumed specific material constitutions.'[12] The ambiguities of this are inordinate. 'Physically determinate', for instance, lends 'socially determined' a hint of mere definition while leaving its late-Marxist determinism intact. And is it the case

---

    9 *Beauty of Inflections*, 178; cf. p. 180.   10 Ibid. 85.

    11 See e.g. Stanley Fish, *Is There a Text in This Class? The Authority of Interpretive Communities* (Cambridge, Mass. 1980).

    12 Jerome J. McGann, *The Textual Condition* (Chicago, 1991), 4–5.

that what cannot be 'understood' cannot be 'understood' as having happened?

McGann's belief that literary texts are characterized by an ability to 'anticipate' or 'call out' different 'readings' allows him to short-circuit historical change when explaining the emergence of new meanings. His model of reading, that is, impoverishes his historicism. 'Every text', he asserts, 'has variants of itself screaming to get out, or antithetical texts waiting to make themselves known. . . . Various readers and audiences are hidden in our texts, and the traces of their multiple presence are scripted at the most material levels.'[13] Behind the mystificatory notion of 'readers . . . hidden in' texts lies an unwillingness to admit that, because of broadly based historical developments to which the 'variants . . . or antithetical texts' of, say, *Clarissa* contribute remarkably little, eighteenth-century approaches to Richardson are quite different from nineteenth- or twentieth-century ones. In other words, McGann's neglect of the active individual reader is compatible with his residually formalistic views about the changing significance of particular texts. For as long as he is thinking about reading acts, his account of the evolution of literary meaning hardly looks beyond the 'readings' already coded into the text.

In this essay I want to show how unfortunate these limitations are, and to suggest that, by supplementing McGann's work, it might be possible to arrive at a more generously defined alternative to the weakened but still dominant mode of formalist-intentionalist editing. Because his literary interests are mostly nineteenth-century, McGann's thinking about textual criticism has concentrated on Romantic, Victorian, and modernist poets. I want to inspect, by contrast, Renaissance texts, partly because the influence of Greg and Bowers remains particularly strong among editors working in that period, but also because early modern writers are revealingly explicit about the variety of responses which they expect from readers. The business of engaging with and managing such responses is so firmly built into their writing that it seems to me impossible to think about how to edit them without attending to the practice and representation of reading.

In 1572–3 Henry Bynneman and his associates printed, for the publisher Richard Smith, an unusually interesting quarto. George Gascoigne's *Hundreth Sundrie Flowres* offers virtually a conspectus of Elizabethan

---

[13] Ibid. 10.

literature. Starting with translations of Ariosto's comedy *I suppositi* and (also through Italian) of Euripides' *Phoenician Women*, it includes an experimental novella entitled 'a pleasant discourse of the aduentures of master F.I.', a gathering of lyrics, all composed by Gascoigne but presented as 'diuers excellent deuises of sundry Gentlemen', plus 'certayne deuises of master Gascoyne', before ending with a set of poems which record 'the dolorous discourse of Dan Bartholmew of Bathe'.[14] Within this heterogeneity, there is further local variety. Although 'the aduentures of master F.I.' is predominantly a prose work, it is organized around a series of lyrics supposedly penned by 'F.I.', while the section called 'diuers excellent deuises of sundry Gentlemen' resembles one of those manuscript or print miscellanies which were so popular during the sixteenth century. In themselves, these features are editorially unremarkable. But they are associated with bibliographical irregularities which heighten the impression of diversity: inconsistencies in typeface, end-of-text arrangements printed long before the end of the book, and, most strikingly, a break in pagination, from 164 to 201, between the plays and the *Adventures*. It would seem unwise to edit Gascoigne without analysing these traits.

The still-standard *Complete Works*, however, edited by John W. Cunliffe in two volumes (1907–10), sidesteps the problem by using as its copytext a later version of the *Flowres* material, *The Posies* (1575). This book (also published by Richard Smith) is of great interest because it shows Gascoigne reordering and revising his work in response to criticisms of *A Hundreth Sundrie Flowres*, and confirming his authorship of the poems previously ascribed to 'sundry Gentlemen'. At many points, however, *The Posies* is unsatisfactory, because the text has been weakened by self-censorship. The poet's desperate search for patronage led him to alter his work[15] in ways which are of major significance in the history of its reception, but which, editorially, make a preference for the 1575 text over that of 1573 unacceptable. As a result, when C. T. Prouty came to edit Gascoigne in 1942, he used the 1573 edition as copy-text. Following classically post-Greg principles, he set out 'to provide a text of *A Hundreth Sundrie Flowres* which would represent as accurately as possible the author's final intention'.[16] Unfortunately the search for that elusive psychological

---

[14] 'The contents of this Booke', A1^v.

[15] See e.g. Richard C. McCoy, 'Gascoigne's "Poëmata castrata": The Wages of Courtly Success', *Criticism*, 27 (1985), 29–55.

[16] *A Hundreth Sundrie Flowres*, University of Missouri Studies, 17/2 (Columbia, Mo., 1942), 221; cf. p. 17.

commodity led Prouty into biographical speculations which were filled out by reading back from presumed confessions, boasts, and riddles in the *Flowres* themselves, so that a historical romance about the author— fitfully documented in the 'Critical Notes'[17]—was produced to provide an intentionalist framework within which the edition could take shape.

The consequences of this approach are most alarming in respect of the plays. Confronted by the jump in pagination which follows them in 1573, Prouty decided—without documentary evidence—that Gascoigne had been driven abroad by financial and legal difficulties during the printing of the *Flowres* and that Bynneman had used the opportunity provided by his absence to include the commercially 'more attractive' play-texts. This explains, apparently, why the book was printed in two sections (though not why the second unit, which starts with 'the aduentures of master F.I.' should not be numbered from page 1). Prouty admits that 'It cannot be said with assurance that Gascoigne was unaware of the printer's intention to include the plays',[18] but the uncertainty does not hamper his editorial decisiveness. Swayed by a New Bibliographical prejudice against publication itself—as a process which contaminates and corrupts authorial intentions—Prouty resolved to right a possible wrong, and entirely excluded the plays.

An edition of *A Hundreth Sundrie Flowres* which cuts about 40 per cent of *A Hundreth Sundrie Flowres* has to be problematic. As it happens, research by Adrian Weiss has shown that the irregularities in Bynneman's quarto were caused by the sharing of work with another printer (Henry Middleton), by the piecemeal provision of copy over a production period which lasted at least eight months, and (it may be) by the poet's failure to complete 'Dan Bartholmew of Bathe' to schedule—since, when the fifty-four stanzas added to that work in *The Posies* are included, it is the only text in the Gascoigne canon which runs to a length which would fill the gap between the plays and 'the aduentures of master F.I.'[19] The claim about 'Dan Bartholmew' is hard to prove, of course, because the poet might have withdrawn another, now lost text, rather than failed to deliver

---

[17] For example, the comments on 'the aduentures of master F.I.', 57 (ll. 26–30), 'deuises of sundry Gentlemen', nos. 8, 38. Prouty was unduly influenced by the rage for interpretation *à clef* which afflicted his unscholarly predecessor B. M. Ward. The latter's edition of the *Flowres* (London, 1926) has been updated and expanded by Ruth Loyd Miller (Port Washington, NY, 1975) to illuminate the early career of that well-known author of Shakespeare's works, Edward de Vere, 17th Earl of Oxford.

[18] *A Hundreth Sundrie Flowres*, ed. Prouty, 18.

[19] 'Shared Printing, Printer's Copy, and the Text(s) of Gascoigne's *A Hundreth Sundrie Flowres*', *Studies in Bibliography*, 45 (1992), 71–104.

at the promised time one which was subsequently and incompletely added to the end of the *Flowres*. But it is clear that, the more we learn about the process of publication in 1573, the more reflective of evolving authorial intentions, hopes, and compromises the quarto appears. The result of such information, however, cannot be a more fully Gregian, or Bowersian, edition, because the principle of changing intent opens the text up to its reception and later history in *The Posies*. To edit Gascoigne in a way which is sensitive to the formation of the 1573 text, it is necessary to look far beyond 'the author's final intention'. This means, first, starting from the McGannish principle that we should reproduce the entirety of the text (including the plays) as it reached print, and, secondly, resolving that relations between the *Flowres* and *The Posies* should be foregrounded by the editor, because how the work was received is essential to its evolution, not just between 1573–5, but within the 1573 edition, given the spectrum of responses which Gascoigne—as I shall presently show—expected to meet when he published the *Flowres*.

The reception of the *Flowres* refutes the idea that 'readings' are lodged inside an Elizabethan text and 'called out' to those who peruse it, not least by showing that responses which go against the grain of the text (as we or the poet might see it) can be potent enough to disgrace the author. *The Posies* begins with no fewer than three addresses: 'To the reuerende Diuines', 'To al yong Gentlemen', and 'To the Readers generally'. All three concede that the *Flowres* has been criticized for immorality, but stress that an author cannot be held responsible for his readers' responses. Gascoigne does not collectivize his audience. After dividing divines from gallant gentlemen, he goes on, when addressing the latter, to discriminate 'curious Carpers, ignorant Readers, and graue Philosophers' (¶¶2^v). While the curiosity of the former makes them variously wayward, the folly of the ignorant renders them equally unpredictable. In every case, a text will be interpreted by different individuals according to their natures. 'As the industrious Bee may gather honie out of the most stinking weede, so the malicious Spider may also gather poyson out of the fayrest floure that growes' (¶¶3^v). His book resembles a garden, Gascoigne says, planted with flowers, herbs, and weeds. Even weeds may be medicinable, and the author should not to be blamed 'if the Chirurgian which should seeke Sorrell to rypen an Vlcer, will take Rewe which may more inflame the Impostume'. In short, 'it is your using (my lustie Gallants) or misusing of these Posies that may make me praysed or dispraysed for publishing of the same' (¶¶3^v).

These claims would be familiar to Gascoigne's admirers not least because they recycle remarks made by 'The Printer to the Reader' in the *Flowres*. Bynneman (ostensibly) tells us that, 'as the venemous spider wil sucke poison out of the most holesome herbe, and the industrious Bee can gather hony out of the most stinking weede: Euen so the discrete reader may take a happie example by the most lasciuious histories.' In this book, we are assured, 'you shall not be constreined to smell of the floures therein conteined all at once . . . But you may take any one flowre by it-selfe, and if that smell not so pleasantly as you wold wish, I doubt not yet but you may find some other which may supplie the defects thereof' (A2ᵛ). These assertions are highly conventional, based on commonplaces derived from Seneca and Horace. They may indeed be the work of Bynneman. But Gascoigne scholars generally agree that 'The Printer to the Reader' was scripted by the poet, extending the editorial role which he plays elsewhere through the figure of that 'G.T.' who (via the agency of one 'H.W.') conveys the story and writings of 'F.I.' to the reader, and through the 'reporter' who frames the tale of 'Dan Bartholmew'. Repeatedly, in the *Flowres*, the editorial presence of the author impinges, recommending responses but conceding that readers cannot be constrained. 'This is but a rough meeter', 'G.T.' will say (of the poem 'A cloud of care . . .'), 'yet haue I seene much worse passe the musters'; 'This Ballade . . . percase you will not like, and yet in my iudgement it hath great good store of deepe inuention . . . leauing it to your and like iudgements'; and again, 'This Sonet treateth of a straung seede, but . . . let it passe amongst the rest, & he that liketh it not, turn ouer the leaf to another, I dout not but in this register he may find some to content him, unlesse he be to curious.'[20]

Gascoigne is far from unique in his attempt to manage reader-responses editorially. To run down a scale from indubitably external commentary to authorial self-annotation, the same practice recurs in Antoine de Muret's glosses on Ronsard's *Amours* (1553), 'E.K.'s remarks on *The Shepheardes Calender* (1579), and Thomas Watson's notes to his *Hekatompathia* (1582). But Gascoigne's case is especially instructive because we know how actual readers responded to the author's prompting, not just from the addresses which preface *The Posies* but from remarks in George Puttenham's *Arte of English Poesie* (1589) and Gabriel Harvey's marginalia.

---

[20] D1ᵛ, E3ᵛ, G1ʳ. On G.T.'s limitations as a reader, and Gascoigne's manipulation of them, see George E. Rowe, Jr., 'Interpretation, Sixteenth-Century Readers, and George Gascoigne's "The Adventures of Master F.J."', *ELH* 48 (1981), 271–89, esp. pp. 278–9.

The latter, for instance, glossed the tale of 'F.I.'s frustrated adulterous affair in *The Posies* with a remarkably pragmatic moral:

The discouerie of his mistres, a false Diamant. His sicknes, & Jealosie did not help the matter, but did marre all. Woomen looue men: & care not for pore harts, that cannot bestead them. Especially at the returne of his riual, her Secretarie; it imported him to emprooue himself more, then before; & not to languish like a milksopp, or to play the pore snake vpon himself. Ladie Elinor woold haue liked the man that woold haue maintained his possession by force of armes, & with braue encounters beat his enimie owt of the feild.[21]

This is typical of Harvey's habit of annotating his books with *aide mémoires* in summary form, and, in terms of application, of his emphasis on patterns of behaviour. He studied Gascoigne, as he studied Caesar and Livy, 'for action',[22] looking for strategies which would advance his own career in the courtly world inhabited by 'F.I.', but also seeking the means of such advancement by identifying exemplary instances of wise or fruitless conduct which could be retailed to those noblemen (such as Philip Sidney) who employed him as an intelligencer. Harvey's closing remarks about 'force of armes, & . . . braue encounters' are particularly characteristic, since they point to a deep identification with the ideology of Leicester's war party. What *this* reader deduces from Gascoigne, somewhere down the line, is that firm and courageous dealing with Spain is the only way to success.

   Puttenham, by contrast, is interested in verbal texture. He repeatedly quotes Gascoigne to show how rhetoric operates, and how epithets, periphrasis, and alliteration can be abused.[23] But his style of close reading differs from that of a modern formalist. He cites 'A cloud of care . . .', for instance, to exemplify 'mixt' allegory, to show the kind of poem which 'discouers withall what the *cloud, storme, waue,* and the rest are, which in a full allegorie should not be discouered, but left at large to the readers iudgement and coniecture'.[24] This interest in what critics now call 'the reader's share' is symptomatic. Citing a Gascoigne poem which begins 'This tenth of March when *Aries* receyud, | Da[n] *Phœbus* rayes, into his horned head', Puttenham objects to the redundancy of expression and

---

[21] *Gabriel Harvey: Marginalia*, ed. G. C. Moore Smith (Stratford-upon-Avon, 1913), 167.

[22] On Harvey's reading in the classics, see Lisa Jardine and Anthony Grafton, '"Studied for Action": How Gabriel Harvey Read his Livy', *Past and Present*, 129 (Nov. 1990), 30–78. For a suggestive attempt to extend this analysis to prose fiction, see Lorna Hutson, 'Fortunate Travelers: Reading for the Plot in Sixteenth-Century England', *Representations*, 41 (1993), 83–103.

[23] *The Arte of English Poesie*, ed. Gladys Doidge Willcock and Alice Walker (Cambridge, 1936), 182, 212, 221, 236, 254, 255, 258–9.   [24] Ibid. 188.

proposes an improvement: 'The month and daie when Aries receiud, | Dan Phœbus raies into his horned head.' This is better, he says, because 'there remaineth for the Reader somewhat to studie and gesse vpon, and yet the spring time to the learned iudgement sufficiently expressed'.[25] Puttenham's mind then passes to Surrey's melancholy pastoral, 'In winters iust returne . . .' Perhaps Gascoigne prompted the association, for in *The Posies*' address 'To al yong Gentlemen' the poet cites as an example of 'ignorant' reading those whose literalism is such that they interpret Surrey's 'pleasant dittie' of rustic life as 'made indeed by a Shepeherd' (¶¶3ʳ). Puttenham's remarks are less robust; they make an early contribution to the subtleties of reader-response theory. Quoting Surrey's opening lines—'In winters iust returne, when Boreas gan his raigne, | And euery tree vnclothed him fast as nature taught them plaine'—he worries at the problem of imputing a sense to 'winters iust returne' which is more than circumlocutionary. Once taken as 'the time which we call the fall of the leafe' (rather than a roundabout way of saying 'winter'), the phrase becomes apt and poignant. If the reader finds this meaning in the text, Puttenham says, he 'may . . . iudge as I do, that this noble Erle wrate excellently well and to purpose'.[26]

Gascoigne was peculiarly alert to the mixed nature of his audience, and to the danger of encountering spiders. But an awareness of reader diversity was widespread among his contemporaries, almost a condition of authorship in the expanding market for print. In the addresses 'To the Reader' printed with early modern literary texts there is a recurrent stress on division. Authors set 'fond curious, or rather currish backbiters' against 'courteous Readers', separate the 'captious' from the 'vertuous', the 'Pretender' from the 'Vnderstander'.[27] They castigate 'scornefull and carpynge Correctours' and 'trust the indifferent Reader'.[28] Sometimes the division is by gender. Lyly, for instance, starts *Euphues and his England* (1580) with epistles 'To the Ladies and Gentlewomen of England' and 'To the Gentlemen Readers'. The former are invited to sport with the novel in between playing with their lapdogs, to nibble at it 'as you doe your Iunckets, that when you can eate no more, you tye some in your napkin for

[25] Ibid. 194.   [26] Ibid. 194–5.

[27] Robert Greene, *Pandosto: The Triumph of Time* (1588), A1ᵛ; Thomas Lodge, *Prosopopeia: Containing the Teares of the Holy, Blessed, and Sanctified Marie, the Mother of God* (1596), A6ᵛ; Ben Jonson, *The Alchemist* (1612), A3ʳ.

[28] Barnabe Googe, *Eglogs, Epytaphes, and Sonettes* (1563), A5ᵛ; William Painter, *The Palace of Pleasure* (1566), ¶¶¶1ᵛ.

children' (¶1ᵛ). Their reading experiences will evidently be quite unlike those of the gentlemen. For though the latter are, like the women, welcomed to variety, being invited (as though by Gascoigne) 'into a Gardeine, some [to] gather Nettles, some Roses, one Tyme, an other Sage', they are expected to show a more commanding involvement with the text: 'Faultes escaped in the Printing, correcte with your pennes: omitted by my neglygence, ouerslippe with patience: committed by ignoraunce, remit with fauour' (¶3ᵛ).

When authors discuss their audiences at length they tend to distinguish ever more groups and sub-categories, approaching the atomism remarked by Robert Greene: 'no book so yll but some will both reade it and praise it; & none againe so curious, but some wil carpe at it. Wel, so many heades, so many wittes.'[29] Thomas Dekker, for instance, observes:

> He that writes, had need to haue the Art of a skilfull Cooke; for there must be those *Condimenta* (seasonings) in his pen, which the other caries on his tongue: A thousand palats must bee pleased with a thousand sawces: and one hundred lines must content fiue hundred dispositions. A hard taske: one says, it is too harsh[:] another, too supple: another too triuiall: another too serious.[30]

It does not diminish the force of Dekker's complaint that it elaborates a commonplace. When Burton, for example, uses the same topoi as Greene and Dekker to characterize the audience of *The Anatomy of Melancholy*, his dependence on classical authority does not make his account of the mixed nature of his readership any the less solidly compatible with his ruling perception, in the *Anatomy* as a whole, of the quirkiness of mankind. 'To say truth with *Erasmus*', he writes,

> *nihil morosius hominum iudiciis*, theirs naught so peeuish as mens iudgements, yet this is some comfort, *vt palata, sic iudicia*, our censures are as various as our Palats.
>
> > *Tres mihi conuiuæ prope dissentire videntur*
> > *Poscentes vario multum diversa palato, &c.* [*Hor.*]
>
> Our writings are as so many Dishes, our Readers Guests; our Bookes like beautie, that which one admires another reiects; so are wee approued as mens fancies are inclined.
>
> > *Pro captu lectoris habent sua fata libelli*,
>
> That which is most pleasing to one is *amaracum sui*, most harsh to another. *Quot homines, tot sententiae*, so many men, so many minds: that which thou condemnest he commends.[31]

---

[29] *Mamillia: A Mirrour or Looking-Glasse for the Ladies of England* (1583), A3ʳ.
[30] *A Strange Horse Race* (1613), A3ʳ.   [31] *Anatomy of Melancholy*, 4th edn. (1632), B1ʳ.

Though Renaissance authors knew that readers' responses could be as various as the readers themselves, they were wary of abandoning their works to misconstruction. That could lead to imprisonment, or worse. It was partly for temperamental and aesthetic reasons that Ben Jonson sought to constrain readers by deploying prefaces, marginal annotation, and author-critic figures in his works;[32] but in the case of *Sejanus*, an apparatus was introduced (in quarto) to refute those ingenious readers— 'those common Torturers, that bring all wit to the Rack'—whose detection of treason in the tragedy was responsible for having its author investigated by the Privy Council.[33] Thomas Nashe could joke about contemporaries who read political allusions into everything: 'Let one but name bread, they will interpret it to be the town of Bredan in the low countreyes; if of beere he talkes, then straight he mocks the Countie Beroune in France.'[34] Others had to worry, though, when reader-responses created a scandal. In *A Free and Offenceles Ivstification, of Andromeda Liberata* (1614), George Chapman protests that, in choosing such an ancient subject for his poem, he had thought himself beyond allusive reading, and 'presum'd, that the application being free, I might *pro meo iure* dispose it (innocen[t]ly) to mine owne obiect: if at least, in mine owne wrighting, I might be reasonablie & conscionablie master of mine owne meaning' (*3ʳ). If a troublesome meaning is brought to the text by a reader, what blame should the author bear? 'Doth any Law therfore cast that meaning vpon me?' Chapman asked, 'Or doth any rule of reason make it good, that let the writer meane what he list, his writing notwithstanding must be construed *in mentem Legentis?* to the intendment of the Reader?' (*4ʳ). It is a question which modern reader-response theory is no closer to resolving.

These notes of dissent are significant, but the general view, fostered by such sources as Plutarch's 'How a yoong man ought to heare poets, and how he may take profit by reading poemes',[35] was that the reader should be allowed considerable latitude in pursuit of the traditional goal of extracting moral benefit from even unpromising texts. Marion Trousdale

---

[32] See e.g. Timothy J. Murray, *Theatrical Legitimation: Allegories of Genius in Seventeenth-Century England and France* (Oxford, 1987), chs. 3 and 4, Joseph Loewenstein, 'Printing and "The Multitudinous Presse": The Contentious Texts of Jonson's Masques', in Jennifer Brady and W. H. Herendeen (eds.), *Ben Jonson's 1616 Folio* (Cranbury, NJ, 1991), 168–91.

[33] ¶2ᵛ; cf. *Volpone* (1607), ¶2ᵛ. On the editorial implications, see John Jowett, '"Fall before this Booke": The 1605 Quarto of *Sejanus*', *TEXT*, 4 (1988), 279–95.

[34] *Christs Teares ouer Ierusalem*, reissue with new prelims. (1594), **1ᵛ.

[35] *The Philosophie, Commonlie Called, The Morals*, trans. Philemon Holland (1603), 17–50.

has written well about Erasmus' skill in moralizing the death of Socrates, drawing from the tale a whole series of mutually incompatible but equally valid axioms. For Erasmus and his followers, the meaning of a fable was neither singular nor defined by the narrative but produced (ultimately from a common store of wisdom) by the reader.[36] This attitude was the more tenaciously held because supported by ancient testimony. Summarizing the message of Plutarch's essay, John Wallace writes:

The reader's profit lay in his powers of discrimination, so that at all times he knew whether to feel raised by the sentiments he encountered or to inoculate himself against their dire effects. Immunity could be obtained by studying the implicit commentary within a work on the bad deeds and characters, by remembering better statements made elsewhere by the author, by paying careful attention to etymological niceties, and so on. If a passage remained impervious to a favorable (i.e., a moral) construction, then it was advisable to tamper with the text or to recall good moral dicta from quite different sources.[37]

These obligations and liberties were widely recognized by early modern writers. The objects of a reader's enquiry were general: truths accessible (and for the most part already familiar) to all. But the means of extracting them were particular, indeed personal. Wallace is right to conclude that, for Renaissance commentators, 'once the explicatory process had begun, then the reader was involved for his own good, and it was immaterial (or only occasionally material) whether one reader's interpretations were the same as another's, or identical with the author's aims'.[38]

We should not be surprised, then, to find a poet like Giles Fletcher the Elder refusing to determine for 'the Reader' what the mistress of his sonnet sequence, *Licia* (1593), stands for: 'it may be shee is Learnings image, or some heavenlie woonder . . . it may bee some Colledge; it may bee my conceit, and portende nothing: whatsoever it be, if thou like it, take it' (B1^r). Such interpretative generosity was commonplace. Occasionally, it is true, reader-responses are envisaged which seem closer to the phenomenology of Georges Poulet[39] than the discrimination urged by Plutarch. The Beaumont and Fletcher Folio, for instance, begins with the claim: 'You may here find passions raised to that excellent pitch and by such

---

[36] 'A Possible Renaissance View of Form', *ELH* 40 (1973), 179–204; cf. John Wallace, '"Examples are Best Precepts": Readers and Meanings in Seventeenth-Century Poetry', *Critical Inquiry*, 1 (1974), 273–90, p. 284.

[37] 'Examples are Best Precepts', 277.   [38] Ibid. 275.

[39] See e.g. his 'Criticism and the Experience of Interiority', in Richard A. Macksey and Eugenio Donato (eds.), *The Structuralist Controversy: The Language of Criticism and the Sciences of Man* (Baltimore, 1972), 56–72.

insinuating degrees that you shall not chuse but consent, & go along with them, finding your self at last grown insensibly the very same person you read, and then stand admiring the subtile Trackes of your engagement.'[40] But this degree of self-loss was rarely proposed. Where identification with the 'person you read' was regularly encouraged, in devotional literature, the aim was to improve, by double involvement, the reader's reading of himself. In this respect, Bunyan's prefatory verses to *Pilgrim's Progress* are orthodox:

> Wouldst read thy self, and read thou know'st not what
> And yet know whether thou art blest or not,
> By reading the same lines? O then come hither,
> And lay my Book, thy head, and heart, together.[41]

The puritan writer joins hands here with the secular strain of reading-theory which descends from Plutarch. Bunyan would have understood McGann's notion of 'readings' being 'called out' to readers, but his own model was more individualized. In his early modern way, he is describing 'the reader's share', a share which, as he interprets human nature, could only ever be particular to that one reader's grace and salvation.

Where does this leave editing? We can return to the issues which began this essay by pondering Plutarch's advice about amending unacceptable text, and Lyly's request that 'Gentlemen Readers' correct 'Faultes escaped in the Printing' while exercising patience and judgement. In both cases the reader has an incipient editorial function—one which, elsewhere, becomes explicit. When Thomas Lodge, for example, introduces 'the Reader' to the 1620 edition of his *Workes of Seneca* (b1^{r-v}), he promises—conventionally enough—'a Garden, wherein . . . thou maiest find many holesome Herbes, goodly flowers, and rich Medicines'. He then adds, however:

yet can it not be but some weedes may ranckly shoote out, which may smoother or obscure the light and lustre of the better. Play the good Gardner I pray thee, and pulling vp the weedes, make thy profit of the flowers. If thou wilt Correct, bee considerate before thou attempt, lest in pretending to roote out one, thou commit many errors.

The editing reader should be prudent, lest he multiply error. But the text is his to use, to modify and select from. 'What a Stoicke hath written', Lodge advises, 'Reade thou like a Christian.' If the reader doubts a

---

[40] *Comedies and Tragedies Written by Francis Beaumont and John Fletcher* (1647), A3^v.
[41] *The Pilgrim's Progress from This World to That Which is to Come*, 2nd edn. (1678), A6^r.

passage, he should 'haue recourse to the sacred Synod of learned and pious Diuines; whose iudgement will select thee out that which is for thy Soules profit'. When Lodge encourages his reader 'to Correct with thy pen, that which other men lesse aduised, haue omitted by ouer hastie labour', textual emendation is only one aspect of an enterprise in which reading and editing go together. Such promptings are ubiquitous. Nathaniel Whiting, for instance, asks his readers,

> . . . where the faultes but whisper, use thy pen
> With the *quod non vis* of the Heathen men.
> And if the crimes doe in loud Ecchoes speake
> Thy sponge . . .[42]

The task of correcting faults involves more than the removal of printer's errors: it implies expunging authorial infelicities, extirpating chunks of text. It is a short step from this to, say, Father Sankey, in the mid-seventeenth century, going through a Shakespeare Folio and deleting unacceptable passages.[43] What looks to us like a monstrous assault on the integrity of a master-text belongs to a set of practices which would have been recognized in the period as normal.

An unfamiliar nexus of relations between writing, reading, and editing begins to come into view. It constitutes a field of textual activity very different from that which took shape in the long century (from Coleridge to Pound) which most interests Jerome McGann. Instead of an author producing a text, inflected by publication, which 'calls out' responses to readers, we have materials rendered 'profitable' by the editorial reading-interventions of writers (e.g. Phineas Fletcher's notes to *The Purple Island*), their annotators (e.g. Selden's commentary on Drayton's *Poly-Olbion*), their printers (e.g. the marginal summaries added by Thomas Snodham to *The Rape of Lucrece*), and, of course, individual readers. The reader might take up his pen in response to nothing more exciting than a list of 'Faultes escaped'—the Renaissance equivalent of an errata slip—but one kind of emendation quickly ran into others. Harvey's correction of typographical errors is not readily separable from his inspection of what is being corrected, his glossing it with marginal comments, his production of 'readings' for action.[44] And if commentary is generated by correction,

---

[42] *Le hore di recreatione: Or, The Pleasant History of Albino and Bellama* (1637), A4ᵛ.

[43] For an account of his expurgations see Roland Mushat Frye, *Shakespeare and Christian Doctrine* (Princeton, 1963), 275–93.

[44] For a short guide to books corrected and annotated by Harvey, see Virginia Stern, *Gabriel Harvey: A Study of his Life, Marginalia and Library* (Oxford, 1979), 198–241.

rewriting follows from both. Drayton was right (at least in spirit) when he assured those readers who amended the printer's errors in their copies of *The Muses Elizium* (1630) that 'the Muses themselues . . . shall in their thankefulnesse inspire thee with some Poeticke rapture' (A4ʳ). The level of textual variation in seventeenth-century manuscripts is too high for us not to conclude that what was transcribed was often corrected in the sense of 'improved'. Suckling's 'A Supplement of an imperfect Copy of Verses of Mr. Will. Shakespears, By the Author' provides just one instance of rewriting growing out of editorial activity by a reader. The poem begins with some (reworked) verses from *Lucrece* before rising to the chance provided, at least fictively, by a torn leaf in the poet's copy to attempt Shakespearian pastiche. What Suckling creates is of a piece with what went on when less talented sixteenth- and seventeenth-century gentlemen transcribed verses into commonplace books and miscellanies[45] and rewrote them in the process, transforming other men's flowers through their interests and aptitudes as readers.

Though Suckling's 'Supplement' looks odd to modern eyes, it is highly indicative. The very fact that its opening might derive not from a contemporary edition of *Lucrece* but from a corrupted or 'corrected' slice of the poem printed in the miscellany *Englands Parnassus* (1600)[46] is a reminder of how user-inflected the reception of Shakespeare's poetry was. Recent work on the *Sonnets* has shown that the adaptation of text was widespread once verses got into manuscript. John Benson's repackaging of most of the sonnets, to resemble cavalier-poet epistles, in his *Poems: Written by Wil. Shake-speare* (1640), looks less perverse when we find Sonnet 106, for instance—apparently addressed to a 'lovely youth' in the 1609 quarto—appearing in one manuscript entitled 'On his Mistris Beauty',[47] and, in another, 'conflated with the text of a lyric that is found also, in

---

[45] The study of commonplace books has hardly begun, but see Hilton Kelliher, 'Contemporary Manuscript Extracts from Shakespeare's *Henry IV, Part I*', *English Manuscript Studies 1100–1700*, 1 (1989), 144–81, 'Unrecorded Extracts from Shakespeare, Sidney and Dyer', *English Manuscript Studies 1100–1700*, 2 (1990), 163–87; and Peter Beal, 'Notions in Garrison: The Seventeenth-Century Commonplace Book', in W. Speed Hill (ed.), *New Ways of Looking at Old Texts: Papers of the Renaissance English Text Society, 1985–1991* (Binghamton, NY, 1993), 131–47. On miscellanies and transcription see e.g. Mary Hobbs, *Early Seventeenth-Century Verse Miscellany Manuscripts* (Aldershot, 1992) and Arthur F. Marotti, 'Malleable and Fixed Texts: Manuscript and Printed Miscellanies and the Transmission of Lyric Poetry in the English Renaissance', in Hill (ed.), *New Ways of Looking at Old Texts*, 159–73.

[46] *Sir John Suckling: The Non-Dramatic Works*, ed. Thomas Clayton (Oxford, 1971), 228.

[47] On this text (in a c.1630s miscellany from Saffron Walden) and other sonnet versions in manuscript, see Peter Beal (comp.), *Index of English Literary Manuscripts*, vol. i: *1450–1625* (London, 1980), pt. 2, pp. 449–63.

slightly different form, in the 1660 poetical anthology pretending to be an edition of the poems of Pembroke and Rudyerd'.[48] One reason why modern editors cannot provide a stable text of the *Sonnets* is that Shakespeare, it seems, revised them. But how far do the variants found in manuscript, or in *The Passionate Pilgrime* (1599), derive from editorial rewriting by readers? We can never be sure. Manuscript texts of Sonnet 2 club together closely enough for their divergence from the 1609 quarto to suggest that traces of two 'authorial' versions survive.[49] But to think of only two forms of the sonnet is to diminish the significance of, for instance, the text in St John's College, Cambridge, MS S23, which transcribes (for the most part) the quarto wording of Sonnet 2 but transposes its meanings by transferring it to another medium (script not print), by placing it between poems by Ben Jonson and Thomas Carew (rather than between Sonnets 1 and 3), and by employing a pattern of punctuation which—varied from the quarto—amounts to a 'reading' recorded by the slow-motion of transcription.

All this should make us more aware of the reader in the modern editor. A textual scholar who corrects, amends, and (in his or her own eyes) 'improves' the 1609 version of the *Sonnets* is doing what Shakespeare's contemporaries did: producing a more or less personalized, or personally adaptable, text, out of already mediated textual evidences, not simply 'getting the text right'. Every practising editor is familiar with the experience of drafting commentary—that is, producing readings—as a way of explaining the text to him- or herself, and then reconstructing the exploration by putting together annotation which provides what other readers might need to reach related ends more swiftly. It is through that process of individual but self-consciously communicative reading that corruptions are identified and textual emendations proposed, not (and certainly not primarily) from thoughts about the print-shop, or the physical oddness of a word on a page. Editions of the *Sonnets* differ because they are produced by particular readers, with different thoughts about other readers. This obvious point is repressed in editorial theory, dominated as it is by the legacy of New Bibliography, while McGann and his followers, striving to collectivize audiences and to present 'readings' as functions of the text, have done little to redress the balance.

---

[48] Arthur F. Marotti, 'Shakespeare's Sonnets as Literary Property', in Elizabeth D. Harvey and Katharine Eisaman Maus (eds.), *Soliciting Interpretation: Literary Theory and Seventeenth-Century English Poetry* (Chicago, 1990), 143–73, p. 149.

[49] Cf. Gary Taylor, 'Some Manuscripts of Shakespeare's Sonnets', *Bulletin of the John Rylands Library*, 68 (1985–6), 210–46.

This is not the place in which to explore the consequences of this suppression of the reader. Nor is there room to do more than gesture towards what would follow if editors took reading more seriously. One current reaction to methodological distress, represented by Randall McLeod's advocacy of un- or anti-editing, can, though, be bracketed off. Random Cloud or Clod (as he calls himself) has produced some erudite and stimulating pieces of bibliographical description,[50] but the texts which would trickle down to readers from editors following his principles could only be more or less in facsimile, with all the problems of accessibility which that entails, and with the questions which it begs about the 'already mediated' yet historically deracinating claims of photographic reproduction. Moreover, Randomness has the paradoxical effect of fixing in textual concrete that which it regards as contingent; it fetishizes what a Gregian would regard as incidental by insufficiently respecting the relational qualities of editions. To promote facsimile, in other words, is to Cloud the scene by neglecting the ultimate lack of historical privilege which attaches to a text's being early, or first, or simply in a particular place, in the chronological run of a work's printings, and, not unrelatedly, it is to underestimate the extent to which the uniqueness of a given edition (what makes it part of an unrepeatable, yet variably renewable, literary phenomenon) is a function of reading practices. There is, of course, no way in which a facsimile text can remain faithful to the dispositions of its source while reordering its material to convey to a modern reader how it struck contemporaries. Yet, as should be apparent by now, Renaissance books have the traits which they possess not simply because of authorial or print-shop peculiarities, but because they have certain designs upon, or hopes of interacting with, readers. McLeod's bibliocentrism discounts the extent to which the characteristics of, say, Harington's Ariosto need to be referred to the kinds of reader that the translator had in mind—considerations which led him, to the confusion (at times) of the printer, to enrich his pages with guides to responses.[51]

[50] McLeod's more editorially directed work has mostly related to Shakespeare. See e.g. Randall McLeod, 'Unemending Shakespeare's Sonnet 111', *Studies in English Literature*, 21 (1981), 75–96, 'UN*Editing* Shak-speare', *Sub-Stance*, 33/4 (1982), 26–55, and Random Cloud, 'The Marriage of Good and Bad Quartos', *Shakespeare Quarterly*, 33 (1982), 421–31.

[51] Representatively lively observations by McLeod, taking in Harington's Ariosto (1591), can be found in Random Clod, 'Information on Information', *TEXT*, 5 (1991), 241–81. On the translator's plans for the book, and its readers, see Simon Cauchi, 'The "Setting Foorth" of Harington's Ariosto', *Studies in Bibliography*, 36 (1983), 137–68, esp. pp. 143–5, Judith Lee, 'The English Ariosto: The Elizabethan Poet and the Marvelous', *Studies in Philology*, 80 (1983), 277–99, and

Another, more practical reaction to the breakdown of Gregian approaches, and the difficulties which inhere in McGann's work, might have us move towards modernized editions. Given that past reading-styles can be hard to recover, never mind inhabit, would not more be gained than lost by concentrating on the responses of the present generation of Shakespeare's 'great Variety of Readers', instead of seeking to reconstitute editorially the reading habits of those who bought his *Workes* in 1623?[52] Unfortunately, modernizing is no solution, because so many determinants of the meaning of a text—and thus of its likely textual readings—are timebound that it is impossible to separate the editorial (and any other adequate) reading process from the composition and reception of the text in its historical moment. The scale of the difficulties involved can be gauged by the results. When Stephen Orgel, for instance, is led by the conventions of the Yale Ben Jonson to squeeze the poet's commentary out of the margins of his masques, so that the layout of his 1969 edition can be modernized to match the modernization of his spelling, the result is a massive erasure of attempts to inform and direct reader-responses which are so characteristic of the poet that, without them on the page before us, we are simply not reading Jonson.

A more appealing prospect is offered by the hope of mediating between Renaissance and modern reading experiences. As it happens, this is what Stephen Booth attempted in his valuable edition of *Shakespeare's Sonnets* (1977). Using facing pages, he set a facsimile version of the 1609 quarto opposite a semi-modernized text which compromised between 'the punctuation and spelling of the Quarto text . . . and modern directive spelling and punctuation (which often pays for its clarity by sacrificing a considerable amount of a poem's substance and energy)'.[53] Punctuation is a particularly important and, until recently,[54] under-examined system of cues and interpretative options which helps individuals produce distinctive readings, and there is no doubt that the tactful lightness of Booth's pointing does free his readers from the constraints which tend to be imposed by modernizing editors. But his commentary damages his attempt to 'give a

Evelyn B. Tribble, *Margins and Marginality: The Printed Page in Early Modern England* (Charlottesville, Va., 1993), esp. pp. 92, 95.

52   John Heminge and Henry Condell address this 'great Variety' in the first Folio: 'From the most able, to him that can but spell: There you are numberd' (A3^r).

53   *Shakespeare's Sonnets* (New Haven, 1977), p. ix.

54   See, now, John Lennard, *But I Digress: The Exploitation of Parentheses in English Printed Verse* (Oxford, 1991) and Malcolm Parkes, *Pause and Effect: An Introduction to the History of Punctuation in the West* (Aldershot, 1992).

modern reader as much as I can resurrect of a Renaissance reader's experience of the 1609 quarto',[55] because its polysemic perversity implies that early modern readers, so far from studying for action, or admiring rhetorical schemes, or seeking moral axioms, were post-structuralists eager to find more ambiguities in the text than could be sustained in any conceivable response. Predictably, Booth neglected the manuscript tradition of the *Sonnets*, despite the listing, collating, and printing of texts from miscellanies by such editors as Tucker Brooke (1936) and H. E. Rollins (1944). The diluted historicism of his semi-modernizing policy is bound up with a late-formalist attitude to the text which, when translated into attitudes to reading, would have considerable difficulty in registering the deflection of the reading-experience created by the expectations which Shakespeare's contemporaries carried to poems recorded in script as well as print,[56] and thus to print in a context of script.

Perhaps the best hope for scholarship lies in critical old-spelling editions produced not along Gregian lines but by developing McGann's method of editing in order to bring out the formative role of individual reading acts in the creation of historically specific meanings. The editor of a post-Romantic author, persuaded of the value of such a venture, might be over-provided with the testimony of readers and have to codify rules of relevance. For those working in earlier periods, the problem would more often be that of deciding how to maximize scarce information. A good edition of Gascoigne, for example, would include, in *A Hundreth Sundrie Flowres*, the plays cast out by Prouty as well as the poems and prose. It would give a full, preferably on-the-page representation of the 1575 changes, and link Gascoigne's revisions to reader-responses by pointing up the significance of *The Posies*' three addresses. Recognizing the importance of manuscript circulation, not just as a source of variants but as a means of audience division and enabler of varying responses in individual readers with access to the same texts in both script and print, the edition would notice manuscript recensions of Gascoigne's poems and prose[57] with the same scrupulousness as the 1575 reworkings. The reactions of

---

[55] *Shakespeare's Sonnets*, p. ix.

[56] For a stimulating attempt to characterize such differences in reader assumptions, see Harold Love, *Scribal Punctuation in Seventeenth-Century England* (Oxford, 1993), esp. ch. 4; cf. D. F. McKenzie, 'Speech-Manuscript-Print', *Library Chronicle of the University of Texas at Austin*, 20 (1990), 87–109.

[57] The sources range from poems in unremarkable miscellanies to presentation texts given to Queen Elizabeth (references to her in gilt, pen and ink drawings of Gascoigne handing over his book, etc.). See Beal, *Index of English Literary Manuscripts*, i/2. 99–100.

Puttenham and Harvey would be woven into the commentary, but also be foregrounded in an introduction. Their reading techniques would be compared with those of other Elizabethans, and attention would be paid to Puttenham's apparent tendency to engage in Sucklingesque editing/ rewriting while producing his readings of Gascoigne—not just when announcing improvements but when quoting, as it were, direct.[58] The editor would have to think hard about 'G.T.'s remarks on 'F.I.'s lyrics, and about the curtailment of that editor-in-the-text's observations in *The Posies*, while pondering the role of the marginalia added in the later book. What meanings do these devices facilitate? How did Gascoigne's readers relate text and gloss?[59] To annotate a literary work always requires historical tact—an awareness of what early readers would *not* have understood, as well as what they would.[60] Where modern annotation has to mesh with Renaissance glosses, these difficulties are compounded, both by the need to establish appropriate hierarchies of commentary and by the theoretical and practical problems contingent on deciding where and how to indicate what is obscure, misleading, or false in notes contemporaneous with the text.

The researches involved in preparing such an edition would be at least as contextual as those associated with McGann's seven-volume *Byron*, for they would add to his attention to socio-historical circumstance and the publishing history of works a wide-ranging analysis of Elizabethan attitudes to manuscript, editorial role-playing by writers, and the function of marginal notes. This would mean (life being short) that the editor would need to draw on the not-yet-existing body of 'Historical Reader-Response Criticism' which Robert D. Hume has called for in another context.[61] But then, so integrally connected are editorial constructions and reader responses that criticism of that sort will not be produced until

---

[58] The first six lines of 'A cloud of care . . .', for instance, are given in a form both elegantly accomplished and markedly variant from *Flowres* and *The Posies* (see *Arte*, 188). Manuscript influence is possible, even though Puttenham's quotations generally appear close to the 1575 edition.

[59] For relevant observations see William W. E. Slights, 'The Edifying Margins of Renaissance English Books', *Renaissance Quarterly*, 42 (1989), 682–716, '"Marginall Notes That Spoile the Text": Scriptural Annotation in the English Renaissance', *Huntington Library Quarterly*, 55 (1992), 255–78, and Tribble, *Margins and Marginality*, 68–70.

[60] Cf. Ian Small, 'The Editor as Annotator as Ideal Reader', in Ian Small and Marcus Walsh (eds.), *The Theory and Practice of Text-Editing: Essays in Honour of James T. Boulton* (Cambridge, 1991), 186–209.

[61] 'Texts within Contexts: Notes toward a Historical Method', *Philological Quarterly*, 71 (1992), 69–100, pp. 80 ff.

textual scholars apply their skills to assessing those features of early books which manage readers' reactions. For the sake of their editing, certainly, but also to help complete what McGann has called 'a finished programme of historicist textual criticism',[62] editors should start thinking harder about the practice and representation of reading.

[62] *Beauty of Inflections*, 82.

CHAPTER 7

Astrophil's Tragicomedy (1992)

Few now read *Astrophil and Stella* as (in C. S. Lewis's words) a 'prolonged lyrical meditation'.[1] Wary of Romantic softening we value those elements in the sequence[2] which are most distinctively Tudor: moralistic *libello* in the manner of Turberville; quasi-autobiographical play recalling *The Adventures of Master F.J.*; *progymnasmata* to supplement the *Apology for Poetry*; extended numerological conceit. Yet the historicizing accounts which have done so much to recover *Astrophil and Stella* as an Elizabethan document have left underexplored that most anti-'lyrical' perspective through which the poems first spoke in print. 'Turn aside into this Theater of pleasure', Nashe invited readers in 1591,[3] 'for here you shal find a paper stage streud with pearle, an artificial heau'n to ouershadow the faire frame, & christal wals to encounter your curious eyes, whiles the tragicommody of loue is performed by starlight.' Having built a 'Theater' from Sidney's imagery, Nashe indicates what it contains. 'The chiefe Actor here is *Melpomene*', he writes, 'whose dusky robes, dipt in the ynke of teares, as yet seeme to drop when I view them neere. The argument cruell chastitie, the Prologue hope, the Epilogue dispaire.' So familiar are these phrases that their significance can be missed. Nashe not only highlights the dramatic dimension of Sidney's verse but concedes that, though the sequence is governed by 'dispaire' and the muse of tragedy, its account of 'loue' is tragicomic.

The dramatic component should not be overstated. Attempts to divide the sequence into three, five, or seven 'Acts', with *protasis*, *epitasis*, and *catastrophe* in the manner of the *Old Arcadia*, have not proved persuasive. It seems symptomatic that, while the sonnets contributed to the intense

---

[1] *English Literature in the Sixteenth Century Excluding Drama* (Oxford, 1954), 327.

[2] The word is used throughout in the spirit of Gascoigne, not Rossetti. See e.g. Germaine Warkentin, '"Love's Sweetest Part, Variety": Petrarch and the Curious Frame of the Renaissance Sonnet Sequence', *Renaissance and Reformation*, 11 (1975), 14–23, esp. n. 5.

[3] Preface to *Syr P.S. His Astrophel and Stella*, in *The Works of Thomas Nashe*, ed. Ronald B. McKerrow, rev. F. P. Wilson, 5 vols. (Oxford, 1958), iii. 329.

world of *The Broken Heart*,[4] they could not, as the prose work did, generate plays directly.[5] Yet 'loue' contrives situations in the sonnets as mixed and heightened as those of the 'Terentian'[6] romance. When Musidorus says to the disguised Pyrocles, 'true love hath that excellent nature in it, that it doth transform the very essence of the lover into the thing loved, uniting and, as it were, incorporating it with a secret and inward working', the reader responds with a flush of Neoplatonic enthusiasm before recalling that Pyrocles has indeed been metamorphosed 'into the thing loved' by dressing as a woman and tending to become, as Musidorus scornfully puts it, 'a launder, a distaff-spinner'.[7] Astrophil is similarly elevated then pitched into comic payoffs—by the equestrian vignettes of 41, 49, and 53, for instance, or in the escalatingly droll *gradatio* of Sonnet 1, which has Astrophil, like Pyrocles in miniature, change sex, get pregnant, beat and taunt himself. Even a cycle as Sidneian as *Pamphilia to Amphilanthus* is 'lyrical' by comparison. Lady Wroth begins with a dream vision of Venus' chariot. In place of Astrophil's clowning she gives us a pageant; emotions find emblematic expression in the igniting of lovers' hearts. When a love god enters *Astrophil and Stella* it is as a fighter who shoots to kill (2), equipped with up-to-date macho hardware:

> Flie, fly, my friends, I have my death wound; fly,
> See there that boy, that murthring boy I say,
> Who like a theefe, hid in darke bush doth ly,
> Till bloudie bullet get him wrongfull pray. . . .[8]

Passivity here is of the active, Zutphen kind which, giving no thought to a 'death wound', thinks only of helping others.[9] Epanalepsis and ploce, patterns often 'recited . . . to no purpose' as Puttenham observes,[10] lend

[4] Anne Barton, 'Oxymoron and the Structure of Ford's *The Broken Heart*', *Essays and Studies*, NS 33 (1980), 70–94, p. 93 n. 1.

[5] e.g. Dennis Kay, 'Introduction: Sidney—A Critical Heritage', in Dennis Kay (ed.), *Sir Philip Sidney: An Anthology of Modern Criticism* (Oxford, 1987), 22–3; 'Early Reception and Influence', in *The Countess of Pembroke's Arcadia (The New Arcadia)*, ed. Victor Skretkowicz (Oxford, 1987), pp. xliii–lii.

[6] Robert W. Parker, 'Terentian Structure and Sidney's Original *Arcadia*', *English Literary Renaissance*, 2 (1972), 61–78.

[7] *The Countess of Pembroke's Arcadia (The Old Arcadia)*, ed. Jean Robertson (Oxford, 1973), 20.

[8] *Astrophil and Stella* 20, in *The Poems of Sir Philip Sidney*, ed. William A. Ringler (Oxford, 1962).

[9] Sidney's exemplary conduct, in giving water to a poor soldier when himself fatally wounded, after the battle of Zutphen (1586), is recorded by Fulke Greville—how authoritatively it must be doubted—in his Life of the poet. See *A Dedication to Sir Philip Sidney*, ch. 12, and notes, in *The Prose Works of Fulke Greville, Lord Brooke*, ed. John Gouws (Oxford, 1986).

[10] *The Arte of English Poesie*, ed. Gladys Doidge Willcock and Alice Walker (Cambridge, 1936), 135, 202.

urgency rather than dilate. The deictic 'See there' and performative 'I say',
which might have been flaccid or random, sacrifice depth to earn insistence. Foregrounding the activity of emphasis, they insist on moral conduct (shun Cupid) so vehemently as to seem undidactic. Renaissance
rhetoricians continually urge that persuasion incite virtuous deeds. The
problem for a poet was to make 'well-doing' an 'ending end'[11] without
blunting the ear with truisms. Sonnet 20 relishes the paradox of flight
being 'virtuous action' (*Apology*, 104), and reverses textbook procedures
by making *docere* seem a vehicle of *movere*.

More narrowly based than *Arcadia*, *Astrophil and Stella* can be more intricate in its analysis of 'loue'. Though numerologically minded scholars
seem to have overlooked this, the word recurs an iconic 108 times,[12] while
the emotion plays through poems which shift, treacherously, between
Virtue and Desire. At first Astrophil claims that his love is utterly chaste
(14), but '*Stella's* face' is already 'Queene *Vertue's* court' (9), and, by the
time we reach 68, a hollow couplet (rhymed on a keyword) is able to
equate the pursuit of virtue with desire for Stella: 'what paradise of joy | It
is, so faire a Vertue to enjoy.' 'Loue' becomes such a nexus of semantic
warping that when, in the next, pivotal sonnet, Astrophil claims to have
won Stella, his egotistical *paenismus* 'I, I, ô I may say, that she is mine' is
notoriously impervious to the qualification 'while vertuous course I take'.
The 'Rubarb words' of the sober friend in 14 are shown to be right, and in
what follows 'loue' proves a source of tragic frustration to the lover,
painful comedy to the reader. Astrophil's critical detachment is eroded;
the poems on writing, exercises in self-consciousness and verbal discipline, fade away. As Stella takes fright at his importunities, Astrophil is
left confronting the epilogue described by Nashe, 'dispaire'. Yet 'loue' remains a force for 'tragicommody'. In the last few sonnets, as the noise of
life begins again and Astrophil observes and appraises his situation with
greater clarity, he finds within his heart a bittersweet confusion of feeling.
'So strangely (alas) thy works in me prevaile', he tells Stella in the closing
tercet, 'That in my woes for thee thou art my joy, | And in my joyes for
thee my only annoy.'

[11]   *An Apology for Poetry or The Defence of Poesy*, ed. Geoffrey Shepherd, rev. edn. (Manchester,
1973), 104.
[12]   On the significance of 108, the number of sonnets in the sequence and of Penelope's suitors in *The Odyssey* (Sidney's depiction of Stella was generally taken to be a compliment to Penelope Devereux, wife of Lord Rich), see Alastair Fowler, *Triumphal Forms: Structural Patterns in
Elizabethan Poetry* (Cambridge, 1970), 175–80.

To close readers that rhyme will be familiar, for Sidney uses it twice before. In Sonnet 44, Astrophil records his astonishment at the pleasure which his 'words' give the reciting Stella. He decides

> That when the breath of my complaints doth tuch
> Those daintie dores unto the Court of blisse,
> The heav'nly nature of that place is such,
>   That once come there, the sobs of mine annoyes
>   Are metamorphosd straight to tunes of joyes.

Sonnet 100 reverses this, and Astrophil draws pleasure from Stella's distress:

> Such teares, sighs, plaints, no sorrow is, but joy:
> Or if such heavenly signes must prove annoy,
> All mirth farewell, let me in sorrow live.

It says much for the truth of the sequence that 44 describes plaints we have heard while 100 does not. Astrophil's 'breath' put into Stella's mouth speaks of griefs which are the stuff of the sonnets; her 'teares, sighs, plaints', like 'vertuous course', are matters for report. Children should be seen and not heard, women heard but not allowed to speak. . . . Sidney registers these social pressures in the asymmetrical speech-distribution which characterizes his use of that male form—at this date, in English—the Sonnet, and in doing so gives scope to action. His texts can feature jousts and pratfalls, cultivate a drama of speech acts, because they centre on a persona able to take the initiative. Stella would not figure so compellingly yet elusively were she allowed to speak in the sonnets. Frustration could not generate the comedy it does were the drive towards masculine 'doing' not felt as culturally appropriate. This holds in verbal detail: 'doth tuch' in 44 is characteristic because of the weight rhyme gives 'tuch', bringing Astrophil's speech action home to Stella, and because of the auxiliary's emphasis on action. To consult the paired epistles of Sidney and Penelope Rich in Bodleian MS Eng. Poet f.9 is to find texts which partly correct the sonnets' inequality of utterance,[13] but also works which, in doing so, drain energy from a situation in which Stella registers as Astrophil 'reeds' her. The contretemps over Virtue and Desire is one aspect of a larger disharmony, in which uneven access to language is compounded with active as against half-silenced divergences in the under-

---

[13] 'The Imaginary Epistles of Sir Philip Sidney and Lady Penelope Rich', ed. Josephine Roberts, *English Literary Renaissance*, 15 (1985), 59–77.

standing of complex words like 'loue'. The linguistic incompatibility of Astrophil and Stella's Greek and Latin names is the tip of a divided iceberg, one where the translation of 'annoy' to 'joy' is joined (rhymed in difference) with failures of empathy.

More is invested in the *contraria*. For Sidney was obsessed with the way sorrow represented yields pleasure. The motif is announced in the first lines of his sequence—'That the deare She might take some pleasure of my paine'—and it finds recurrent expression in those poems where Astrophil is his own auditor. In Sonnet 57 he describes how Stella's singing of his love-plaints, 'So sweets my paines, that my paines me rejoyce.' As though aware that to 'reed' her might be to read himself, 58 declares more fully that

> in piercing phrases late,
> Th' anatomy of all my woes I wrate,
> *Stella's* sweete breath the same to me did reed.
> O voice, ô face, maugre my speeche's might,
> Which wooed wo, most ravishing delight
> Even those sad words even in sad me did breed.

From this and other passages it is clear that contrariety is not just dependent on misunderstanding. The Ramist detachment of *elocutio* and *pronunciatio* from logic encouraged Sidney to regard rhetoric as entailing re-presentation. Language, broadcasting matter, was a glass but not a transparency, a thick medium through which the sad passage of life could be transposed into manageable pleasure. From this, for readers, grows the enriching thought that, the further his sonnets travel from topicality before modulating annoy to joy, the more they adumbrate and witness an intensity in the experiences which formed them. The tribute to Penelope Rich is eloquent in indirection. 'Come let me write', the lover says in 34,

> 'And to what end?' To ease
> A burthned hart. 'How can words ease, which are
> The glasses of thy dayly vexing care?'
> Oft cruell fights well pictured forth do please.

One reason why Astrophil feels inextricable from Sidney at this point is that he works material also found in the *Apology*. There the conceit of joyful distress is raised into a literary principle. Invoking authority the poet asserts 'that, as Aristotle saith, those things which in themselves are horrible, as cruel battles, unnatural monsters, are made in poetical imitation delightful' (p. 114).

But then, it is hard to resist the conclusion when reading the *Apology* that, despite the conventional priority given to 'high and excellent Tragedy' (p. 117), the centre of Sidney's imagination is occupied by 'tragicommody'. When the former is discussed an oxymoronic idiom of 'soursweetness' and 'sweet violence' supervenes (pp. 108, 118); when he turns to tragicomedy Sidney combines adulation and possessive stricture. 'Now in his parts, kinds, or species (as you list to term them)', he writes of the poet,

> it is to be noted that some poesies have coupled together two or three kinds, as tragical and comical, whereupon is risen the tragi-comical. Some, in the like manner, have mingled prose and verse, as Sannazzaro and Boethius. Some have mingled matters heroical and pastoral. But that cometh all to one in this question, for, if severed they be good, the conjunction cannot be hurtful. (p. 116)

The argument is so insubstantial that to find William Temple acquiescing in it in his analysis of the *Apology* speaks more of a secretary's loyalty than the logician's rigour.[14] Caviar and treacle tart are 'good' when 'severed', but few would eat them 'together'. 'Severed' pre-emptively assumes unity, and 'cannot be hurtful' is evasively bland. Sidney begins by saying that artists 'couple' kinds to produce tragicomedy, yet ends up calling it a natural 'conjunction'. It begins to look as though his hostility to the Elizabethan stage might be explained in some part by his feeling for unsevered tragicomedy. 'All their plays be neither right tragedies, nor right comedies', he says of 'mongrel tragi-comedy', 'mingling kings and clowns, not because the matter so carrieth it, but thrust in clowns by head and shoulders' (p. 135). The qualification 'not because the matter so carrieth it' deserves more weight than it usually receives, since it reconciles this passage with the earlier, zealous defence of 'mingled matters'. Sidney is not objecting to Cinthio, Guarini, and the like, but is frustrated that English theatre should bungle and cross-breed its way into a travesty of something so central.

Towards the end of 'The first Book or Act' of the *Old Arcadia*, in a sequence which was to help father those dramatic 'mongrels' *Mucedorus* and *The Winter's Tale*, Pyrocles, Musidorus, and their mistresses gather in a glade. 'Round about the meadow', Sidney writes,

> as if it had been to enclose a theatre, grew all such sorts of trees as either excellency of fruit, stateliness of growth, continual greenness, or poetical fancies have made at any time famous. In most part of which trees there had been framed by art such

---

[14] *William Temple's 'Analysis' of Sir Philip Sidney's 'Apology for Poetry'*, ed. and trans. John Webster (Binghamton, NY, 1984), 125.

pleasant arbours that it became a gallery aloft, from one tree to the other, almost round about, which below yielded a perfect shadow, in those hot countries counted a great pleasure. (p. 46)

Hardly have the lovers assembled in this shady scene than a 'monstrous lion' and 'she-bear' burst out of the trees, ravening for blood. The local rustics, intelligently enough, dash for cover; but Sidney's lovers freeze into an exquisite dumb-show of mixed emotions:

There might one have seen at one instant all sorts of passions lively painted out in the young lovers' faces—an extremity of love shining in their eyes; fear for their mistresses; assured hope in their own virtue; anger against the beasts; joy that occasion employed their service; sorrow to see their ladies in agony. (pp. 46–7)

It is a brilliant *pragmatographia*: as 'graphic' as those canvases by Titian and Veronese which Sidney encountered in continental Europe, yet as 'pragmatically' a work of frozen action (i.e., 'praxis') as the tableaux in Euripides' *Hecabe*—that drama admired in the *Apology* and, surely, rendered tragicomic in one of the most tonally volatile episodes of the *New Arcadia*.[15] All the artful traits in the scene, however, are harnessed to a humanist impulse to characterize moral attitudes: love, fear, hope, anger, the desire to undertake service.

Interestingly, Sidney begins the fine Eighth Song of *Astrophil and Stella* in an almost identical way. First the shadowed scene of drama; then a language of gesture, 'lively painted out':

> In a grove most rich of shade,
> Where birds wanton musicke made,
> May then yong his pide weedes showing,
> New perfumed with flowers fresh growing,
>
> *Astrophil* with *Stella* sweete,
> Did for mutuall comfort meete,
> Both within themselves oppressed,
> But each in the other blessed. . . .

The beautiful mutuality of this proceeds to a *synoeciosis* which, in the spirit of *The Winter's Tale* ('their Ioy waded in teares'),[16] crosses each feeling with its opposite:

---

[15] *Apology*, ed. Shepherd, 112, 135; *New Arcadia*, ed. Skretkowicz, 236–41, cf. *Hecabe*, ll. 960 ff.
[16] v. ii. 50–1; quotations from *The First Folio of Shakespeare: The Norton Facsimile*, ed. Charlton Hinman (New York, 1968).

Wept they had, alas the while,
But now teares themselves did smile,
While their eyes by love directed,
Enterchangeably reflected.

Sigh they did, but now betwixt
Sighs of woes were glad sighs mixt,
With armes crost, yet testifying
Restlesse rest, and living dying. . . .

What should be made of these busy features, limbs, and moods? In a well-known discussion of 'The Legible Body', Norman Bryson claims that 'no lexicon of the body exists' before della Porta's *Della fisionomia dell'uomo* and the visual studies of Charles LeBrun—who used Descartes's *Traité sur les passions de l'âme* to establish, in the late seventeenth century, a language of countenance and gesture.[17] Like most accounts of origin this is largely a fiction, because the study of physiognomy went back centuries[18] and was entangled with practices of reading the body derived from classical rhetoric. Every educated reader knew that, when asked '*What was the Chiefe Part of an Oratour?*', Demosthenes 'answered, *Action*; what next? *Action*; what next again? *Action*.'[19] For a gloss we can turn to Thomas Wright's *Passions of the Minde*. 'Action', he says in the 1604 edition,

is either a certaine visible eloquence, or an eloquence of the bodie, or a comely grace in deliuering conceits, or an externall image of an internall mind, or a shaddow of affections, or three springs which flow from one fountaine, called *vox, vultus, vita*, voice, countenance, life . . . (M8ᵛ)

Wright thinks of 'action' as uttering what is within, but knows that it can feign; his mediating term (as often in the period) is the Ciceronian idea that an orator best 'acts' forth a cause which he feels as his own. Accounts of the 'visible eloquence, or . . . eloquence of the bodie' which a passionate speaker would employ, such as John Bulwer's illustrated *Chirologia*, suggest how early readers would have visualized the *Supplico, Admiror, Tristitiam animi signo, Adoro*, and so forth[20] 'lively painted out' in the grove by Sidney.

---

[17] *Word and Image: French Painting of the Ancien Régime* (Cambridge, 1981), ch. 2, p. 55.

[18] Nurtured by the pseudo-Aristotle *Secreta secretorum* (widely translated), it was advanced after the Renaissance by such works as Bartholomaeus Cocles, *Brief and Most Pleasaunt Epitomye of the Whole Art of Phisiognomie* (in English with illustrations from 1556).

[19] Cited by Francis Bacon, 'Of Boldnesse', in *The Essayes or Counsels, Civill and Morall*, ed. Michael Kiernan (Oxford, 1985), 37.

[20] *Chirologia: Or the Naturall Language of the Hand* (1644), 151, 155, 189.

Certainly the song would have been taken as an exercise in 'visible' as well as audible 'eloquence'. Sidney was known as a poet with a keen sense of gesture. Abraham Fraunce's *Arcadian Rhetorike* (1588), which draws repeatedly on his work, is notable among Elizabethan manuals for the attention it pays to posture and projection. Chapters like '*Of the gesture of the head, eyes, lipps, &c.*' and '*Of the gesture of the arme, hand, fingers, &c.*' overlap with Sidneian creativity as much as Bulwer's *Chirologia*. 'Gesture and action', says Fraunce,

is both more excellent and more vniuersall than voyce: as belonging not onelie to those that vse the same speach, but generallie to all people, yea to beasts and senceles creatures, as the verie pictures which being dumme, yet speake by gesture and action. The gesture must followe the change and varietie of the voyce, answering thereunto in euerie respect: yet not parasiticallie as stage plaiers vse, but grauelie and decentlie . . . (17^{v})

This appeal to 'verie pictures' is suggestive in the light of the Arcadian *pragmatographia*; but Fraunce's attack on 'plaiers' is still more striking. Being 'parasitical', they are not only (in the classical sense) lowly and insinuating performers but—prizing open what Cicero secured for Wright—bloodsuckers on the art of action. One recalls Sidney's hatred of Clinias, who 'in his youth . . . had used to be an actor in tragedies (where he had learned, besides a slidingness of language, acquaintance with many passions, and to frame his face to bear the figure of them), long used to the eyes and ears of men' (*New Arcadia*, 288). Here again, antagonism towards the theatre is consistent with, and perhaps fuelled by, a respect for its resources. Sidney approved signifying action if it led to 'well-doing', but feared the power of acting to stir up vice and disorder.

Without doubt, Astrophil's sighs and folded arms in the Eighth Song are stage vocabulary. Jaques's stock 'Louer' is imagined 'Sighing like Furnace' (*As You Like It* II. vii. 147–8), and Moth in *Love's Labour's Lost* advises Armado to pose 'with your armes crost on your thinbellie doublet, like a Rabbet on a spit' (III. i. 17–18). Verbally, too, 'Restlesse rest, and living dying' is tainted by the posturing which Sonnet 6 finds in 'living deaths, deare wounds, faire stormes and freesing fires'. Conceding the suasive force of Astrophil's performance, Sidney hints at doubts which will become urgent at the end of the song. Meanwhile indication and touch figure strongly. Words come late and less than adequately, making way for gesture. When Astrophil attempts to praise Stella, epideictic 'fails' him, faced with 'the legible body':

'*Stella*, in whose body is
Writ each character of blisse,
Whose face all, all beauty passeth,
Save thy mind which yet surpasseth.

'Graunt, ô graunt, but speech alas,
Failes me fearing on to passe . . .'

Deeply influenced by this, Donne in 'The Exstasie' will nevertheless not be short of words when reading the 'booke' of his mistress' 'body'. As Astrophil reads Stella's person, however, her idiom of 'blisse'—what Wright calls 'an eloquence of the bodie'—silences persuasion. Sidney tags his plight with a stage-direction, comically deliberated in its auxiliary 'did', 'Graunt, ô deere, on knees I pray, | (Knees on ground he then did stay) . . .', and leaves the lover to find speech from another quarter than himself. Astrophil appeals to nature, finding a sense in birdsong, an utterance in the rustling of leaves, communication in the mere 'action' of water seeping into the soil. 'And if dumbe things be so witty', he asks (like Fraunce on gesture), 'Shall a heavenly grace want pitty?' Inevitably Astrophil turns to touch, the natural 'action' of lovers and a forcibly expressive sign-language:

There his hands in their speech, faine
Would have made tongue's language plaine;
But her hands his hands repelling,
Gave repulse all grace excelling. . . .

The most decisive exchange in this poem—if not the entire collection—is uttered by gesture. To adumbrate the touching moment, feminine endings fumble and pleonasm works with an initial trochee ('her hands his hands repelling, | Gave repulse') to impress the feel of awkwardness. When Stella's reply comes, it retains the tactile quality of Astrophil's silent speech: 'Then she spake; her speech was such, | As not eares but hart did tuch . . .' Her 'tuch' stirs Astrophil deeply as she alludes to unfeignable action:

'Trust me while I thee deny,
In my selfe the smart I try,
Tyran honour doth thus use thee,
Stella's selfe might not refuse thee.

'Therefore, Deere, this no more move,
Least, though I leave not thy love,
Which too deep in me is framed,
I should blush when thou art named.'

Stella fears that love's most dramatic yet least dissemblable act, blushing, will declare the heart, and on this the lovers separate:

> Therewithall away she went,
> Leaving him so passion rent,
> With what she had done and spoken,
> That therewith my song is broken.

After 103 lines of third-person narration, 'him' becomes 'my' and a new perspective opens. Is this the usual fluctuating Astrophilip or does the shift serve to indicate Sidney's judgemental aloofness? A moralistic view[21] would hold that we have been swayed by the art of a Clinias. The song is 'broken' for Astrophil because Stella resists his adulterous performance, and for us because we are 'surprised by sin' in the Edenic grove, jolted back to a larger context by the final line. Yet the 'him . . . my' change would not be so compelling were it not fraught with recognition that being in love puts you beside yourself. Acting can be a means of survival under stress, until the inwardly hinged relation between 'him' and 'my' flaps wide in a gust of passion. Recall 'The Third Eclogues', where lovesick Philisides (another Philip) 'began to utter that wherewith his thoughts were then (as always) most busied; and to show what a stranger he was to himself spake of himself as of a third person'.[22] Sidney both insists that we recognize the virtue of what Stella has 'done and spoken' and implicitly underwrites the occasion with feelings too violent for a first-person voice to cope with.

When Lamb, intentionally or not, echoed the stagy 'Knees on ground' stanza in his judgement of Astrophil's sonnets—'Time and place appropriates every one of them'[23]—his critical instincts were just. The specificity and actualness of the song recur in those traits of sonnet style by which Sidney cultivates 'tragicommody'. Contemporary poets, he famously complained, wrote 'coldly', as though drawing on other 'lovers' writings': they lacked 'that same forcibleness or *energia* (as the Greeks call it) of the writer' (*Apology*, 137–8). His account of mid-Tudor poetry is polemically bleak, but it is not difficult to find texts which support his diagnosis. Thomas Watson's *Hekatompathia*, the first long sequence of love sonnets in English, was going through the press as Sidney wrote *Astrophil and Stella*. Far from concealing dependence, Watson embroiders his text

---

[21] See, most notably, Thomas Roche, Jr., '*Astrophil and Stella*: A Radical Reading', *Spenser Studies*, 3 (1982), 139–91.

[22] *Old Arcadia*, ed. Robertson, 254, crit. app.

[23] '*Essays of Elia*' and '*Last Essays of Elia*', introd. Geoffrey Tillotson (London, 1962), 254; cf. Eighth Song, l. 52.

with notes which boast his reliance on others. A 'passion of loue' like *Hekatompathia* VII is not just 'parasiticallie' written, but boasts its Clinias-like servility by embracing the description 'ἄινη παρασιτική'.[24] Sidney seems to have parodied the poem in advance even of perusing it, in the mock-blazon of Mopsa 'What length of verse can serve . . .?'[25] When Watson's 'passion' is read, it contrives an audible or tacitly heard shape little different from that of the lines on the page because syntax and form chime with such regularity. His poems aspire towards the concrete figuring which *Hekatompathia* LXXXI, '*A Pasquine Piller erected in the despite of Loue*', displays. The look of an Astrophil text, by contrast, diverges from the shape it utters. Admittedly, Sidney's best-known sonnet, 'My true love hath my hart . . .', is one of the most poised and mellifluous of Elizabethan lyrics. But that is part of its point: the neat quatrains and couplet are meant to seem faintly factitious. Musidorus composes it in the *Old Arcadia* to persuade Miso that her spouse (its supposed author) is being unfaithful, the idea being that when she runs off to find the miscreant he will be left with Pamela (pp. 190–1). It seems appropriate that when the text is quoted by Puttenham[26] it should have lost its residual sonnet asymmetry to become an example of '*versus intercalaris*'. Unforcible, lacking the intellectual pressure of what Astrophil calls 'inward tuch' (15), the sonnet had been tidied by 1589 into a quatrain song with refrain.

Among the dislocations involved in reading an Astrophil sonnet, sudden changes of pronoun (as between 'him' and 'my') are probably the most telling. In Sonnet 74, for example, Sidney makes play with 'lovers' writings', following Persius, du Bellay, and Ronsard to declare that Astrophil is no poet at all. But a poem which begins, 'I never dranke of *Aganippe* well' suddenly turns plural: 'Guesse we the cause: "What, is it thus?" Fie no: | "Or so?" Much lesse: "How then?" . . .' The sequence has featured crowds earlier, to witness jousting or fill out the court. But where does that 'we' come from? Astrophil cannot talk to himself without imagining an interlocutor—a whole audience of them. As it fractures into abrupt jostling dialogue, scarcely contained by line and rhyme, his poem becomes a theatre for speech. 'Sonnet' derives from *suono*, 'sound': Sidney writes a form which, by virtue of its ability to generate and contain competing sound-patterns, can dramatize the very 'action' of the voice. Hence

[24] *The Hekatompathia or Passionate Centurie of Loue* (1582), A4^r.
[25] Cf. Shakespeare, *Sonnets and A Lover's Complaint*, ed. John Kerrigan (Harmondsworth, 1986), 19–21.
[26] *Arte of English Poesie*, ed. Willcock and Walker, 225.

the celebrated Sonnet 47, which starts with decorous *ratiocinatio*, 'What, have I thus betrayed my libertie? | Can those blacke beames such burning markes engrave | In my free side? . . .', but ends in dramatic irregularity (a shift measured between 'blacke beames' and the bare specific 'that eye'):

> Vertue awake, Beautie but beautie is,
> I may, I must, I can, I will, I do
> Leave following that, which it is gaine to misse.
> Let her go. Soft, but here she comes. Go to,
> Unkind, I love you not: O me, that eye
> Doth make my heart give to my tongue the lie.

The conscience-stirring figures of the octave seem vain when contrasted with the syntactical impact of Stella's entry. While Astrophil's octave prompts 'well-doing' by means of persuasion, the sestet shows desire, his 'old companion' (72), stirring the will. The poem devolves towards what has seemed to some a weak link in Elizabethan theories of rhetoric, a weakness which would have struck Sidney as that of human nature: 'The crucial intermediary between hearing and doing is willing,' writes Brian Vickers, 'and it is no accident that a new stress on the will and voluntaristic psychology accompanied the revival of rhetoric.'[27] Sidney does not flinch from enacting the difficulty of *flectere* and *movere*, of stirring to good, and in doing so creates a drama of Will which is his least noticed but most interesting legacy to Shakespeare's *Sonnets*.[28]

Vickers adds, of Renaissance commentators: 'Any power ascribed to rhetoric was automatically transferred to poetry.' Sidney is no exception to this rule, yet 47 shows a tendency to pitch speech-patterns against form in ways which give the modern debased sense of 'rhetoric' some relevance. The poet's hostility to embellishment for its own sake can be traced through his various anti-Ciceronian statements, and underlies his claim in *An Apology* that versing does not make a poet (p. 103). Sidney transcends his time more successfully than most sonneteers because he risks greater variety within the form—the *gravitas* of kings and mirth of clowns—than would be possible were each line an end in itself. Even the octave of 47 has the felt irregularity of a lover trying to be Watson and not succeeding: the move from line 1's pentameter question, to one which

---

[27] 'Rhetoric and Poetics', in Charles B. Schmitt (gen. ed.), *The Cambridge History of Renaissance Philosophy* (Cambridge, 1988), 715–45, p. 736.

[28] The quibbling sonnets on Shakespeare's Christian name, 135–6, flag an issue variously engaged in his sequence and in the long poem, *A Lover's Complaint*, that follows it in the first (1609) edition.

urgently enjambs ('Can those blacke beames . . . free side?'), sets up a pattern of syncopation sustained until the sestet. Equally characteristic is the way Sidney's couplet eschews the consolation of sententious rhyme. His endings are generally unlike those of (for instance) Wyatt as translator, whose couplet closure of Petrarchan rhyme schemes implies a stoic control denied by the drift of argument (above, p. 32). What rhyme delivers in Sonnet 47, syntax takes away. The impetuous run-on from line 13 unbalances the couplet, and, in so far as the mind can grapple back from 'lie' to 'eye', it discovers only the source of Astrophil's self-betrayal. 'O me, that eye I Doth make my heart give to my tongue the lie.' The lover is left in a state of despairing self-division, and the reader in pitying amusement since the predicament is half-comic. An older line comes to mind: 'My tongue (γλῶσσα) spoke it, not my heart (Φρήν).' This, from the *Hippolytos* (612), was Euripides' most widely quoted verse in the ancient world. It was felt to show, with particular clarity, the dramatist's sophistic yet convincing sense of tragic inner life, the discrepancy between show and feeling. Yet the same words, taken by Aristophanes and given to Dionysus in *The Frogs* (1467–71), are irresistibly comic. Why do you promise me the prize yet deny it me now?, Euripides asks. 'Our old friendship! you can't go back on an oath!' To which Dionysus replies: 'My tongue swore it . . .' It is in this company—among dramatists, but allied to both tragedy and comedy—that Astrophilip, like Astrophil, belongs.

CHAPTER 8

William Drummond and the British Problem

When James VI left Scotland to assume the English throne in 1603, he promised to return to his native land every three years. In the event, it was not until 1617 that time, inclination, and money (most of it borrowed) made a visit possible. For the Scots this was an important event. The honour of the country required a display of hospitality that would persuade the often patronizing English in the entourage that Scotland offered more than 'fowle linen, fowle dishes and potts'.[1] It is also evident, however, that honour required an assertion of national self-esteem which did not comfortably fit the policy of British unity that the King had promoted in England. James was hardly across the border before he was reminded in a Latin oration that the Scots had never been conquered, by the Britons, Saxons, Picts, Danes, Normans, or Romans. In Edinburgh, he was praised for appointing responsible officers to act in his absence. But at Paisley he was welcomed to the home-parish of the patriot William Wallace, 'that worthie warrier, to whome, under God, wee owe that you ar ours, and Britanne yours', and treated to an Ovidian fable which cast him as a sun god who had abandoned his first love, Clytia or Scotland, in favour of Leucothoe, England. Though the orator conceded that this triangle could be resolved by the two ladies becoming wholly one, he ended his speech with an image of the rejected Clytia gazing after Phoebus' chariot until she turned into a heliotrope.[2]

The finest literary work produced for this visit, William Drummond's long poem *Forth Feasting*, is less aggressively ambivalent about the union.

This essay was researched and written during my tenure of a British Academy Research Readership, 1998–2000.

[1] Sir Anthony Weldon, 'A Description of Scotland', in John Nichols (ed.), *The Progresses, Processions, and Magnificent Festivities of King James the First*, 4 vols. (London, 1828), iii. 338–43, p. 338.

[2] Nichols (ed.), *Progresses*, iii. 302, 321–2, 383–5.

Even so, as soon as the King began to read the copy presented to him,[3] he will have noticed problems:

> What blustring Noise now interrupts my Sleepe?
> What echoing Shouts thus cleaue my chrystal Deep?
> And call mee hence from out my watrie Court?
> What Melodie, what Sounds of Ioy and Sport,
> Bee these heere hurl'd from eu'rie neighbour Spring?[4]

Ideologically the River Forth is perfectly attuned to the visit. She has a court not a parliament, and raises no puritanical objections to the pleasures of sport. After fourteen years of neglect, however, she finds it hard to recognize the King's 'glittring' train (9). Once she realizes that a progress is afoot, the Forth summons the rivers of Scotland. But regret at James's absence looms larger than the occasion requires. While he was away, we are told, the fields were cursed with frost and the kingdom became as dull as a portrait stripped of colours. To point the contrast, Drummond recalls the years before 1603 when James ruled only in Scotland. Praising his abilities as huntsman, philosopher-king, and poet, he mounts a celebration of the Scottish Renaissance of the 1580s and 1590s that qualifies the panegyric which follows on James's pacification of Britain as a whole.

When Ben Jonson paid his celebrated visit to Drummond at Hawthornden, his country house just south of Edinburgh, a few months after James's progress, he said 'that he wished to please the King, that piece of Forth-Feasting had been his owne'.[5] Like other remarks in the 'Conversations with Drummond', this is potentially misleading. We know from the draft of a letter preserved in the Hawthornden Manuscripts that the poem did not entirely 'please the King'. Objecting to the Forth's declaration, 'No Guard so sure as Loue vnto a Crowne' (246), James 'argued that it is better to gouerne a people by feare than by loue'. This has been interpreted as a passing disagreement about a maxim,[6] but the King surely recognized that in context Drummond's line stirred the thought that a

---

[3] A text was presented at Seton, home of the Earl of Winton, on 15 May 1617 (ibid. 306–7); published in quarto by Andro Hart (Edinburgh, 1617), with an equestrian engraving of the King, the poem quickly reappeared in John Adamson's *Τα των μουσων εισοδια: The Muses Welcome* (Edinburgh, 1618).

[4] Lines 1–5, quoting from the text in *The Poetical Works of William Drummond of Hawthornden*, ed. L. E. Kastner, 2 vols. (Edinburgh, 1913), i. 141–53.

[5] 'Ben Jonson's Conversations with William Drummond of Hawthornden' (more correctly, 'Informations be Ben Johnston to W.D. when he came to Scotland upon foot') in *Ben Jonson*, ed. C. H. Herford, Percy and Evelyn Simpson, 11 vols. (Oxford, 1925–52), i. 132–51, p. 135.

[6] Robert H. MacDonald, 'A Disputed Maxim of State in "Forth Feasting" (1619)', *Journal of the History of Ideas*, 32 (1971), 295–8, from which I quote Drummond's draft letter.

monarch hardly known to his people could not easily be loved and was the less secure. When *Forth Feasting* heightens the value of the King by emphasizing Scotland's grief at his absence, it makes that absence seem unfortunate; and the more it compensates by extrapolating James's success as a Scottish king into his achievements after 1603, the more his northern kingdom seems to be lost in a British polity.

In his *Schort Treatise, Conteining Some Reulis and Cautelis to be Obseruit and Eschewit in Scottis Poesie* (1584), James had advised the poets of his Castalian circle to 'be warre with composing ony thing in the same maner as hes bene ower oft vsit of before'.[7] In this respect at least, *Forth Feasting* should have pleased him, because it diverges so sharply from the conventions of welcome-poetry.[8] It was traditional to give some account of the sufferings of the welcomer during the absence of the arrivee. Drummond so emphasizes the cost of union, however, that his panegyric edges into elegy.[9] As innovative are the turns that come when the Forth urges James to remain in Scotland. At first, the attractions of the country are partly attributed to the King, whose presence is said to make the woods and silver brooks more alluring. But the verse then shifts uneasily between the suggestion that, secure in its liberty behind high mountains, the country does not need the King to protect it, and the hope that, because it is so full of attractions (especially animals for hunting), it can entice him to stay.

In a self-consciously climactic passage, Drummond describes what seagoing Scots and the poet himself can provide by way of enticement:

> The *Tritons*, Heards-men of the glassie Field,
> Shall giue Thee what farre-distant Shores can yeeld,
> The *Serean* Fleeces, *Erythrean* Gemmes,
> Vaste *Platas* Siluer, Gold of *Peru* Streames,
> Antarticke Parrots, *Aethiopian* Plumes,
> *Sabæan* Odours, Myrrhe, and sweet Perfumes:
> And I my selfe, wrapt in a watchet Gowne,
> Of Reedes and Lillies on mine Head a Crowne,
> Shall Incense to Thee burne, greene Altars raise,
> And yearly sing due *Pæans* to Thy Praise. (373–82)

---

7 G. Gregory Smith (ed.), *Elizabethan Critical Essays*, 2 vols. (1904; London, 1950), i. 208–25, p. 220.

8 On these rules see e.g. Francis Cairns, *Generic Composition in Greek and Roman Poetry* (Edinburgh, 1972), 16–31, J. W. Binns, *Intellectual Culture in Elizabethan and Jacobean England: The Latin Writings of the Age* (Leeds, 1990), 70, 73–4.

9 Cf. Robert Cummings, 'Drummond's *Forth Feasting*: A Panegyric for King James in Scotland', *Seventeenth Century*, 2 (1987), 1–18, esp. pp. 7–12.

Those unlikely sounding 'Antarticke Parrots' are ornithologically correct because the adjective (as in Latin *antarcticus*) can mean 'southern' as well as 'south polar',[10] but the choiceness of the epithet adds to an impression of misplaced indulgence. The King who warned against the use of trisyllables at the start of verse lines[11] could only be discomfited to find 'Antarticke Parrots' followed by '*Sabæan* Odours'. Not just the Forth but the poet runs to excess in his desire to get James to stay; the verse escalates from persuasion to the promise of lavish bribes.

It is a measure of Drummond's sophistication that he should build into the passage an ebbing sense of conviction. The accumulating polysyllables ring emptily with an awareness that Scotland can offer no gifts that will work, and the imagined revival in Scottish poetry is circumscribed by isolation. The poem finally abandons the conventions of prosphoneticon when it moves from arguing against departure to accepting its inevitability. The Thames has more wealth to offer the King than the Forth, and all the poet can plead is that James should

> Loathe not to thinke on Thy much-louing FORTH:
> O loue these Bounds, whereof Thy royall Stemme
> More then an hundreth wore a Diademe. (398–400)

It is indeed a strange welcome. When the Forth roused the rivers of Scotland, she included the '*Tweed* which no more our Kingdomes shall deuide' (60). Now the bounds are reinstated, and the Forth fears that the King will be reluctant even to remember her, despite a line of Scottish ancestors running back (in the traditional genealogy) to Fergus I.

These tensions are typical of Drummond, whose work was conditioned by the relative isolation of Scotland within a culturally conflicted regal union. At first, those circumstances attracted him to *otium* and *contemptus mundi*, and his work showed the often felicitous self-involvement of an art practised in solitude. During the 1630s and 1640s, however, as Scotland triggered and was swept into the political and military crises that afflicted all three Stuart kingdoms[12]—crises that were at least compounded by what historians call 'the British problem'[13]—his work became more engaged and polemical. Like a number of early modern

---

[10] *OED a.* and *sb.* 1.   [11] *Ane Schort Treatise*, 212–13.

[12] The best accounts are Peter Donald, *An Uncounselled King: Charles I and the Scottish Troubles, 1637–1641* (Cambridge, 1990) and Mark Charles Fissell, *The Bishops' Wars: Charles I's Campaigns against Scotland, 1638–1640* (Cambridge, 1994).

[13] See e.g. Steven G. Ellis and Sarah Barber (eds.), *Conquest and Union: Fashioning a British State, 1485–1725* (London, 1995), Brendan Bradshaw and John Morrill (eds.), *The British Problem, c.1534–1707: State Formation in the Atlantic Archipelago* (Basingstoke, 1996).

writers based in Wales, Scotland, and Ireland (such as Henry Vaughan, Iain Lom, and the Earl of Orrery) he developed in ways that are hard to make sense of without reference to the multi-faceted 'problem' that centred on the difficulty of governing a multiple monarchy.

It is true that Drummond's verse has recently found prestigious admirers capable of looking beyond the timeless, lyrical poet constructed by Palgrave's *Golden Treasury*,[14] but his œuvre remains neglected on the one hand because its British traits can make it appear too 'English' to satisfy nationalistic depictions of Scottish literature[15] and on the other because our still Anglocentric maps of cultural history tend to make it seem peripheral and anachronistic. His early verse has been misconstrued as a hang-over from Elizabethan Petrarchism, and his later, often pungent verse satires and prose tracts remain obscure to readers who might know about the English civil wars but who lack the necessary grounding in Scottish and more largely Three-Kingdoms history. It is the contention of this essay that, once his British contexts are understood, Drummond emerges as a more complex and pressured figure than has been realized, and as a grossly undervalued writer.

James did not leave a desert when he went south. Scotland kept its law courts, major universities, a Privy Council, a functioning Parliament. The nobility sustained a network of country houses, and exercised considerable patronage.[16] In any case, Drummond's estrangement from the royal milieu was qualified. His uncle, the poet William Fowler, secretary to Queen Anne, went to London, with other Scots, in 1603, and Drummond apparently stayed with him three years later, when he witnessed the celebrations that surrounded a visit by the King of Denmark. His first published poem, an elegy on the death of Prince Henry, appeared or was reprinted in the pan-British and Irish collection *Mausoleum* (1613). He may not have been employed at court, but he corresponded with and entertained such Scottish writers as Sir Robert Kerr of Ancram, who

---

[14] See Edwin Morgan, 'How Good a Poet is Drummond?', *Scottish Literary Journal*, 15/1 (May 1988), 14–24, the inclusion of twenty-seven items in Alastair Fowler (ed.), *The New Oxford Book of Seventeenth Century Verse* (Oxford, 1991), and Karl Miller, *Rebecca's Vest: A Memoir* (London, 1993), ch. 6.

[15] Against these misunderstandings see R. D. S. Jack, in the 'Introduction' to R. D. S. Jack and P. A. T. Rozendaal (eds.), *The Mercat Anthology of Early Scottish Literature 1375–1707* (Edinburgh, 1997), pp. vii–xxxix, pp. vii–xi.

[16] Keith Brown, 'Scottish Identity in the Seventeenth Century', in Brendan Bradshaw and Peter Roberts (eds.), *British Consciousness and Identity: The Making of Britain, 1533–1707* (Cambridge, 1998), 236–58, pp. 253–4.

enjoyed a post in King James's Bedchamber, and Sir William Alexander of Menstrie, who rose through the households of Prince Henry and Charles I, and who helped Drummond network with English poets. The lists of 'Bookes red be me' that survive among his papers, and the contents of his extensive library, show that his literary world was at least as full as that of any courtier;[17] and a patent from 1627, which allowed him to develop ingenious weapons of war, not to mention a machine for creating perpetual motion,[18] indicates that, like royalist gentlemen elsewhere in Britain, he was curious about science, and wanted to be a virtuoso.

This is not to say that his culture was homogenized to a new British ideal. Jonson told him that his verses 'were not after the Fancie of ye tyme'[19] because his literary tastes (including his passion for the sonnet) appeared out-of-date to a Jacobean Londoner; but Drummond's grounding in the Scottish Renaissance[20] led him to look to continental Europe for models—advancing beyond Ronsard and du Bartas to the fashionable Guarini and Marino.[21] In this as in other respects, the polyglot, often highly imitative Drummond[22] can be seen as the beneficiary of the internationalism of earlier Scottish poetry.[23] When he writes,

> Slide soft faire FORTH, and make a christall Plaine,
> Cut your white Lockes, and on your foamie Face
> Let not a Wrinckle bee, when you embrace
> The Boat that *Earths Perfections* doth containe.[24]

readers are meant to remember Sidney's Stella on the Thames, and Tasso's mistress on the River Po, placing the Forth among the centres of European literature.

---

[17] Robert H. MacDonald, *The Library of Drummond of Hawthornden* (Edinburgh, 1971), 228–32, 149–228.

[18] Translated from Latin in what remains the fullest biographical source, David Masson, *Drummond of Hawthornden: The Story of his Life and Writings* (1873; New York, 1969), 156–61.

[19] 'Conversations', 135.

[20] See Ronald D. S. Jack, 'Drummond of Hawthornden: The Major Scottish Sources', *Studies in Scottish Literature*, 6 (1968–9), 36–46 and *William Drummond of Hawthornden: Poems and Prose*, ed. Robert H. MacDonald (Edinburgh, 1976), p. xix.

[21] R. D. S. Jack, *The Italian Influence on Scottish Literature* (Edinburgh, 1972), ch. 4, esp. pp. 113–44.

[22] He read, translated, and imitated Latin, Italian, French, and Spanish poetry, praised Alexander in French, and in Latin composed an elegy on King James and an eight-line poem to Drayton.

[23] On the Three-Kingdom personnel and linguistic pluralism of James's court poets see e.g. Helena Mennie Shire, *Song, Dance and Poetry of the Court of Scotland under King James VI* (Cambridge, 1969).

[24] *Poetical Works of Drummond*, i. 35.

So the localism of Drummond, who was described by his contemporaries as a swan singing on the banks of the Esk, a Grampian shepherd,[25] was by no means naively provincial. Like his correspondent Drayton he relished writing about places unexplored in verse, and he composed commendatory poems and epitaphs for Scots unknown beyond their country.[26] But when he announces in a sonnet, 'Thrise happie hee, who by some shadie Groue, | Farre from the clamarous World doth liue his owne' and says that rustic birdsong is sweeter than 'smoothe Whisp'rings neare a Princes Throne', the lines are loosely translated from the latest Italian poetry,[27] they have classical roots in Horace, and they are sustained by familiarity with the courtly life they reject. They are engaged in a dialogue that becomes explicit when Kerr of Ancram sends Drummond his own '*Sonnet* in praise of a Solitary Life' written from that storm centre of the politics of regal union, '*the very Bed-chamber* [of King James], *where I could not Sleep*'.[28]

It is clear, however, that Drummond's highly sophisticated acceptance of obscurity[29] was mixed with real frustration at life in a country that was geographically remote and so small that it encouraged envy among its inhabitants at those who achieved excellence. With the neglect of the Scottish humanist George Buchanan in mind, he writes, 'Alas! . . . What can we perform in this remote part of the earth . . . Many noble pieces of our countrymen are drowned in oblivion περσκοτιαν Scotorum.'[30] In some of his strongest poems, the possibility of retirement as a rewarding alternative to court fails to alleviate isolation. The poet is not a wild bird warbling in the forest[31] but a voice crying in the wilderness—as in his sonnet on St John the Baptist:

[25] *Poetical Works of Drummond*, i., pp. ci, cx.

[26] See esp. 'Commendatory Verses' and 'Posthumous Poems', ibid., vol. ii.

[27] Ibid. i. 90, 224–5.

[28] Quoted in *The Works of William Drummond of Hawthornden* (Edinburgh, 1711), 152–3; on the contentiously Scottish composition of the Bedchamber see Neil Cuddy, 'The Revival of the Entourage: The Bedchamber of James I, 1603–1625', in David Starkey et al., *The English Court: From the Wars of the Roses to the Civil War* (London, 1987), 173–225, esp. pp. 177, 185–204, and 'Anglo-Scottish Union and the Court of James I, 1603–1625', *Transactions of the Royal Historical Society*, 5th ser. 39 (1989), 107–24, pp. 110–11, 120–3.

[29] e.g. XXVI 'A dedication of som[e] poems to Cra[i]gmiller', XXVIII, in Eloisa Paganelli, 'Lettere e note inedite di William Drummond of Hawthornden', *English Miscellany* (Rome), 19 (1968), 295–333, pp. 328–9.

[30] Masson, *Drummond*, 34–5.

[31] See his letter to William, Earl of Morton, sending madrigals, in *Works of Drummond*, 156 ('yet know I, that sometimes, to the most delicate Ear, the Warblings of the Wild Birds in the Solitary Forrests, are wont to be as delightful as the Artificial Notes of the learned Popingayes in the Guilt Cages').

The last and greatest Herauld of Heauens King,
Girt with rough Skinnes, hyes to the Desarts wilde,
Among that sauage brood the Woods foorth bring,
Which hee than Man more harmlesse found and milde:
His food was Blossomes, and what yong doth spring,
With Honey that from virgine Hiues distil'd;
Parcht Bodie, hollow Eyes, some vncouth thing
Made him appeare, long since from Earth exilde.
There burst hee foorth; All yee whose Hopes relye
On GOD, with mee amidst these Desarts mourne,
Repent, repent, and from olde errours turne.
Who listned to his voyce, obey'd his crye?
    Onelie the Ecchoes which hee made relent,
    Rung from their Marble Caues, repent, repent.[32]

In this finely wrought poem, almost Miltonic in the intensity it contrives from syntactical foldings and suspensions, flight from society brings suffering, and the saint gets no response to his virtuous message, except that wrung (the pun is expressive) from stones, from the marble of caves that mockingly empty the keyword of the sonnet into echoes.

The relationship between these feelings of provincial isolation and national sentiment in a British context can be tracked through Drummond's dealings with English poets. Alert to their interest in their own country, he was sensitive to possible slights to his own. His very first note on Jonson's table-talk, for instance, says 'that he had ane jntention to perfect ane Epick Poeme jntitled Heroologia of the Worthies of his [*or* this] Country, rowsed by fame, and was to dedicate it to his Country'—which by its variant alone educes the British problem[33]—and he recorded his dislike of the way his visitor 'thinketh nothing well bot what either he himself, or some of his friends and Countrymen hath said or done'.[34] His approval of *Poly-Olbion* was heightened by Drayton's plan to extend its range beyond England and Wales, and when Drayton died he asked Alexander to acquire 'those fragmentes . . . of his Worke which concerne Scotland' so as to 'endevour to put them in this country to the presse . . .

---

[32] *Poetical Works of Drummond*, ii. 12.

[33] 'Conversations', 132. Modern editions of this text are based on a transcript of Drummond's lost holograph made by Sir Robert Sibbald (1641–1722) collated with the reduced version published in the 1711 *Works of Drummond*. Rarely following 1711, the Oxford *Ben Jonson* prefers its 'his' over MS 'this' at this point, making Jonson's plans seem memorable to Drummond because consistently English-patriotic rather than, as 'this' would suggest, King-James-pleasingly Anglo-Scots with a provokingly insisted-upon dedication to England.

[34] 'Conversations', 151.

with the best remembrances his love to this countrey did deserve'.[35] But even Drayton could stir resentment: 'I find in him, which is in most part of my Compatriots, too great an Admiration of their Country; on the History of which, whilst they muse, as wondering, they forget sometimes to be good Poets.'[36] In other words, Drayton's chauvinism led him to forget his Aristotle and to weaken poetry by elevating history. But 'my Compatriots' is at odds with 'their Country'. Was Drayton a fellow-Briton or an alien Englishmen?

For English writers the trappings of a British identity could be acquired by, for instance, claiming Scottish ancestry, as Jonson did shortly after 1603, by accepting patronage and lodging from highly placed Scots, which he also did, and, come to that, by walking to Scotland to gather materials for a poem about the country and a piscatory or pastoral play set in Loch Lomond—schemes which Jonson was careful to outline to King James on his return to London.[37] The situation was rather different for Scottish poets at Whitehall: not just Kerr of Ancram and Sir William Alexander but Sir Robert Ayton, who succeeded Fowler as private secretary to the Queen, Sir David Murray, and others. They were entering a country large and powerful enough to dictate the terms of union, at a time when English nationalism (already practised in Scotophobia) was stirred by threats from Counter-Reformation Europe. Later history has also been against them, since any refashioning of their Scottishness designed to cope with the new situation has been interpreted as a culpable dilution of identity at a moment when Scotland (with hindsight) began to relinquish its independence.

Scottish nationalists might think it the more deplorable that the court poets who went south anticipated the long-term loss that Scotland would suffer. Writing in that mood in 1603, Ayton asked the Tweed to carry James's 'last farewell' to his native kingdom 'To that Religious place whose stately walls | Does keepe the heart which all our hearts inthralls'—that is, to Melrose Abbey, where the heart of Robert Bruce was buried.[38] Yet it is possible to read this elegiac sonnet as signalling, in its obscure-to-out-

[35] Bernard H. Newdigate, *Michael Drayton and his Circle* (Oxford, 1961), 162, 189.

[36] 'Character of Several Authors' (prob. 1613–16), in *Works of Drummond*, 226–7, p. 227.

[37] David Riggs, *Ben Jonson: A Life* (Cambridge, Mass., 1989), 115–16, 125–6; 'Conversations', 143; letter of Jonson to Drummond (10 May 1619), quoted in Masson, *Drummond*, 109. For a contemporaneous and equally celebrated walking tour see John Taylor, *The Pennyles Pilgrimage: Or, The Moneylesse Perambulation* (London, 1618).

[38] '[Sonnet: On the River Tweed]', *The English and Latin Poems of Sir Robert Aytoun*, ed. Charles B. Gullans (Edinburgh, 1963), 167.

siders allusion, Ayton's attachment to an identity that he would preserve. For the careers of the court poets do fit the general picture that Keith M. Brown has established for the early seventeenth-century Scottish nobility. Although they sometimes married English wives, and became involved in the British dimension of Stuart politics, the court-based élite continued to visit Scotland, used their income to buy or improve Scottish estates, and remained Scottish in their cultural assumptions.[39] Kerr of Ancram became a member of the English Privy Council, but his correspondence 'reveals a sustained interest in his home locality'.[40] Sir William Alexander, the acclaimed author of love sonnets, political closet dramas, and the encyclopaedic *Doomes-day* (1614), was even more successful, acquiring mining rights in Scotland, land in Ulster, and the governorship of Nova Scotia. Yet he published books in Edinburgh, built a new house in Stirling, and was not just made an earl by Charles I but became chief of the MacAlexander Clan.

To descend from this big picture to the finer grain of literature is to find clearer signs of hybridity. From a sonnet apparently composed in 1604 or later we know that King James discouraged Alexander from writing 'harshe vearses after the Inglische fasone'. Reminding Alexander that he had been 'bath'd . . . in Castalias fountaine cleare', the King objected to him adopting the irregularities of a Sidneian or metaphysical style:

> Although your neighbours haue conspir'd to spill
> That art which did the Laurel crowne obtaine
> And borowing from the raven there ragged quill
> Bewray there harsh hard trotting tumbling wayne
> Such hamring hard the mettalls hard require
> Our songs ar fil'd with smoothly flowing fire[41]

That Alexander responded obediently is clear from a letter that he wrote to Drummond in 1616 to keep him in touch with poetic debate. At Newmarket, he explains, while bad weather delayed hunting, he and the King discussed how the same syllables could function in one place as long and

---

[39] 'Courtiers and Cavaliers: Service, Anglicization and Loyalty among the Royalist Nobility', in John Morrill (ed.), *The Scottish National Covenant in its British Context* (Edinburgh, 1990), 155–92, 'The Scottish Aristocracy, Anglicization and the Court, 1603–38', *Historical Journal*, 36 (1993), 543–76.

[40] 'Courtiers and Cavaliers', 164.

[41] *The Poems of James VI of Scotland*, ed. James Craigie, 2 vols. (Edinburgh, 1955–8), ii. 114. For a capable discussion see Michael R. G. Spiller, 'The Scottish Court and the Scottish Sonnet at the Union of the Crowns', in Sally Mapstone and Juliette Wood (eds.), *The Rose and the Thistle: Essays on the Culture of Late Medieval and Renaissance Scotland* (East Lothian, 1998), 101–15.

in another as short—a doctrine in happy conformity with what James had said in his *Reulis and Cautelis* (pp. 215–16). It is probably significant that the poem Alexander wrote on this occasion, 'When *Britain's* Monarch, in true Greatness great', follows the recommendation of the *Reulis* in using the sonnet form for panegryic (p. 223). Flattering the King's mastery of smooth, Castalian numbers, it implies that this accomplishment contributes to his excellence as a monarch of the union.[42]

The survival of a Castalian bias in élite conceptions of British poetry might seem thinly 'Scottish' beside the vigorous Scots of such Lowland ballads as 'The Laird of Logie' and 'The Lads of Wamphray' (not to mention the vitality of Gaelic poetry as it evolved beyond bardic conventions). But that raises the question of why Drummond and his contemporaries Anglicized their verse. The manuscripts show Ayton writing Scots in the 1580s, being associated with 'a peculiar Scoto-English orthography' after 1603, and subsequently being circulated in 'polished and anglicised' texts.[43] King James, even before the union, arranged for his works to be Anglicized. And the presence of more Scots in Drummond's manuscript drafts than in his printed texts[44] again points to a desire to project a public voice closer to southern English than was idiomatic for the writer.

What the poets said about this situation could be insecure. Introducing his first tragedy, *Darius*, in the Edinburgh edition of 1603, Alexander wrote:

The language of this Poeme is (as thou seest) mixt of the English and Scottish Dialects; which perhaps may be un-pleasant and irksome to some readers of both nations. But I hope the gentle and Judicious Englishe reader will beare with me, if I retaine some badge of mine owne countrie, by using sometimes words that are peculiar thereunto, especiallie when I finde them propre, and significant. As for my owne country-men, they may not justly finde fault with me, if for the more parte I vse the English phrase, as worthie to be preferred before our owne for the elegance and perfection thereof. Yea I am perswaded that both countrie-men will take in good part the mixture of their Dialects, the rather for that the bountiful providence of God doth invite them both to a straiter union and conjunction as well in language, as in other respects.[45]

---

[42] *Works of Drummond,* 149–50, p. 150.

[43] Mary Jane Wittstock Scott, 'Robert Ayton: Scottish Metaphysical', *Scottish Literary Journal,* 2/1 (July 1975), 5–16, p. 8.

[44] Cf. e.g. the sonnet prefixed to Alexander's *Doomes-day* with the version in the Hawthornden MSS: *Poetical Works of Drummond,* ii. 161, 371.

[45] *The Poetical Works of Sir William Alexander, Earl of Stirling,* ed. L. E. Kastner and H. B. Charlton, 2 vols. (Manchester, 1921–9), i, p. cxcvi.

In its edgy and uneven way—insinuating to the English and a touch defiant on the home front—this proposes a merger of tongues as the concomitant of union. It advances an ideal of synthesis, comforting to the Scots, that ran on at least until Alexander Hume's treatise *Of the Orthographie and Congruitie of the Britan Tonge* (*c.*1619). Yet the unpatriotic assertion that southern English is superior in elegance and perfection makes Alexander's further reduction of Scots in the 1604 (London) and later editions of *Darius*, as well as in other plays and poems,[46] seem less a compromise than a dilution.

If Alexander's appeal to the union was to some extent an opportunistic rationalization, however, it does not follow that his Anglicizing was the product of cultural cringe. His primary motive was almost certainly the pragmatic one of not alienating his potentially large English readership, and he will have been encouraged in his policy by a drift to Anglicization which began in Scottish printing long before 1603.[47] This process has a prehistory, but it is usually related to the mid-sixteenth-century introduction into Scotland of the Geneva Bible and other Protestant texts in English. So, if there was an element of British identity-formation in Alexander's practice, its roots should be sought in the hopes of Kirk reformers that they would be strengthened by an alliance with the godly in the south.[48] What we call Anglicization was easier to accept because writers could see themselves as shifting not between languages but between what Alexander calls 'Dialects'. In a linguistic context the term 'Scots' does not appear until the late fifteenth century, and it then accompanied rather than replaced 'Inglis' to describe the Lowland tongue. Drummond and his contemporaries knew that their speech was close to that spoken in northern England, and they regarded themselves as speaking the same 'Inglis' as their fellow-Britons.[49]

In any case, the Scottish élite was competent in several tongues, including Latin for educational purposes, French at court, Gaelic in some regions, Scots for dealing with Lowland tenants and for many official documents; and just as Scotland's architectural idiom was distinctively

[46] Ibid. i, pp. cxciv–cc, ii, pp. xi–xvi.

[47] M. A. Bald, 'The Anglicisation of Scottish Printing', *Scottish Historical Review*, 23 (1925–6), 107–15.

[48] For a sceptical investigation see Mairi Robinson, 'Language Choice in the Reformation: The Scots Confession of 1560', in J. Derrick McLure (ed.), *Scotland and the Lowland Tongue: Studies in the Language and Literature of Scotland in Honour of David D. Murison* (Aberdeen, 1983), 59–78.

[49] For contexts see J. Derrick McClure, 'Scottis, Inglis, Suddroun: Language Labels and Language Attitudes' (1981), repr. in his *Scots and its Literature* (Amsterdam, 1995), 44–56.

mixed, so its linguistic character was defined by the nature of its eclecticism.[50] Southern English could be added to this repertoire, as the lingua franca of the King's new British state, without it seeming a betrayal. Here it should be remembered that, although some of the texts circulating in Scots during Drummond's lifetime—such as Blind Harry's *Wallace*— were anti-English, it was not until the early eighteenth century that publication in Scots *per se* took on a patriotic colouring, and not until much later, and then but patchily, that Scots became privileged, with Gaelic, as an authenticator of national identity.[51] In the early modern period, pride in Scottish culture was if anything more naturally displayed in Latin, because that language could raise the country's profile throughout educated Europe. That is one reason why so many of the poems and speeches welcoming James in 1617 are in Latin, and were published in John Adamson's erudite *Τα των μουσων εισοδια: The Muses Welcome* (1618), and why the anthology *Delitiæ poetarum Scotorum* (1637), partly assembled by Drummond's friend Scot of Scotstarvet, is such a landmark.

In short, while the Scottish court poets employed some British motifs, there is little more evidence among them of regal union encouraging cultural synthesis than there is among their English contemporaries. Like the more distantly removed Drummond, they could be associated with Whitehall without compromising their Scottishness—at least until the late 1630s, when political breakdown led them (and especially Alexander) to be viewed as Anglicized drones. When the travel-writer William Lithgow wrote about King James's 1617 visit, in a poem about his own departure from Scotland, he declared:

> Amongst these long Goodnightes, farewell yee *Poets* deare,
> Graue *Menstrie* true *Castalian* fire, quicke *Drummond* in his spheare.
> Braue *Murray* ah is dead, *Aiton* supplies his place,
> And *Alens* high *Pernassian* veine, rare Poems doth embrace.[52]

No discrimination is made between Scottish poets north and south of the border. All belong to Scotland; and if Lithgow partly wrote (as seems

⁵⁰ Cf. Deborah Howard, 'Languages and Architecture in Scotland, 1500–1660', in Georgia Clarke and Paul Crossley (eds.), *Architecture and Language: Constructing Identity in European Architecture, c.1000–c.1660* (Cambridge, 2000), 162–77.

⁵¹ See J. Derrick McClure, 'Lowland Scots: An Ambivalent National Tongue' (1984), repr. in his *Scots and its Literature*, 5–19.

⁵² 'An Elegie, Containing the Pilgrimes Most Humble Farewell to his Natiue and Neuer Conquered Kingdome of Scotland', in *The Pilgrimes Farewell to his Natiue Countrey of Scotland* (Edinburgh, 1618), H3ᵛ–4ᵛ, H4ʳ.

likely) in the hope of attracting their patronage, that makes the more significant the cultural map he expected these poets to favour.

English historians began to investigate the seventeenth-century British problem after revisionism had seriously damaged Whig and Marxist explanations for the outbreak of the Civil War. If long-term political friction between the Stuart crown and Parliament, and socio-economic difficulties, could not account for the crisis, then the complications of governing a multiple monarchy—evident elsewhere in Europe—seemed the likeliest trigger, if not cause, of the chaos which so quickly engulfed the Three Kingdoms.[53] Because of its background in revisionism, the new British history of Conrad Russell and his followers has focused on high politics, the Church, and military history, and tended to neglect popular grievances.

Yet literary evidence shows that the problems of regal union could galvanize socio-economic discontent in Scotland during the decades that English-based historians used to regard as leading to civil war. A sense that the country was 'maymed' without its monarch[54] grew, if anything, after 1617; it found a focus in the rise of Buckingham (subject of at least one scornful epigram by Drummond),[55] and it was exacerbated, after the death of James, by the failure of his successor not only to be crowned initially in Scotland, the country of his birth, but to avoid coming north for eight years after his accession. When Charles did finally travel to Edinburgh to be crowned, in 1633, his arrival was even more extravagantly celebrated than the progress of 1617. But the visit also prompted petitioning about grievances real and anticipated, and it was handled so badly by the court that it escalated the distrust of Anglican England that would light the touchpaper of war when the Scottish Presbyterians signed their National Covenant in 1638.

The commonplace William Lithgow is once again helpful. No doubt revisionist historians were right to urge against reading the crises of

[53] The classic exposition is Conrad Russell, *The Causes of the English Civil War* (Oxford, 1990), esp. chs. 2 and 5.

[54] Alexander Craig, 'Scotlands Teares', in his *Poeticall Essayes* (London, 1604), C1ᵛ–2ᵛ— though the predominant sentiment in this volume is pro-union.

[55] 'On the Isle of Rhe', *Poetical Works of Drummond*, ii. 245. His authorship of the satire on James I and VI's corrupted senses ('For the Kinge', *Poetical Works of Drummond*, ii. 296–99), which dates from the period of Buckingham's dominance, is extremely doubtful; see Robert H. MacDonald, 'Amendments to L. E. Kastner's Edition of Drummond's Poems', *Studies in Scottish Literature*, 7 (1969), 102–22, p. 118 and the Drummond section in Peter Beal (comp.), *Index of English Literary Manuscripts*, vol. i, pt. 2 (London, 1980), 17–47, p. 18.

1638–42 back into earlier data, but when he says, in *Scotlands Welcome to her Natiue Sonne*, that Charles has not come 'with sterne bloody collours flying', like a Turkish prince seeking to subdue, one wonders why the idea should have been raised only to be denied. And when Lithgow points out that the Scots have great military strength, not least in Ireland, why does his obedience sound minatory? 'Then slight mee not (Dread Sir) since I, and Myne, | Still vow, to serue *Thee*.'[56] By the end of the decade, Charles would indeed come like a Turkish prince, to fight (and lose) two Bishops' Wars, and the Scots would develop their presence in Ireland, arming the Ulster Presbyterians and, in due course, reinforcing them in a multi-angled conflict that required them to take on the Irish Catholics who sometimes fought in support of the King.

Meanwhile, Lithgow grumbles, the Scottish nobility and gentry go to London to squander money exacted from their tenants that should support merchants at home. The courts and Privy Council are being undermined because people take their complaints to Whitehall. Berwick, as a frontier town, is full of 'Slaughter, Adultry, Incest'.[57] Youngsters are slipping to England to marry without parental consent. The English are buying up Scottish cattle, sheep, and horses. Scotsmen are being infected with southern effeminacy and smoking tobacco. Folk sit in alehouses, telling disaffected stories about Robin Hood and Wallace. They are slow to pay their bills, and because of a shortage of Scottish copper coin little is given to charity. Overall, the country is decaying. Fortifications and ports are neglected. Bridges are not being built. And Sunday is not properly observed. Many of these complaints can be paralleled in English satire, but they do not cluster there around the disadvantages of union. The problems of multiple monarchy provided a magnet for feelings that, south of the border, took on a different inflection.

If the magnificent pageant that Drummond wrote to welcome the King to Edinburgh—*The Entertainment of the High and Mighty Monarch Charles*—is read with Lithgow in mind, it looks even less likely to 'please' than the 1617 *Forth Feasting*. As he rode into the city, Charles met actors playing the parts of Religion and Superstition, Justice and Oppression, Caledonia and Nova Scotia—innocuous-sounding pairs, but, as we shall see, provocative. After hearing a speech from his never-conquered Caledonia, Charles then advanced to an arch decorated with the devices of war and peace and the iconography of Great Britain. This might have been

---

[56] *Scotlands Welcome to her Native Sonne, and Soveraigne Lord, King Charles* (Edinburgh, (1633)), A3^v, A4^v.   [57] Ibid. C3^v.

the climax of the day. As the King approached, however, a theatre disclosed Mercury 'with an hundred and seven Scottish Kings, which hee had brought from the Elisian fields' and '*Fergus* the first had a speech in Latine'.[58] We know that, of the huge amount of money spent, a large proportion was lavished on these pictures of the Scottish kings. A manuscript quoted in David M. Bergeron's *English Civic Pageantry* suggests that the King's inspection of the portraits, and Fergus' now-lost speech, were time-consuming affairs,[59] though, because they hardly figure in the printed text,[60] Bergeron fails to make the obvious deduction. Together, they made up the core of a pageant that was 'civic' but by no means 'English'—which is why the King was next shown a display of the 'ancient Worthies of Scotland', before being introduced by Endymion to the seven planets, each of which made a speech about the future of the northern kingdom. The Dunfermline-born but English-bred King was being given a crash course in Scottishness.

Awkward issues were raised by each of Drummond's initial tableaux. Religion had created difficulties in 1617, when King James had insisted on the public use of church ornaments and organs and had pressed the General Assembly of the Kirk to accept a number of Anglican measures.[61] Worse was expected in 1633, because of Charles's known determination to push Laudian policies through the Scottish Parliament, and because the coronation service (with its surplices, altar, and crucifix)[62] was a planned affront to Presbyterian sensibilities. Drummond was no Kirk radical, but he shared the wariness of many Episcopalians[63] towards the authority of Canterbury, and was proud of the primitive independence of the Scottish Church from Rome.[64] In the *Entertainment* he signalled his preference for simplicity over Laudian-papistical antiquated ceremony by present-

---

[58] *The Entertainment of the High and Mighty Monarch Charles*, in *Poetical Works of Drummond*, ii. 113–36, p. 123.

[59] *English Civic Pageantry 1558–1642* (London, 1971), 112–31; British Library Harleian MS 4707, art. 3 (fos. 59ᵛ–60ᵛ). Cf. British Library Additional MS 40885, fos. 2ʳ–20ʳ; Edinburgh University Library MS D.C.4,3.

[60] First published in Edinburgh, in 1633, by the John Wreittoun who produced William Lithgow's *Scotlands Welcome*.

[61] Alan R. MacDonald, *The Jacobean Kirk, 1567–1625* (Aldershot, 1998), 158–61.

[62] See John Spalding, *History of the Troubles and Memorable Transactions in Scotland from the Years 1624 to 1645*, quoted e.g. by John Morrill, 'The National Covenant in its British Context', in Morrill (ed.), *Scottish National Covenant*, 1–30, pp. 2–3.

[63] Colin Kidd, *British Identities before Nationalism: Ethnicity and Nationhood in the Atlantic World, 1600–1800* (Cambridge, 1999), 129.

[64] Cf. the early pages of Archbishop John Spottiswoode, *The History of the Church of Scotland, Beginning in the Year of Our Lord 203 and Continued to the End of the Reign of King James the VI* (London, 1655).

ing Religion as a maiden in white taffeta trampling Superstition, 'a woman blind, in old and worne garments' (pp. 114–15). Later, Caledonia warns the King that ' *Faith* (milke-white *Faith*) of old belov'd so well, | Yet in this corner of the World doth dwell | With her pure Sisters, *Truth, Simplicitie*' (p. 119).

When it comes to Justice and Oppression, the *Entertainment* boldly addresses abuses of royal power. More firmly than the London lawyers who a few months earlier had funded Shirley's *Triumph of Peace*, Drummond points out that a good prince 'first subjects himselfe to his owne law' (p. 120). Charles, according to Jove, will relieve ' *Iustice* kept low by grants, and wrongs', avoid promoting favourites like Buckingham, and find ways of funding good causes:

> Thou shalt no Paranymph raise to high place,
> For frizl'd locks, quaint pace, or painted face;
> On gorgeous rayments, womanising toyes,
> The workes of wormes, and what a Moth destroyes,
> The Maze of fooles, thou shalt no treasure spend,
> Thy charge to immortality shall tend,
> Raise *Pallaces*, and *Temples* vaulted high,
> Rivers ore arch, of hospitality,
> Of Sciences the ruin'd Innes restore,
> With walls and ports incircle *Neptunes* shore . . . (pp. 129–30)

This is strikingly close to Lithgow's round-up of grievances, regarding English effeminacy and the lack of proper expenditure on bridges, ports, fortifications, and colleges. In the *Entertainment*, as in *Forth Feasting*, Drummond says that a king should be loved rather than feared. As Jove ringingly puts it: 'Thou fear'd of none, shalt not thy people feare, | Thy peoples love thy greatnesse shall up-reare' (p. 130). But how could subjects love a king who sought to fund colleges and hospitals by a Revocation of Grants[65] and to build 'walls and ports' along the Firth of Forth by imposing new duties on coal and salt?[66] The tax burden, already high in Edinburgh, was doubled during the King's visit, and provocative methods of collection were applied.[67] When Jove speaks of this, prediction modulates

---

[65] See e.g. Donald, *An Uncounselled King*, 16–20.

[66] Allan I. Macinnes, *Charles I and the Making of the Covenanting Movement 1625–1641* (Edinburgh, 1991), 104, notes the general scepticism about, and lack of enthusiasm for collecting, this impost, announced in 1627.

[67] See e.g. Maurice Lee, *The Road to Revolution: Scotland under Charles I, 1625–37* (Urbana, Ill., 1985), 133–5.

into injunction: 'New and vast taxes thou shalt not extort, | Load heavy those thy bounty should support' (p. 130).

The other topic announced in Drummond's opening tableaux, that of empire, was even more delicate. In one sense the appearance of a woman clad in 'divers coloured feathers, which shew her to bee an *American*, and to represent new *Scotland*' is not surprising. New World iconography was not unknown in pageants;[68] and Lithgow emphasized Scotland's pride in the possession of Nova Scotia near the end of *Scotlands Welcome* (G2ᵛ). Drummond, as a friend of Alexander, the Governor, had particular reason to celebrate a colony that he had already, in *Forth Feasting*, praised as a Scottish achievement (319–34), and to do so in terms reminiscent of those used to describe that bleak part of Canada—'Lands which passe *Arabian* fields | In fragrant Wood and Muske' (*Entertainment*, 130)—in Alexander's *Encouragement to Colonies* (1624) and *The Mapp and Description of New-England* (1630).[69]

Nova Scotia was peopled by English Dissenters as well as Highlanders and Lowland Scots: it had a British aspect. But the colony was primarily Scottish, bound up with patriotic emotion, and its prominence in the *Entertainment* confirms what David Armitage has argued, that the growth of the British Empire needs to be understood in relation to interaction between the Three Kingdoms, because it was fragmented, during the seventeenth century, by the ambitions of the Scots and English within a political structure that did not always serve them equally.[70] And if Nova Scotia was topical in 1629, when Drummond first wrote his *Entertainment*, in expectation of the King's long-awaited arrival,[71] by 1633 it was politically explosive, because the colony had been ceded to France in 1631 in order to release Henrietta Maria's dowry to her husband.[72] It was by no means the last time that the interests of an absentee king would damage Scottish enterprise overseas, but it was a peculiarly stark example of the

---

[68] e.g. the New World arch (designed by Thomas Dekker) that greeted King James in Fleet Street when he ceremoniously entered London; Stephen Harrison, *The Arch's of Triumph Erected in Honor of the High and Mighty Prince James* (London, 1604), H1ʳ.

[69] For evidence of his interest see the item in the Hawthornden MSS (perhaps raw material for a poem), transcribed in McGrail, *Alexander*, 236–8, and now known to derive from a report written by a Scot who went to Nova Scotia in 1629 (N. E. S. Griffiths and John G. Reid, 'New Evidence on New Scotland, 1629', *William and Mary Quarterly*, 3rd ser. 49 (1992)), 492–508.

[70] 'Making the Empire British: Scotland in the Atlantic World 1542–1707', *Past and Present*, 155 (May 1997), 34–63.

[71] 'Memorialls', in *Drummond: Poems and Prose*, ed. MacDonald, 193–5, pp. 193–4.

[72] See Daniel Cobb Harvey, 'Sir William Alexander and Nova Scotia', Nova Scotia Historical Society, *Collections*, 30 (1954), 1–26, p. 25.

drawbacks of regal union, and however Drummond might have claimed to be taking his cue from the King's specious insistence that he had not finally sacrificed Scotland's claims to its American namesake, an Edinburgh audience could only have reacted sardonically to the idea that Charles

> rising high
> To grace this throne makes *Scotlands* name to flie
> On *Halcyons* wings (her glory which restores)
> Beyond the Ocean to *Columbus* shores, . . . (p. 120)

Charles had been warned, but he did little to charm the Scots, who found him stiff and aloof, in the manner of the English élite, and pettily resentful towards those who opposed him.[73] He forced his Laudian reforms and his tax increases through a reluctant Parliament, and estranged much of the Scottish nobility. As a result, support was patchy when, in the following year, he sought to prosecute the Presbyterian Lord Balmerino for possessing a document that challenged his policy on the Kirk. At this point turning to prose, Drummond sent an *Apologetical Letter* about the case to Kerr of Ancram, with the intention of reaching if not the King then at least those closest to him. Noting that poverty makes people rebellious, he accused the King's officers of not so much fleecing as skinning the Scots, and concluded: 'it were not evil for a Prince to read *Jan Marianai* [Juan de Mariana] and *George Buchanans* piece *de jure Regni apud Scotos*, for his own private and the publick good.'[74] Given Buchanan's notorious preference for limiting royal power, this is startling advice to have from a writer who has often been regarded—since the 1711 edition of his *Works* (which omitted this *Letter*)—as 'a great Cavalier, and much addicted to the King's Party'.[75]

Poetry hampered the efforts of Alexander, now Earl of Stirling and Secretary of State for Scotland, to defuse the mistrust created by the Balmerino affair. As early as 1620, he had corresponded with Drummond about King James's translation of the Psalms, and the impossibility of cor-

---

[73] David Stevenson, 'The English Devil of Keeping State: Élite Manners and the Downfall of Charles I in Scotland', repr. in his *Union, Revolution and Religion in 17th-Century Scotland* (Aldershot, 1997), (126–44); Lee, *Road to Revolution*, 136.

[74] 'An Apologetical Letter', in William Drummond, *The History of Scotland* (London, (1656)), 238–44, p. 242.

[75] Bishop John Sage, 'The Life of William Drummond of Hawthornden', in *Works of Drummond*, pp. i–xi, p. ix. For the ongoing belief, even among perceptive scholars, that Drummond only distrusted and rejected Buchanan, see MacDonald, 'A Disputed Maxim of State', 298 and Miller, *Rebecca's Vest*, 91.

recting the royal efforts with propriety.[76] On James's death, Alexander was encouraged by Charles to revise and consolidate the translation,[77] and granted the privilege of printing it. The first (1631) edition appeared at a time when Alexander was trying to make good his fortunes after the collapse of the Nova Scotia colony. But Charles's efforts to have the familiar, sixteenth-century version of the Psalms replaced in his Three Kingdoms met with a mixed reaction, and positive hostility in Scotland. Only too aware that Alexander shared the King's desire to advance Laudianism, the General Assembly of the Kirk resisted his Psalms on doctrinal but also poetic grounds. They objected to the 'heathenish libertie and poeticall conceats in this new metaphrase', and said that its 'French, Latine, and hard Englisch tearmes' baffled the common people.[78]

The King was not greatly moved. He forbad further publication in Scotland of the old version of the Psalms; then a second edition of 'Menstrie's psalms' was published, and bound together with a new Scottish prayerbook. This was the infamous volume that started the slide into war, when, on 23 July 1637, its use provoked a riot in St Giles's Cathedral, Edinburgh. That Alexander was busy at the time preparing his *Recreations with the Muses* (1637) for publication encouraged further carping about the part played by his poetry in the troubles of the union. Plainly out of touch, he was excluded from the negotiations which Charles undertook to stem the tide of Presbyterian feeling, and he died with his standing almost as low in court as it was in Scotland, where Drummond only mourned him in draft[79] and others were scathing about his misuse of his literary talents (despoiling the psalter), his farming and milling of revenues, and his monopoly of copper coin:

> Hier layes a fermer and a millar,
> A poet and a psalme book spillar,
> A purchessour by hooke and crooke,
> A forger of the service booke,
> A coppersmithe quho did much evill,
> A friend to bischopes and ye devill,
> A waine ambitious flattering thing,
> Late secretary for a kinge;

[76] *Works of Drummond*, 151.

[77] On the poverty of the work see Gary F. Waller, 'Sir William Alexander and Renaissance Court Culture', *Aevum*, 51 (1977), 505–15, p. 514.

[78] Thomas H. McGrail, *Sir William Alexander, First Earl of Stirling: A Biographical Study* (Edinburgh, 1940), 167.

[79] Ibid. 199.

> Soum tragedies in verse he pen'd,
> At last he made a tragicke end.[80]

This anonymous mock-epitaph is a reminder that topical satire and verse abuse (flyting) had sturdy roots in Scotland. Its social, vigorous manner seems far removed from the Drummond who figures in literary history as a 'fastidious', 'somewhat prim' straight man to the exuberant Jonson of the 'Conversations'.[81] Yet the Hawthornden Manuscripts are not short of rough jokes and bawdy satires, composed as well as gathered by Drummond—like the one about the equestrian girl who, when she got to puberty, thought she was growing horsehair between her thighs.[82] He wrote prefatory verse for an edition of *The Flyting betwixt Montgomery and Polwart*,[83] and was by repute the author of a poem in Scots and pidgin Latin about a scatological battle between the folk of Scotstarvet and Newbarns.[84] Sharp, ribald poetry was provoked in him by political upheavals; his verse became harsher, and closer to popular genres—as in 'A Prouerbe', his response to the prayerbook riots:

> God neuer had a Church but there, Men say,
> The Diuell a chapell hath raised by some wyles.
> I doubted of this saw, till on a day
> I Westward spied great Edinbroughs Saint Gyles.[85]

It is typical that this attack on the Presbyterians should leave scope for disapproval of the bishops for bringing disorder into the Kirk. Though Drummond never sided with the radical reformers, he could be animated, as a poet, by their anger. An early example would seem to be 'Drummonds Lines One the Bischopes: 14 Appryll 1638', which assumes with Swiftian savagery an anti-episcopalianism voice:

---

[80]   *Sir William Alexander*, 187.

[81]   Anne Barton, *Ben Jonson, Dramatist* (Cambridge, 1984), 7, Ian Donaldson, *Jonson's Magic Houses: Essays in Interpretation* (Oxford, 1997), 19.

[82]   'Anecdotes, &c. Selected from Drummond of Hawthornden's Miscellanies, Vol. II', in David Laing, 'A Brief Account of the Hawthornden Manuscripts in the Possession of the Society of Antiquaries of Scotland', *Archaeologia Scotica: Or, Transactions of the Society of Antiquaries of Scotland*, 4 ((1831) 1857), 57–116, 225–40, pp. 78–82; *Poetical Works of Drummond*, ii. 208, 285–7; French Rowe Fogle, *A Critical Study of William Drummond of Hawthornden* (New York, 1952), 205, 208; MacDonald, 'Amendments', 107–11, *Drummond: Poems and Prose*, ed. MacDonald, 141–3. 'The Country Maid', *Poetical Works of Drummond*, ii. 210.

[83]   'To the Reader', *Poetical Works of Drummond*, 327.

[84]   'Polemo-Middinia', *Poetical Works of Drummond*, ii. 321–6; there is a parallel-text translation in Allan H. MacLaine (ed.), *The Christis Kirk Tradition: Scots Poems of Folk Festivity* (Glasgow, 1996), 39–49. Against Drummond's authorship see MacDonald, 'Amendments', 120.

[85]   *Poetical Works of Drummond*, ii. 245.

Naye, pray you Heauens, once lend me bot your thunder,
Ile crusch and teare thesse sordid slaues assunder,
And leuell with the dust ther Altars horne,
With the lascivious organs, pieties scorne;
Or lett me be as king, then of their skine
Ile causse dresse lether and fyne Marikin,
To couer coatches (quher they wount to ryde)
And valk in bootes and shoes made of ther hyde,
Vhipe them at neighbour princes courts to show,
That No Nouations Scotts zeall can allow.[86]

The speaker says that the bishops' pride makes 'poore Brittane smart, | Confound the church, the stait, and all the nation' (46–7). This slyly suggests that the Presbyterians who opposed the pan-British ambitions of the Laudians had similarly imperialistic plans of their own; and it is true that, even though their first step was to sign a National Covenant in Scotland, they exported Scots-language and Anglicized pamphlets to bring round English puritans.[87] They recognized that if the Kirk was to be safe, a British settlement would be needed across what Drummond provocatively calls 'all the nation'.[88]

Developing this fear in *Irene*, a manuscript treatise far-sighted enough to be a candidate for printing seven years later, Drummond argued that 'If thus, the Protestants of this Isle of Great-*Britain*, who are now united in Religion, and All of one Mind with their King, shall inconsiderately, without his Consent, make a League, they cannot but divide.' Some will go with Charles, others with the Covenanters, and this division, he points out, will simply advantage Rome, and make Britain 'a Bait for Strangers to feed upon'. Having discouraged the Covenanters, he finishes with a section in which Scotia apologizes to the King for the disloyalty of her people but also advises him to 'vanquish and subdue them by Mercy. The impregnable fortress of a Prince', Scotia reflects—in the vein of *Forth Feasting* and the *Entertainment*—'is the Love of his Subjects, which doth only arise from the Height of his Clemency.' Reassuring, or warning, Charles that 'It was not Religion alone which did occasion these Troubles', Drummond repeats the socio-economic complaints of 1633–4,

[86] Ibid. 293–5, ll. 31–40; for a similarly ventriloquized poem see 'A Character of the Anti-Couenanter, or Malignant' (ii. 218–21).

[87] See e.g. Conrad Russell, *The Fall of the British Monarchies 1637–1642* (Oxford, 1991), 43–4, 61, 69.

[88] Key contexts (including the Low Countries) are established by Donald, *An Uncounselled King*, ch. 5; for one revealing career see John Coffey, *Politics, Religion and the British Revolutions: The Mind of Samuel Rutherford* (Cambridge, 1997), 229–30, 243–6, 202–19.

that the Scots were clipped too close, and that poverty was 'the principal Ground of Novations and Alterations'.[89]

It was a time of duress. Scotsmen in London were compelled to disown the Covenant, and Wentworth rigorously enforced the same test on the Scots in Ireland. On the other side, Montrose (not yet a royalist hero) forced the reluctant academics of Aberdeen University to sign it. With the King preparing to launch the first Bishops' War, Drummond challenged his enemies in *Queries of State*. Asking 'Whether this war may renew the old National Quarrels between *Scotland* and *England*, and divide this Island in it self, to be a Prey to Foreign Conquest?', he advanced from the prediction that there would be disunity within Britain between different kinds of Protestants to the possibility that war would break up the regal union along national lines.[90] It is a sign of the contradictory priorities set up within royalism by multiple monarchy that a process feared by him was welcomed by the King: faced with a Covenanting movement too united to be broken from within, Charles came to hope that inherited antagonisms would allow him to use the English against the Scots.

In *A Speech . . . to the Noblemen . . . who have Leagu'd themselves for the Defence of the Religion and Liberties of Scotland*, dated 2 May 1639, Drummond declared that, if war came, the Scots would lose because the King had enough resources to survive short-term defeats, whereas the Scots only had to lose one battle, as at Pinkie and Flodden, to finish their campaign for good.[91] He could not have been more wrong. Once the Scots set out their forces at Duns Law, Charles—unsure of his strength, and ambivalent about accepting Irish Catholic reinforcements[92]—moved to a negotiated settlement. He cravenly yet temporizingly yielded to the substance of the rebels' demands, and a General Assembly of the Kirk persuaded the Scottish Privy Council to pass an Act requiring all Scots to sign the Covenant.

Drummond, who had reluctantly sent men to fight the English, and asked the King in verse to send them back in pieces,[93] satirized this Act[94] and the protracted Parliament that capitalized on the Scottish victory. Lashing out with a scornful epigram,

---

[89] *Works of Drummond*, 163–73, pp. 166–7, 173.

[90] Ibid. 177–8, p. 178.　　　　　　　　　[91] Ibid. 179–82, p. 181.

[92] Jane H. Ohlmeyer, *Civil War and Restoration in the Three Stuart Kingdoms: The Career of Randal MacDonnell, Marquis of Antrim, 1609–1683* (Cambridge, 1993), ch. 3.

[93] *Poetical Works of Drummond*, ii. 223.

[94] This seems the likeliest occasion for 'Bold Scotes, at Bannochburne yee killd your king' and the 'Reply' attached (ibid. 207).

The parlament lordes haue sitten twice fiue weekes,
Yet will not leaue their stooles, knit vp their breekes;
Winter is come, dysenteryes preuaile:
Rise, fooles, and with this paper wype your taile.[95]

he proposed fifty-nine mock measures for the Parliament to pass. That
the provost of Edinburgh should pray in St Giles's Cathedral to the sound
of pistol shots rather than organs. That Buchanan's *De jure regni* (no
longer just a book for a prince) should be bound into copies of the Bible.
Poetry would play its part: 'That the Books of *Wallace* and King *Robert
the Bruce* be printed over again, against our old Enemies of *England*, and
Pensions be given to some learned Rhimers, to write XII. Books of our
Expedition and Victory at *Dunslaw*, or *DUNSLAIDOS Libri* 12.'[96]

If Drummond found it galling that the Covenanters claimed an epic
victory without enduring the heat of battle, the events of 1640 would
change that. When the King brought his forces north to fight a second
Bishops' War, the Scots marched into England, defeated the royal forces
at Newburn, and took over Newcastle. In Three-Kingdom terms it was a
significant victory because, as Conrad Russell says, with only some exag-
geration, it determined that Scotland would not be Anglicized in religion
and implied that any Act of Union that came would have to allow for diversity. Given the revived threat to use Irish troops to support the crown,
it probably also contributed to a long-term Scottish ambition to Protes-
tantize Ireland.[97] Above all, in the immediate crisis, victory meant that
when the King, pressurized by the Long Parliament, came north to woo
the Scots in 1641, it was on terms highly advantageous to the Covenanters.

Drummond's reaction can be gauged from the *Speech for Edinburgh to
the King* that was published in the 1711 *Works* but was most unlikely to
have been spoken in 1641 because it absolved the King from so much.[98]
Pointing out that religious and political conflicts racked much of Europe,
Drummond reassured Charles that there were bound to be tremors in
Scotland. Against the background of Covenanter moves to establish 'a
perfect amity' between England and Scotland,[99] he also struck a chord
that became familiar in Scottish royalism—one that was compatible with

---

[95] *Poetical Works of Drummond*, ii. 242; my dating is again only probable.
[96] *Considerations to the Parliament September 1639*, in *Works of Drummond*, 185–7, pp. 185–6.
[97] *Fall of the British Monarchies*, 145.
[98] *Works of Drummond*, 216–17; contrast the apologia for Covenanting Scotland in *A Relation
of the Kings Entertainment into Scotland* ((London), 1641).
[99] Keith Brown, *Kingdom or Province? Scotland and the Regal Union, 1603–1715* (Basingstoke,
1992), 121–2.

Forth Feasting and the 1633 *Entertainment*, though it tended to erode the integrity of the regal union—that Scotland would be loyal to its monarch regardless of the rest of Great Britain. Writing as, by now, the author of an ongoing *History of Scotland* from James I to James V, in which he was covertly analysing elements of the contemporary crisis,[100] Drummond cites as precedents how Edinburgh stood by James II, James III, and Mary Queen of Scots. The displaced King of England was being reconstructed as a Scottish monarch.

Charles was forcibly reminded, however, that his Scottish crown was unsafe without control of his other kingdoms, when, in October 1641, news reached him of the Irish Rebellion, and he had to return to England to gather resources to suppress it. To pacify Scotland on his departure, he freed a number of royalists who had allegedly plotted to murder leading Covenanters, but he also placated and promoted his most prominent opponents. Trying to react incisively to the mixed news, Drummond drafted an epigram:

> Behold (O Scots!) the reueryes of your King;
> Those hee makes Lordes who should on gibbetes hing.[101]

The Scots rhyme of 'King' with 'hing' makes it clear where the piece is written from, yet the replacement in manuscript of 'Behold (O Scots!) . . .' by 'Britannes, admire the extravagancyes of your King . . .'[102] shows how hard it was to disentangle Scottish from British politics. Try as Drummond might to cast Charles as the king of an ancient, independent Scotland, his future clearly depended on his fortunes south of the border.

Those quickly unravelled after Charles raised his standard at Nottingham, on 22 August 1642, and he was defeated at Edgehill. Disagreement in Scotland over how to resolve or exploit the situation led Drummond to compose, in January 1643, a tract called *Skiamachia* ('fighting with shadows') that was hot in support of the crown. On the British problem, however, it took a step into paradox, arguing that because Scotland was physically conjoined to England it could not maintain its religious dis-

---

[100] e.g. *History of Scotland*, 5 (moderate taxation), 7 (avoidance of faction), 17 (the decadence of peace and English mores at the Scottish court), 20–2 (the English case for a league with Scotland), 114 ff. (the rashness of noble rebellion), 117–19 (flaws in James III resembling those of Charles I), 210–15 (the wise counsellors of James V urge religious toleration, but, as in the 1630s, clerics prevail and create divisions); for a more generalized account see Thomas I. Rae, 'The Historical Writing of Drummond of Hawthornden', *Scottish Historical Review*, 54 (1975), 22–62, pp. 37–44.

[101] *Poetical Works of Drummond*, ii. 243.

[102] Hawthornden MSS; National Library of Scotland MS 2062, 185^r.

tinctiveness if it got involved in English affairs.[103] Drummond feared that the Scots would do a deal to help the English Parliament against the King, which is, in fact, what happened, when, on 25 October 1643, a Solemn League and Covenant was sealed, 'to bring the Churches of God in the three kingdoms to the nearest conjunction and uniformity in religion'.[104] In due course Drummond was proved partly right, in that the agreement did contribute to the undoing of Scotland by the English Republic when the Independents or sectarians rose up against Presbyterianism.

Now the Scots made their second major incursion into England, intervening militarily on the side of Parliament. It had an acute effect on English opinion. Symptomatic is John Cleveland's '*The Rebell* Scot', which asks 'What? shall our Nation be in bondage thus | Unto a Land that truckles under us?'[105] The Scotophobia curbed in royalists by their respect for the principle of regal union was unleashed, and Cleveland satirized the Covenanters as sub-human ('A *Scot* within a beast is no disguise'), saying that, because of the Scots plantation in Ulster, Ireland had lost its claim to be a nation free of snakes. It is ironic that this tirade should so resemble that of Milton at the end of the decade, in his *Observations on the Articles of Peace* (1649), where he excoriates the Presbyterians of Belfast, and Scottish opinion more largely, for renewed royalism after Charles I's execution. Only in Cleveland's approval of '*Montrose* and *Crawfords* loyall Band' is there any liking for the Scots.

Both distinct and interactive, each Stuart kingdom was also subdivided by regional allegiances which, in some areas, extended into transnational ethnic units. Although the old continuity between Scottish and Irish Gaeldom had been (as a matter of crown policy) disrupted by the Jacobean plantation in Ulster, the turbulent mid-1640s revived the prospect of a royalist alliance between the mere Irish and Scottish Gaels. The dashing Earl of Montrose, fine poet as well as brilliant general, in 1644 joined forces with Alasdair Mac Colla, an expropriated gentleman of the Clandonald South, who had led a couple of thousand Irishmen (mostly MacDonnells) and Islesmen from Wexford to Atholl, whence they marched through central and eastern Scotland, winning a string of victories.[106] For

---

[103] *Works of Drummond*, 190–205, p. 197.

[104] David L. Smith, *A History of the Modern British Isles, 1603–1707: The Double Crown* (Oxford, 1998), 141.

[105] *The Poems of John Cleveland*, ed. Brian Morris and Eleanor Withington (Oxford, 1967), 29–32.

[106] On these successes but also the limits of pan-Celtic solidarity see David Stevenson, *Alasdair MacColla and the Highland Problem in the Seventeenth Century* (Edinburgh, 1980).

many of those involved, as the Gaelic poetry shows, these battles were part of a clan feud, or a local quarrel with kale-eating Lowlanders.[107] But larger alliances were formed, and members of Drummond's own family were drawn into an army whose leadership understood the Three-Kingdom predicament of the King.

What the poet thought of Mac Colla's men is not clear. In the *Entertainment* he had generalized the martial prowess of the Scots from the Highland-sounding resilience of those who 'Runne over panting Mountaines crown'd with Ice' (p. 120), and among the measures that he drafted to mock the 1639 Parliament was a proposal 'That School-Masters be placed in the remotest High-Lands to instruct Youth in Civility and the *English* Language.'[108] Such scraps of evidence suggest a sympathy with aspects of Gaeldom that began to harden into approval when the long-standing royal mission to civilize and Anglicize clan leaders was translated into a parliamentary, evangelizing design to bring them within the pale of the Covenant. At all events there is no doubt that Drummond supported Montrose's campaign. He offered him *Irene* for publication and received his military protection;[109] he wrote a dialogue-epigram relishing the discomfiture of the Covenanters at his success.[110]

It is thus a measure both of how badly things turned out for Scottish royalism, and of how tangled political interests became when the war between the crown and its enemies was cut across by different national dynamics and dispositions of loyalty, that, only two years later, Drummond was seeking approval from the English for the fact that Montrose had been defeated by a Scottish Covenanting army. The event which changed his tack was the King's surrender of himself to the Scots on English soil, in May 1646, rather than fall into the clutches of the New Model army. The Covenanters then had to decide whether to deal with Charles themselves in his role as King of Scotland, or to hand him over to the English Parliament. Drummond's *Objections against the Scots Answer'd* was written to assert the independence of the Scots while insisting that they were

---

[107] See Allan I. Macinnes, 'Scottish Gaeldom, 1638–1651: The Vernacular Response to the Covenanting Dynamic', in John Dwyer, Roger A. Mason, and Alexander Murdoch (eds.), *New Perspectives on the Politics and Culture of Early Modern Scotland* (Edinburgh, 1982), 59–94, pp. 76–82, and parallel-texts of poems by Iain Lom, 'Oran air Latha Blàir Inbhir Lóchaidh eadar Clann Dòmhnaill agus na Caimbeulaich' ('A Song on the Day of the Battle of Inverlochy') and perhaps by Fionnghal Maclean, 'Turas mo chreiche thug mi Chola' ('The Journey of my Undoing I Made to Coll') in Colm Ó Baoill (ed.), *Gàir nan Clàrsach: The Harps' Cry*, trans. Meg Bateman (Edinburgh, 1994), 106–17.

[108] *Considerations to the Parliament*, 186.

[109] Masson, *Drummond,* 404.

[110] *Poetical Works of Drummond*, ii. 243.

no threat to the English in defending their King. To hand him over, he says, would not just go against their homage and fidelity as subjects, but would break the terms of the National Covenant of 1638. As for the objection that the Scottish army in England had not earned its pay from London, part of it did, he says, march north to defeat Montrose, without which 'the State of the Affairs of *England*, had fallen to as low an Ebb as now they swell in a high Tide'.[III]

These unscrupulous arguments did not persuade the Scottish Presbyterians—and they were only tactically addressed to the English—to protect the King. Defeated in June 1646 by the Catholic Irish at Benburb, Co. Tyrone, and ineffective elsewhere, the Covenanters had lost their ability to produce a favourable outcome to events; so, in January 1647, they pulled out of Newcastle, leaving Charles I to the English Parliament. This was not even in the short term the end of Scottish royalism because the rise of Covenanting conservatism led to the signing of a secret engagement with the imprisoned King during the winter of 1647–8. But the Duke of Hamilton's attempt to lead a Scottish force to victory in the Second Civil War—supported by Drummond in his *Vindication of the Hamiltons*—failed because appetite for resistance was flagging even in royalist Gaeldom, while a godly rising in south-west Scotland underlined the impossibility of converting the nation as a whole to the cause of the King. After Hamilton's defeat at Preston, on 3 September 1648, Cromwell came to Edinburgh, where a diehard regime of Covenanters was installed. The British union of crowns was dying, and what promised to replace it was the worst option that Drummond could imagine: the reduction of Scotland to a province under the control of the English Parliament.

The 'Life' that introduces the 1711 *Works* says that Drummond 'was so overwhelmed with extreme Grief and Anguish' at the execution of Charles I 'that he Died' (p. x). Since the poet passed away on 4 December 1649, about ten months after the King, the story is medically implausible, but it is also politically unlikely. It was perhaps a freak of fate that his poems should have been edited in 1656 by a nephew of the regicide Milton.[112] But he would not have relished the fact that his prose works were first brought out in the same year by the anti-royalist Englishman John

---

[III] *Works of Drummond*, 212–15, p. 214.

[112] The likely poetic influence of Drummond on Milton (e.g. H. Neville Davies, 'Milton's Nativity Ode and Drummond's "An Hymne of the Ascension"', *Scottish Literary Journal*, 12/1 (May 1985), 5–23) has been debated at least since Masson's *Drummond*, 472–4, proposed a role for Milton in the preparation of Edward Phillips's edition.

Hall. The appearance of that collection mostly highlights the difference between the British kingdoms which meant that, while Drummond could attack Presbyterian intolerance in Scotland without thinking he would give succour to Independency (which hardly existed north of the border), at least parts of his work could find such English admirers as Cromwell whose anti-Presbyterianism was far from royalist.[113] It is also instructive, however, that Hall's choice of texts was only somewhat more selective than that of the Tory editors of the 1711 works, who sought to project a very different image.

As a Three-Kingdom perspective brings out, and partly explains, Drummond was a far more multi-faceted figure than has been recognized, and the rapidly changing and personally dangerous circumstances of his final decade did nothing to simplify his work. What did remain constant, despite the Anglicization of his language, was an identification with Scotland, its ancient monarchy, and the distinctive culture of its élite. This infused him, as a young writer, with an internationalist localism that finds an echo in such modern Scottish poets as his admirer Edwin Morgan.[114] In his later work, the eventualities which spur him into frustrated pragmatism and even savagery are also those of Scotland, but a country that has advanced from the almost harmless neglect complained of in *Forth Feasting* into the labyrinth of the British problem.

[113] On Hall and Drummond see David Norbrook, *Writing the English Republic: Poetry, Rhetoric and Politics, 1627–1660* (Cambridge, 1999), 221; on Cromwell's liking for the discourse on toleration in the James V section of the *History of Scotland* (above, n. 100), see Derek Hirst, 'The English Republic and the Meaning of Britain' (1994), repr. in Bradshaw and Morrill (eds.), *The British Problem, c.1534–1707*, 192–219, p. 210 and n. 114.

[114] See n. 14 above.

CHAPTER 9

Thomas Carew (1988)

Early one morning in February 1623, two horsemen set off from New Hall, Essex, and made for the Gravesend ferry. The boatman, paid with a twenty-shilling piece, became suspicious of the pair—'John' and 'Thomas Smith', as they called themselves, muffled under false beards— and reported them to the authorities. A note of Quixotic comedy had entered the quest of Buckingham and the Prince of Wales to woo the Spanish Infanta. For the Duke of Savoy, 'it was a Trick of those ancient Knight Errands who went up and down the World after that manner to undoe Inchantments'.[1] The usually down-to-earth Secretary Conway called it a 'voyage of the Knights of Adventure'.[2] Whether sceptical or sanguine, observers invoked the language of chivalry. King James himself, despondent and elated by turns, addressed 'Tom' and 'Jacke' as 'My sweet boys and venturous knights, worthy to be put in a new romance'.[3] He thoughtfully sent them their Garter robes, and scraped the royal coffers to fund tilting gear and horses.[4] For the Infanta he provided a looking-glass fancifully 'enchanted by art magic'.[5] She, in turn, wore a 'ribbon about her arm'—blue, for love and sign of the Garter—so that the Prince might distinguish her in the royal train, and fall for her, by this favour.[6] Mendoza describes the Easter games at which Charles ('with the George about his necke, hanging by a watchet riban') was diverted by jousts, and a Pentecost 'Festivitie' which offered further feats of arms.[7] A chivalrous spectacle was played out in Madrid, almost a diplomatic masquerade.

---

[1] *The Life of Edward, First Lord Herbert of Cherbury, Written by Himself,* ed. J. M. Shuttleworth (Oxford, 1976), 118.

[2] 3 Mar. 1623, State Papers (SP) 14/139/26. Quoted by Charles Carlton, *Charles I: The Personal Monarch* (London, 1983), 34.

[3] *The Poems of James VI of Scotland,* ed. James Craigie, 2 vols. (Edinburgh, 1955–8), ii. 192–3; *Letters of King James VI and I,* ed. G. V. P. Akrigg (Berkeley, 1984), No. 190 (27 Feb. 1623), p. 388.

[4] *Letters,* No. 197, 1 Apr. (1623), p. 403, No. 199, 10 Apr. (1623), p. 407, No. 200, 18 Apr. (1623), p. 408. [5] Ibid., No. 195, 17 Mar. (1623), p. 398.

[6] According to James Howell, who witnessed events in Madrid; *Epistolæ Ho-Elianæ: Familiar Letters,* ed. Joseph Jacobs (London, 1890), I. iii. 15.

[7] Andrés de Almansa y Mendoza, *Two Royal Entertainments, Lately Given to the Most Illvstrious Prince Charles . . . Translated out of the Spanish originals Printed at Madrid* (1623), esp. pp. 6–7.

Elsewhere in the entourage, mock-chivalry took on wilder forms. One group of blades, in the fleet sent to bring Charles and Buckingham home, formed a society called 'the Order of the Bugle'.[8] Together with a set known as 'Tittere tu', they became notorious in the taverns of London. Sporting ribbons of 'blew or yellow', 'wetched', and 'Orendge Tornye', with officers and watchwords, they gleefully parodied knightly codes. In place of the gravity of the Garter, these 'orders' went in for tobacco-smoking, wenching, and scuffling with the watch. John Chamberlain, in his letters, gives us a taste of their 'ridiculous toyes' by telling us they had 'a Prince whom they call Ottoman', while Walter Yonge records a ritual oath sworn on a dagger thrust in a bottle.[9] It sounds like harmless roistering, tricked out with youthful wit.[10] But the King, anxious about recusants and conspiracy, ordered an investigation.[11] Amusingly, papers surviving in the Public Record Office show that, while the Order of the Bugle did not slay many dragons, it took a lively interest in giants. In a catalogue of ponderous nicknames—'Giant. Asdriasdust . . . Giant. Drinkittupall . . . Giant. Neuerbegood'—are sobriquets that will recur in the anti-puritan books of drollery.[12] There is also a list of members of the order; among them, 'M^r: Tho: Carew'.[13]

[8] 'The examinacon of michael Constable of West Raison in the Countie of Lincolne gent . . . this 19th daie of december 1623', SP 14/155/82.

[9] 'Examinacon'; cf. Walter Yonge, *Diary at Coyton and Axminster, 1604–1628*, Camden Society Publications 184/8 (London, 1848), 70–1; *The Letters of John Chamberlain*, ed. Norman E. McClure, 2 vols. (Philadelphia, 1939), ii. 530.

[10] On the Virgilian conceit of Tittere tu see Walton B. McDaniel, 'Some Greek, Roman and English Tityretus', *American Journal of Philology*, 35 (1914), 52–66, pp. 62 ff., Thornton Shirley Graves, 'Some Pre-Mohock Clansmen', *Studies in Philology*, 20 (1923), 395–421, p. 399 n. 15, and Annabel Patterson, 'Pastoral versus Georgic', in Barbara Lewalski (ed.), *Renaissance Genres* (Cambridge, Mass., 1986), 241–67, pp. 250–2.

[11] Chamberlain links Tittere tu with 'Our papists of Cheshire and Lancashire' and reports that 'This combination began first in the Low Countries in the Lord Vaulx his regiment' (*Letters*, ii. 530), forces which were largely Catholic. Yonge records rumours of Catholicism in the fleet sent to Spain (*Diary*, 68–9). Constable of the Bugle was a suspected Jesuit; cf. *Calendar of State Papers Domestic* (*CSPD*), *1619–1623*, 180, 199, 272. These and other evidences (see Graves, 'Some Pre-Mohock Clansmen', 402–4) refute Patterson's attempt to align Tittere tu with agitation against Spain.

[12] *Wit Revived: Or, A New and Excellent way of Divertisment digested into most ingenious Questions and Answers. By Asdryasdust Tossoffacan* (1674). In the PRO 'Giant. Tossacan . . . Giant. Drunckzadoge/Giant. Drun[k]assaratt' and 'Giant. Drinkittupall' indicate the Bugle's preferred activity. Cf. *Wit Restor'd* (1656), esp. 'The Tytere-Tues, or A Mock-*Songe to the tune of* Chive Chase. By Mr *George Chambers*'—known to be of the Bugle—p. 29; and, for generally boisterous Garterism, 'St. George for England', in *Wit and Drollery* (enlarged edn., 1682), 273–7.

[13] These lists follow 'examinacon' in State Papers (14/155/84–5). Graves prints them, accurately enough, but ignores Carew. The position of this name near the bottom of a register organized by rank rules out confusion with 'Tho: Carie the Lord Lepingtons younger sonne', though the latter's involvement in the Madrid venture is attested, e.g. by Chamberlain (*Letters*, ii. 482).

A very different story ran its course in that same year, 1623. Folded into the papers of Boxley Abbey, Kent, in a miscellany compiled by Sir Francis Wyatt, are three elegies on Wyatt's sister Eleanor. Herself a poet of merit, though for centuries passed over and unpublished,[14] she was the first wife of that John Finch who would, during the personal rule, brand Prynne and defend the prerogative. In the early 1620s, however, neither these Wyatts nor Finch held high office. Their interests revolved around the Virginia Company, while John Finch was making a name for himself as a 'puritan and moderate' MP.[15] Culturally they belonged to that fraction of the gentry which could favour, in the 1640s, insurrection. The anti-Spanish rebel Sir Thomas Wyatt was a proudly acknowledged ancestor; Sir Francis married Margaret Sandys, kinswoman to parliamentary colonels.[16] The year 1621, indeed, found Margaret's brother Sir Edwin restrained for using his influence in the Commons against rapprochement with Madrid.[17] And by 1623, the MP who once declared 'No successive King, but First elected. Election . . . by Consent of People' had earned, along with the Virginia Company as a whole, a decided reputation for opposing royal interests.[18] Economic recession, including a disastrous local harvest in the year of Eleanor's death,[19] did nothing to modify this stance. Nor did subsequent controversy pass Boxley by. Later decades found the area a Brownist stronghold, associated perhaps with Digger activity.[20]

---

[14] The miscellany in BL Add. MS 62135 pt. ii includes four texts attributed to 'E': a twenty-three stanza autobiographical poem (fos. 334^r–7^r), a sestet (fo. 337^r), advice to a rival in trochaic tetrameters (fos. 337^v–9^r), and 'Sooner the number or the value . . .' (339^v–40^r). The poems recur, ascribed 'E.F.', in a seemingly later Kent anthology, Harvard MS Eng. 703. On the county's literary culture see Peter Laslett, 'The Gentry of Kent in 1640', *Cambridge Historical Journal*, 9 (1947–9), 148–64.

[15] Peter Clark, *English Provincial Society from the Reformation to the Revolution: Religion, Politics and Society in Kent, 1500–1640* (Hassocks, 1977), 336, noting Finch's persistence in this role through the election of 1624. Wilfrid R. Prest sketches his Presbyterian background in 'Sir Henry Finch (1558–1625)', in Donald Pennington and Keith Thomas (eds.), *Puritans and Revolutionaries: Essays in Seventeenth-Century History Presented to Christopher Hill* (Oxford, 1978), 94–117. The biography by W. H. Terry, *The Life and Times of John, Lord Finch* (London, 1936), is unreliable but usefully prints a Latin elegy on Eleanor Finch from the Boxley church register, p. 65.

[16] Alan Everitt, *The Community of Kent and the Great Rebellion 1640–60* (Leicester, 1973), 63, 117.

[17] Conrad Russell, *Parliaments and English Politics 1621–1629* (Oxford, 1979), ch. 2, pp. 122–3, 'The Examination of Mr Mallory after the Parliament of 1621', *Bulletin of the Institute of Historical Research*, 50 (1977), 125–32.

[18] Quoted by Noel Malcolm, 'Hobbes, Sandys, and the Virginia Company', *Historical Journal*, 24 (1981), 297–321, p. 302.

[19] Clark, *English Provincial Society*, 317 ff., relates Kentish involvement in the Virginia Company to the need for economic diversification.

[20] Ibid. 370, 393.

That Eleanor did not live to see these developments is less painful than the nature of her death, while heavily pregnant or in childbirth. Thus much is clear from her elegies. One of them is attributed to a certain 'C.A.' The second is ascribed to, and known to be by, Carew; but it appears in other places as 'An Elegie on the La[dy] Pen[iston]'.[21] Paradoxically, the unlikeliness of that poem's being 'An Elegie on E.F.' lends weight to the third elegy's subscription, though hesitant and later deleted, 'T.C.'[22] Sir Francis Wyatt probably knew the poet, who was born a few miles from Boxley and had a sister married nearby.[23] His other Carew ascriptions are sound. And do we not find, in this modest provincial text, an anticipation of the poet's Caroline images of vulnerable bowered calm?[24]

> Coward death thy Stigian dart
> Now let fly at any heart.
> Thou hast slaine at once in those
> All that earth could feare to loose. . . .
> She from whom earth hop't to see
> Fruit befitting such a tree.
> Whose sweet branches might afford
> More content then Jonah's guord. . . .

But the poem itself does not concern me, nor even (quite) its ascription. What matters is Wyatt's recollection that Carew had written *an* elegy for his sister. For it points up the 'country' dimension of this poet:

[21] In the posthumous edition of Carew's *Poems* (1640), and half a dozen manuscripts listed on pp. 57–8 of the *Index of English Literary Manuscripts*, vol. ii, pt. i, compiled by Peter Beal (London, 1987). Most quotations below are, contrastedly, from manuscripts with a high proportion of Carew material (e.g. Rosenbach MS 1083/17 (Carey MS), Bodleian MS Don. b. 9 (Wyburd MS)) and from miscellanies which contain fewer poems but witness Carew's range of circulation in the decades after 1623. Contractions have been expanded, upper case imposed at the start of certain verse lines; for ease of reference a few titles are regularized from *Poems*.

[22] The attribution reads 'Qu [space] By T.C. on E.F.', with 'T.C.' crossed through at some later stage, fo. 348ᵛ. In Harvard MS Eng. 703 the text is not ascribed. That MS includes on p. 15, beside the 'C.A.' poem (under the title 'An Epitaph made vpon yᵉ same woemans death by C:', preceded by a love poem and part of another, from 'A'), a touching 'in obitum sobolis'.

[23] The family lived at West Wickham, until about 1598 (when Carew was 3 or 4 years old) when they moved to London, taking up residence in Chancery Lane. The poet matriculated as a Kentishman (C. W. Boase and Andrew Clark (eds.), *Register of the University of Oxford*, 2 vols. (Oxford, 1885–9), vol. ii, pt. 2, p. 301). Martha married James Cromer of Tunstall, then Sir Edward Hales of Tenterden, *c*.7 and 16 miles from Boxley.

[24] Cf. the epistle on Gustavus Adolphus (i.e. 'In answer of an Elegiacall Letter . . .'), where 'Myrtle bowers' are the more vulnerable for their overprotested 'securitie' (quoting St John's College, Cambridge MS S23, fos. 73ʳ–5ʳ). Also the erotic shades of 'A Pastorall Dialogue' (both texts) and 'A Rapture', and the association with illness in 'Vpon the sicknesse of (E.S.)', 'Must Feavors shake this goodly Tree and all | That ripened fruite from the fayre branches fall? | Which Princes haue desirde to tast?' (quoting BL Add. MS 25303, fos. 140ᵛ–1ʳ).

the Carew who stayed at Wrest Park, Bedfordshire, Selden's rural retreat; the lyricist who, in his poems on the green sickness, praises Katharine and Mary Neville, a family associated with Protestant and republican politics; the poet anthologized by Lucy Hutchinson.[25] That Carew and his writings enjoyed such a variety of connections does not raise him above the conflicts of his age, but it reminds us how complex they were. In so far as he was a court poet, élite culture was articulate with more ironies than meet the eye. Behind the masquerade cult of the Garter in *Cælum Britanicum*—to take an extreme instance—with its jesting at 'the annuall celebration of the Gygantomachy',[26] lies the parodic cult of the Bugle. But also in so far as he became a courtier, Carew preserved 'country' affinities. To read 'Vpon my Lord Chiefe Iustice', or the prefatory poem to George Sandys's *Psalms*, outstanding works from the 1630s, is not only to encounter Finch of the prerogative and Sandys the Privy Chamberer, but the *'J.F'* of Wyatt's miscellany, and the brother of Margaret Sandys who ventured to Virginia and later lived at Boxley—and both poems are changed by that.[27] What the manuscript evidences of 1623 show is Carew capable of mourning with one hand an obscure provincial lady while toasting 'Prince Ottoman' with the other.

Yet repeatedly in criticism and historical writing, from Hazlitt to the latest textbooks, Carew is presented as 'the negligent courtier', a poet of 'pusillanimous hedonism', all lace and velvet.[28] Tarred with the brush of

---

[25] On Wrest Park see below, pp. 211–12; on the Nevilles e.g. *DNB*; Lucy Hutchinson's anthology is in Nottinghamshire Record Office, HU/3.

[26] Quoting the first edn. (1634), B4ᵛ. In Carew's source, *Lo spaccio della bestia trionfante* (below, pp. 214–15), Heaven is purified on 'la festa de la Gigantoteomachia'. Given the overtones of papist conspiracy generated by the Bugle and Tittere tu (above, n. 11), it is interesting that the poet should relocate that feast, away from the occasion of his masque, Shrove Tuesday, to 'the fift of *November* last'.

[27] Strikingly, when Carew's poem appeared, in Sandys's second edition (1638), it was with work by Sir Francis Wyatt. That the *'J.F.'* to whom two poems are ascribed in the Boxley Abbey papers is Finch ('I will sooner hope to know . . .', fos. 340ᵛ–1ʳ, 'Alas I am content, resolue thou then', fo. 341ʳ⁻ᵛ) appears confirmed by 'J.Fin.' after the latter in Harvard MS Eng. 703 (pp. 30–1). His lasting love of rhetoric is remarked e.g. by *DNB*. Such sophistication puts in doubt the flatly political reading of 'Vpon my Lord Chiefe Iustice' proposed by Kevin Sharpe, *Criticism and Compliment: The Politics of Literature in the England of Charles I* (Cambridge, 1987), 142–3, 283, 288, 299 (which also overlooks Finch's early remarriage). For an index of *'J.F.'*'s cultural consistency, protested to the Long Parliament, see Prest, 'Sir Henry Finch (1558–1625)', 116, recalling that when Evelyn met him in exile at The Hague he was lodged at the house of a Brownist.

[28] Hazlitt calls Carew 'an elegant court-trifler' in his *Lectures Chiefly on the Dramatic Literature of the Age of Elizabeth* (London, 1820), 251. Negligence is glancingly imputed by Alastair Fowler, 'Country House Poems: The Politics of a Genre', *Seventeenth Century*, 1 (1986), 1–14, p. 10, while hedonism is charged in P. W. Thomas's less considerable 'Two Cultures? Court and

royal 'complacency' and 'ruthlessness',[29] he is accused of having 'almost no qualities of his own',[30] and selected as the author of a handful of poems in which Jonson and Donne are said to combine.[31] When larger perspectives are proposed, analysis tends, in the strict sense, to the preposterous: later things come first, and Carew is read in the light of a Revolution or Rebellion he did not live to see.[32] Even now, as the poet begins to feature in freshly informed studies of court culture,[33] the shape of his achievement is overwritten by dubious assumptions. High among the reasons for this is a neglect of his medium, and hence relation with his readers. It will be one of my claims here that an intelligible Carew emerges only when early printed texts (the basis of every edition and account so far) are

Country under Charles I', in Conrad Russell (ed.), *The Origins of the English Civil War* (London, 1973), 168–93, p. 179. The tradition of Whig commentary invoked by 'lace and velvet' (e.g. C. V. Wedgwood, 'Cavalier Poetry and Cavalier Politics', in *Velvet Studies* (London, 1946), *Poetry and Politics under the Stuarts* (Cambridge, 1960)) is often pronounced dead, but its influence remains evident in e.g. Graham Parry's discussion of masque, *The Golden Age Restor'd: The Culture of the Stuart Court, 1603–42* (Manchester, 1981), 184–203, and in Derek Hirst's uncharacteristic gesture, *Authority and Conflict: England 1603–1658* (London, 1986), 164: 'the revelling cavalier poetry of the likes of Thomas Carew contrasted dangerously with the desperate certainty of puritan sermons that God was turning his back on England.'

[29] John Creaser, '"The present aid of this occasion": The Setting of *Comus*', in David Lindley (ed.), *The Court Masque* (Manchester, 1984), 111–34, pp. 118–19; Martin Butler, *Theatre and Crisis 1632–1642* (Cambridge, 1984), 78.

[30] Hardin Craig (ed.), *A History of English Literature* (New York, 1950), 304.

[31] Leavis insists in *Revaluation* (1936; Harmondsworth, 1972), 21–3, that Carew 'should be . . . more than an anthology poet', then reduces to an anthology one of his most achieved epitaphs (pp. 40–2). Disintegrative knowingness disables much subsequent criticism.

[32] Hence the chronological drift which postdates *Cælum Britanicum* to 1637 (Hirst, *Authority and Conflict*, 163), or reserves it for the closing pages of Stephen Orgel's survey of Stuart court theatre: 'That such forms of expression should now seem to us at best obscure, at worst insincere, says much for the success of the Puritan revolution. History has vindicated William Prynne' (*The Illusion of Power* (Berkeley, 1975), 88).

[33] Much can be learned from Kevin Sharpe's *Criticism and Compliment*, from the scholarly essays of Raymond A. Anselment—notably 'Thomas Carew and the "Harmlesse Pastimes" of Caroline Peace', *Philological Quarterly*, 62 (1983), 201–19—and from the outstanding work of R. Malcolm Smuts: 'The Puritan Followers of Henrietta Maria in the 1630s', *English Historical Review*, 93 (1978), 26–45; 'The Political Failure of Stuart Cultural Patronage', in Guy Fitch Lytle and Stephen Orgel (eds.), *Patronage in the Renaissance* (Princeton, 1981), 165–87; *Court Culture and the Origins of a Royalist Tradition in Early Stuart England* (Philadelphia, 1987). Among literary critics, Michael P. Parker has shown himself most alert to the possibilities of reassessment. His Ph.D., '"Comely Gestures": Thomas Carew and the Creation of a Caroline Poetic' (Yale, 1979), is extracted and developed in: '"All are not born (Sir) to the Bay": "Jack" Suckling, "Tom" Carew, and the Making of a Poet', *English Literary Renaissance*, 12 (1982), 341–68; 'Carew's Politic Pastoral: Virgilian Pretexts in the "Answer to Aurelian Townsend"', *John Donne Journal*, 1 (1982), 101–16; '"To my friend G.N. from Wrest": Carew's Secular Masque', in Claude J. Summers and Ted-Larry Pebworth (eds.), *Classic and Cavalier: Essays on Jonson and the Sons of Ben* (Pittsburgh, 1982), 171–91; and 'Diamond's Dust: Carew, King, and the Legacy of Donne', in the same editors' *The Eagle and the Dove: Reassessing John Donne* (Columbia, Mo., 1986), 191–200.

supplemented by manuscript.[34] As well as recovering a poet peculiarly sensitive to what it means to be read—alert to the ways in which script, music, and print modify the significance of language—Carew then shows himself capable of intricate development. In place of the 'THOMAS CAREVV | Esquire' who authorizes *Poems* (1640) there appears an intelligence that defines and refines itself by dispersal as much as concentration. The sophisticated young translator from Italian, born in late-Elizabethan Kent and flourishing by 1623, seems not quite the same figure as the theatre wit of the late 1620s, or Sewer in Ordinary of the 1630s, while the veteran of the Berwick campaign, writing his last, great country-house poem before death in 1640, elaborates the apologist of Charles's personal rule.

That Carew's development seems less to possess its own trajectory than dissolve in social circumstance is unsurprising. It is because they have looked for an unique life story that scholars have imagined they know so little about him—and what they have learned, often, misconstrued. Both in general outline (as one of a generation of Kentish lawyers gaining preferment),[35] and in the patterns of kinship and patronage which supported him, Carew's career was typical for his period. He matriculated from Merton College in 1608, for example, just as he went into Chambers at the Middle Temple 'bound with . . . George Carew' in 1612,[36] because of family tradition. His father, Sir Matthew, was a distinguished lawyer. Warden Savile of Merton was a kinsman by marriage.[37] The poet's first employment, in 1613, was with Sir Dudley Carleton in Venice: protégé and stepson-in-law of Savile, joint-translator and disseminator of his Chrysostom, patron of Merton graduates.[38] Significantly, we hear of Carew reporting back to Savile in 1616 upon his return from Carleton's mission to the Hague.[39] Such connections were largely to remain intact. It is in Carleton's circle, for example, that we encounter John Hales, fellow of Merton and another relative of the poet by marriage, who will be associated with Carew in Suckling's 'The Wits', who links him (along with George Sandys) to the culture of Great Tew, and who eventually

---

[34] Only ten of Carew's poems, plus the masque, were published during his lifetime. They are listed by Rhodes Dunlap (ed.), *The Poems of Thomas Carew* (Oxford, 1949), pp. lix–lxii.

[35] Clark, *English Provincial Society*, 271 ff.

[36] Dunlap, in Carew, *Poems*, p. xvii, quoting the Temple records.

[37] Cf. H. W. Garrod, 'Sir Henry Savile: 1549–1949', repr. in his posthumous *The Study of Good Letters*, ed. John Jones (Oxford, 1963), esp. p. 103.

[38] At Venice, for instance, Carleton employed Nathaniel Brent, Isaac Wake as Secretary, and Thomas Horne as Chaplain, all three fellows of Merton.

[39] *Poems*, ed. Dunlap, p. xxiii.

attends the poet—with a dramatic refusal of absolution (according to Walton)—on his deathbed.[40]

Carew's relations with Carleton also reach across two decades. This is worth emphasis, since the received life story, established in Rhodes Dunlap's edition, presents the poet's difficulties in 1616—when he was edged out of employment for writing satirical notes on the Carletons—as a decisive rupture, a moment of 'disgrace'.[41] In its wake, Dunlap believes, Carew came down with the pox and began to write the Psalm translations reserved by Victorian commentators for a late phase of recantation. To read at all widely in the Public Record Office, however, is not only to hear elevating news from Venice, with visits by Hobbes and Cavendish, Arundel and Inigo Jones, but to register Carleton's disapproving fascination with a whole series of drunken wards and kinsmen, among whom Carew was but one.[42] We learn of paintings and marbles procured, but in Carleton's handling of them find an insecure diplomat, eager to trade art for court favour. Carleton's appointment as ambassador to the United Provinces makes him seem a powerful employer, not a man to alienate. But his financial difficulties were compounded by the post, religious turmoil in the Low Countries hampered his efforts, while intrigues over the cloth trade and Treaty of Xanten drove Carleton into political embarassment. The year 1616, indeed, brought several problems to a head. Philip Lytton, known associate of Carew, who had been left drunkenly concussed in Venice, arrived in The Hague expecting maintenance. Carleton's protracted effort, following the fall of his patron Somerset, to sell his marbles to Arundel foundered.[43] The ambassador, never in the best of health, was afflicted with gout and the stone. It was not a good time for the poet to commit critical thoughts to paper.

Certain remarks by Carleton complement Dunlap's account of Carew. One letter to Chamberlain overlooked by the Oxford editor warns of

---

[40] *Poems*, ed. Dunlap, pp. xl–xli.

[41] Ibid., p. xxi. For an attractive, though finally unpersuasive, interpretation, see Joanne Altieri, 'Responses to a Waning Mythology in Carew's Political Poetry', *Studies in English Literature*, 26 (1986), 107–24.

[42] Informative Carleton correspondence from this period bulks large in SP 84/72–7 and 99/9–20. Limited selections are available in Philip Yorke (ed.), *Letters from and to Sir Dudley Carleton, Knt. during his Embassy in Holland, from January 1615, to December 1620* (London, 1757) and in *Dudley Carleton to John Chamberlain, 1603–1624*, ed. Maurice Lee, Jr. (Princeton, 1972). His early career has been examined by Albert Henry Marshall: 'Sir Dudley Carleton: James I's Ambassador to Venice, 1610–1615' (MA, Wake Forest, 1973); 'Sir Dudley Carleton and English Diplomacy in the United Provinces, 1616–1628' (Ph.D., Rutgers, 1978).

[43] Evidence in Carleton's letters is now supplemented by David Howarth, *Lord Arundel and his Circle* (New Haven, 1985), 58–63.

'faults and close knaueries, wch are of so high a nature in him as you would little imagine'.[44] But this same missive does not deny the poet's fitness to serve one of the new Privy Counsellors; and it must surely be discounted by what Carleton's biographer describes as 'a propensity toward priggishness'.[45] Interestingly Carew was not the only kinsman shown the door in 1616. Lytton was sent off to make his way in the world.[46] Yet the pair turn up shortly afterwards, seemingly no worse for their liberty, as strikingly elegant attendants at the investiture of the Prince of Wales[47]—that festival of pageantry memorialized in *Ciuitatis amor*. By 1619 Carew would be secure in the train of Sir Edward Herbert, ambassador to Paris. Temporary setbacks of one sort or another were expected in diplomatic life. Carleton had fallen out with his first employer, Parry, in 1603 and he almost exactly duplicated Carew's blunder in 1616 by criticizing Secretary Winwood on paper. If the note-taking poet was, in the words of his distressed father, 'an Aristarchus, to fynd faultes in other', far more so was Carleton in that tactless letter to his superior.[48] We should think of them less as master and miscreant servant and more as mutual players in the game of patronage, their motives not quite their own.[49] Certainly, we must consider them in a new light when we learn that the only known Carew poem in holograph—his reply to Jonson's 1631 'Ode to Himselfe'—survives in Carleton's papers.[50] It is an example of manuscript socializing biography. Whatever may be deduced from the poem being where it is, it cannot suggest an irreparable breach.

Exculpating Carew from 'disgrace' is, though, a minor satisfaction. Of far greater interest is the picture early documents provide of virtuoso culture in the making. From directions given to Inigo Jones, and a list of

[44] To Chamberlain from The Hague, 5/15 Sept. 1616, SP 84/73/201–4, 204^r. Compare his relief, and that of Lady Carleton (she had been 'passionatly affected and troubled'), at the discrediting of 'a voice . . . here spred' that he would marry a kinswoman, née Lytton, widow of Sir George Smith, 16/26 Nov. 1624, SP 84/121/98–9, 98^r.

[45] Marshall, 'Carleton and English Diplomacy', 16.

[46] To Chamberlain, 1 May 1616, SP 84/72/169–70.

[47] *Poems*, ed. Dunlap, pp. xxix–xxx.

[48] Dunlap quotes Sir Matthew's letter, *Poems*, pp. xxvi–vii; Marshall, 'Carleton and English Diplomacy', gives Carleton's critique of Winwood, pp. 44–5 (4 Mar. 1616, SP 84/72/92); Carleton admits the damage done in a letter of 2 Dec. 1617, SP 84/81/12–13.

[49] e.g. in their mutual cultivation of Buckingham. 'To the Countesse of Anglesey' shows that Carew, presumably introduced by Herbert, was acting for the Villiers family in 1622 (the marriage of Kit and Elizabeth Sheldon), a time when Carleton, much less successfully (cf. John H. Barcroft, 'Carleton and Buckingham: The Quest for Office', in H. S. Reinmuth (ed.), *Early Stuart Studies* (Minneapolis, 1970), 122–36), was wooing the Duke as an alternative to Arundel.

[50] Beal, *Index of English Literary Manuscripts*, ii/1. 39.

holdings by Daniel Nys, we can identify works purchased during Carew's stay in Venice: Tintorettos, Veroneses, a Bassano Vecchio, an Andrea Schiavone.[51] From papers relating to Somerset and Arundel, Buckingham and the acquisitive Rubens, we can gauge the wealth of Carleton's statuary.[52] In Italy, The Hague, and Paris, Carew was initiated into systems of taste which would not find their codification in England until Junius' *Painting of the Ancients*.[53] Art and life come into subtler relations, approaching the kind of equivalence that leads Suckling to declare, 'a gallerie hung with *Titians* or *Vandikes* hand, and a chamber filled with living Excellence, are the same things to me'.[54] Delicacy of effect becomes more than Tudor daintiness: it is a means to the sublime.[55] In verse born of such virtuosity—small in scale to be large of implication—voice and the body aspire to song and sculpture, while script becomes painterly. Hence the lyric subtitled 'Celia singing' in 1640 and our editions, but associated in manuscript with 'Arundel Garden' and (Buckingham's residence) 'a Gallery at Yorke house':[56]

> Harke how my Cælia with the choice
> Musick of her hand and voice
> Stills the lowd wind and makes the wild
> Incensed Bore and panther mild
> Marke how those statues like men mou'd
> Whilst men with wonder statues prou'd
> The stiff Rock bends to worshipp her
> The Idol turns Idolater. . . .

If this modulation of stone to flesh recalls another event of 1623—the printing of the Shakespeare Folio—the idiom of Leontes' court is per-

---

[51] Arundel required that £200 be given to Sherburn, Carleton's agent, for *Susanna and the Elders*, the *Benediction of Jacob*, the *Queen of Sheba*, the *Samaritan Woman*, and *Ceres, Bacchus, and Venus* by Tintoretto (see Howarth, *Arundel*, 60–1). Cf. '3 by Paul Veronese, the Life of Hercules . . . 1 by Bassano Vecchio, the Beheading of St. John . . . 1 The Venus of Titian . . . 1 by Andrea Schiavone, Shepherds', quoting 'Danyel Nys his list of pictures', 8 Feb. 1614–15, in W. Noël Sainsbury (ed.), *Original Unpublished Papers Illustrative of the Life of Sir Peter Paul Rubens, as an Artist and a Diplomatist* (London, 1859), 275.

[52] Sainsbury (ed.), *Papers*, 9–44, 273–80, 299–303 (cf. Howarth, *Arundel*, 60 and 62, Barcroft, 'Carleton and Buckingham', 130–2). Twenty-four chests, each containing several pieces, are listed in the 'Note of ye Statues' (shipped in the *Falcon* of Dort) endorsed by Carleton.

[53] *De pictura veterum* (1637); the English translation, dedicated to the Countess of Arundel, appeared the following year.

[54] *Sir John Suckling: The Non-Dramatic Works*, ed. Thomas Clayton (Oxford, 1971), Letter 2, p. 108.   [55] Junius, *Painting*, 330–1.

[56] Beal, *Index of English Literary Manuscripts*, ii/1. 93–5, here quoting the untitled text in BL Add. MS 25707, fo. 7ʳ.

plexed by comparison. Shakespeare anxiously discriminates between 'Faith', 'Oyly Painting', and 'Magick' in the 'Chappell' near Paulina's 'Gallerie'.[57] Carew, with travelled insouciance, turns his gallery into a crypto-Laudian chapel and embraces the puritan slur that connoisseurship is idolatry.[58] His may be a quasi-dramatic poem—one Oxford manuscript has notes suggestive of performance[59]—but its artistry is miniature beside Shakespeare's, condensing its marvels into compact tetrameters continuous with the lyricism they celebrate.

Such conceits of scale and instantiations of the medium are a hallmark of virtuosity. In Dutch and Italian painting, contemporaries are fascinated by convoluted lines and spaces, by the unstable perspectives of Titian—much in evidence at York House—detailed with jewels, laces, stars that resolve into knots of pigment, by Still Lives, not read through the photograph, but as feats of the pencilled surface. In such a context, the poet's script (trace of Celia's voice and body) will resemble ' *Titians* or *Vandikes* hand' because it uses signs spatially to dispose meanings compact with 'living Excellence'. Carew's being a manuscript poet here becomes as much a creative matter as an aspect of reception; what palaeographers call his 'accomplished italic'[60] metonymically participates in, for example, 'A Fancy':[61]

> Marke how this polisht Easterne sheet
> Doth with our Northerne tincture meet,
> For though the paper seeme to sinke,
> Yet it receives, and bears the Inke;
> And on her smooth soft brow these spots,
> Seeme rather ornaments then blots;
> Like those you Ladies use to place
> Mysteriously about your face . . .

Writing on oriental paper, the poet displays a calligraphic intentness which would seem Buddhist were it not so worldly. At first, paper-fine

---

[57] *The Winters Tale*, v. ii (Cc^v).

[58] The Romanist sympathies of the Arundels were notorious. Buckingham's stance remained ambivalent, though he inclined to the Arminians at the York House conference, 1626. Some idea of likely reaction to Carew's lyric can be had by comparing the song in Middleton's *A Game at Chesse* v. i.

[59] In 'Early Seventeenth-Century Verse Miscellanies and their Value for Textual Editors', *English Manuscript Studies 1100–1700*, 1 (1989), 182–210, n. 29, Mary Hobbs instructively records marginal comments at ll. 5 and 18, in Corpus Christi College MS 328, 'Here these co: in', 'here these fall'.

[60] P. J. Croft, *Autograph Poetry in the English Language: Facsimiles of Original Manuscripts from the Fourteenth to the Twentieth Century*, 2 vols. (London, 1973), i. 36.

[61] Quoting, accidentals edited, the 1642 edition of *Poems*.

distinctions prevent a dispersal of meaning across the work's ornamented surface. The 'Characters' are not 'carelesse', we are told, "cause you underneath may find I A sence that can enforme the mind'. Yet the poem concludes with a typically startling twist: 'So what at first was only fit I To fold up silkes, may wrap up wit.' What will 'enforme', by wrapping up turns its actual 'underneath' outside, leaving the written surfaces of 'wit' inside like a folded letter. This suggestion is the more problematic given the hint of revised fair copy in 'polisht . . . sheet', as though the revealed blankness were itself opaquely glossed, all script as well as none. There being a fullness in candour is more remarkable than blankness: complexity is exhausted before writing begins, and what Carew disposes is unhurried, supplementary, with a spareness which reaches beyond the mannerist. As 'A Fancy' comes to mean 'delicate contrivance' (ahead of general usage), the text seems less 'a curious thought' with the structure of 'musical impromptu'[62] than a painting which has depths by virtue of imagined internal surfaces.

Herrick, Lovelace, and other poets of the generation after Carew will domesticate this love of line and whorl and planisphere in the shoestrings, fans, dewdrops, and compendious snails that fill their cabinets of fancy. But such a troping of minutiae into foldings articulate round the inside (emblems becoming monads?), through the motif of *multum in parvo*, barely figures in Jacobean writing. When Peacham enthuses about 'a cherrie stone cut in the forme of a basket' or 'the *Ilias* of *Homer* . . . enclosed within a nut'[63] his astonishment—'*Cicero* tels vs he saw it with his eyes'— seems insular. The native appetite that can digest Donne's 'The Flea' strains at Scaliger, 'whether in iest or earnest I know not' (as Peacham admits), reporting 'a flea he saw with a long chaine of gold about his necke, kept very daintily in a boxe, and being taken forth, could skip with his chaine, and sometime suck his mistresses white hand.' For Carew the Grand Tourist such curiosities are familiar. He is fluent in extravagance. One miscellany calls his most popular youthful lyric, on 'A flye that flew into my Mistris her eye', 'extempory', something 'perform'd',[64] and dramatic in a Marinesque sense it is.[65] As in 'Celia singing', or that later

[62] *OED*, 'fancy', *sb.* 5.

[63] This, and following quotations, from *The Compleat Gentleman* (1622), 75.

[64] Yale, Osborn MS b. 197, pp. 52–3. Compiled by Tobias Alston of Sayham Hall near Sudbury, this manuscript is linked in content as well as social geography to friends of Carew at Little Saxham. See below, p. 209. The poem itself is quoted from the superior Boxley Abbey text, BL Add. MS 62135 part ii, fo. 354[r].

[65] Marino came to Paris in 1615 and published in the year of Carew's French employment

exercise 'A Fancy', rhyme points up Carew's conceits so lightly as to indicate the shaping rather than completion of contrivance. One is reminded of Junius on the beauty of unfinished art, on canvases in the making.[66] The means by which Carew's poem becomes an object, wraps itself up, is deftly reinforced as the fly's carefree movement ('She did from hand to bosome skipp') inclines toward resolution in the 'polisht' mobility of his favourite ornament,[67] the pearl:

> At last into her ey she flew,
> There scorch't in flames, and drown'd in dew.
> Like Phaeton from the Sunnes spheare,
> She fell and with her drop't a teare.
> Of which a pearle was straight compos'd,
> Wherein her ashes ly enclos'd.
>> Thus she recieu'd from Celia's ey,
>> Funerall flame, tombe, obsequy.

'In iest or earnest?' would be Peacham's question. But the poem so busies itself with being lucid that doubt hardly registers, just as wonder supplants surprise. 'Lucidity' in this context might be rendered *arguzia* or *acutezza* since the language of Italian criticism is apter than anything Jacobean: *meraviglia* for artful extraordinariness; *novità*, despite the poem's derivation from Guarini.[68] The word 'ingenuity' recurs in criticism of the 1620s. Linked to another art term, *ingegno*, it has the advantage in Stuart English of implying almost its opposite: ingenuousness.[69] Cadenced to elicit (by assuming) consent, the lyric is suavely neglectful of its own brilliance, which outstrips that of its source both in range of reference and dexterity. The compacting of sun and eye, for example, in the simile of Phaeton, is not in Guarini. It satisfies that enthusiasm for cosmographical diminution which leads Peacham, in his paragraphs on tiny things, to celebrate the astrolabe,[70] while hinting at the mythological wit which will

Galeria, a collection which glitters with spiders, ants, butterflies entombed in verse. Rivalling the delights of York House and Arundel Garden, it has sections entitled *Pitture* and *Sculture*. That Carew, and Sir Edward Herbert, read Marino is clear from imitation and translation. It is unlikely that they would have omitted to attend one or other of the public improvisations which helped establish his fame.

[66] *Painting*, 120–1, 187.

[67] e.g. 'Lips and Eyes', 'To my Rivall', and, in scriptural vein, 'Epitaph on the Lady S. Wife to Sir W.S.' Bejewelled insects, often petrified in amber, were prized by virtuosi; see e.g. Evelyn's *Diary*, ed. E. S. de Beer, 6 vols. (Oxford, 1955), ii. 47 (26 Sept. 1645).

[68] The original is reprinted by Dunlap, *Poems*, 231.

[69] e.g. Carew's question 'When didst thou flie | From hence, cleare, candid Ingenuity?' in 'To my worthy Friend, M. D'Avenant, Vpon his Excellent Play, The Iust Italian' ((1630), A3ᵛ).

[70] *Compleat Gentleman*, 75–6.

prove sublimely reductive in *Cœlum Britanicum*. Carew's lyric displays in little qualities explored in that largest miniature. Indeed it suggests how means justified beginnings, sending the poet to particular, often particularized, matter: subjects which permitted an elegant volution of manner. Confirmed to whatever degree by the arts of Venice and the Low Countries, those priorities would remain, circumscribing yet defining the detail of his work.

The 'perform'd', the scripted yet 'extempory' aspect of Carew will have struck even early readers with no access to manuscript. His few initial printed works are prefatory verses to plays. In the opening pages of Tom May's *The Heire*, puffed by him in 1622, we seem to eavesdrop on the Order of the Bugle as Philocles and Clerimont dispute 'the Authenticke histories of chiualrie . . . where those braue men whom neither Enchantments, Gyants, Wind-mils, nor flockes of sheepe could vanquish, are made the trophyes of tryumphing loue'.[71] Eight years later and he is more securely audible in the echoes of his verse which adorn Davenant's *The Just Italian*.[72] Interestingly, Carew's printed defence of that play provoked an exchange of paper bullets in which his art was challenged wholesale, from its encomiastic and erotic matter to the praise it guaranteed for itself by coterie circulation.[73] Given the interaction of 'subiect' and implied occasion apparent in, for instance, 'A flye . . .', the hostile polemic—penned by Massinger—may be apt as well as intemperate in claiming such broad scope. For the dramatist, as Peter Beal has shown, Carew's 'tribe', which scribbles 'In corners and amonge yo[r] selues recite', cannot claim out of its exclusiveness the right to determine taste. Yet this exquisite clique treats theatre as its own domain: virtuosi in a muse's cabinet.[74] A large cultural shift is at issue here, with Aristarchus becoming a fashionable social animal. Discount for a moment Massinger's vehemence and it is possible to reflect that Carew's poems on Jonson and Donne make him our first great critic in verse.[75]

---

[71] 1622, B3[r].

[72] e.g. of 'A Rapture'; ed. cit., A4[r–v].

[73] Peter Beal, 'Massinger at Bay: Unpublished Verses in a War of the Theatres', *Yearbook of English Studies*, 10 (1980), 190–203.

[74] Cf. Michael Neill, '"Wits most accomplished Senate": The Audience of the Caroline Private Theaters', *Studies in English Literature*, 18 (1978), 341–60.

[75] Variants in the autograph of the former, and between the 1640 and (later) 1633 texts of the Donne elegy, display Carew's genius in practical as well as descriptive criticism. Cf. Junius' *Painting*, 208–9—and elsewhere, for instance pp. 348–9, together with Sir Henry Wotton's *Elements of Architecture* (1624), 84 ff., for the emergence of criticism from virtuosity.

But Massinger has more pressing concerns. What finally outrages him is the suggestion that the dilettante translator of 'loose raptures brought | In a Mart. booke from Italy' might enjoy what one of his admirers calls 'a more glorious charge' in 'the state'.[76] The quarrel glances at Carew's preferment to the Privy Chamber,[77] yet it carries larger implications. For the harshest of Massinger's lines, and a barbed sheaf against him, are written in the back of a journal of the 1629 Parliament: that turbulent last gathering before the personal rule, which ended with Sir John Finch pinned to the speaker's chair as Denzil Holles, Sir John Eliot, and other rebels passed 'the three resolutions' on Arminianism, tonnage, and poundage. It is a reminder of how inextricable were the arts of poetry and politics. What is to be deduced from the appearance in this journal of Carew's best-known lyric, 'Aske mee noe more', under the title 'verses on the Queene of Bohemia'?[78] How political does the dialogue implicit in that poem become? Martin Butler has cited the imprisonment of Eliot after the 1629 Parliament to characterize Carew's age as 'pre-political in the sense that it did not occur readily to men that society could tolerate dissenting opinion within itself as a matter of course'.[79] The Trumbull papers, with their avid recording of discord, suggest the importance of this being but a half-truth. 'Aske mee noe more', a lyric always in mid-argument, speaks from a culture as well as for the poet. More than tolerant of dissent, Carew devolves toward disputation. But then, poetic disputes dramatize the consensus which allows of disagreement, while 'Aske mee noe more' assumes an encompassing celebration, no matter how outrageously it makes a mistress, or Queen of Bohemia, the phoenix's nest. What such a lyric has to do with politics reaches beyond the unlikely notion that its author wrote propaganda for the Palatinate. In Carew, the obliquities of love poetry are continuous with such arguments of state as *Cœlum Britanicum*. The poet's elusive accomplishment depends not on

[76] Quoted in 'Massinger at Bay', 192, 195. These shafts against 'A Rapture' are far from unique; see, e.g., Paul Delany, 'Attacks on Carew in William Habington's Poems', *Seventeenth Century News*, 26 (1968), 36. Carew's own retraction comes in 'To the Queene'.

[77] 6 Apr. 1630; see Dunlap, *Poems*, p. xxxv. Carew became Sewer in Ordinary shortly afterwards, despite fierce competition (Clarendon notes) from a Scottish candidate. Kevin Sharpe indicates the degree of privilege by citing from SP 16/154/76 (1629) a list of thirty-two Privy Chamberers, four of them Sewers; see 'The Image of Virtue: The Court and Household of Charles I, 1625–1642', in David Starkey (ed.), *The English Court* (London, 1987), 226–60, p. 244.

[78] A unique title, though the manuscript (BL Add. MS 70639, fo. 66ʳ) is an early witness and textually orthodox, beginning with the stanza which comes second in 1640, 'Aske mee noe more whether doe straie . . . .'.

[79] *Theatre and Crisis*, 19. Butler is following Russell, *Parliaments and English Politics*, 416.

some anachronistic quarrel with himself but on a capacity for self-rehearsal in texts which imply other voices.

What is at stake here is clarified by Suckling, two of whose images of Carew take the significant form of dialogue. In the prose example, '*Jack*' and '*Tom*' dispute the advisability of the latter wedding a widow. The twin epistles, printed in parallel columns in *Fragmenta aurea*,[80] are read together, and their both being disagreements—Jack with Tom's intentions, Tom with Jack's dissent—reinforces the pleasure to be had in each voice shaping and confirming the other. '*Jack*' and '*Tom*', like the 'Tom' and 'Jacke' who went to Madrid, become visors of, or countenance, a situation. 'Upon my Lady Carliles walking in Hampton-Court garden'[81] goes further. Against a barrage of dissent from '*J.S.*', '*Thom*', author of 'Aske mee noe more', blazons another mistress who scatters 'rare perfumes all about | Such as bean-blossoms newly out | Or chafed spices give'. The poem contrives parody of the subtlest kind, *self*-mockery almost, because dialogue, not travesty, edges '*Thom*' (also 'T.C.') into vulnerable over-statement:

> Dull and insensible, could'st see
> A thing so near a Deity
> Move up and down, and feel no change?

Ultimately the interaction of '*Thom*' and '*J.S.*' is such as to persuade a Rawlinson manuscript to subscribe the poem 'T:C:'. Since that text is variant, and includes such 'Carewan' readings as 'Arabian gumtrees' for 'bean-blossoms', it is possible, as Suckling's editor notes, that it 'incorporates alterations or suggested revisions made by Carew'.[82] In a letter tellingly addressed from Wrest Park, Anne Merricke writes of 'the newe playe a ffreind of mine sent to Sr Iohn Sucklyn, and Tom: Carew (the best witts of the time) to correct'.[83] The idea of texts circulating for revision through the hands of Carew and Suckling writes dissent within consensus into the details of their literary activity. The likelihood that only a rhetorical Carew introduced variant readings suggests his ability, as 'T.C.', to rehearse himself in dialogues not quite his own. Certainly, even

---

80 Though not in Clayton's edition; Letters 51 (a) and (b), pp. 155–8.

81 *Suckling: Non-Dramatic Works*, 30–2.

82 Bod. MS Rawl. poet. 199; collated by Clayton, discussed p. 238.

83 That the epistle may be a faction (*Suckling: Non-Dramatic Works*, p. xlvi n. 3) complicates, mostly to its advantage, my argument. Even provisionally to examine 'correction' as a creative concept in this period (cf. n. 75) is to find the terms in which we customarily discuss, e.g., post-Jacobean versions of Shakespeare—Benson's *Poems* of 1640, Suckling's 'A Supplement of an imperfect Copy of Verses . . .'—inappropriate.

more than with 'Aske mee noe more', the drift of '*Thom*''s and '*J.S.*''s disputation cannot be separated from politics: the Countess of Carlisle's exercise of her charms at court, for and against Henrietta Maria and the King, contrary to the interests of Suckling, responsive to wooing by Carew.[84]

That manuscript variation should offer itself under the scheme of dialogue suggests how deeply the principle ran. English Renaissance minds were, through continued rehearsal, 'enformed' by it. At school, at Merton and the Middle Temple, Carew will have disputed. Several of his mature poems are quasi-academic dialogues refined by song, lyrics designed to cope with 'dissenting opinion' at court. 'Of iealousie', for instance, had its beginnings, Thomas Killigrew tells us, in 'a dispute held betwixt M[res] Cicilia Crofts and my self'.[85] In imagery highly political, it recurs in two manuscripts of poems on affairs of state.[86] Jealousy 'sitting on the usurped Throne', and ruling 'like a Tyrant', sufficiently explains that. Yet the word 'dispute' also implies private difficulties between Killigrew and his future wife, reminding us (in Caroline usage) that the structure of the song was already present in court conversation. Dialogue was so ubiquitous that even poems avoiding the form are spiced by disagreement. On reading at random in *Poems* (1640), 'In *Celia's* face a question did arise . . .', we expect the quarreling 'Lips and Eyes' to be a pretext for the pleasures of dissent, take the barely interrogative 'question' to speak from a world in which the 'matter of disputation' is more significant than any 'answer' in the emergent sense 'solution' could be.

Our habit of reading Caroline poetry in author-shaped parcels obscures the quality of its disagreements. To encounter Carew's reply to Townshend's 'vpon the death of the King of Sweden' in a collected edition makes for a poorer response than finding it side by side with the original—in, say, St John's College, Cambridge MS S23, where the antiphonal logic of the poem is rationalized and amplified by its interrelations with Townshend. That same miscellany begins with Jonson's 'Ode to him selfe' and Carew's 'To Benn Jo[h]nson'. The tactful firmness of Carew's dissent ('Tis true (deare Benn) . . . and yet tis true') is far more pointed in

---

[84] See Raymond A. Anselment, 'The Countess of Carlisle and Caroline Praise: Convention and Reality', *Studies in Philology*, 82 (1985), 212–33.

[85] Quoted by Beal, *Index of English Literary Manuscripts*, ii/1. 65, from the autograph of Killigrew's *Cicilia and Clorinda*, Folger MS V.b.209, pp. 50–1. The text here cited is Bod. MS Don. b. 9, fo. 4[r].

[86] Österreichische Nationalbibliothek, Vienna MS 14090, Victoria and Albert Museum, Dyce Collection, Cat. No. 43. It also, interestingly, features in Lucy Hutchinson's miscellany.

juxtaposition. Its rebarbative praise, 'Tis true . . . thy iust chastising hand | Hath fixed uppon this sotted age a brand', depends not only on the sottishness and branded thumb of Jonson, but on succeeding the evidences of that 'hand' in manus/script. Two poems change in meaning by being together—gain intimacy and equality, as between '*J.S.*' and '*Thom*'—and by heading a manuscript so much concerned with both leaders of a 'tribe'. Almost any arrangement of Carew poems demonstrates, however, that 'To *x*' is his commonest title, that his standard first line is imperative or vocative, positing an interlocutor. He naturally implies relations, what students of pragmatics call 'dialogue games',[87] and his intelligence gets to work by knowing in advance (though unspoken) that to which his writing answers. His lucidity is social ellipsis, and his verse is glossed with implications not to be mined out as ambiguity. Manuscript elaborates this by virtue of coterie exclusiveness, underwriting texts with the message that a short chain of transcription leads to the poet, overwriting them with courteous knowingness. You are one, manuscript flatters, who can decipher 'To T.H.' or 'To my friend G.N.' You are one of few, because manuscript publishes yet maintains the fiction that the reader is specially privileged. To examine a lyric such as 'Secrecy protested' is to find little of significance 'in the poem' but much generated by there being dozens of manuscripts which, beginning 'Feare not deere Loue that Ile reueale | Those houres of pleasure wee two steale', discreetly betray the protestation, trust us with it.[88]

First and last, though, dialogue is what its root in Greek declares: discourse going across against, *dia-*, joined in separation. This paradox is explored by Carew in a series of erotic poems which are among his best yet least discussed. In all of them the Blackfriars theatre-goer is evident, not only in the speech prefixes, inset observers, echoes of Shakespearian drama,[89] but in a rhetoric that extends into doing. 'A Pastorall Dialogue: Celia: Cleon',[90] for instance, moves from vocalized paradoxical embraces—

> Then thus my willing armes I winde
> About thee, and am soe
> Thy pris'ner,

---

[87] See e.g. the book of that title by Lauri Carlson (Dordrecht, 1983).

[88] BL Add. MS 25303, fo. 153ʳ. Agreeably endorsing this some manuscripts (e.g. Bod. MS Eng. poet. e. 14, fo. 12ʳ) begin 'Think not', admitting a shadow of duplicity. Bod. MS Rawl. poet. 65 even reads 'Doubt not, my Dear . . .', fo. 29ʳ.

[89] e.g. *Romeo and Juliet*, *The Tempest*, in 'This mossie bank . . .'

[90] BL Harley MS 6917, fos. 5ᵛ–6ᵛ.

—through a wreathed exchange of lovelocks, her favours, his 'ryme', into affections fraught with Petrarchan contraries, interrupted by a shepherd. Even when voices lose distinction, and only a reader eavesdrops, Carew is interested in fertile apartness. In 'A hymenæal Dialogue', the bride replies to a singing groom,[91] 'whose wordes were those, | For though your voyce the ayre did breake . . . through your lipps my hart did speake'—a pretty sentiment which does not prepare us for the 'disunion' which ends the poem, dividing bodies from souls, 'As two doe one, and one fowre growe | Each by contraction multiplyde.' Implosiveness of dialogue achieves the miniature sublime. As compound obliquity, double scope of indirection, dialogue converges on that inexplicit centre which is for Carew a reflex of movement rather than determinate point. At its most refined it is voiceless not because 'disunion' vanishes but because words recoil, eddy, and reticulate away. 'Though our bodyes are disioynd', the poet appeals 'To his mistress in absence',[92] 'lett vs work a mystique wreath . . . lett our secrett thoughts vnseene | Like netts be weav'd and entertwin'd.'

The audible influence of that 'dialogue of one', 'The Exstasie',[93] on these lyrics is ponderable, because Carew's eroticism is usually related to a different strain in Donne: egotistical and urbane. Part of the achievement of Carew's elegy on the Monarch of Wit, though, beside others of 1633, is its awareness of the Augustan sway he exercised over several realms of writing. To inspect the poem most attacked in the Trumbull papers, and since, 'A Rapture',[94] is to find a good deal that is Donnean yet not in its immediate model, 'To his Mistris Going to Bed': mutuality, implied dialogue, an aestheticism (as in 'The Exstasie') which relates the physical to the spiritual: 'Loves mysteries in soules doe grow, | But yet the body is his booke.' Beyond Donne's 'I', indeed beyond 'we', Carew is free with 'our': something shared, including 'our discourse'. He imagines, in his Arcadian grove, 'our actiue play', 'our soules | In stedfast peace'. If Celia has no reported speech, that at least avoids the betrayal which Randolph perpetrates in 'A Pastoral Courtship',[95] by giving Phyllis right of reply. What a seduced mistress can say in this period belongs, for the most part, to Complaint. Randolph is less aggressive than Donne *erectus*, 'having the foe in sight', but his assurance seems to threaten despite itself: 'No wasp

---

[91] St John's College, Cambridge MS S23, fos. 60ᵛ–1ʳ.

[92] Bod. MS Don. b. 9, fo. 20ʳ–ᵛ.

[93] Donne quotations from *The Elegies and The Songs and Sonnets*, ed. Helen Gardner (Oxford, 1965).

[94] Rosenbach MS 1083/17, fos. 49ᵛ–53ʳ.

[95] *Poems with the Muses Looking-Glasse: and Amyntas* (1638), 103–10.

nor hornet haunts this grove,' he tells Phyllis, 'Nothing that wears a sting, but I.' The violence implicit in the title of 'A Rapture' (i.e. 'rape') is modified by Celia's responsiveness into 'ecstasy' and 'poetic exaltation'. When Carew 'wears a sting' it is to become a creative emblem out of the rhetoric books.[96] Like a bee, that 'Flyes 'bout the paynted feild with nimble winge | Deflowringe the fresh virgins of the spring,' he will kiss his way down Celia's person,

> weareing as I goe
> A tract for louers one the printed snowe.
> Thenc climbing ore the swellinge Appenine,
> Retire into the groue of Eglantine:
> Where I will all those rauisht sweets destill
> Through Loues Alembique, and with Chimique skill
> From the mixt mass, one soueraigne Balme deriue,
> Then bring that great Eli[x]ar to thy hiue.

The most outrageous sexual act in the poem is substantively rhetorical. Tacit dialogue condenses eroticism into a lustrous reticence. Having buzzed across the body's book, rifling the florilegium and lipping his prints as tracts, Carew means to tongue that 'rich myne' which, in the exequy on Donne, is 'a Mine | Of rich and pregnant phansie'.[97] He may be active, but Celia's 'dumbe eloquence' (another phrase from the Donne elegy) provides his matter. Behind the passage are such lyrics as 'A Prayer to the winde',[98] in which a sigh, gusted down the mistress's nectarous body returns to the poet, replies wordlessly, having acquired the power to 'chainge . . . Every weede into a flower'.

Hence the expressive climax of 'A Rapture'. Lucrece, reading Aretine, 'hurles | Her limnes into a thousand windinge Curles, | And studyes Artfull postures'—attitudes 'Caru'd one the bark of euery neighbring tree': not Marvell's oak inscribed on oak, but erotically articulate windings. When Suckling rewrote Shakespeare's *Lucrece*,[99] he turned the heroine's modesty into passive display. Carew, by contrast, has her sexualize herself in art. Penelope actively chooses to 'display | Herself before the youth of Ithaca', while Daphne, still more energetic, breaks 'her barke, and . . . doth now unfetter'd, rune | To meete the embraces of the youthfull Sunn'.

96 e.g. *Discoveries* ll. 2466–82; *Ben Jonson*, ed. C. H. Herford, Percy and Evelyn Simpson, 11 vols. (Oxford, 1925–52), viii. 638–9. On the diffusion of this commonplace see Richard S. Peterson, *Imitation and Praise in the Poems of Ben Jonson* (New Haven, 1981), 6–9.

97 Quoting *Poems, By J.D. With Elegies on the Authors Death* (1633), 385–8.

98 BL Sloane MS 1792, fos. 130ʳ–1ʳ.

99 'A Supplement of an imperfect Copy of Verses . . .'

With her, the poem's imaginary inscribed verdure bursts out in unheard song:

> Full of her God she sings inspired layes
> Sweet Odes of loue such as deserue the Bayes
> Which shee herself was.

Chasteningly this reflexive conceit, though it again seems Marvellian, leaves an impure residue. 'A Rapture' has too many hints of doubtful wreathing (as when the poet hymns 'our twisted loues') not to recall (such is Carew's integrity), beyond the wound arms, exchanged curls, and 'ryme' of 'A Pastorall Dialogue: Celia: Cleon', the 'Nets of passions finest thred, | Snareing poems' in his 'Good counsel to a young Maid'.[100] Dialogue is not transcended by virtue of 'dumbe eloquence', not saved from involving persuasion, verbal 'rape'. It could not honour Celia's side of the encounter were it not startled as well as elated by the effect of erotic writing on Lucrece. But then, 'Honour', we are told, is a 'Goblyn'. It is the 'Gyant . . . Masquer' who keeps lovers out of Arcady. One reason why 'A Rapture' concerns itself with rhetoric is that, to imagine sexual liberty, it must posit a world beyond convention. There wishes, bodies, and the signs of art can be one, and a nymph's desiring song is crowned (as it were already) with 'the Bayes | Which shee herself was'. Such raptures lie beyond 'A Rapture', must be written out blankly, over the horizons of experience, from a poem whose language is fallen. Carew begins and ends in the social 'Pageant', the 'Gyant''s kingdom, where dislocations between desire and words, warps of 'Honour' which make twined loves twisted, open gaps in which flourish an exalted or risible symbolism: the semiotics of a Garter or the Bugle. It is to Carew's redemption of 'Honour', his attempt to purify the 'Pageant' by a writing out of words, that the argument must now turn.

Consider 'A Ribban',[101] further debt to Donne, continuous with much that has been quoted:

> This silken wreath, which Circles in myne arme
> Is but an Embleme of that Mistick charme,
> Wherewith the Mag[i]que of your beautie bindes
> My Captive Soule, and round about it winds
> Fetters of lasting Loue . . .

---

[100] 'Gaze not . . .'; BL Add. MS 53723, fo. 109^r.
[101] Bod. MS Don. b. 9, fo. 30^r.

Carew calls his token an 'order', as 'The Relique' does not, relating it to a whole series of chivalrous devices from the ribbons of the Bugle (with its 'Giant' names) through the Infanta's knotted favour to the 'Wreathe of bay' deposited in 'For a Pictu[re] whe[re] a Queen Laments over the Tombe of a slain knight'.[102] It is one of the more obvious lacunae in Caroline research that so little attention should have been paid to chivalry and its codes.[103] From English Cervantes to the 'Mock Romansa' of *Britannia Triumphans*—mentioning only burlesques—romantic knighthood charmed and diverted. The success of *Arcadia* and its offshoots was phenomenal.[104] For Charles himself, lately masquer to Spain, the Prince Astiagés and Basilino of court romance,[105] chivalry held immense appeal. The Order of the Garter, elaborated by him, satisfied a deep ceremoniousness in his nature.[106] Even in minute detail, ritual 'order' shaped Carew's life from 1630, as Sewer in Ordinary to the King. BL Stowe MS 561, for instance, catalogues the handwashing, toasting in wine, and three-times triple-bowing required of Carvers and Cupbearers before serving, as though the royal table were a eucharistic altar.[107] That such procedures, verging into transcendence, were congenial to the poet is suggested by 'A Ribban', where the 'Ceremonie' due to his 'order' allows of 'Faith' to the 'Loue' it enshrines: 'This order as a lay Man I may beare | But I become loues Preist, when that I weare.' Chivalrous ritual lent, then, an aura to its subjects. The looking-glass 'enchanted by art magic' sent by King James to Madrid is no odder than the 'enchanted Crystall', with 'ayrie repercussive sorceries', which 'thy Glasse' becomes in 'To a Ladye mistrustfull of hir owne beautie'.[108] Carew's poetry is continually interested in things which, like a mirror or curl of hair (not to be cracked or given to witches),

---

[102] BL Sloane MS 739, fo. 100ʳ.

[103] Useful first steps are taken by Mervyn James, 'The Changing Emphasis of Honour', in *English Politics and the Concept of Honour 1485–1642, Past and Present*, Supplement 3 (1978) and Annabel Patterson, *Censorship and Interpretation: The Conditions of Writing and Reading in Early Modern England* (Madison, 1984), ch. 4.

[104] For Sidney's Caroline efflorescence see *STC*, Patterson (*Censorship and Interpretation*, 171) adding dramatizations by James Shirley (1632) and Henry Glapthorne (1638). Cf. the reception and multiple reprints of Francis Quarles's *Argalus and Parthenia* (1629), discussed by David Freeman in his edition (Cranbury, NJ, 1986).

[105] See Antoine Rémy, *La Galatee et les adventures du Prince Astiagés. Histoire de nostre temps, ou sous noms feints sont representez les amours du Roy et de la Reyne d'Angleterre. Avec tous les voyages qu'il a fait, tant en France qu'en Espagne* (1625), a wedding present for Henrietta Maria, and Walter Montague, *The Shepheard's Paradise*, perf. 1633 ((1659)).

[106] Kevin Sharpe, 'The Personal Rule of Charles I', in Howard Tomlinson (ed.), *Before the English Civil War* (London, 1983), 53–78, esp. pp. 59–60.

[107] Fo. 4ᵛ. Cf. Prynne on Laud, quoted by Smuts, *Court Culture*, 228.

[108] St John's College, Cambridge MS S23, fos. 83ᵛ–5ᵛ ('To A.D. . . .' in *Poems*).

extend the human into the marvellous. The pearl exalted in his lapidary is an example: most organic of stones, 'geniture of a shell-fish',[109] it is imagined as viscously forming from a dewdrop, tear, or smile, it was held to participate in the character of its wearer. At times his feeling for such tokens smacks of the primitive power anthropologists find in ritual gifts. The jewels and wreaths of Carew's highly civilized verse might almost be the *vaygu'a* or strings of shell-treasure, at once property, pledge, and sacred loan—with all the medicinable virtue ascribed to gems in Renaissance digests—given by Trobriand islanders in Marcel Mauss's *Essai sur le don.*[110]

Certainly Carew's milieu was one in which gifts were significant. Ritualized exchanges helped organize court life. Especially on New Year's Day, presents were reciprocated between patrons and their clients. King Charles, not the most assiduous reader of state papers, took care to annotate the annual list.[111] Gold, pearl, and other ornaments were accepted. But as the career of Dudley Carleton reminds us, paintings and sculptures were also used to acquire favour. Poems supplemented gifts,[112] or were themselves the art-objects given.[113] Father Ong observes that the word 'ornament' described in the period not only jewelled adornments but the attire and equipage of a poem—as 'a "praise" (*laus*) or an "honor" (*honos* or *honor*) or a "light" (*lumen*) of words'—and also, in social application, a 'gift' or 'honorarium', as with the annual *ornamentum* which equipped Ramus to discharge his Regius professorship.[114] Carew's 'New-yeares gift. To the King' thus constitutes the same kind of honouring ornament as the band of 'whiter stone' which it urges Janus to wreathe, pearl-like, about the King's year:[115]

---

[109] Thomas Nicols, *A Lapidary: Or, The History of Pretious Stones* (1652), 75. The emphasis on parturition goes back to Pliny, who classes the pearl apart from gemstones (*Natural History* 9. 54–60).

[110] 1925; quotations from *The Gift: Forms and Functions of Exchange in Archaic Societies*, trans. Ian Cunnison (London, 1954).

[111] Carlton, *Charles I*, 107, 158. A list of New Year's gifts given by the King, such as that in BL Harley Roll T2, details exchanges more ceremonial than substantial, yet part of a system which involved large benefits.

[112] An example by Carew appears to be 'Red, and white roses'.

[113] In addition to Carew's texts note e.g. 'A New-yeares-Gift sung to King Charles, 1635' by Jonson, Herrick's 'The New-yeeres-Gift, or Circumcisions Song', 'Another New-yeeres Gift, or Song for the Circumcision' and 'A New-yeares gift sent to Sir Simeon Steward', Davenant's 'To the King on New-yeares day 1630' and his three New Year's gift poems 'To the Queen'.

[114] Walter J. Ong, SJ, *Ramus: Method and the Decay of Dialogue* (Cambridge, Mass., 1958), 277–8.

[115] No manuscripts extant; *Poems*, 151–2.

> let them shine
> In this succeeding circles twine,
> Till it be round with glories spread,
> Then with it crowne our *Charles* his head . . .

Manuscript, again, alters meaning. 'To *x*' now implies a thing given as well as address; relations between the poet and his verse change by virtue of his praise-emanating accomplishment finding expression in an object. When Carew's holograph of 'To the King', or an ornate fair copy, was presented, wreathed writing marked the *res* with those signs of the giver which Mauss looks for in the archaic *rah* or 'gift';[116] ornament was invested with the honour and praise which it was the Renaissance poet's to give. Subtly, and as in 'A Fancy', verse's writtenness was refined into something more beautiful than what it said.

'The whole field over which *laus, honor, lumen,* and *ornamentum* play', notes Ong, 'is . . . one where the distinctions between persons and objects now made automatically . . . are more or less blurred.'[117] If we return to the '*Thom*' depicted by Suckling 'in Hampton-Court garden', both the versatility of court ritual informed by these ambiguities, and its tendency to polish away the poetry it generates, come clear. For Carew's radiant address 'To the New-yeare, for the Countesse of Carlile'[118] develops its genre by insisting that, since a Countess called Lucy is her own *lumen*, nothing need be given:

> Give Lucinda pearle, nor Stone
> Lend them light who els have none
> Let her Beauty shine, alone . . .
>
> No attire thou canst invent
> Shall to grace her forme be sent,
> She adorns all ornament.

Like the mistress or Queen of 'Aske mee noe more', the Countess is called a phoenix's nest: twined centre of political influence. Such exaltation may threaten dialogue, yet attributing 'grace'—active principle in Renaissance usage—invites reciprocation. Lamenting the 'frowne' which has marred Lucinda's favour (a bodily pun is palpable), Carew declares:

> Janus, if when next I trace
> Those sweete lines, I in her face
> Reade the Charter of my grace

---

[116] *The Gift,* 48–50.   [117] *Ramus,* 278.
[118] BL Sloane MS 739, fos. 99ᵛ–100ʳ rev.

> Then from bright Appollo'es tree
> Such a garland wreathd shalbe
> As shall crowne both her, and thee.

Carew imagines the Countess as the kind of honour-radiating text which his court poems might be: they speak the same language, that of patronage and 'grace''s cognate, 'gratitude'. Even more than 'To the King', the poem is sheened away, exceeds itself in exchanges: the real text is still to be written.[119] In the standard Renaissance treatise on gifts, *De beneficiis*, such a subordination of the object to the mystique of exchange is assumed. Seneca's image of the dancing Graces, as much as Mauss on the *kula* or 'ring' around which *vaygu'a* pass,[120] explains why the rhetoric of Carew's Arcadian dialogues, with their empty centres of wreathing and curling, should articulate so fluently Charles's year, his *anulus* or 'circle',[121] the crowning of the Countess of Carlisle. 'What meaneth this dance of theirs, in which hand in hand they trip it alwaies in a round [*chorus*]?' Seneca asks. 'Because the order and processe of benefits . . . is such, that they returne again to the giuer, and should wholly loose the grace of all which they should effect, if euer they should bee interrupted.'[122]

Carew's appeal to Janus is suggestive. For the dialogues and gift poems have as their corollary prayer, the refinement of 'Ceremonie' into 'Faith', and objects becoming messages in sacrifice:

> Leade the black Bull to slaughter with the Bore
> And Lambe, then purple with their mingled gore
> The Oceans curled browe, that so wee may
> The Sea Gods for their carefull waftage pay.
> Send gratefull incense up in pious smoake
> To those mild spiritts . . .

Celebrating the return of Walter Montague from the Continent,[123] Carew heightens Caroline ritual into a neoclassicism which honours his friend's incipient or actual conversion to Rome. Imaginatively his prosphoneticon belongs in the Queen's chapel at Somerset House, designed

---

[119] BL Harley MS 4955, fos. 206^(r–v), 'when next I trace, | These smooth lines', though probably corrupt, makes still more intimate the object and means of annual address.

[120] *The Gift*, 19–29.

[121] John Swan, *Speculum mundi* (1635): 'In Latin the yeare is called *Annus*, because we may say of it, *revolvitur ut annulus*. For as in a ring the parts touch one another, circularly joyning each to other, so also the yeare rolleth it self back again by the same steps it ever went.' Quoted by S. K. Heninger in *The Cosmographical Glass* (San Marino, Calif., 1977), 3–4.

[122] *De beneficiis* 1.3; *The Workes of Lucius Annæus Seneca*, trans. Thomas Lodge (1614), 4.

[123] 'Vppon M^r. W. Mount: his returne from trauell', Rosenbach MS 1083/17, fos. 75^(v)–6^(r).

by Inigo Jones to Vitruvian principles, with Doric entablatures drawn from 'an antique marble at Arundel house' and scrolled up into 'Mannerist ornamentalism'.[124] Brilliant was the effect there, when Mass was held for the court, of Dieussart's machine for displaying the eucharist, painted with angels lent voice by a concealed chorus.[125] Exquisite, likewise, in the poem is the 'Muses Quire' that blesses Montague's 'waftage', and eucharistic Carew's address to his fellow-poet: 'Thus whilst you deale your body 'mongst your friends . . . As Laymen clapse their hands wee ioyne our feete.' Such an explicit pun (on prosody) is rare in Carew, and this acknowledgement of the medium serves to articulate the transition implicit in 'A Ribban' between the 'Ceremonie' of a 'lay Man' and 'Faith' inspired by 'loues Preist', here between 'Laymen' and 'wee of Delphos'. It makes sacerdotal claims for the poet, underpinned by Horatian phrasing. The shrines and altars of Carew's lyrics are not conventional props; embedded in an organized and transcendent view of life, they belong to that 'order and processe' out of which 'grace' is wreathed. The 'pearly drops' of 'smooth soft language', which should (he tells a rival) be offered at Celia's 'Altars', partake in priestly sacrifice.[126] His verse aspires to yield itself in aromatic melting, it gives up its mass as scripted object in curlèd wreaths of rhetoric. We should remember that Massinger gibed not only at manuscript circulation but at poems uttered aloud to a 'tribe' of adoring believers. Nor should we forget the unusually large number of Carew lyrics (about a third of the entire canon) which gravitated to song-books— verses 'perform'd' as airs, of the air, losing verbal distinction as the winding music of William Lawes and Walter Porter suffused and exalted the text.[127] It was what the lyrics sought, most declared themselves as.

The 'round' or *kula* of givingness resolves in those poems which identify addressee and godhead. In them, the fascination in *De beneficiis* with prayer escalates into transcendently lucent utterance, imaginary unseen smoke:

> Those that can give open theire hands this day
> Those that cannot, yet hould them upp to pray
> That health may Crowne the Seasons of this yeare
> And myrth dance round the Circle . . .

[124] Sir John Summerson, *Inigo Jones* (Harmondsworth, 1966), 78.

[125] Thomas Birch, *The Court and Times of Charles I*, ed. Robert Folkestone Williams, 2 vols. (London, 1848), ii. 311–14.   [126] 'To my Rivall', BL Harley MS 6917, fos. 4ᵛ–5ʳ.

[127] The list in *Poems*, ed. Dunlap, 289–93, has now been extended by Scott Nixon, 'The Sources of Musical Settings of Thomas Carew's Poetry', *Review of English Studies*, NS 49 (1990), 424–60.

Carew begins 'A New yeares Sacrifice to Lucinda'[128] by rehearsing the *chorus*, but then exaltedly deprecates its tokens. Like the *vaygu'a* thrown at the feet of a great man in Mauss's account,[129] the poems which stand in for gold and pearl are dismissed as 'cheape and vulgar wishes I could lay | As triviall offrings at your feete this day'. Instead the text projects to an extreme that sacerdotalism which privileges the poet yet abases him at a shrine, his works becoming functions 'of' the gratitude which grace elicits:

> Such Incence vowes and holy rites as were
> To the involued Serpent of the yeare
> Payd by Egiptian Preists lay I before
> Lucindas sacred shrine, whilst I adore
> Her beautious Eyes, and her pure Altars dresse
> With Gumms and Spice of humble thankfulness. . . .

No need to invoke Mauss again, on absolute gifts as sacrifice. The Carew of 'Egiptian Preists' is demonstrably in touch with the new interest in comparative religion and anthropology which informs Sandys's Ovid and Carew's former employer, Lord Herbert of Cherbury's *De religione gentilium*. No need, either, to stress process and dissolution as measures of textual value. 'Incence vowes' and 'Gumms' are but materials of art; it is for Lucinda, Carew concludes, to 'inspire' those tokens with 'Delphique fire' into a 'blaze' that will manifest her 'name'.

Such writing may seem far removed from the Carew of 1623, elegist of 'E.F.' But the poet's provincial reach not only remained intact: breadth of political vision made court and 'country' inextricable. That generality of reference is apparent even in 'To the King at his Entrance into Saxham, By Master Io[hn] Crofts',[130] a poem usually dated back to the period in which we started, when Carew's imaginative allegiances included the likes of 'Prince Ottoman'. Undoubtedly its speaker—Crofts the poet, colleague of Carew at the embassy in Paris—had access to the King at that time. In 1620, for instance, he carried a book from his master Herbert

---

[128] Bod. MS Don. b. 9, fo. 27^{r–v} (where it is dated '1632').

[129] *The Gift*, 21.

[130] Brotherton Collection MS Lt.q 48, fo. 37^r. This early text, which Beal dates '*c*.1620s–30s' (*Index of English Literary Manuscripts*, ii/1. 114), can be found among papers relating to the Sebright and Crofts families. Sir John Sebright, 7th bart. (as Christopher Sheppard informs me), married in 1793 Harriet Crofts, daughter of Richard Crofts of West Harling, Norfolk, originally of Little Saxham itself.

(another gift text) to James at his family seat.[131] Oddly enough, it was rumoured that the King was often at Little Saxham because he had contracted a marriage, after the death of Queen Anne, to that daughter of the household, Cicilia Crofts, who would later become a Maid of Honour and 'dispute' with Thomas Killigrew. If, as E. E. Duncan-Jones has argued, the chambermaid dubbed Queen Cis in *The New Inne* was a satirical barb in her direction,[132] then Carew's reply to Jonson's 'Ode' in defence of that play will have been in part precipitated by long-standing provincial loyalties. Certainly the Crofts, while not quite a family of servingmen, were better placed by geography, near the hunting fields of Newmarket, than by wealth or breeding:[133]

> Sir
> 'Ere you passe this Threshold, stay,
> And give your Creature leave to pay
> Those pious Rites, which unto you,
> As to our Houshold Gods, are due.
>
>   Instead of Sacrifice, each Breast
> Is like a flaming Altar drest
> With zealous fires, which from pure Hearts
> Love mixt with Loyalty imparts.
>
>   Incense, nor Gold have we, yet bring
> As rich, and sweet an Offering;
> And such as doth both These express,
> Which is our humble Thankfulness . . .

What Carew's speaker offers, yields up in address, is ethically as well as verbally continuous with court gift poems. His climactic 'two-edg'd' verb, for example—which has gold and incense 'expresse' the 'humble thankfulness' of 'A New yeares Sacrifice' until it does them—adumbrates a round-dance in which giving takes predominance over gifts. Also

---

[131] *Poems*, ed. Dunlap, p. xxxii. Herbert's bookish influence on Carew himself has been neglected (cf. Francis W. Fry on 'Aske mee noe more', *Notes and Queries*, NS 24 (1977), 140–1); yet he was completing *De veritate* during the poet's years of employment. Its model of faculties (inchoate, but more sympathetic to the imagination than Scholastic or Baconian schemes) and hostility to predestinarianism must have been congenial. There are pre-shocks of *libertin* speculation in Herbert's circle (the Lucretian Carew of 'Loves Force'), a flux of ideas aided by Parisian civility. For some suggestive remarks, especially in relation to Herbert's secretary William Boswell (atomist, Galileist, virtuoso, Arminian), see Nicholas Tyacke, 'Arminianism and English Culture', in A. C. Duke and E. A. Tamse (eds.), *Britain and the Netherlands*, vol. vii (The Hague, 1981), 94–117.

[132] Unpublished typescript; now available as 'Jonson's Queen Cis', *Ben Jonson Journal*, 3 (1996), 147–51.

[133] For a genealogy sparse with honours until the Stuart period, see John Gage, *The History and Antiquities of Suffolk. Thingoe Hundred* (London, 1838), 134.

Senecan, though newer in Carew, is the negotiation of a difficulty which exercises *De beneficiis*: how to place, in a system of giving, the 'Caesar' who (in some sense) 'omnia habet'.[134] Carew's answer lies in 'Rites . . . As to our Houshold Gods'. The devotion which is Lucinda's at court, Celia's in love poetry, at Saxham is due in the house to the King. As with Walter Montague, the classical 'order and processe' which greets arrival becomes eucharistic, points beyond 'Ceremonie'. Wittily, 'the Gore | Which should be dasht on ev'ry door', at Saxham, 'We change into the lusty Bloud | Of youthfull Vines.' Magical provision is a commonplace in country-house poems. Yet Carew's emphases are different from those of, for example, 'To Penshurst'.[135] The 'open table', the 'liberall boord', of the Sidneys is no altar. Jonson's '*Penates. . .* entertayne' but are not compared with the King. There is scarcely that sense, as in Carew, that 'your servants . . . bear sway | Here in your Absence'. Continuity with the court is still clearer in what follows: 'having supt', Crofts says, 'We may perchance | Present you with a Country Dance.' The Graces put their clogs on, but a celebration of the *chorus*, the Senecan *kula*, at Saxham, seems intended. Osborn MS b. 197 includes 'Maske of Sʳ John Crofts at the Kings being entertained there' which shows what Carew had in mind.[136] More than itself 'presented', its dances end with the deities of country life (Diana, Ceres, Pan, and so on) bestowing their gifts on the monarch: game, foison, wool.

Significantly Carew's other Crofts poem, always printed as 'To Saxham', survives in most manuscripts under the title 'A winters entertainement . . .'.[137] That the poet was, like James and Charles, wreathed by the

---

[134] VII. v and vi. In the Cambridge University Library copy of Lodge's trans. (*Workes*, 144–5), this claim is underlined by an early hand in both chapters of the treatise.

[135] *Ben Jonson*, viii. 93–6.

[136] pp. 169–73. It is possible, though unlikely, that Carew wrote the masque—now edited and discussed by C. E. McGee, '"The Visit of the Nine Goddesses": A Masque at Sir John Crofts's House', *English Literary Renaissance*, 21 (1991), 371–84. Internal evidence points to an early Caroline date, before the death of Buckingham, yet the emphasis on youth and a bright future is not incompatible with one of James's visits to Saxham, *c*.1620. Cf. 'sober, strong, and young' in 'Vppon the kings Sicknesse' (quoting Bod. MS Don. b. 9, fos. 15ᵛ–16ᵛ), apparently the text catalogued 'when k: James was sicke' at the back of St John's College, Cambridge MS S23.

[137] Fourteen out of twenty-one complete texts—I include the version of 'To Saxham' recently noted by Peter Beal in 'An Authorial Collection of Poems by Thomas Carew: The Gower Manuscript', *English Manuscript Studies 1100–1700*, 8 (2000), 160–85, p. 177—mention 'entertainement', four with the qualifying season (significant in that 'winter' found gentry less laudable than the Crofts, contrary to proclamation, 'entertaining' in London). That the seven manuscripts which grant Saxham (or 'Taxum', 'Saxum', 'Sarum') a locale place it in 'Kent' supports the claim that Carew maintained contact with his native region, and underlines the relative obscurity of the Crofts' establishment. The text is quoted here from Bod. MS Don. b. 9, fos. 14ᵛ–15ᵛ.

Graces in Suffolk, and over a long period, is clear. A Latin epigram, printed in *Nympha Libethris, or, the Cotswold Muse* (1651), finds him being sent Davenant's works 'apud J.C.'[138]—yet another textual gift, this one pointing to the 1630s. The political message of 'To Saxham', however, is that more than kings and poets are 'entertained':

> thy Gates haue beene
> Made onely to lett strangers in
> Vntaught to shutt they doe not feare
> To stand wide open all the yeare
> Careless whoe enters for they know
> Thou neuer didst deserue a foe
> And as for theeues thie bounties such,
> They cannot steale thou giu'st soe much.

As in the epistle on Gustavus Adolphus and the elegies for Buckingham, Carew takes his politics seriously enough to admit objections. It is one of the ironies of his subsequent misconstruction that this urge to acknowledge difficulties, to gain edge and obliquity by sailing close to the wind, should be taken as inept apologetics. Does not deserving them, Carew wonders, prevent us having foes? Can stealing be trumped by the gift? The play of sceptical wit does not obscure an engagement with live issues. Entertainment was political; Felicity Heal has shown that conventions of hospitality were under pressure.[139] 'A winters entertainement' belongs in a larger social dialogue, and should be read against those sternly Protestant treatises which distinguish between locals and strangers, worthy and idle poor. The poet's own stance, where not ambivalent, may seem primitive. Alms in his text relate to sacrifice, as in Mauss; they are a displacement of aristocratic excess as much as an alleviation of popular hardship. But at least the circuit of gratitude avoids means-testing:

> The could and frozen ayre had steru'd
> Much poore, unless by thee preseru'd;
> Whose prayers haue made thy table blest
> With plentie farr aboue the rest . . .

All readings mistake which hypostatize the text. It is involved in the 'round' of benefits described. The printed title, 'To Saxham', has this to recommend it, that it adumbrates a rendering of *laus* and *honor*, tribute being paid to, prayer at, the Crofts's 'table'.

---

[138] Repr. *Poems*, ed. Dunlap, 210.
[139] 'The Idea of Hospitality in Early Modern England', *Past and Present*, 102 (1984), 66–93.

Among Carew's estate poems, though, it is 'To my friend G.N. from Wrest'[140] that best demonstrates his continuity of vision and socialized poetic. Far more than Little Saxham, Wrest speaks from the political 'country'. Its owner, Henry Grey, refused the forced loan in 1626–7, lived mostly in retirement thereafter, and did not accompany the King during 1639 in his campaign against the Scots.[141] Poetic 'address' is reversible. Writing 'from Wrest' is as indicative as 'To Saxham'. At this point, frustratingly, our inherited assumptions risk pushing Carew too far from court, as though his discomfort during the Scottish expedition, grimly depicted in the opening lines of his epistle, left him nowhere to go but Nun Appleton. This analogy is advanced, indeed, in the best account of the poem we have, by Michael P. Parker. Symptomatically, however, it needs support from such evidences as 'the presence of the opposition leader Selden at the de Grey estate'[142]—a misleading description of the great lawyer's role at this, and perhaps any, time. Grey was not decisively retired. In November 1633, for example, the Earl and Countess of Kent featured prominently at the christening of James, Duke of York.[143] Nor should retirement be taken to indicate a particular ideological stance. Carew had already praised seclusion in a far from 'oppositional' context: his consoling poem 'To the Countesse of Anglesey' compares Kit Villiers's life away from court to an 'Eddye' that 'turnes his water round, | And in continuall Circles dances, free'[144]—a passage anticipating, across the detail of Carew's work, Wrest's

> spacious channells, where they slowly creepe
> In snakie windings, as the shelving ground
> Leades them in circles, till they twice surround
> This Island Mansion, which i'th'centre plac'd,
> Is with a double Crystall heaven embrac'd,
> In which our watery constellations floate,
> Our Fishes, Swans, our Water-man and Boate,
> Envy'd by those above, which wish to slake
> Their starre-burnt limbes, in our refreshing lake . . .

Much could be said about the cultural politics of this, touching as it does on such late 1630s issues as Italianate gardening, fen drainage, and the

---

[140] No manuscripts extant; quoting *Poems*, 146–50.

[141] Richard Cust, *The Forced Loan and English Politics 1626–1628* (Oxford, 1987), 102 n. 13; *CSPD, 1638–1639*, 621–2, cf. *CSPD, 1639*, 221.

[142] 'Carew's Secular Masque', 176.

[143] *CSPD, 1633–1634*, 297.

[144] BL Harley MS 6917, fos. 24ʳ–5ᵛ.

wholesomeness of Wrest water compared with the disease-ridden Tweed, complained of by Suckling in his letters from Scotland.[145] When the moat is described as 'the circuit of our narrow Seas' the allusion is to Selden's *Mare clausum* (1619, rev. and printed 1635)—his scholarly assertion of the right of the Stuart kings to command their territorial waters. But the whorled 'channells' that figure retired life and intimate a political agenda also define an imaginative landscape. Like winding teardrops forming pearl, the double crystal 'channells' are jewels in movement, an involved lucid serpent. Partly because 'To my friend G.N.' is a late work, it is tempting to produce it to a creative limit, to render it, as Parker does, a point of 'rest'. But there is no pun on this estate without the 'W' which centres a reflex, nor any creativity, however magical, which is not alive with 'order and processe': 'Wee presse the juycie God, and quaffe his blood, I And grinde the Yeallow Goddesse into food.' Above all, while meat, drink, and the disposition of ornament make 'Wrest' a chorography of 'entertainement', the conceited zodiac which it shares with *Cœlum Britanicum* cannot be made to render in rustic sufficiency a 'protection' which the masque grants 'solely to the court'—the phrasing, again, is Parker's[146]—because, given the integrity of Carew's politics, the masque does nothing of the kind.

But then, Carew's greatest achievement has been, more than any other of his works, pre-emptively undervalued. It requires a trust in the poet's range of sympathy to grant the masque's big names—the Three Kingdoms, Genius, Eternity—the breadth of reference they claim. Read in political context, though, this playful purging of the zodiac and its peopling with British heroes is Carew's ultimate investment of the *anulus*. Proposing the heavens themselves as ornament, it graces poetry with a radiance which gives of the stars, and offers itself to an addressee who is, by divine right, an image of God. We should not call the heavens, unconceitedly, 'an *Ornament*'. But Junius does, in the opening sentence of his treatise. We hardly think of the zodiac as giving. Yet *De beneficiis* describes planets, star, and the gods they enshrine as exemplars of a generosity man should emulate.[147] Above all, acting tends, for us, to 'representation'. But the aesthetics and economics of the masque—short braveries seen once, rarely more, as part of a larger festival—translate into the seasonal gift. The congruence with country 'entertainement' is finely observed by Herrick: Pemberton's laden spits, he declares, 'Not represent but give

145 *Suckling: Non-Dramatic Works*, Letter 40, pp. 145–6.
146 'Carew's Secular Masque', 184.   147 e.g. IV. xxiii–viii.

relief'.[148] Masque title-pages, unlike theatre quartos, read: 'presented by *x*, to *y*, on *z*.' *Cœlum Britanicum* goes further, writing this into its text: 'The first thing that presented it selfe to the sight', it begins, 'was a rich Ornament, that enclosed the Scæne.' Spectacle becomes jewellery, purified as light and yielded to an audience: 'All this Ornament was heightned with Gold, and . . . was the newest and most gracious that hath beene done in this place' (B1ᵛ). Here the words 'was', 'this place', and 'done' are as important as the gift word 'gracious'. The elaborate description which begins *Cœlum Britanicum*, printed in 1634, simply makes the more evident its not delivering up the masque given at Whitehall. Royal policy will have encouraged publication of a work which, typically, answered in its writing to the not yet witnessed *Triumph of Peace*, performed a few weeks before it.[149] But the manuscript poet also seems to welcome print—its definite, almost emblematic disposition, but also leaden-typed fixedness—as a way of enforcing limits familiar from the gift poems. *Cœlum Britanicum* begins with 'address', to the extent of staging an introductory leaf, yet presents itself as closed, inert without the 'Delphique flame' which only occasion and the King can give: 'over al was a broken Frontispice, wrought with scrowles and masque heads of Children; and within this a Table adorn'd with a lesser Compartiment, with this inscription, *COELVM BRITANNICVM*' (B1ʳ).

Yet who, or what, says so? No name appears on the printed title-page except that of the 'Cæsar' who commanded the masque. 'Carew' remains an attribute of script. And what of the 'broken Frontispice'? Its description may be the poet's, but Inigo Jones *fecit*. Certainly the images and issues of the masque's opening 'Scæne' interested the King's Surveyor before and after the 1630s: 'old Arches, old Palaces, decayed walls, parts of Temples, Theaters . . . altogether resembling the ruines of some great City of the ancient Romanes, or civiliz'd Brittaines' (B1ᵛ). Visually this recalls the fallen house of chivalry in *Prince Henry's Barriers*—the design for which was classed by Herford and Bell as belonging to *Cœlum Britanicum*; historically, its 'Romanes, or civiliz'd Brittaines' sound very like the builders on Salisbury plain imagined in Jones's posthumous *Stone-Heng Restored*. As a result, the chivalric plot which helps organize the masque, from the Picts who 'dance a Perica or Marshall dance' (E1ᵛ) through the

[148] 'A Panegyrick to Sir Lewis Pemberton', *Poetical Works*, ed. L. C. Martin (Oxford, 1956), 146–9.

[149] For an excellent analysis of relations between the two see Martin Butler, 'Politics and the Masque: *The Triumph of Peace*', *Seventeenth Century*, 2 (1987), 117–41.

chief Masquers, disguised as 'ancient Heroes' (E2ᵛ), to the hallowed advent of '*Prince* Arthur, *or the brave* | St. George *himselfe*' (E4ʳ), appears to stem from Jones as well as Carew, from 'Cæsar''s commitment to the Garter. Indeed, when we learn in the treatise that Stonehenge was built as a temple to Coelus, god of the heavens, that '*Factotum fuisse ad formam coronae*', that it was 'termed . . . the Giants Dance', was 'orderly disposed' as a zodiac of stones, we seem to be in another 'Hampton-Court Garden', with Carewan material not written by his hand.¹⁵⁰ We return, in short, to the problem of life stories. What we know of Carew whets yet disappoints our appetite for vivid biography resolved on a deathbed. That Clarendon wrote, 'after fifty Years of his Life, spent with less Severity or Exactness than it ought to have been, He died with the greatest Remorse',¹⁵¹ tantalizes but cannot justify the recollection at this point of John Hales (above, pp. 187–8). Carew scatters his traces too well, covers his tracks, lips prints, dance steps. Writing or written out, he is '*Thom*', 'T.C.', is deleted, deletes himself. As surely as his smallest lyrics, set like gems in miscellanies, *Cœlum Britanicum* displays a not at all inward ability to tread 'Lyrique feet' (Carew's self-description, granted him by Townshend)¹⁵² through congeries of dialogue.

For reciprocal 'order and processe' remains fundamental. In the exchange between Mercury and Momus which unfolds on Jones's set, informed spectators will have recognized a disputation derived from Giordano Bruno. Carew had precedents in Jonson's *Love's Triumph through Callipolis* for a masque employing Brunesque material.¹⁵³ But it seems characteristic of him to choose a dialogue as source, and a problematic one (cited for heresy) at that. The classical republican sympathies of *Lo spaccio della bestia trionfante*, its notion that metempsychosis makes Jove fluid and subject to fate, hardly promise a celebration of that royal asterism, the King as Defender of the Faith. Scholarship inclines to overlook this. As Mercury and Momus sinuously debate the rigour and implausibility of Charles's efforts to spread his reforming 'order' to an ungrateful kingdom, their indirectness is polarized by commentary, or

---

¹⁵⁰ *Stone-Heng Restored* (1655), esp. pp. 19, 22, 67 ff., 70 ff., quoting Camden, Polydore Vergil, et al. The work was edited from Jones's notes by John Webb; opinions differ as to the extent of his contribution. That influence by Carew on *Stone-Heng Restored*, in turn, cannot be ruled out, is part of the argument for impersonality.

¹⁵¹ *Poems*, ed. Dunlap, p. xxxix.

¹⁵² See the Gustavus Adolphus epistle, echoing Townshend's 'vppon the death of the King of Sweden', and 'To my worthy friend Master Geo. Sands, on his translation of the Psalmes'.

¹⁵³ *De gli eroici furori.*

glossed as 'sycophantic', or we are solemnly reminded that 'Momus'
proclamation . . . comes less than a decade before 1642. . . . All are teeter-
ing on the brink of Cromwell's power.'[154] The claim is more than historically ill-judged. By neglecting the openness and volatility of dialogue, it
obscures a distinctive dynamic. Carew's extended antimasques become
formless, where, in practice, they proceed with elegant logic, starting
from Riches and her opposite Poverty (both dismissed, neither moder-
ated), followed by Fortune (her contraries enacted in battle), to culminate
in a figure who herself enshrines extremes: that cynosure of the 'negligent
courtier', Hedone. 'Bewitching Syren', Mercury calls her:

> guilded rottennesse,
> Thou hast with cunning artifice display'd
> Th'enameld outside, and the honied verge
> Of the faire cup, where deadly poyson lurkes.
> Within, a thousand sorrowes dance the round;
> And like a shell, Paine circles thee without.
> Griefe is the shadow waiting on thy steps,
> Which, as thy joyes 'ginne tow'rds their West decline,
> Doth to a Gyants spreading forme extend
> Thy Dwarfish stature. Thou thy selfe art Paine,
> Greedy, intense Desire . . . (D4ᵛ)

This magnificent passage belongs to a family of Anatomies of Pleasure
written in the early 1630s: Randolph's *Aristippus*, for example, Townshend's *Tempe Restor'd*. But the richness and flexibility of its blank verse—
the '*Cyrcæan*' cup, the dancing round—most recall, and anticipate by
only months, *A Maske Presented at Ludlow Castle*. It may seem eccentric
to end by invoking Milton, for all that the presence of Thomas Egerton
in Carew's cast list prompts it (F2ʳ). Yet the affinities are extensive and
they run deep enough to discount what remains of 'pusillanimous', poxy
Carew. It matters, after all, that Hedone should not appear in *Lo spaccio*,
that she is Carew's addition to Bruno, and that her dismissal should meta-
morphose the masque in ways which make her central to the poet's diagnosis of the ills of Charles's state. What follows is familiar to Miltonists: a
dance of ancient Britons, songs of Druids and Rivers. As ponderable,
however, is the common structural extendedness. Because of its principles
of address and dialogue, *Cælum Britanicum* diverges from Jonsonian

---

[154] For the polarizing tendency, even in distinguished work, see e.g. Sharpe, *Criticism and
Compliment*, 234–42; 'sycophantic' is P. W. Thomas, 'Two Cultures?', 181; 'Cromwell's power',
R. Chris Hassell, *Renaissance Drama and the English Church Year* (Lincoln, Nebr., 1979), 135.

models by not reserving the monarch to hinge the spectacle, and it develops, *Comus*-like, transformations which spread its politics across three realms. Its last phase may not be so bafflingly protracted as Milton's printed text. But the dances of chivalry which begin with Hedone's exit lead to the glittering awkwardness of the Kingdoms' reluctance to have their heroes stellified. Genius has to insist on the mystery which allows, by '*grace*', the stars to be both up and down, in a dialogue of what Carew (inflecting constitutional theory) calls 'Homonoia', before the scene can be '*With wreathes of Starres circled about*'. It is a culminating vision of the *kula*, a realization, out of song, of the '*chorus*' (Fi^{r-v}).

The Milton who read this grandest of Carew's dialogues was not a courtier and would never, we may safely speculate, have joined an Order of the Bugle. But he belonged to a culture which found the pious Quarles writing the verse-romance *Argalus and Parthenia* as well as Rubens painting Charles as St George, which counted among its Spenserians both Sir Kenelm Digby and William Browne. Nothing but hindsight makes such contrasts seem paradoxical. When Mervyn James notes that Arcadian chivalric codes appealed to 'oppositional' as well as 'court' elements, or John Creaser argues that Milton's 'reforming' masque was composed for an occasion of 'royalism' and 'splendour',[155] there are pressures within the vocabulary working to distort remarkable scholarship. We should think less of dialectic than of dialogue, of trans-shifting in a social 'Pageant'— the 'Gyant''s realm, Comus' kingdom—rather than cultural division imposed by some logic of history. When Milton's 'Scene changes, presenting Ludlow towne, and the Presidents Castell'[156] there is no sharp break from that 'prospect of *Windsor* Castell, the famous seat of the most honourable Order of the Garter' which helps resolve *Cœlum Britanicum* (Fi^{v}). Carew the Privy Chamberer and Milton the author of *Comus* may not, for us, stand easily together; but unless we can accommodate them to a shared historical moment, we shall continue to underestimate the coherence of Caroline culture, the complexity of its political centre, the integrity and oblique brilliance of those manuscript traces marked 'T.C.'

---

[155] *English Politics and the Concept of Honour*, 72–91; 'The Setting of *Comus*', 116.
[156] 1637, Fi^{r}.

CHAPTER 10

Milton and the Nightingale (1992)

There is a curious moment in Shakespeare's Sonnet 102 when a nightingale changes sex. 'Our loue was new, and then but in the spring,' the poet writes to his friend, 'When I was wont to greet it with my laies, | As *Philomell* in summers front doth singe, | And stops his pipe in growth of riper daies.'[1] That 'his' conflicts with Philomel's gender, and some scholars emend it to 'her'. Others invoke ornithology and point out that cock nightingales, not hen birds, sing. But at its volta the sonnet reverts to 'her':

> Not that the summer is lesse pleasant now
> Then when her mournefull himns did hush the night,
> But that wild musick burthens every bow . . .

Having identified the nightingale with his eloquence, the poet, registering loss ('now' the friend is wooed by others), recovers decorum in detachment. A sonneteer like Thomas Watson might routinely 'compare' himself with '*Philomela*' and say that 'her . . . night-complaints' resemble his laments to his '*Saint*'.[2] Shakespeare is more like the Keats of 'Ode to a Nightingale', who aspires to join an inspired bird—'Already with thee! tender is the night'[3]—only to find himself apart.

Milton's first sonnet has a creative imbalance which achieves fresh cogency when read in the light of Keats and Shakespeare:

> O Nightingale, that on yon bloomy Spray
> Warbl'st at eeve, when all the Woods are still,
> Thou with fresh hope the Lovers heart dost fill,
> While the jolly hours lead on propitious *May*,
> Thy liquid notes that close the eye of Day,
> First heard before the shallow Cuccoo's bill,

---

[1] *Shake-speares Sonnets* (1609), G2ʳ.

[2] Thomas Watson, *The Hekatompathia or Passionate Centurie of Loue* (1582), XXVI (D1ᵛ).

[3] Line 35, in John Keats, *The Complete Poems*, ed. John Barnard, 2nd edn. (Harmondsworth, 1977).

Portend success in love; O if *Jove's* will
Have linkt that amorous power to thy soft lay,
Now timely sing, ere the rude Bird of Hate
Foretell my hopeles doom in som Grove ny:
As thou from yeer to yeer hast sung too late
For my relief; yet hadst no reason why:
Whether the Muse, or Love call thee his mate,
Both them I serve, and of their train am I.[4]

It has become a convention to refer these ardent but contained lines to 'Sir Thomas Clanvowe's *The Cuckoo and the Nightingale* ... found in Speght's edition of Chaucer'.[5] Yet it matters that, in manuscript tradition, that *débat* is called *The Boke of Cupide, God of Loue*. Clanvowe's (or Roos's) themes are amatory: Milton is more interested in song. For all its talk of 'the Lovers heart', his octave is alliteratively and close-rhymedly given over to 'liquid notes', Shakespearian echo,[6] and what Keats calls 'full-throated ease'. Temporal anxiety is allayed by a prosodic coherence which 'jolly hours' and 'timely'—words used in rhetorical treatises (*horae, tempus*) to describe the placing of feet—point up. Especially in the sestet solemn monosyllables lend quasi-Tuscan[7] amplitude. Elaborate syntax, apostrophically sustained by the empty 'O's of lines 1 and 7, intimates a nightingale's song-flow. And of course, the weight of the poem, through its Italianate turn, falls on performance: 'Now timely sing'. In this, the work is typical: one of a series concerned with Miltonic tardiness, and the first in a group of sonnets written between 1629 and 1631 (two English, five Italian) in which the young poet, ostensibly amorous but preoccupied with song, is drawn to Italy.

In '*Donna leggiadra. . .*', Sonnet II, the mistress charms less by her looks than by an Orphic ability to shift alpine timber. 'When you speak', the poet insists at the volta, '*o lieta canti*', everyone should guard eyes and ears against a music so potent that only grace from heaven can prevent "*l disio amoroso*" from rooting itself in the heart—strange end to a love poem, that reminder of higher things. Sonnet V reduces the desiring heart to a baroque steam engine, shuddering with hot vapour and surrounded by icy mist, while VI says that *amor* meshes with ambition to

---

[4] Unless indicated, verse quotations are taken—for want of a better, old-spelling edn.—from *The Poetical Works of John Milton*, ed. Helen Darbishire, 2 vols. (Oxford, 1952–5).

[5] *John Milton: Complete Poems and Major Prose*, ed. Merritt Y. Hughes (New York, 1957), 53.

[6] e.g. 'eye of Day' (*Sonnets* 18.5, 25.6).

[7] Cf. C. C. Abbott (ed.), *The Correspondence of Gerard Manley Hopkins and Richard Watson Dixon*, rev. edn. (Oxford, 1955), 86.

sound the lyre. Eager for eloquence, Milton is attracted to his Beatrice or Laura as a figure of inspiration. Hence the lucid intensity of III and IV. When the poet celebrates his lady, love nurtures on his tongue the new flower ('*il fior novo*') of foreign speech. Such discourse might not be understood by his countrymen, but it brings rhetorical release: instead of urging 'timely' song in another, III turns on 'Canto', 'I sing'. A '*nova idea*', the *donna* of IV comprises '*Parole adorne di lingua più d'una*' and song that would draw the labouring moon from the heavens. Enriching language with the voice of Keats's 'warm South', her very name, Emilia, is cognate with 'emulation'—a quality incident not only to poets but (as readers knew from Pliny)[8] to Philomel. 'Nightingales *emulate one another, and other birds*', we are told: 'Many stories we have of *Nightingales* emulating and striving to outvie one another, and other birds, yea, and men too in singing.'[9]

The rivalry was much discussed. Pliny said that nightingales would die rather than be out-performed; a widely read poem by Famiamus Strada has Philomel emulate a lutenist playing beneath a shady oak until, exhausted by virtuosity, she falls from the branches.[10] The learned were interested because of arguments about *imitatio* and *aemulatio* in rhetoric,[11] but also because the motif brought song to bear on the question of nature vs. nurture. Most scholars followed Pliny in holding nurture to be decisive. Fledglings were said to imitate older birds, receiving criticism from their betters in a kind of Erasmian singing school. Others, emboldened by Pliny's attention to the individuality of nightingale song-patterns, maintained that birds bred alone were eloquent, 'Nature without any other teacher instructing them to utter the notes proper to their own kind'.[12] This is clearly relevant to a poet who, at about the time of writing 'O Nightingale', praised the untaught author of Sonnet 102 as 'fancies childe', a 'Warble[r]' of 'native Wood-notes wilde' (*L'Allegro* 133–4). Milton was an assiduous imitator when young, as well as intensely emulous, yet the sway of his creative personality owes much to his cultivation of inspired separateness.[13] When Shelley declares, 'A poet is a nightingale, who

---

[8] *Natural History* 10. 43. 81–5.

[9] John Ray, *The Ornithology of Francis Willughby* (1678), 223, 226.

[10] *Prolusiones Academicae, Oratoriae, Historicae, Poeticae* (1617), Liber 2, Prolusio 6, Academicae 2. Repr. 1619, 1625, 1631; for an early trans. see John Ford, *The Lovers Melancholy* (1629), I. i.

[11] On this distinction see G. W. Pigman III, 'Versions of Imitation in the Renaissance', *Renaissance Quarterly*, 33 (1980), 1–32, esp. pp. 22 ff.

[12] Olina, quoted in Ray, *Ornithology of Francis Willughby*, 223.

[13] Contrast John Guillory's influential remarks, *Poetic Authority: Spenser, Milton, and Literary History* (New York, 1983), 18–21.

sits in darkness and sings to cheer its own solitude with sweet sounds',[14] it is Milton as 'the wakeful Bird' which 'Sings darkling, and in shadiest Covert hid | Tunes her nocturnal Note' that he has in mind. The story of Milton's inward growth can be traced towards that assertion, in *Paradise Lost* III (38–40), of his distinct, rival-silencing voice. For it was not until the late 1650s, after travel to Italy and travail for the Republic, that the poet could think of himself, in a vernacular text, as the fledged songster, Philomel.

In his amusing story 'Why I Changed into a Nightingale', Wolfgang Hildesheimer presents a narrator who, uncertain which profession he might virtuously pursue, retires into obscure study.[15] 'It was during this period', the hero explains, 'that I first felt the wish to become a bird.' This odd desire—fulfilled by the end of the tale—would have been frustrated were it not for the acquisition of magical powers, gifts founded on the kind of imaginative literalism which prompts the narrator to reward a journalist's grumble, 'I wish I were a toad', with metamorphosis. The Miltonic authority which can turn Satan into a toad with one simile (*PL* IV. 800) grew out of a period of similar obscurity, troubled by thoughts of a career. When he returned from the Italian to the vernacular sonnet in 1631, Milton wrote a text in retirement which, by worrying about timely song, plumbed depths of emulous anxiety:

> How soon hath Time the suttle theef of youth,
> Stoln on his wing my three and twentith yeer!
> My hasting dayes flie on with full career,
> But my late spring no bud or blossom shew'th. . .

Though this begins in fear of Time it is, by lines 7–8, describing the 'inward ripenes . . . That som more timely-happy spirits indu'th'. The poet looks for a tardy nightingale, but finds 'no bud or blossom' in his 'late spring'. Significantly, the letter which conveyed this sonnet to the world in 1633 speaks of 'solid good flowing from due & tymely obedience to that command in the gospell set out by the terrible seasing of him that hid the talent'.[16] Though the parable of the vineyard reassures, Milton cannot ignore 'a certaine belatednesse in me'. The poem eases doubt by accepting that what is 'less or more, or soon or slow' will be 'eev'n' in God's bal-

---

[14] 'A Defence of Poetry' in *Shelley's Prose*, ed. David Lee Clark, rev. edn. (London, 1988), 282.

[15] Trans. Joachim Neugroschel, repr. in Alberto Manguel (ed.), *White Fire: More Tales of the Fantastic* (London, 1991), 642–7.

[16] *The Works of John Milton*, ed. Frank A. Patterson et al., 18 vols. (New York, 1931–8), xii. 324–5; all prose quotations from this edn.

ance—humility rewarded by the enjambed ambivalence which finds a de-ferred object in 'lot': 'eev'n, | To that same lot . . . Toward which Time leads me, and the will of Heav'n.' Its close further subordinates Time: 'All is, if I have grace to use it so, | As ever in my great task-Masters eye.' Yet timeliness is not forgotten, because the quiescent calm of 'grace to use it so' cannot suppress active 'use', drawing from 'it' not 'lot' but 'All' to pro-duce 'if I am graced enough to make use of the "talent" which is my lot as that lot deserves'. God's control of Time may be absolute and caring, but for 'timely-happiness' labour is required.

Milton did not dread Time's passing in the same way as earlier son-neteers. 'Fly envious *Time*' (written shortly after 'How soon hath Time') might begin with an alternate-rhymed, Shakespearian opening, but it dwindles in numerologically ordered[17] assurance. Far from blunting lion's paws, Time in this poem will 'lead' to a 'long Eternity' of 'bliss'. Vic-tory over temporality is not earned by bland abstraction. Like Shake-speare's Sonnet 12, 'When I doe count the clock . . .', Milton's is grounded in mechanics. Its 'hours' are 'leaden-stepping' because meted out by a pendulum; though published with the title 'On Time', it began in manu-script under the words 'set on a clock case'. Less devouring than provi-dential, however, 'envious *Time*' moves towards that timeless order which Michael shows Adam 'Replete with joy' at the end of *Paradise Lost*.[18] From this follows Milton's resistance to *carpe florem*. The arguments that Shake-speare gives Venus and advances in his early sonnets become the property of Comus, as he ineffectually tests Alice Egerton's virginity: 'If you let slip time, like a neglected rose | It withers on the stalk' (743–4). A 'cavalier' might urge 'Virgins, to Make Much of Time' by saying, 'Gather ye Rose-buds while ye may, | Old Time is still a flying'. For Milton, even paradise is subject (though chronically unbelated, in 'Eternal Spring') to Time, and the withering of roses—as in Adam's garland—commands attention as a moral, not temporal, event (*PL* IV. 268, IX. 892–3). Fragility was no sign of merit; to 'let slip time' was only wrong if that time was timely.

The sonnets are full of this concern. Number IX praises a 'timely-happy' lady who 'in the prime of earliest youth' has started up the 'Hill of heav'nly Truth' and now need only wait for that mystic time—'at the mid hour of night'—when God will admit her to Heaven. XV and XVI pre-sent Fairfax and Cromwell as men who succeed because they act with

[17] Cf. Edward W. Tayler, *Milton's Poetry: Its Development in Time* (Pittsburgh, 1979), 41–2.
[18] Cf. Stanley Eugene Fish, *Surprised by Sin: The Reader in 'Paradise Lost'* (Berkeley, 1967), 323–4.

dispatch. Even the slighter, occasional poems to Lawrence and Skinner, XX and XXI, return to timeliness. In XX, Milton encourages Lawrence to make Time run faster, not more slowly—by eating, drinking, and music. Strikingly, he characterizes the latter with the timely nightingale's trill, and associates song with Italy: 'artfull voice', he says, should 'Warble immortal Notes and *Tuskan* Ayre'. XXI likewise urges Skinner not to be too strenuous, introducing a vocabulary of 'measure', timely-betiming, and (that phrase from the letter of 1633) 'solid good'. The danger is that, while lost time may be redeemed, a timely hour missed is gone forever. At some points this anxiety is projected into historical loss, so that VIII recalls Alexander and the enviably renowned '*Pindarus*', while, more immediately, X laments that the poet was 'later born' than 'the dayes' in which Margaret Ley's 'Father flourisht'. But in a number of texts, as in 'O Nightingale', the roots of anxiety are exposed: 'Now timely sing . . . As thou . . . hast sung too late.' The poet is oppressed to think that, like Edward King or Charles Diodati, he might be called or killed before he had used his talent. 'I envie no mans nightingale or spring', wrote Herbert in 'Jordan (I)';[19] Milton, brooding on the fame of Arthur Johnston or Abraham Cowley, could hardly have said so. Scholars have long noticed his habit of pre-dating juvenilia, implying a precocity he lacked.[20] Yet when he falsely tells us in 'When I consider . . .' that he has not passed 'half his days', the impulse to under-date does not come (as LeComte implies) from vanity or alarm at *tempus fugit* but in what lines 3–6 reveal:

> And that one Talent which is death to hide,
> Lodg'd with me useless, though my Soul more bent
> To serve therewith my Maker, and present
> My true account, least he returning chide . . .

'All is, if I have grace to use it so . . .'. Time passes, God guides it; but with it passes, perhaps, that time in which the 'talent' should be put to 'use'. What Edward Phillips recorded in worldly terms—Milton's loss of '2000 l. which he had put for Security and improvement into the Excise Office, but neglecting to recal it in time, could never after get it out'[21]—recalls what was, spiritually, the central drama of his life.

Two lines, jotted on an envelope *c*.1638–9, epitomize this. Milton had just lamented in verse the death of Edward King, and he was undertaking

---

[19] Line 13, in *The Works of George Herbert*, ed. F. E. Hutchinson (Oxford, 1941).
[20] e.g. Edward LeComte, *Milton's Unchanging Mind: Three Essays* (Port Washington, NY, 1973), 16–17, 20–4, 31–3, 41–2.
[21] Helen Darbishire (ed.), *The Early Lives of Milton* (London, 1932), 78.

a journey to Italy, associated with that sonnet Muse. It was a period of anxiety allayed by hope about a venture which Milton thought might end his apprenticeship and make him an artist of European stature. His passport came in a letter from Henry Lawes, and on its cover he wrote: 'Fix here ye overdated spheres | That wing the restless foot of time.' Significantly, the word 'overdated' is not recorded before this; Milton seems to have invented it under the pressure of occasion. 'Antiquated, out of date', say the editors;[22] but, while this seems adequate for its use in *Of Reformation* and *The Doctrine and Discipline of Divorce* (III. 1, 469), it misses the Miltonic texture of the gibe in *Eikonoklastes* that Charles I (a jumped-up child) had not 'redeem'd his overdated minority from a Pupillage under Bishops' (V. 185), and it falls short of the couplet's complexity. There is a leap in 'over', and resonance to 'dated'. A 'date' was the time when a contract ran out or debt became due. Those 'spheres', the circling planets that measure the hours, give Time's foot wings because they vault dates—not just the ten spring days of 1638 lost between English and continental calendars when Milton crossed the channel, but the scripturally awesome times when a poet's 'talent' should be put to 'use', settling his 'account' with 'God'. Vaulting so, the 'spheres' put Time ahead of itself and give 'overdated' a second implication: that the planets overestimate dates, seeming later than they should. The lines catch Milton's sense that he must surely be younger than he is, but are precipitated by alarm that, as he begins another preparation, he might already have missed his time. Iconographically, of course, the reference is to *kairos*, Latin *occasio*.[23] Integral to this motif are scales (like those made 'eev'n' in Sonnet VII), a forelock to be grasped by timely spirits, and one or more 'spheres' winging the feet. Renaissance versions of *kairos* often merge these last with the 'ever moving Spheares of heaven' that Faustus bids 'Stand' at the end of his tragedy.[24] In the early Prolusion II, *De sphærarum concentu*, Milton depicts the nightingale as a bird which 'spend[s] the whole lonely night in song, in order [to] adjust [its] strains to the harmonic mode of the sky, to which [it] listen[s] attentively' (XII. 152–5). This is a harmony enjoyed by the Genius of the Wood 'in deep of night' (*Arcades* 61). But though the youthful Milton yearned, as he said, to hear the 'silver chime' of the

---

[22] The lines are quoted (as modernized and corrected) from *The Poems of John Milton*, ed. John Carey and Alastair Fowler (London, 1968), 254; Carey's gloss is followed by LeComte, *Milton's Unchanging Mind*, 20 and Mother M. Christopher Pecheux, 'Milton and *Kairos*', *Milton Studies*, 12 (1978), 197–211, pp. 204–5.

[23] Cf. Pecheux, 'Milton and *Kairos*', 201–6.

[24] Christopher Marlowe, *Doctor Faustus* (1616), H2ᵛ.

'Crystall sphears'—the sound of which would make Time 'run back' to 'the age of gold' ('On the Morning of Christs Nativity', 125–35)—he could not harmonize his song with heavenly music. 'Deep of night' would find him 'warbling' as an inspired solitary in the 1650s. But the revolutions which inspired the nightingale filled his ears in 1638–9 with what Empson called the 'poison' of 'Missing Dates'.[25]

To claim that Milton gained creative assurance in Italy is not novel: he tells us as much himself (III. 235–7). More intriguing is the evidence that southerly migration allowed him to enact and partly exorcize the nightingale drama of 'belatednesse'. Over the whole journey into Keats's 'sun-burnt . . . South' hangs the late asseveration, 'the Sun which we want, ripens Wits as well as Fruits' (XVIII. 254). Italy could be seen as a home of Jesuitical intrigue (VIII. 125–7). A vulnerable migrating bird in *Mansus* (27–9), Milton casts himself as a 'poor hapless Nightingale' (like Alice Egerton) in 1639 by inscribing, in the album of Count Cerdogni: 'if Virtue feeble were, Heaven itself would stoop to her.'[26] One test of virtue bound up with song came when Antonio Malatesti dedicated and presented to Milton his bawdy sonnets, *La Tina*. Much preoccupied with the plucking of fruit, with sexual *carpe florem*,[27] the *Equivoci rusticali* quibble about their heroine in ways which bear upon such playful descriptions as 'Defac't, deflourd, and now to Death devote' (*PL* IX, 901), where ' "Deflourd" is one of those serious puns, like "fruitless" . . . used to good effect' in *Paradise Lost*.[28] More openly retained[29] were the encomiums which the juvenilia attracted. To be dubbed by Selvaggi the equal of Homer, Virgil, and Tasso rolled into one, having written little more than 'Lycidas' and *A Mask*, was agreeable, but to print such compliments before *Poemata* 1645, and then reprint them in 1673 with the 'solid good' of *Paradise Lost* achieved, betrays a formidable mix of self-doubt and pride. The poems recited from memory and praised in Florence must have included the Italian sonnets, II–VI, 'Now' uttered in Italy. And the tributes paid to the visitor were calculated to assuage root fears. '*Non batta il Tempo l'ale*,' writes Francini, '*Fermisi immoto*'; the young poet, declares Dati, hears '*Harmonicos celestium Sphærarum*'—commonplace, but used

[25] See the villanelle of that title in William Empson, *Collected Poems* (London, 1949).

[26] The final lines of *A Mask Presented at Ludlow-Castle*; see William Riley Parker, *Milton: A Biography*, 2 vols. (Oxford, 1968), i. 181.

[27] e.g. nos. 7, 23, 25, 26, 35, 37, 44.

[28] John R. Knott, Jr., *Milton's Pastoral Vision: An Approach to 'Paradise Lost'* (Chicago, 1971), 120.

[29] Milton kept Malatesti's manuscript but suppressed his name at VIII. 123.

of the nightingale in Prolusion II.[30] That bird was never far from Milton's imagination. '*Ad Leonoram Romæ canentem*' and its two pendants, above all, recapitulate earlier fictions. Not without sinister allure, like the ear-inveigling mistress of Sonnets II and IV, the singer Leonora Baroni is a Philomel-resembling warbler ('*serpit agens; | Serpit agens*') traced back to and heard in the 'warm South'. Since Warton she has been associated with the subject of the Italian sonnets.[31] What romantic biography has said of the 'incognita' as mistress and Muse[32] makes literal the psychological allegory which Milton contrived in Italy.

The prose works written on his return to England demonstrate the new assurance. Worried that 'I should not write thus out of mine own season' in *Church-Government* II, Milton goes on to 'covnant with any knowing reader' for 'the payment of what I am now indebted' (III. 234, 240–1), and declares himself a 'timely spirit'.[33] A sense of timeliness attained emerges in verse as early as 'When I consider . . .' (1652?), where the poet asks 'Doth God exact day-labour, light deny'd', and Patience replies, 'They also serve who only stand and waite.' Herbert's lessons are being learned: not only technically in the unforced yet syncopated exchange with a personified virtue but in humility. Shortly after writing this sonnet, Milton apparently began *Paradise Lost*. In its earliest surviving part (IV. 32–41), Satan debates the grounds of his disobedience. The lines issue into a reminder that merely to be grateful for a debt is to repay it (55–7). Philomela, meanwhile, recurs. 'Her amorous descant' (IV. 602–3) sounds through this conjugal fourth book. Appealed to twice in Eve's embedded sonnet on 'silent Night | With this her solemn Bird' (IV. 647–8, 655), 'Nightingales' lull the embracing couple in their bower (771). In Eden at least, this is very much Philomel's poem. And we find in Book V:

> Why sleepst thou *Eve*? now is the pleasant time,
> The cool, the silent, save where silence yeilds
> To the night-warbling Bird, that now awake
> Tunes sweetest his love-labord song . . . (38–41)

While the poet warbles in his house near St James's Park, 'Her' becomes 'his' (through 'now . . . time . . . song') and a nightingale changes sex.

---

[30] '*Al Signor Gio. Miltoni Nobile Inglese* Ode' 67–8 (cf. Pecheux, 'Milton and *Kairos*', 206–8), '*Joanni Miltoni Londiniensi*' 13–14.

[31] *Poems Upon Several Occasions . . . by John Milton*, ed. Thomas Warton (1785), 334.

[32] e.g. George Steevens, recorded by James Sutherland (ed.), *The Oxford Book of Literary Anecdotes* (Oxford, 1975), 105–6.

[33] III. 282; Cf. LeComte, *Milton's Unchanging Mind*, 32.

In his patchy account of 'Milton among the Nightingales', John Leon Lievsay remarks: 'The change of gender, I take it, has no significance.'[34] It is, in fact, a matrix of significances, not least because anxiety about *kairos* proved double-edged. From about 1641 the poet began to 'crave excuse' for claims 'that urgent reason hath pluckt from me by an abortive and foredated discovery' (III. 240)—a reversal of 'overdated' equally un-recorded before Milton. During the same period, warbling song, which 'harmonizes' in the early work,[35] becomes the voice of fallen splendour. Not by accident is it Satan who, in Eve's account, renders Philomel 'he', putting Milton's sensual music into the devil's camp. With hindsight, Leonora's '*serpit agens . . .*' discloses an interlingual snaky creepiness. Al-most as insidious is the way those great lines on the 'wakeful Bird' in *Par-adise Lost* III are prefaced by allusions to the blind poets Thamyris and Maeonides. 'Is it coincidence', Alastair Fowler wonders, 'that the soul of Thamyris passed into a nightingale?' (38 n.). Probably not, since (accord-ing to Homer and Plato) this poet lost his sight and underwent meta-morphosis for competing with the Muses themselves. The lines show Milton, now sure of his powers, wondering what emulous success amounts to in the sight of Urania and God. Shelley responds to an in-spired blindness which is, for Milton, touched with potential sin in being self-absorbed and rival-silencing. Even Hildesheimer's narrator had scru-ples about his metamorphosis. Apart from anything else, he reflects, a nightingale is 'one who interferes with someone else's life by disturbing his sleep'.

Dr Johnson was clearly right to believe that, 'beginning late', Milton was 'not without some fear' that *Paradise Lost* was itself untimely, written 'in *an age too late* for heroick poetry'.[36] Yet the signs are that Milton began to dread foredating more than 'belatednesse' once the epic unfolded in his mind. By 1652, in '*Cromwell*, our cheif of men', the mood is changing. This sonnet is laudatory; but it cannot be read for long without disclos-ing the kind of modified admiration which Marvell brings to the theme. It is partly that 'thy glorious way hast plough'd' calls to mind the cut worm. Like the 'three-fork'd Lightning' in the 'Horatian *Ode*', which cuts

[34] *Renaissance Papers 1958, 1959, 1960*, 36–45, p. 45.

[35] e.g. *Elegia quinta* 25–30, with its symptomatically placed '*Jam*'. For musicological com-ment, see James D. Brophy, 'Milton's "Warble": The Trill as Metaphor of Concord', *Milton Quarterly*, 19 (1985), 105–9.

[36] *Lives of the English Poets*, ed. Arthur Waugh, 2 vols. (Oxford, 1906), i. 96, paraphrasing *PL* IX. 13–47.

a 'fiery way' through 'the Clouds where it was nurst',[37] the initial image of sundered 'cloud' suggests a ruthlessness to the *virtù* which has made '*Darwen* stream' run with 'blood'. But the most telling instability registers at lines 5–6. 'Gods Trophies' have been 'reard' 'on the neck of crowned Fortune proud', but only God knows how justly. By this date icons of 'Fortune' had merged with *kairos*. In emblem books Fortuna has Occasion's winged sphere at her feet, and, bald behind, must, like her, be grasped by the forelock. After standing and waiting, Cromwell—much given to tactics of preparatory delay—has seized his time. Milton is dazzled by his success, but the violent image of Occasion/Fortune mastered has more than a glint of Machiavellian[38] boldness. The republican poet is already beginning to distance himself from a figure who, for all his righteousness, will prove constitutionally threatening and a less than distant analogue of Satan in *Paradise Lost*. The best gloss is retrospective: when Satan urges Christ, with offers of fame and praise, 'on Occasions forelock watchful wait' (*PR* III. 173), the latter recognizes his twisting of 'stand and waite', and responds: 'All things are best fulfilld in thir due time, | And time there is for all things, Truth hath said . . .' (182–3).

There is a formal corollary. Encouraged by hints of chronological order in 1645 and 1673, some have tried to read Milton's sonnets as a sequence. Others have emphasized the miscellaneity of the 1673 title-page: *Poems, &c. Upon Several Occasions*. Evidently internal links can be found, and not just in I to VII. But the largest principle of coherence lies in *Occasions* giving the godly life significance by virtue of discontinuity. In such works as *Astrophil and Stella* and Shakespeare's *Sonnets*, Milton found 'occasional' poems: they describe tournaments and anniversaries, begin 'When I . . .', turn on 'Now'. This association between timeliness and the Sonnet no doubt helped draw him to the form. After all, his first substantial work in print, 'Lycidas', begins with an irregular sonnet which addresses 'sad occasion dear': 'sad' because King is dead 'ere his prime' (though 25), 'dear' because 'occasion' is both 'grievous' (in Caroline English) and 'precious'. Celebrating the individual's freedom to grasp, or miss, 'timely-happiness', while craving what *A Treatise of Civil Power* calls 'timely reading' (VI. 1), Milton's sonnets promulgate (in Bacon's phrase) 'a doctrine of scattered occasions'. Their priorities are thus inseparable

---

[37] '*An* Horatian *Ode upon* Cromwel's *Return from* Ireland', 13–16, in *The Poems and Letters of Andrew Marvell*, ed. H. M. Margoliouth, 2nd edn., 2 vols. (Oxford, 1963).

[38] On *fortuna, virtù,* and *occasione* see J. G. A. Pocock, *The Machiavellian Moment: Florentine Political Thought and the Atlantic Republican Tradition* (Princeton, 1975).

from his dissenting spiritual life. When Presbyterians '*under the Long PARLAMENT*' sought to impose times and patterns of worship—regular, collective means for paying God his 'tribute'—the anti-sabbatarian rebelled by writing a sonnet which was most tautly disciplined where least regular, Italianately tailed. Nor did Milton's movement beyond sureness to patience change his seasonal gappiness. 'His Invention was much more free and easie in the Æquinoxes than at the Solstices', Edward Phillips told Aubrey.[39] When invention fused the timely with the eternal, the 'season'd life of man' was quibblingly said to be 'preserv'd . . . in Books' (IV. 298). At first, in occasional poems, talents were put to 'use' and 'tributes' paid—always, implicitly, to God, but, when the moment called, to deserving men and women. In the 1640s and 1650s sonnet-form was thus employed to honour Margaret Ley, Catharine Thomason, Fairfax, Henry Lawes, and the rest. Yet 'the desire of honour & repute & immortall fame' conceded in that 1633 letter is already a 'last infirmity' in 'Lycidas', and, by the time of *Paradise Regained*, 'praise' is matter for the submerged sonnets[40] with which Satan flatters Jesus. Christ does not doubt the 'true glory and renown, when God, | Looking on th' Earth, with approbation marks | The just man' (III. 60–2), yet such distant acclaim is very different from that of the Italian panegyrics. Partly because *Paradise Regained* can begin with the assurance 'I . . . now sing', the late poetics move, beyond anxieties of occasion, into the impersonality of scriptural paraphrase.

Milton's abandonment of the Sonnet follows. Indeed, the form can be seen losing its temporal and personal immediacy in the dateless, softly focused poem which, whatever its occasion, belongs where Milton put it: at the end of his 1673 grouping. For who is praised in 'Methought I saw my late espoused Saint'? The poem points towards Mary Powell as well as Katharine Woodcock, and beyond both. A tribute paid in public remains private, and owes much of its beauty to Milton's not himself quite knowing her to whom he pays homage. 'Vested all in white', the woman's face is concealed by a veil which, among other intimations, recalls that 'candida gonna' which (as others have noted) clothes Petrarch's elusive Laura in the *Trionfo della pudicizia*. As tantalizing is a sense of corrective imitation, of *retractatio*, exercised on *Canzoniere* 311, 'Quel rosigniuol . . .'[41]

[39] Darbishire, *Early Lives*, 13.

[40] e.g. I. 321–34, 383–96, III. 7–20; cf. Lee M. Johnson, 'Milton's Blank Verse Sonnet', *Milton Studies*, 5 (1973), 129–53, pp. 147–8.

[41] Quoting *Le rime del Petrarca*, ed. Lodovico Castelvetro (Basel, 1582); Parte seconda, p. 67.

and, before that, *Georgics* 4. 494–520. In his unusually nocturnal sonnet Petrarch (changing the gender of Virgil's nightingale) compares his lament over Laura's death to Orpheus' Philomel-like grief for Eurydice. Like Virgil's Orpheus, 'twice robbed of his wife' (literally by 1658), Milton tacitly alludes—though this has been neglected by editors—to Eurydice's last attempt to reach out to her spouse (494–504), while promoting the Christological typology of Hercules and Alcestis, and, it may be, referring Laura's dead blindness to himself: 'Those two lights far brighter than the sun, | whoever thought to see them become dark clay [*veder far terra oscura*]?' It is sometimes said that 'O Nightingale' is Milton's only 'love poem'.[42] The claim is wrong for that sonnet, yet it might be true of this. For the first time Milton feels able to use of an 'incognita' that term applied so freely by poetasters like Watson (in his sonnet on Philomel), 'Saint'. The whole text is reticent yet resolving in this way. In the very first line, 'late' can be included without the reflex of self-rebuke inescapable in the early poems. Likewise 'Methought I saw' conveys a flash of hope that, when dreaming that he saw, he thought he did; and the consolation is that, in what *Areopagitica* calls 'midnight watchings' (IV. 324), Milton 'saw' what he asked to see in Book III of *Paradise Lost*: 'things invisible to mortal sight' (55). During the hours in which, 'darkling', he composed his epic, tuning 'his nocturnal note', the sonneteer was visited by a gleam of the 'Celestial Light' he had thought 'spent'. It is worth adding that, if you look up that passage on the 'wakeful Bird' in the epic, you will find a verse paragraph in fourteen lines (III. 37–50)—yet another nightingale sonnet, rehearsing but assuaging 'belatednesse'.

---

[42] e.g. David Parker, 'The Love Poems of *Paradise Lost* and the Petrarchan Tradition', *Ariel*, 3/1 (1972), 34–43, p. 35.

CHAPTER 11

Revenge Tragedy Revisited,
1649–1683 (1997)

The purged House of Commons sentenced Charles I to death for seeking 'tyrannical power' and for waging a cruel war in which 'many thousands' were 'slain'.[1] During the trial, John Bradshaw declared, with retributive vehemence, that the spilling of 'innocent blood' had left a stain which could not 'be cleansed but with the shedding of the blood of him that shed this blood'.[2] On the scaffold Charles spoke of a punishment equally sanguinary but more particular. Recalling the arraignment and execution of Strafford, in 1641, he said: 'God forbid that I should be so ill a Christian as not to say God's judgements are just upon me. . . . an unjust sentence that I suffered for to take effect, is punished now by an unjust sentence on me.'[3] The more closely one looks at these events, the more they seem structured by retributive sentiment. Even Charles's quip to the executioner—in the line of More and Ralegh—'Hurt not the Axe that may hurt me' shows a fascination with reciprocal violence, and what it does to things, which is a hallmark of revenge tragedy. Like the ghost in *Hamlet*, urging fidelity on the Prince, the King's final injunction was 'Remember'. He gave his Garter badge and ribbon as remembrances to Bishop Juxon, and, once the axe had fallen, the troubled crowd thronged forward to snatch more lurid tokens: to take hairs from his head and beard, to dip their handkerchiefs (like Kyd's Hieronimo) in blood.[4]

That theatrical metaphors shaped perceptions of public life in the 1640s is agreed.[5] Scholarly readers of Marvell are aware that his figuring of

[1] David Iagomarsino and Charles T. Wood (eds.), *The Trial of Charles I: A Documentary History* (Hanover, NH, 1989), 106–7.

[2] Quoted by Stephen Baskerville—with numerous contemporary analogues—in 'Blood Guilt in the English Revolution', *Seventeenth Century*, 8 (1993), 181–202, p. 181.

[3] Quoted by Pauline Gregg, *King Charles I* (London, 1981), 444. Cf. Matthew 7: 1–2, Luke 6: 37–8.

[4] Gregg, *King Charles I*, 444–5; cf. Charles Carlton, *Charles I: The Personal Monarch* (London, 1983), 358–60. *Hamlet*, ed. Harold Jenkins (London, 1982), I. v. 91; *The Spanish Tragedy*, ed. Philip Edwards (London, 1959), II. v. 51–2.

[5] Cf. Nancy Klein Maguire, 'The Theatrical Mask/Masque of Politics: The Case of Charles I', *Journal of British Studies*, 28 (1989), 1–22.

the King's execution—'That thence the royal actor borne I The tragic scaffold might adorn'[6]—is elegantly of its time. What interests me, more specifically, is why an outraged loyalist, such as the author of *The Famous Tragedie of King Charles I* (1649), should shape his view of the King's death theatrically by revisiting the conventions of revenge tragedy. The Cromwell of his quasi-dramatic pamphlet has the hallmarks of a stage Machiavel, and Rainsborough is a hellish villain struck down by 'divine justice' (p. 37); in the manner of Webster and Ford, the anonymous writer introduces 'six Masquers, habited for ambition, treason, lust, revenge, perjury, sacriledge' (p. 35); and he ends with the Chorus (in a Kydian touch)[7] discovering '*behind the travers the dead body of the* King' (p. 42). More exaltedly, though as symptomatically, the royalist Christopher Wase sought to 'vindicate' the King's 'right' by translating Sophocles. Cromwell was for him an Aegisthus figure, seducing the people and 'twining' a 'net' (as Marvell put it),[8] like the one used at Mycenae, to catch his royal prey. In his version of *Electra* (1649), Wase makes the allegory explicit, with Charles as Agamemnon and the deluded nation Clytemnestra, the future Charles II in the role of Orestes, Prince Rupert as Pylades, the Princess Elizabeth, Electra, and Cromwell (in a wishful prediction) the usurping adulterer struck down by the dead King's kin.

In this essay I want to argue that Wase's political application of revenge tragedy is far from unique. Like *The Famous Tragedie of King Charles I*, his *Electra* helps refute the still widely held belief that the development of the genre in England was an essentially 'literary' phenomenon: the product of Senecan imitation.[9] It is apt that when Nashe—in a passage often cited in support of this view—says that 'English Seneca . . . will afford you whole Hamlets, I should say handfuls, of tragical speeches. But oh grief! *Tempus edax rerum*: what's that will last always?', he is both stressing the exhaustibility of this source and (*pace* his Penguin editor) citing not Seneca but Ovid.[10] The attractions of Seneca were always partial—Tudor translators of his plays adapted them—and in themselves political. He

---

[6] 'An Horatian Ode upon Cromwell's Return from Ireland', in *The Oxford Authors: Andrew Marvell*, ed. Frank Kermode and Keith Walker (Oxford, 1990), ll. 53–4.

[7] *Spanish Tragedy* IV. iv. 88–97; cf. Anne Barton, ' "He that Plays the King": Ford's *Perkin Warbeck* and the Stuart History Play', repr. in her *Essays, Mainly Shakespearean* (Cambridge, 1994), 234–60, p. 260.   [8] 'Horatian Ode', ll. 62, 49–50.

[9] e.g. Anthony Burgess, 'European Literature', Cheltenham Festival of Literature 1993 inaugural lecture, abridged in *Independent*, 27 Nov. 1993, p. 31.

[10] *Metamorphoses* 15. 234; *'The Unfortunate Traveller' and Other Works*, ed. J. B. Steane (Harmondsworth, 1972), 474.

appealed to those early humanists who wanted to counsel great men because, as a philosopher near the throne (adviser and victim of Nero), he understood the dangers of that desire for 'tyrannical power' which Bradshaw and his fellows diagnosed in Charles I. When Alexander Neville, for example, introduced his patron (a Privy Counsellor) to his translation of Seneca's *Oedipus* (1563), he equated his own intentions with those of the Roman author: 'to admonish all men of theyr fickle Estates . . . And lyuely to expresse the iust reuenge, and fearful punishments of horrible Crimes' (a3^v). Neville is almost as interested as post-Freudian readers in Oedipus' 'incestuous lothsome lust'.[11] But he is also preoccupied with aspects of tyrannical government. For him, the tragedy is that, before Laius is 'reuenged', Oedipus has caused the 'destruction of the Nobilitie . . . and spoyle of the Cominaltie' of Thebes (a5^v–6^r). In language which King Charles would recognize, Neville says that the play shows the 'wrathfull vengeaunce of God', the 'deepe hidden secret Iudgements of God' (ibid.), upon a prince and his polity.

What has been called 'the revenger's madness'[12] could be mobilized on the early modern stage by a variety of passions, by no means excluding incest. As I have shown in *Revenge Tragedy: Aeschylus to Armageddon*,[13] the genre has been, since antiquity, so psychologically and dramaturgically resourceful that its manifestation, in any one period, cannot be tidily explained by reference to immediate contexts. Yet it is a sign of the importance of politics to the life of the genre in England that, if you look for its beginnings,[14] what you find is another Oresteian *drame à clef* about the death of princes—for most scholars now accept that, in John Pykeryng's *Horestes* (1567), Elizabeth I is being urged to execute Mary Queen of Scots (Clytemnestra) for her role in the murder of her husband, Darnley (Agamemnon), by the Earl of Bothwell (Aegisthus).[15] It is a point of great significance for the future of revenge tragedy in England that the topic was an appealingly difficult one for the lawyer Pykeryng—a future Lord Keeper—and his contemporaries because the hostility of Scottish Protestants towards Mary could, and did, inform Catholic debates about

---

[11] Cf. Richard A. McCabe, *Incest, Drama and Nature's Law 1550–1700* (Cambridge, 1993), 110.

[12] See Charles A. Hallett and Elaine S. Hallett, *The Revenger's Madness: A Study of Revenge Tragedy Motifs* (Lincoln, Nebr., 1980).

[13] Oxford, 1996.

[14] On precursors see Julia Dietrich, 'Justice in this World: The Background of the Revenger in the English Morality Drama', *Journal of Medieval and Renaissance Studies*, 12 (1982), 99–111.

[15] See e.g. Marie Axton (ed.), *Three Tudor Classical Interludes: 'Thersites', 'Jacke Jugeler', 'Horestes'* (Cambridge, 1982), 29–30.

the legitimacy of rebellion against Elizabeth. This period saw the development and dissemination of those theories of resistance which would fuel religious and political unrest right through the seventeenth century,[16] and debate about that subject was inextricable from the question of revenge because the biblical passage most often cited in arguments about obedience was also concerned with the difference between private and divinely justified vengeance. As tracts and homilies note,[17] after citing, from Deuteronomy, 'Vengeance is mine; I will repay, saith the Lord', St Paul goes on to urge: 'Let every soul be subject unto the higher powers. For there is no power but of God; the powers that be are ordained of God. . . . if thou do that which is evil, be afraid; for he beareth not the sword in vain: for he is the minister of God, a revenger to execute wrath upon him that doeth evil' (Romans 12: 19–13: 6).

That the emergence of revenge tragedy in England was encouraged by post-Reformation providentialism is by now almost a truism.[18] What has been less securely grasped is that the recurrent tension in early modern drama between the rightness of what Neville calls 'Gods horryble vengeance for Sin' (a7^v) and the questionable claim of individuals to be acting as his scourge and minister was cross-cut—from Pykeryng's *Horestes* to the Lee–Dryden *Duke of Guise* (1682)—with political argument about tyranny and the limits of just rebellion. In making that claim I am, of course, pushing revenge tragedy beyond its usual terminus. For a second misconception which Wase's *Electra* and *The Famous Tragedie of King Charles I* help lay to rest is the idea that work in the genre stopped with the closure of the theatres in 1642. This tenacious error[19] ignores continuities in the translation,[20] composition,[21] first

---

[16] See e.g. Quentin Skinner, *The Foundations of Modern Political Thought*, 2 vols. (Cambridge, 1978), ii, pt. 3.

[17] Cf. e.g. Eleanor Prosser, *Hamlet and Revenge*, 2nd edn. (Stanford, Calif., 1971), 6–7.

[18] See e.g. Lily B. Campbell, 'Theories of Revenge in Renaissance England', *Modern Philology*, 28 (1930–1), 281–96.

[19] See e.g. Fredson Bowers's influential, and paradoxically entitled, *Elizabethan Revenge Tragedy 1587–1642* (Princeton, 1940), esp. pp. 283–4, Prosser, *Hamlet and Revenge*, ch. 2 and app. B, Hallett and Hallett, *The Revenger's Madness*, ch. 11, and Wendy Griswold, *Renaissance Revivals: City Comedy and Revenge Tragedy in the London Theater, 1576–1980* (Chicago, 1987), 55.

[20] *Agamemnon* (BL Add. MS 60276) and *Hercules Furens* (BL Add. MSS 60276 and 60277), trans. James Compton; *Medea*, trans. Edward Sherburne (1648); *Hippolytus*, trans. Edward Prestwich (1651); *Troades*, trans. Samuel Pordage (1660)—all from Seneca.

[21] Among works published later see e.g. J.S., *Andromana; or, The Merchant's Wife* (early 1640s; pub. 1660), Thomas Fuller, *Andronicus: A Tragedy. Impiety's Long Success, or Heaven's Late Revenge* (c.1643; pub. 1646, citing here 1661 title-page), and, if W. R. Parker's dating (1646–7, 1652–3) is accepted, Milton, *Samson Agonistes* (1671).

publication,[22] reprinting,[23] and performance[24] of revenge tragedy between 1642 and 1659, and its stage prominence after the Restoration. Some play-texts dealing with vengeance from the 1640s and 1650s have already been recognized as topical;[25] but I want to argue that the ambiguities of Romans 12–13 made the genre tellingly resurgent during the Restoration and Exclusion crises.

Because the political perplexities are so pervasive, it would be arbitrary to construct too fixed a pre-1642 genealogy for post-1649 revenge drama. Yet a case can be made for identifying a key tradition of plays about resistance to authority in those lustful monarch tragedies which were anticipated by Neville's *Oedipus* but which start about 1600 in such plays as Shakespeare's *Hamlet* and, with greater formulaic directness, in Dekker, Haughton, and Day's *Lust's Dominion*. There, as in Beaumont and Fletcher's *The Maid's Tragedy* (1608–11), Fletcher's *Valentinian* (1610–14), and Suckling's *Aglaura* (1637–8), revenge is a spur to rebellion in principled or ambitious opponents of a king who shows his tyrannical tendencies in sexual intrigue. These protagonists—wronged husbands and brothers—set themselves against monarchs who are associated with the sword of wrath attributed to kings and magistrates in Romans 13.

---

[22] Works written and published within the period include e.g. *The Tragedy of that Famous Roman Oratour Marcus Tullius Cicero* (1651), which focuses on historical retribution—a copy survives, in Worcester College Library, Oxford, among the future Charles II's books; *The Bastard* (1652); George Gerbier D'Ouvilley, *The False Favourite Disgrac'd* (1657)—a tragicomedy with vengeful elements. Examples of pre-1642 revenge plays published for the first time are: Shirley, *The Cardinal* (1641), in his *Six New Plays* (1653), and *The Politician* (1639?; pub. 1655); William Heminges, *The Fatal Contract: A French Tragedy* (1639; pub. 1653); Henry Glapthorne (?), *Revenge for Honour* (c.1637–41; pub. 1654); *Alphonsus Emperor of Germany* (1590s; pub. 1654); Middleton, *Women Beware Women* (c.1620–7), in his *Two New Plays* (1657); and Lodowick Carlell's ultra-loyal contribution to lustful monarch drama, *Osmond the Great Turk; or, The Noble Servant* (1622/37; pub. 1657).

[23] e.g. Chapman, *Bussy D'Ambois* (pub. 1607–8), reappeared 1646 and 1657; Suckling, *Aglaura* (pub. 1638), in his *Fragmenta aurea*, 1646, 1648, and 1658; Marston, *Antonio's Revenge* (pub. 1602), in his *Comedies, Tragi-comedies; and Tragedies* (1652); Thomas Rawlins, *The Rebellion* (pub. 1640), in 1652; Webster, *The Duchess of Malfi* (pub. 1623), in 1657–64.

[24] The records are patchy, but, for a colourful and indicative account, see James Wright, *Historia histrionica: An Historical Account of the English-Stage* (1699), 8–9, on 'the Tragedy of the *Bloudy Brother*' (i.e. *Rollo, Duke of Normandy*, by Fletcher and others), played at the Cockpit during the winter of 1648.

[25] e.g. Henry Burkhead's thinly veiled account of conflict in Ireland, *Cola's Fury; or, Lirenda's Misery* (1645; pub. 1646), where Revenge appears as a character (p. 46). For analysis see Patricia Coughlan, ' "Enter Revenge": Henry Burkhead and *Cola's Furie*', *Theatre Research International*, 15 (1990), 1–17. Cf. Dale B. J. Randall's remarks on *Alphonsus Emperor of Germany* and the politics of 1653–4, and on how Sherburne's *Medea* and Pordage's *Troades* address the cruelties of 1648 and the Restoration: *Winter Fruit: English Drama, 1642–1660* (Lexington, Ky; 1995), 240–1, 214–15.

Amintor, in *The Maid's Tragedy*, may be willing to brandish his weapon in quarrel with his brother-in-law Melantius ('As justly as our magistrates their swords I To cut offenders off'),[26] but, when blades are drawn in the course of an interview with the King, Amintor is disabled by Pauline obedience and an awestruck sense of divine right (III. i. 245–9). This caution is shown to be justified when, at the end of the play, those involved in regicide are extirpated, and a conclusive moral is produced: 'on lustful kings I Unlook'd-for sudden deaths from God are sent; I But curs'd is he that is their instrument.' Disaster is not invariable. In *Aglaura*, as first conceived, a 'Lustfull and cruell'[27] King of Persia is murdered by a group of rebels led by the vengeful Ziriff, angered at the King's part in his father's death and by his attempts on the virtue of his sister Aglaura. Yet when Charles I 'expressed concern at the unhappy ending',[28] Suckling, it seems, revised it, sparing the lives of both the King (who is merely subjected to shaming rebukes) and Ziriff. Though early Stuart lustful monarch plays were fundamentally conservative, they could incorporate enough 'political criticism'[29] to trouble the crown.

The afterlife of these tragedies provides an index of continuity. *Lust's Dominion*, for example, was not published until 1657, when it helped console royalist readers resentful of Cromwell's yoke. Hence the gloss on the rebel Eleazar's death, provided by a prefatory poem:

> So may they Fall, that seek for to Betray,
> And Lead the People in an Unknown Way:
> As in a Glasse, thus We may Clearly See,
> All Vanishes That's Built on Tyranny.[30]

The uncertainties associated with Cromwell's sickness and death, in the following year, made it possible to believe that the English people might now turn from their 'Unknown Way', and the newly topical play was reissued in 1658, and again in 1661. Meanwhile, *The Maid's Tragedy* and *Valentinian*—published during the closure, and thereafter[31]—were being

---

[26] *The Maid's Tragedy*, ed. Howard B. Norland (London, 1968), III. ii. 162–3.
[27] Dramatis Personae, in *The Works of Sir John Suckling: The Plays*, ed. L. A. Beaurline (Oxford, 1971).
[28] 'Sir John Suckling', *DNB*.
[29] Martin Butler on *Aglaura*, in his *Theatre and Crisis 1632–1642* (Cambridge, 1984), 56.
[30] 'To my honored Friend Mr. F. K. on the publishing this Tragedie', ll. 21–4, in *The Dramatic Works of Thomas Dekker*, ed. Fredson Bowers, 4 vols. (Cambridge, 1953–61), iv. 130.
[31] *Valentinian* was first published in the 1647 Folio of Beaumont and Fletcher's *Comedies and Tragedies*; *The Maid's Tragedy* (pub. 1619) joined it in the 1679 Folio. The 6th edn. of *The Maid's Tragedy*, dated 1650 (actually 1660), was followed by printings in 1661 (?) and 1686; Waller's

revived on stage. Productions of the former began as early as August 1660. Pepys liked the play well enough to see it five times between 1661 and 1668. But Charles II must have been less gratified when he viewed it in 1667. No audience would have confused the married chastity of Charles I with the lust of Beaumont and Fletcher's King. During the second half of the 1660s, however, his son's love affairs were becoming a scandal. As a result, this warning against rebellion 'was by private Order from the Court silenc'd'.[32] Gerard Langbaine tells us that, when Edmund Waller produced his tragicomic adaptation of the play, the last act was (in the manner of *Aglaura*) 'wholly alter'd to please the Court'.[33] Waller's version does not excise the King's affair with Evadne, but when Melantius protests about it to Lucippus, the monarch's brother, the latter asks (as though Nell Gwyn or Moll Davis were in question), 'shou'd a Prince, because he does comply | With one that's Fair, and not unwilling, die?'[34] Waller plainly thought not, and the main action ends with Lucippus and the King duelling their way to reconciliation with Melantius and his brother.

Robert D. Hume has proposed *c.*1664 as the date of *The Maid's Tragedy Alter'd*.[35] Waller's handling of Lucippus, however, suggests a later occasion. In the original his role is small, but much is made in revision of Melantius' attempt to win him over to rebellion. 'A present Crown', the rebel reflects, 'Cannot but tempt a Prince so near the Throne.' And if he refuses to join in the 'Revenge', 'He's full of Honour: tho' he like it not, | If once he swear, he'll not reveal the Plot' (p. 193). Lucippus not only resists these blandishments, but sides with his brother in combat. As the King, rather heavily, remarks: 'O! what an Happiness it is to find | A Friend of our own Blood, a Brother kind!' (p. 199). All this smacks of a desire to reassure audiences that James, Duke of York, was not interested in deposing Charles II, his brother, and that a 'Plot' to assassinate the sovereign and put the papist James on the throne could have no support from the Duke. Rumours about such a 'Plot' were growing in the mid-1670s, and this would be the obvious date (just compatible with Waller's old-

---

adaptation first appeared in *The Second Part of Mr. Waller's Poems and The Maid's Tragedy Altered. With Some Other Pieces* (both 1690). Rochester's version of *Valentinian* was published in quarto in 1685 (while also circulating in MS); texts were included in his *Poems, &c. on Several Occasions* from 1691 and 1696 onwards.

[32] Preface to *The Works of Mr. Francis Beaumont and Mr. John Fletcher*, 7 vols. (1711), i. 8.

[33] Gerard Langbaine, *An Account of the English Dramatick Poets* (1691), 212.

[34] *The Maid's Tragedy Alter'd*, in Edmund Waller, *Poems, &c. Written Upon Several Occasions, and to Several Persons*, 9th edn. (1712), 197.

[35] '*The Maid's Tragedy* and Censorship in the Restoration Theatre', *Philological Quarterly*, 61 (1982), 484–90.

fashioned dramatic couplets) for an adaptation to seek to supplant the original. Certainly it seems likely that it was at the height of the panic about Jesuit conspiracy, during the 'Popish plot' and the attempts to exclude the Duke of York from succession (1678–81), that *The Maid's Tragedy* was removed from the stage.[36] This was also the period in which Rochester's subversive rewrite of *Valentinian*—it leaves the chief rebel, Maximus, at the end, unpoisoned—was denied performance.[37]

The Exclusion Crisis, and the culture of vengeance associated with it, cannot be understood in isolation. It has recently been dubbed 'the Restoration crisis'[38] to emphasize how much of its turmoil was the legacy of 1660. That earlier year was itself, of course, a season in which scores were settled. So many ex-royalists (including Waller) had compromised with Cromwell that it would have been 'impractical' to provide all 'the vengeance which the old cavaliers wanted'.[39] But Pepys caught the temper of the time when he wrote, of the executed regicides, 'it was my chance to see the King beheaded at White-hall and to see the first blood shed in revenge for the blood of the King at Charing-cross.'[40] As Paul Hammond notes, 'The trial and execution of Charles I were restaged with different actors when the bodies of Bradshaw, Cromwell and Ireton were exhumed and hanged at Tyburn . . . It was evidently important that vengeance, or justice, should be carried out upon the bodies of the republicans.'[41] Nancy Klein Maguire is surely right to speculate that, during performances of *Hamlet* in 1661, 'the ghost of Hamlet's father resonated with the "ghost" of Charles I'.[42] Orrery's double concern, in *The History of Henry the Fifth* (1664), with vengeance for a dead father and the reclamation of a kingdom[43] reflects the same political dynamic. Maguire has plausibly suggested that tragicomedy is more current than tragedy during the 1660s because it deals in things restored; but, of all tragic scenarios, those which turn on vengeance—using recapitulative

---

[36] See ibid.

[37] For publication see n. 31 above; on the play's apparent preparation for the 1675–6 or 1676–7 season, and its first known performance in 1684, see Larry Carver, 'Rochester's *Valentinian*', *Restoration and Eighteenth-Century Theatre Research*, 2nd ser. 4/1 (Summer 1989), 25–38, p. 26.

[38] Jonathan Scott, *Algernon Sidney and the Restoration Crisis, 1677–1683* (Cambridge, 1991).

[39] Susan J. Owen, 'Interpreting the Politics of Restoration Drama', *Seventeenth Century*, 8 (1993), 67–97, p. 90.

[40] *The Diary of Samuel Pepys*, ed. Robert Latham and William Matthews, 11 vols. (London, 1970–83), i. 265.

[41] 'The King's Two Bodies: Representations of Charles II', in Jeremy Black and Jeremy Gregory (eds.), *Culture, Politics and Society in Britain, 1660–1800* (Manchester, 1991), 13–48, p. 17.

[42] *Regicide and Restoration: English Tragicomedy, 1660–1671* (Cambridge, 1992), 121.

[43] Cf. Derek Hughes, *English Drama 1660–1700* (Oxford, 1996), 32.

acts to extirpate evil—most resemble, and are most compatible with, tragicomedy.[44] That, it seems to me, is why revenge plots are plentiful (as Maguire's own evidence demonstrates) in the early tragicomedies of Dryden, the plays of James Howard and John Dover—plays which no doubt do show 'the culture's guilty attempt to rehabilitate Charles I in the person of his son'.[45]

It was 1678–83 which saw, however, the last great efflorescence of revenge tragedy on the English stage. 'As religious anxieties mounted throughout the 1670s,' Jonathan Scott writes, 'the country realised that it was slipping back again into a repetition of the crisis of Charles I.' As Scott notes, this period saw a return to the political literature of the earlier crisis, including republished descriptions of the Irish rebellion of 1641 and the printing of Sir Robert Filmer's defence of Caroline absolutism, *Patriarcha*.[46] Writing for the theatre proved equally recapitulative. The heroic drama of the Restoration not only sounded overblown by this date ('Some Verses of my own *Maximin* and *Almanzor*', Dryden admitted in 1681, 'cry Vengeance upon me for their Extravagance'),[47] its black-and-white morality was too inflexible for dealing with the urgent questions of factional duplicity and parliamentary infighting. Shakespeare set a better precedent. It was now that Edward Ravenscroft rewrote *Titus Andronicus* to reflect on the Popish plot, while tragedies were frequently marked by the influence of *Julius Caesar*: that many-times reprinted revenge drama[48] based on conspiracy and centring on a struggle between the aspiring absolutism of Caesar and the late republican fidelity of Brutus. It cannot be accidental that the two tragedies of the Exclusion Crisis which speak most powerfully today, Lee's *Lucius Junius Brutus* (1680) and Otway's *Venice Preserved* (1682), are both works in this mode, that the most topically explicit play of the period, the Lee–Dryden *Duke of Guise* (1682), is galvanized by factional vengeance, and that the tragedy which seems to have reached the largest audience—written as news of the Popish plot was breaking—the Dryden–Lee *Oedipus* (1678)—brings a drama of vengeful conspiracy into vivid conjunction with the lustful monarch formula.

[44] Kerrigan, *Revenge Tragedy*, 208–16.

[45] Maguire, *Regicide and Restoration*, 162.

[46] *Algernon Sidney and the Restoration Crisis*, 31 and 7.

[47] Epistle dedicatory to *The Spanish Fryar; or, The Double Discovery*, in *The Works of John Dryden*, gen. eds. Edward Niles Hooker, H. T. Swedenberg, Jr., et al. (Berkeley, 1956–), xiv. 100.

[48] There were at least six quartos between the Exclusion Crisis and 1700, plus appearances in issues of the fourth Folio (1685).

Charles II's enemies accused him of more than adultery. Rumoured to be the illegitimate offspring of Henry Jermyn and Henrietta Maria, he was also said to have slept with his mother.[49] In *The Speech of Hodge the Clown* (1679), sometimes attributed to Marvell, 'the Goatish king' is spied in 'scenes of . . . incestuous Love' and urged, 'Cease, cease, O Charles, thus to pollute our Isle; | Return, return to thy long wisht Exile.'[50] It was thus rather bold of Dryden and Lee to write a play about a Theban monarch who was not the son of his ostensible father and who combined undoubted incest with having been an exile when he secured the throne. But this kind of high-risk irony is typical of the author of *Absalom and Achitophel*, the masterpiece of the Exclusion Crisis. Indeed, the awkwardness from which that poem starts—Charles's multiple amours, which have 'Scatter'd his Maker's Image through the Land'[51]—relates to another difficulty associated with *Oedipus*. Echoing one of the play's characters, Dryden, in his preface, calls Oedipus 'a Father of his Country'.[52] This chimes with the doctrine of Filmer's *Patriarcha* (published in the same year as the play), that 'Kings are either Fathers of their People, or Heirs of such Fathers, or the Usurpers of the Rights of such Fathers.'[53] But it also faces down the common quip that Charles was 'The Truest *Pater Patriae* e'er was yet, | For all, or most of's subjects, does beget.'[54]

Equally bold is the handling of the plague. We know from Thucydides that Athens was smitten with pestilence before Sophocles wrote *Oedipus Tyrannus*. Dryden and Lee were in a similar position. For many, the plague of 1665 had been caused by divine anger against a court which served 'to pollute our Isle'. The 1678 *Oedipus* suggests, however, that plague afflicts Thebes/London because the city has not exorcized the ghost of Laius/Charles I. Sophocles includes no apparition; but the Dryden–Lee play, owing much to Seneca, does. In a Dryden-composed scene at once hellish and reminiscent of triumphal Caroline masque, Laius rises through a stage trap '*arm'd in his Chariot, as he was slain*' (III. i. 344). This is the nightmare of a traumatized body politic. Oedipus and the English Thebans have not come to terms with '*Blood-Royal unreveng'd*' (I. i. 437).

[49] Richard L. Greaves, *Deliver Us from Evil: The Radical Underground in Britain, 1660–1663* (New York, 1986), 23.

[50] Quoted by Scott, *Algernon Sidney and the Restoration Crisis*, 145.

[51] Line 10, in *Works of Dryden*, ii.

[52] *Works of Dryden*, xiii. 115 and I. i. 409.

[53] Title of ch. 5, in *'Patriarcha' and Other Political Works of Sir Robert Filmer*, ed. Peter Laslett (Oxford, 1949), 60.

[54] *A Satyr upon the Mistresses* ll. 16–17; quoted by Hammond, 'The King's Two Bodies', 17.

As the old cavaliers complained, sufficiently 'ample vengeance' (II. i. 106) had not been exacted in 1660. Dryden, who worked for Cromwell's regime, had more reason than many to feel guilt about this, but he also believed that collaborator and cavalier were now so interwoven that to resurrect old conflicts, through talk of a Popish plot, and through threats of Whig insurrection, was to conjure up spectres of 1640s violence that put all in jeopardy. These are the ghosts, politically speaking, which flit about the stage when Tiresias raises Laius. It is a past which, for Dryden, should not be remembered—which can only produce tragedy if disinterred—but which continues to haunt. From that scene, ominously, rings the dead King's cry for retribution. The episode has been shaped to recall the Prince of Denmark's first encounter with his father's spirit.[55] 'Remember *Lajus*' is the cry (III. i. 465, 468-9), echoing not only the ghost's words to Hamlet, but Charles I's valediction to Juxon.

What kind of king inherits this burden? As in Alexander Neville's Tudor translation from Seneca, the protagonist's legitimacy and effectiveness in government are necessary questions of the play. The Lee–Dryden *Oedipus* is not called *Oedipus Tyrannus*, despite the primary debt to Sophocles, because the protagonist is neither (in the words of 1649) 'unlimited' nor 'tyrannical' in 'power'. Though a Tory-sounding Priest calls Oedipus one to whom 'knees are bent . . . As to a visible Divinity' (I. i. 410-11), there is an equally striking passage in which a mob (a Popish plot version of the crowd in *Julius Caesar*) is reminded by Tiresias that Oedipus was, like Charles II in 1659-60, 'By publick voice elected' (I. i. 283). The ancient Greek protagonist is still the irascible figure who, years before the action of the play, murdered several men at a crossroads for some slight. 'Insolence [*hubris*] breeds the tyrant', says Sophocles' chorus: 'insolence | if it is glutted with a surfeit, unseasonable, unprofitable.'[56] In Dryden and Lee this quality is associated with Creon in the subplot: a vindictive, misshapen character intriguing his way to power. No one doubts that Dryden had in mind here the broken, brilliant figure of Shaftesbury—the Whig leader kept alive by a silver tube and tap implanted in his gut by the physician and philosopher Locke: chief refuter, appropriately enough, with Algernon Sidney, of Filmer's *Patriarcha*.

The rebel-as-potential-tyrant is staple in early modern revenge tragedy. In Lee, Lucius Junius Brutus responds to Lucrece's cry, 'Revenge me,

[55] Cf. Maximillian E. Novak's note to III. i. 468–79, in *Works of Dryden*, viii. 486.

[56] *Oedipus the King*, trans. David Grene, ll. 874–5, in *The Complete Greek Tragedies*, ed. Grene and Richmond Lattimore, 4 vols. (Chicago, 1959).

Father, Husband, Oh revenge me: | Revenge me, Brutus; you his Sons revenge me'[57] by overthrowing the Tarquins, and resisting a cavalier conspiracy for their early restoration. But once a republic has been secured, this *Father of his Country* (as Lee's subtitle sardonically puts it) becomes 'Tyrannick Brutus', a 'pittyless avenger'[58] whose virtue consists in displaying the ruthless integrity of Cromwell. Shaftesbury/Creon is an even less worthy rebel, a man who, like the Duke of Guise in that other Lee–Dryden tragedy, is fired in his ambition not by royal abuse of a woman but by a jealous lover's 'Lust, and revenge'.[59] Creon makes the people an instrument of this 'revenge' (IV. i. 20, V. i. 83), employing an eloquence derived from Shakespeare's Mark Antony to rouse them into a 'Rabble' which 'with a thousand Antick mouths | Gabbled revenge, *Revenge* was all the cry' (IV. i. 33–5). As fears of a Popish plot gained momentum, with the discovery of the corpse of Sir Edmund Berry Godfrey, supposedly murdered by Jesuits, elements of the populace did become 'vindictive, unhinged or just plain terrified'.[60] When the Whigs used their strength in London to press for the trial of implicated papists, Charles told his Council (in another echo of 1649) 'that when they were so busy in revenging the innocent blood of Godfrey, it was hard for him to consent to the shedding of more, and that he well remembered what his father suffered for consenting to the Earl of Strafford's death'.[61]

Henry III, in *The Duke of Guise*, exhibits similar scruples. When his life seems threatened by a 'Plot', he is slow to take 'Revenge' (II. i. 94–5); and even after he has resolved to 'push . . . slack'nd vengeance home', he is careful to ask, 'Is my Revenge Unjust, or Tyrannous? | Heaven knows, I love not Blood' (V. i. 251, 305–6; cf. 272–6). What makes Henry agreeable to Tory fantasy, however, is that he does, in fact, crush the Guise, who dies at the hands of eight assassins. As Dryden observes in his *Vindication of 'The Duke of Guise'*, 'You may see through the whole conduct of the Play, a *King* naturally *severe*, and a *resolution* carried on to *revenge* himself to the uttermost on the *Rebellious Conspirators*.'[62] By the time Dryden published these words, in 1683, mercy was ebbing at court. What historians call 'Stuart revenge'[63] was under way. In the winter of 1681–2, when *The*

---

[57] *Lucius Junius Brutus* I. i. 408–9; in *The Works of Nathaniel Lee*, ed. Thomas B. Stroup and Arthur L. Cooke, 2 vols. (New Brunswick, NJ, 1954–5).   [58] V. ii. 133, 138.

[59] II. i. 325; cf. e.g. V. i. 19, 325; and *The Duke of Guise* I. ii. 196–201 (in *Works of Dryden*, xiv).

[60] John Kenyon, *The Popish Plot* (1972; Harmondsworth, 1974), 114.

[61] Quoted ibid. 154.   [62] *Works of Dryden*, xiv. 317.

[63] e.g. David Ogg, *England in the Reign of Charles II*, 2 vols. (Oxford, 1934), ch. 17; J. R. Jones, *Country and Court: England 1658–1714* (London, 1978), 217.

Duke of Guise was drafted, the text looked so provocative that permission to perform it was refused. The Tories made such headway during 1682, however, that in October of that year 'there were Orders given for the *Acting* of it'.[64] If those asserting the existence of a Popish plot had been willing to use plays to publish their evidence,[65] Tories would now use the theatre to press for retribution. Across every front, Shaftesbury was routed. Locke went into exile. In a 'precisely organised act of political revenge',[66] Algernon Sidney was executed.

The Duke of Guise is resourceful but it turns revenge drama into an opportunistic vehicle for current affairs. It also takes such pleasure in using the Guise's death to anticipate Whig defeat that it hardly deserves its subtitle, *A Tragedy. Oedipus* is that more interesting phenomenon: a revenge play which deepens into tragedy the more politically it is construed. It does this because it celebrates Carolean power not only in so far as Oedipus/Charles II is sympathetic but in so far as he is not. As a lustful monarch and regicide—both at once—Oedipus must 'call . . . Vengeance down' (IV. i. 574), exact 'Vengeance' on himself (IV. i. 607), give '*ample satisfaction | For bloudiest Murder, and for burning Lust*' (V. i. 55–6). In the final minutes of the play, he also veers into mad competitiveness with Jocasta to perpetrate acts of 'Revenge' (V. i. 443). Yet the guilt which unhinges his wits simultaneously endorses his legitimacy. The more the ghost and his agents clamour for vengeance against 'The first of *Lajus* blood' (II. i. 172; cf. 177, 226, etc.), the more they discredit the rebel view that Oedipus is merely a monarch by circumstance, 'A stranger to [*Lajus*] Blood' (I. i. 298). Charles II, in other words, could not be so burdened with the consequences of his father's execution, could not be the catalyst of political strife in such an innocent yet blame-stirring way, were he not, in Filmer's formulation, 'the successor by blood' (p. 83) of a line which ran back through Charles I to King Adam. Meanwhile, the fact that a king-killer suffers so grievously, even though himself of royal blood, is dramatic proof that rebellion should never be attempted—by, for instance, Charles II's illegitimate first-born, Monmouth (or were his claims, like those of Oedipus to Laius' throne, actually legitimate?),[67] who consorted with

[64] *The Vindication of 'The Duke of Guise'*, 310.

[65] William Bedloe, a Popish plot intriguer, published *The Excommunicated Prince; or, The False Relic* in 1679, and the anonymous *Rome's Folly; or, The Amorous Friar*, dedicated to Shaftesbury and Lord Howard of Escrick, was performed in 1681. Cf. Tim Harris, *London Crowds in the Reign of Charles II: Propaganda and Politics from the Restoration until the Exclusion Crisis* (Cambridge, 1987), 103.   [66] Scott, *Algernon Sidney and the Restoration Crisis*, 173; cf. p. 329.

[67] See e.g. Ronald Hutton, *Charles the Second: King of England, Scotland, and Ireland* (Oxford, 1989), 25–6.

Whigs and republicans during the Exclusion Crisis, and who later, of course, rose against James II.

The 'Stuart revenge' was short-lived. Though Jonathan Clark has valuably shown how far Filmerian ideology persisted into the eighteenth century,[68] power increasingly passed to the descendants of Shaftesbury and Locke. After 1688, Sidney's attainder was repealed and he was celebrated as a Whig martyr. Anti-Tory views were advanced in the theatre. Sympathetic heroes, rather than mobs and devious plotters, began to clamour on stage for 'Liberty!'[69] Strong Whig views about authority owed much to those Calvinistic theories of resistance which had, earlier, fuelled revenge drama—and which, in the sixteenth-century setting of Lee and Dryden's *The Duke of Guise*, continue to inspire rebellion (I. i. 9–71). Yet Algernon Sidney and Locke developed elements of the Protestant tradition, around the themes of conscience, property, and justice, in ways which diminished the power of revenge tragedy. As I now want to show, while recurrent political crises sustained the genre for longer than has usually been recognized, a slow but irreversible shift in the ideology which triggered those crises was working to change and erode it.

In the final scene of *The Atheist's Tragedy* (1611), D'Amville overreaches himself. Thanks to his machinations his virtuous nephew has been condemned to death. Disregarding the protests of two judges, Tourneur's villain now announces that he will mount the scaffold on stage before us and personally execute Charlemont. Appealing to that pride in his blood-line which characterizes him—sometimes in manic and incestuous forms—throughout, he insists that 'The instrument that strikes my nephew's blood | Shall be as noble as his blood.'[70] Charlemont is unruffled, and, with something of the resolved insouciance of Marvell's 'royal actor', he agrees to let his uncle 'crown my resolution with | An unexampled dignity of death' (236–7). When D'Amville swings into action, however, Heaven intervenes. '*As he raises up the axe* [*he*] *strikes out his own brains,* [*and then*] *staggers off the scaffold*' (241). Tourneur's catastrophe may have been inspired by the death of that 'atheist' Marlowe, as described by Thomas Beard in his widely read book of retributive histories, *The Theatre of God's Judgements* (1597);[71] but we need not look outside the play for signs of an

[68] J. C. D. Clark, *English Society 1688–1832: Ideology, Social Structure and Political Practice during the Ancien Regime* (Cambridge, 1985), esp. ch. 3.

[69] Susan Staves, *Players' Scepters: Fictions of Authority in the Restoration* (Lincoln, Nebr., 1979), 100.   [70] Ed. Irving Ribner (London, 1964); V. ii. 227–8.

[71] McCabe, *Incest, Drama and Nature's Law*, 221.

active providence. When the dying D'Amville confesses his crimes, the leading judge speaks of 'The power of that eternal providence | Which overthrew his projects in their pride', and Charlemont (still in Charles I vein) declares, 'Only to Heav'n I attribute the work' (270–5).

Some seventy years later, another 'atheist' met his death on a scaffold in revenge tragedy. The climactic scene of *Venice Preserved*, however, does not take place in a theatre of God's judgements. Though the word 'providence' occasionally ornaments a wishful speech in the body of the drama, there is no sign of its hand at work either for or against Pierre and Jaffeir. Instead, Otway's conspirators are subject to an all-too-human system of (apparently Whiggish) justice. When Jaffeir saves Pierre from execution by stabbing him to death on the scaffold, and nobly immolates himself for having betrayed their conspiracy, the episode is theatrically stunning, but it has no metaphysical resonance, any more than the following sequence, in which Belvedira (Jaffeir's wife) enters raving and '*The Ghosts of* Jaffeir *and* Pierre *rise together both bloody*' to meet her.[72] This is the sort of spectacle which can only be potent—as it is when Laius' ghost appears in *Oedipus*—when more is involved dramatically than a recycling of Elizabethan devices.

The actual executions of the 'Stuart revenge' were less melodramatic than those envisaged by Otway. Even so, they bear a likeness. Whatever views would have been imputed to Jaffeir by original audiences,[73] and however he related for Otway to the duplicitous conspiracies of the early 1680s, his hope that the 'blood . . . shed' by the Venetian authorities 'may . . . rest upon you | And all your race' (v. iii. 101–3) can be read as a more eloquently aggressive version of Algernon Sidney's prayer, when he was sentenced in 1683: 'O God . . . if . . . the shedding of blood that is innocent must be revenged, let the weight of it fall upon those that maliciously persecute me for righteousness sake.'[74] Though Sidney remained silent on the scaffold, the widely circulated treatise which he substituted for a speech, *The Very Copy of a Paper Delivered to the Sheriffs* (1683), was defiant. Making none of the usual gestures of regret and fidelity to the King, it spelled out Sidney's objections to *Patriarcha*, insisting 'That the right and power of magistrates in every country was that which the laws of that country made it to be', and that constitutions were established by

---

[72]   *Venice Preserved*, ed. Malcolm Kelsall (London, 1969), V. iv. 19.
[73]   For a fresh account of the politics of the play see Jessica Munns, *Restoration Politics and Drama: The Plays of Thomas Otway, 1675–1683* (Newark, Del., 1995), ch. 5.
[74]   Scott, *Algernon Sidney and the Restoration Crisis*, 336; cf. p. 315.

means of 'a contract between Magistrate and people'.[75] This was not the only blow to Filmer. Just as bystanders dipped their handkerchiefs in the blood of Charles I—descended from King Adam—so, after Sidney's decapitation, a soldier broke ranks 'and got his Handkerchif diped in his bloud'. The fact that he did this under the misapprehension that the executed man was a papist martyr[76] simply makes the more piquant this comic-sad parody of royalist blood-mystification.

Filmerian blood-claims were in any case coming under pressure because of scientific advances. The unselfconscious identification with paternal blood which characterizes, for instance, Beatrice-Joanna's address to her father in *The Changeling*—'I am that of your blood was taken from you | For your better health'[77]—was scarcely tenable by the 1680s. The literalism of the idea that, by means of a lance and cupping glass, paternal gore could be extracted from a daughter's body would have seemed highly questionable in the context of Restoration medicine. Well might the aura of blood be dispelled when—as Shadwell's *Virtuoso* reminded audiences in 1676—experimental transfusion had begun, leaving scientists of the Royal Society disturbed by Thomas Coxe's cure of a mangy dog by the use of blood from a healthy spaniel, and by John Wilkins's bizarre introduction of twelve ounces of sheep's gore into the veins of a madman.[78] (The patient's hair did not curl, and neither did he bleat, but—the more because of that disappointment—thoughts of blood as a sacred bond were shaken.) Coxe and Wilkins can hardly be held responsible for the ousting of James II by William III, but the claims of '*Lajus* blood' were being exposed as little more than superstition: understandable in ancient Thebes, but not in late seventeenth-century London.

It was Sidney's emphasis on 'laws' and 'a contract between Magistrate and people', however, which was most pregnant with the political future. The gradual extension of state control over punishment for crimes of blood goes back to the Norman conquest, but those Elizabethan appeals to Romans 12–13 which lie behind *Hamlet* and *Lust's Dominion* are symptomatic of its reinforcement during the Tudor period.[79] Whether or not

---

[75] Quoted ibid. 344.

[76] Ibid. 347.

[77] Thomas Middleton and William Rowley, *The Changeling*, ed. N. W. Bawcutt (London, 1958), v. iii. 150–1.

[78] See *The Virtuoso*, ed. Marjorie Hope Nicholson and David Rodes (Lincoln, Nebr., 1966), II. ii. 108–33, 179–237 and pp. xxiii–iv.

[79] For an overview see e.g. Ronald Broude, 'Revenge and Revenge Tragedy in Renaissance England', *Renaissance Quarterly*, 28 (1975), 38–58, pp. 43–52.

there was 'a Growth of Order'[80]—a decline of feuding and faction, and related shift in the honour code—in early Stuart England,[81] there was certainly a greater appeal to the law, both at the level of constitutional theory, to check the encroachments of prerogative government, and, in the Assizes and Quarter Sessions, to bring godly order to the localities. The procedures of these courts were not calculated to satisfy an appetite for drama (the histrionic mode of Charles I's trial was unusual),[82] but John Smyth of Nibley nonetheless strikes a suggestive note when he calls the courts at Westminster 'our cockpitt of revenge'[83]—given that the term 'cockpit' was both generically and specifically used of early Stuart theatre.[84] This period saw a partial translation of social conflict into the legal arena compatible with the theatre's flourishing interest in vengeance. 'Societies being weaned from habits of private revenge', Lawrence Stone remarks, 'always turn to the law with intemperate enthusiasm, but by any standards the growth of litigation between 1550 and 1625 was something rather exceptional.'[85]

What ideas of punishment were operative in the sphere (if not the invariable practice) of law? Here Algernon Sidney's talk of 'a contract' is loaded, since, despite its origins in pre-civil war political theory,[86] it recalls the contemporaneous argument of Hobbes and Locke that society emerges from a state of nature because man agrees to submit himself to

---

[80] Lawrence Stone, *The Crisis of the Aristocracy, 1558–1641* (Oxford, 1965), 234–50.

[81] For indications of change see Mervyn James, 'English Politics and the Concept of Honour, 1485–1642', *Past and Present*, Supplement no. 3 (1978), repr. in his *Society, Politics and Culture: Studies in Early Modern England* (Cambridge, 1986), 308–415, but also, on the persistence of honour disputes and duels, Caroline Hibbard, 'The Theatre of Dynasty', in R. Malcolm Smuts (ed.), *The Stuart Court and Europe: Essays in Politics and Political Culture* (Cambridge, 1996), 156–76, pp. 160–6.

[82] See e.g. Cynthia Herrup, *The Common Peace: Participation and the Criminal Law in Seventeenth-Century England* (Cambridge, 1987), chs. 4–7.

[83] Quoted by Stone, *Crisis of the Aristocracy*, 240.

[84] The Cockpit rivalled Blackfriars, after about 1619, as a venue for moneyed audiences, while the Cockpit-at-Court (built under Henry VIII) continued to be used for plays.

[85] *Crisis of the Aristocracy*, 240. Stone's primarily English evidence finds parallels in Wales; see Peter Roberts, 'The English Crown, the Principality of Wales and the Council in the Marches, 1534–1641', in Brendan Bradshaw and John Morrill (eds.), *The British Problem, c.1534–1707* (London, 1996), 118–47, p. 135. On Scotland, where feuding persisted and the legal code worked differently, see e.g. Jenny Wormald, 'Bloodfeud, Kindred and Government in Early Modern Scotland', *Past and Present*, 87 (1980), 54–97, and Keith Brown, *Bloodfeud in Scotland 1573–1625: Violence, Justice and Politics in an Early Modern Society* (Edinburgh, 1986).

[86] On an original contract between sovereign and people in John Pym, Robert Mason, and others see Conrad Russell, *Parliaments and English Politics 1621–1629* (Oxford, 1979), 355, and J. G. A. Pocock, *The Ancient Constitution and the Feudal Law: A Study of English Historical Thought in the Seventeenth Century*, 2nd edn. (Cambridge, 1987), 302–4.

sanctions for the sake of the advantages that this yields. Though there are patriarchal strains in Hobbes (as well as a philosophy of the virtues which complicates his contractarianism),[87] he explicitly denies that one man's blood is better than another's.[88] Societies involve rank and depend on different human competences, but they are not hierarchically established by a descent of blood-lines from Adam. Sidney boldly asserted that society could revert to a state of nature (though not quite in Hobbesian terms) if the monarch broke his contract with the people. In that lawless condition, 'No guards can preserve a hated prince from the vengeance of one resolute hand.'[89] This sounds like the fiery voice of Melantius or Maximus, but it is based on Romans 12–13. For Sidney maintained against Filmer that, according to St Paul, 'He . . . is only the minister of God, who is not a terror to good works, but to evil.' When the king-as-magistrate does evil, the founding 'contract' is broken and *'every man is a magistrate'*.[90] Locke, attacking Filmer with less rebellious zeal, also argued against the notion of a monarch as God's image on earth from whose sole hands justice flowed.[91] Filmer 'vindicated the right of Kings' (p. 54) by insisting that St Paul had anticipated 'strained' readings of Romans 13 and had 'let it be known that by power he understood a monarch that carried a sword' (pp. 100–1). Locke sought to refute this, substituting a theory of consent as the basis of civil society which owed more than a little to Hobbes.

Though Catherine Belsey's attempt to show that revenge tragedy helps install 'liberal humanism' in the seventeenth century is marred by more than anachronistic terminology, she is right to associate the cries of 'Liberty!' and 'Revenge!' in *Venice Preserved* with a change in views of authority which can be paralleled in Locke.[92] More significant, however, are shifts in the ideology of justice. Like the regicides of 1649, Sidney's political rhetoric is seamed with references to blood and vengeance.[93] His

---

[87] See Quentin Skinner, *Reason and Rhetoric in the Philosophy of Hobbes* (Cambridge, 1996), 11 and chs. 8–9.

[88] See e.g. Keith Thomas, 'The Social Origins of Hobbes's Political Thought', in K. C. Brown (ed.), *Hobbes Studies* (Oxford, 1965), 185–236, pp. 188–9, 191–2.

[89] *Discourses Concerning Government* (1681–3, pub. 1698), quoted by Scott, *Algernon Sidney and the Restoration Crisis*, 243.

[90] *Discourses*; Scott, *Algernon Sidney and the Restoration Crisis*, 250, 264.

[91] His views in 1660 had been rather different. See e.g. C. B. Macpherson, *The Political Theory of Possessive Individualism: Hobbes to Locke* (Oxford, 1962), 260–1.

[92] *The Subject of Tragedy* (London, 1985), ch. 4, esp. pp. 116–24.

[93] Their execution after Charles II's return prompted him to inscribe 'SIT SANGUINIS ULTOR JUSTORUM' ('Let there be revenge for the blood of the just'): see Jonathan Scott, *Algernon Sidney and the English Republic, 1623–1677* (Cambridge, 1988), 171. Cf. Scott, *Algernon Sidney and the*

views are representatively Pauline to the extent of being retributive. Yet it tended to follow from contract and consent that punishment should not be the reflex of divine retribution. Vengeance might be the way of God, but it brought no advantage to man. Punishment was only useful if it corrected and deterred. 'We are forbidden to inflict punishment with any other design than for correction of the offender or direction of others,' wrote Hobbes: 'Revenge without respect to the Example, and profit to come, is a triumph, or glorying in the hurt of another, tending to no end; (for the End is always somewhat to Come;) and glorying to no end, is vain-glory, and contrary to reason.'[94] 'Each Transgression', Locke declared, 'may be *punished* to that *degree*, and with so much *Severity* as will suffice to make it an ill bargain to the Offender, give him cause to repent, and terrifie others from doing the like.'[95] Restraining and deterring, punishment should be pragmatic rather than retributively symmetrical.

Such opinions were gaining acceptance by the 1680s, but many Elizabethans and Jacobeans would have found them impious. The earlier view, which flowed out of late medieval providentialism, but which was fostered by Reformation theology, was that justice derived from God and that divine punishment was retributive. 'Vengeance is mine; I will repay' was read as promising heavenly intervention, as well as forbidding private revenge.[96] Seeking to endorse St Paul, believers looked about them for signs of retribution.[97] Earthquakes, fires, and famine provided evidence of divine wrath. In diaries and autobiographies, sermons and chapbooks, endless examples of God's providence were collected: the incestuous villain struck down by lightning (as in Massinger's *The Unnatural Combat*); the drunkard choked by his own ale. On a more exalted level, Protestant apologists like Foxe explained the history of entire nations in terms of divine favour and revenge. Massive and persuasive, too, were such case-history compilations as John Reynolds's *Triumphs of God's Revenge, Against the Crying, and Execrable Sin of Murder* (in three volumes, 1621–3) —Middleton's source for *The Changeling*—and, of course, Thomas Beard's regularly augmented *Theatre of God's Judgements*.

Like T. S. Eliot's 'dissociation of sensibility', the much-discussed cultural crisis which William R. Elton calls 'the skeptical disintegration of

Restoration Crisis, 190, 194, 238–40, 257, and Patricia Crawford, ' "Charles Stuart, That Man of Blood" ', *Journal of British Studies*, 16/2 (Spring 1977), 41–61.

94 *Leviathan*, ed. C. B. Macpherson (Harmondsworth, 1968), 210 (I. xv).
95 *John Locke: Two Treatises of Government*, ed. Peter Laslett, 2nd edn. (Cambridge, 1967), 293 (II. §12).   96 Campbell, 'Theories of Revenge', 285.
97 See e.g. Keith Thomas, *Religion and the Decline of Magic* (London, 1971), ch. 4.

providential belief'[98] moves around the early modern period, finding its place (or being denied altogether) according to the preconceptions of the observer and the nature of the material inspected. For Jonathan Dollimore, following Elton, providentialism was being eroded by 1600. He thinks such vindictive tragedies as Marston's *Antonio's Revenge* 'radical' because they subvert 'the dramatic conventions which embody a providentialist perspective', and he reads D'Amville's death as parodic.[99] Given the full-blown moralism which is ubiquitous in *The Atheist's Tragedy*, the latter claim is hardly persuasive—however melodramatic Tourneur's handling of the scaffold scene. Historically, too, Dollimore runs up against the evidence that providentialism remained commonplace in mid-seventeenth-century England.[100] After the Restoration, the picture clouds. Aubrey Williams's well-documented *Approach to Congreve* maintains that, as late as the 1690s, providential belief was widespread and theatrically vital.[101] Derek Hughes, however, has cogently challenged Williams's interpretation of statements made by Stillingfleet, Tillotson, and others. Valuably discriminating between different strains of providentialism, and noting that declarations from the pulpit, and in the playhouse, cannot prove that what is preached is generally accepted (it might indicate the contrary), he identifies a range of attitudes and dramatic practices—espousing, defying, and it seems ignoring providentialism—among late seventeenth-century tragedians.[102]

The rise of anti-providentialism may have been fostered among royalist gentlemen by the grim experience of war's chances and by the defeat of Charles I's just cause. To understand the process more philosophically would involve exploring the European-wide influence of Epicurus and Gassendi,[103] and, in England, the relationship between Arminianism and

[98] *'King Lear' and the Gods* (San Marino, Calif., 1966), 335.

[99] *Radical Tragedy: Religion, Ideology and Power in the Drama of Shakespeare and his Contemporaries* (Brighton, 1984), 39, 88–9.

[100] e.g. Thomas, *Religion and the Decline of Magic*, ch. 4; Blair Worden, 'Providence and Politics in Cromwellian England', *Past and Present*, 109 (1985), 55–99; Peter Lake, 'Deeds against Nature: Cheap Print, Protestantism and Murder in Early Seventeenth Century England', in Kevin Sharpe and Peter Lake (eds.), *Culture and Politics in Early Stuart England* (Basingstoke, 1994), 257–83; Alexandra Walsham, '"The Fatal Vesper": Providentialism and Anti-Popery in Late Jacobean London', *Past and Present*, 144 (1994), 36–87, and, now, *Providentialism in Early Modern England* (Oxford, 1999).

[101] Aubrey L. Williams, *An Approach to Congreve* (New Haven, 1979), esp. ch. 1.

[102] 'Providential Justice and English Comedy 1660–1700: A Review of the External Evidence', *Modern Language Review*, 81 (1986), 273–89, esp. pp. 288–9.

[103] Cf. Charles Kay Smith, 'French Philosophy and English Politics in Interregnum Poetry', in Smuts (ed.), *The Stuart Court and Europe*, 177–209.

virtuoso science, as it shaped the Royal Society and created the experimental culture in which—whatever their views during the interregnum—Coxe and Wilkins flourished.[104] It would also encounter paradoxes. For a start, the growing tendency of Restoration science to 'recast Providence as a benign and distant spectator on events rather than a wrathful meddler in earthly affairs' went along with a reinforcement of providential story-telling which placed fresh emphasis on the rewarding of virtue as well as the punishment of sin. This change—which might be dated from Samuel Clarke's *A Mirror or Looking-glass both for Saints and Sinners* (1646)—reaches its late seventeenth-century climax in William Turner's *Complete History of the Most Remarkable Providences* (1697) and the popular works of Nathaniel Crouch (i.e. 'Robert Burton').[105]

The idea that divine providence was directed towards contriving happiness was given political force, for Anglicans and Dissenters, by the circumstances of the Williamite invasion. It is a second paradox worth noting that the breakthrough of contractarian thinking into mainstream opinion, associated (sometimes too heedlessly) with the Revolution of 1688, coincided with, and was facilitated by, a revival in providentialism. Gilbert Burnet was not unique when he used contractarian arguments against James II but revived the more obedient language of providential election when consolidating the authority of William III. Not only were both approaches to the crisis in government available: the latter might rationalize the former. Certainly such Anglican apologists as William Sherlock (in *The Case of the Allegiance Due to Sovereign Powers* (1691)) cited Romans 13 to prove that, because all power came from God, the prodigious success of William of Orange showed that he was divinely chosen to rule. The danger of this approach was that it risked interpreting as providential the ungoverned course of events: it appeared to set little distance between comprehensive divine involvement and heavenly indifference. As Burnet faithfully put it, in *A Sermon Preached before the King and Queen, at Whitehall, On the 19th Day of October, 1690* (1690), 'there is such a Chain in all things, the most Important Matters taking oft their rise or turn from very inconsiderable Circumstances, that it is certain that either

---

[104] See e.g. Nicholas Tyacke, 'Science and Religion at Oxford before the Civil War', in Donald Pennington and Keith Thomas (eds.), *Puritans and Revolutionaries: Essays in Seventeenth-Century History Presented to Christopher Hill* (Oxford, 1978), 73–93.

[105] Alexandra Walsham; private communication.

there is no Providence at all, or that it has no limits, and takes all things within its care'.[106]

This points to a further difficulty: one which had been integral to providentialist thought about nature since at least the late sixteenth century. For the 'paradoxical aspects of puritan views of causation' were such that the providential rigour of firm Protestants[107] contained the seeds of its own subversion. 'Towards the end of the Cromwellian Protectorate', Keith Thomas notes, 'an ... elaborate "Designe for registring of Illustrious Providences" was initiated by the Presbyterian minister, Matthew Poole, in collaboration with other divines at home and in New England.' The plan was for local secretaries to gather evidence of divine intervention and to send it on to Poole, at Syon College, for collation and analysis. As Thomas says, 'The close parallel with the methods used by the scientists of the Royal Society for collecting and classifying natural phenomena is obvious enough, and it is worth recalling that Francis Bacon had himself urged the desirability of compiling a definitive history of the workings of providence.'[108] This sort of enterprise can be interpreted too whiggishly, but if divine influence was regarded as ubiquitous and just, if the operation of nature was (in Bishop Cooper's words) 'nothing but the very finger of God working in his creatures',[109] then studying the world was studying its maker and theology was an adjunct of natural philosophy. To that extent, Thomas Cooper and Matthew Poole gave birth, through Burnet and his contemporaries, to eighteenth-century rationalism.

All this might seem distant from politics and drama; but the softening of, and resistance to, providentialism did more than anything else to sap revenge tragedy in England. That doctrine supported the idea of a Pauline divinity, punishing evil, and thus reinforced the assumption that justice should be retributive. As a minister of God the magistrate was a channel of divine anger. Hence the vehement tone of early seventeenth-century assize sermons—texts like Hannibal Gamon's *God's Smiting to Amendment, or, Revengement* (1628) where all the righteousness of fear and faith underwrites 'auenging Iustice' (p. 30). The piecemeal decay of retributive providentialism encouraged more pragmatic reasons for punishment to

---

[106] pp. 6–7; cf., for informative contexts, Gerald Straka, 'The Final Phase of Divine Right Theory in England, 1688–1702', *English Historical Review*, 77 (1962), 638–58, p. 656.

[107] Barbara Donagan, 'Providence, Chance and Explanation: Some Paradoxical Aspects of Puritan Views of Causation', *Journal of Religious History*, 11 (1981), 385–403.

[108] *Religion and the Decline of Magic*, 94–5.

[109] Thomas Cooper, *Certain Sermons* (1580), 163; quoted by Thomas, *Religion and the Decline of Magic*, 80.

be found, along the lines of Hobbes and Locke. To punish was no longer a religious duty: it was social prudence. From that came such assize sermons as Henry Downes's *The Necessity and Usefulness of Laws* (1708), which uses St Paul as a way into confirming 'the Happiness of our National Establishment and Constitution' and the value of 'publick rules to fix and guard private Property' (pp. 4, 8). Attitudes to natural law underwent related changes. When D'Amville invokes his appetites and his reason as guides, Tourneur shows them encouraging incest, greed, and murder. In this the play is typical of much written before 1660. 'Your blood, your very nature', puritans warned, 'is stained and tainted with original corruption.'[110] Locke had more faith in natural law, and he argued that reason unaided by revelation could discover the human obligations required by it, while his pupil, the third Earl of Shaftesbury, had, of course, a view of human nature so benign as to seem Pelagian.

Revenge tragedy did not vanish from the English stage in 1683, or 1688, any more than it did after 1642: the narrative energy and moral ambiguity of a theme which had attracted dramatists since Aeschylus would not be lost overnight. In some respects, in fact, the potency of the theatrical formula ensured that talk of providential retribution was kept alive on stage as it faded out of other contexts. Old works in the genre were revived and adapted,[111] and new ones, both domestic and more largely political, were written—not just in the 1690s[112] but as late as, for instance, the high-flown tragedies of Aaron Hill. Yet, as Susan Staves points out, the late seventeenth-century view that 'Man . . . is not essentially a creature of lust and vengeance, but a tranquil social animal animated by benevolence', encouraged the composition of plays which turn on the discovery of a suspected character's innocence.[113] In these circumstances, the typical catastrophe was no longer the betrayal of a conspiracy or the revenge killing of a villain. Rather than deriving the principles of justice from St Paul, Shaftesbury and his followers held that man is a self-punishing creature,

---

[110]   Francis Cheynell, *The Man of Honour* (1645), 30–1, quoted by Baskerville, 'Blood Guilt in the English Revolution', 186.

[111]   e.g. *Hamlet* and *Othello*, repeatedly, the manuscript *The Rape Reveng'd; or, The Spanish Revolution* by W.C., a version of Rowley's *All's Lost by Lust* (*c.*1690); D'Urfey, *Bussy D'Ambois; or, The Husband's Revenge* (1690; pub. 1691), based on Chapman; 'Mr Rivers', *The Traitor* (1692), and Christopher Bullock, *The Traitor* (1718), modified from Shirley; also, looking back to Euripides, Charles Gildon's version of the Medea story—instructively justified in his preface—in *Phaeton; or, The Fatal Divorce* (1698).

[112]   e.g. Edward Ravenscroft, *The Italian Husband* (1697); Charles Gildon, *The Roman Bride's Revenge* (1696); William Philips, *The Revengeful Queen* (1698).

[113]   *Players' Scepters*, 302, 305.

to the extent that, when he does wrong, he suffers in his heart for it. Christian moralists had, for centuries, emphasized the anguish of a guilty conscience, but Shaftesbury's philosophy of punishment anticipates a very different, and recognizably Enlightenment, dispensation.

Elizabethan and Jacobean dramatists such as Tourneur could see the world as a theatre of God's judgements, and the stage as representing a problematic microcosm of that world. It is no accident that Kyd's *Spanish Tragedy* should be, at large, a play within a play—supernaturally overseen by a character called Revenge, and expressing a goddess's 'doom' (both judgement and destiny)[114]—nor that, within that structure, Hieronimo should avenge his son's death by staging an inset drama which he, its providential mover, has penned. In the later seventeenth century, that metaphysical dimension was vitiated. The theatrical reflexivity which registers the possibility of a metadramatic perspective at moments of impious vaunting and impending judgement in *Lust's Dominion* is assiduously stripped away when Aphra Behn revises the play as *Abdelazar; or, The Moor's Revenge* (1676) and Edward Young the frequently performed and reprinted *Revenge* (1719). We might detect an impulse towards providential reflexivity when Milton, at the climax of his late revenge tragedy[115] *Samson Agonistes*, has the Philistines punished with death not in the 'house' of Judges 16: 27 but a 'theatre'. Yet the Chorus's reflections on the inscrutable ways of providence and Milton's own allegiance to what has been called 'contingent predestination'[116] both show how far radical Protestantism had moved from ideas of divine direction.

Belief in an active providence did persist (for some it still does). Hence, in part, the eighteenth-century reprints, and the 1778 abridgement and revision (by Philip Batteson), of Reynolds's *Triumphs of God's Revenge*, and hence the fascination with ambiguous signs of divine plotting in prose fiction beyond Defoe—a susceptibility which helps explain the migration of revenge tragedy into the novel.[117] It indicates change, however, that critics should increasingly urge authors 'after 1688'[118] to adumbrate 'the Punishment of Vice, and Reward Virtue' in tragedy not because those

---

[114] *Spanish Tragedy* I. i. 79.

[115] For general reflections see John F. Andrews, ' "Dearly Bought Revenge": *Samson Agonistes, Hamlet*, and Elizabethan Revenge Tragedy', *Milton Studies*, 13 (1979), 81–107.

[116] ll. 667–704, in *The Poems of John Milton*, ed. John Carey and Alastair Fowler (London, 1968); Mary Ann Radzinowicz, *Toward 'Samson Agonistes': The Growth of Milton's Mind* (Princeton, 1978), 339.

[117] Kerrigan, *Revenge Tragedy*, 217 ff.

[118] Robert D. Hume, *The Development of English Drama in the Late Seventeenth Century* (Oxford, 1976), 152.

outcomes were considered a given of experience but because such a procedure was judged 'most conducing to good Example of Life'.[119] Theories
of deterrence were taking over the playhouse. What remained were the
lasting achievements of those post-1649 dramatists—above all, play-
wrights of the Exclusion Crisis—who, in politically charged, if not meta-
physically transcendent, works, revisited revenge tragedy.

---

[119] Dryden, 'Heads of an Answer to Rymer' (1678), *Works of Dryden*, xvii. 191; cf. Thomas
Rymer, *The Tragedies of the Last Age Consider'd and Examin'd* (1677), in *The Critical Works of
Thomas Rymer*, ed. Curt A. Zimansky (New Haven, 1956), 17–76, esp. pp. 22–3.

Index